D1594435

Amiri Baraka / LeRoi Jones:
The Quest for a "Populist Modernism"

Amiri Baraka / LeRoi Jones:
The Quest for a "Populist Modernism"

Werner Sollors

Columbia University Press
New York 1978

Columbia University Press
New York—Guildford, Surrey

Copyright © 1978 Columbia University Press
Printed in the United States of America

D 188

LIBRARY OF CONGRESS CATALOGING IN PUBLICATION DATA

Sollors, Werner.
  Amiri Baraka/LeRoi Jones : the quest for a
"populist modernism."

  Bibliography: p.
  Includes index.
  1. Baraka, Imamu Amiri, 1934-   —Criticism and
interpretation.
PS3552.A583Z88   818'.5'409   78-7499
ISBN 0-231-04226-4

Grateful acknowledgment is made to the following: The Sterling Lord
Agency and Amiri Baraka, for permission to reprint excerpts from Baraka's
works; the James Weldon Johnson Collection, Beinecke Rare Book and
Manuscript Library, Yale University, for sections from letters by Baraka;
Viking Press, for lines from James Weldon Johnson, *St. Peter Relates an
Incident* © 1917; Harcourt Brace Jovanovich, for quotes from T. S. Eliot's
Complete Poems and Plays: 1909–1950; and the University of Michigan
Press, for permission to reprint a section from André Breton's *Manifestoes
of Surrealism* (1969).

For Robbie and David

Contents

viii
Contents

Illustrations facing p. 184

Abbreviations

A   *Arm Yourself or Harm Yourself*
AC *African Congress*
B   *Black Magic: Collected Poetry, 1961–1967*
BF *Black Fire*
BM *Black Music*
BP *Blues People*
BT *The Baptism and The Toilet*
DS *Dutchman and The Slave*
DL *The Dead Lecturer*
F   *Four Black Revolutionary Plays*
H   *Home: Social Essays*
HF *Hard Facts*
IN *It's Nation Time*
J   *Jello*
M   *The Moderns*
P   *Preface to a Twenty Volume Suicide Note*
R   *Raise Race Rays Raze: Essays Since 1965*
SD *The System of Dante's Hell*
SR *Spirit Reach*
SS *Slave Ship*
T   *Tales*
UD Uncollected Drama (Bibliography section II. C)
UF Uncollected Fiction (Bibliography section II. D)
UI Interviews (Bibliography section II. G)
UM Uncollected Music Criticism (Bibliography section II. F)
UN Uncollected Nonfiction (Bibliography section II. E)
UP Uncollected Poetry (Bibliography section II. B)

Prefatory Remarks and Acknowledgments

This study is an interpretive survey of Baraka's collected and uncollected works. The introduction is a brief biographical sketch. Chapters one and two are concerned with Baraka's artistic socialization and maturation in the Bohemian 1950s. Chapter three discusses the nonfiction after 1960. Chapters four through seven form the center of the book and deal with Baraka's most famous literary works in the first half of the 1960s, a period of increasing ethnic and political polarization. Chapters eight and nine follow Baraka's cultural politics and literary works in the phase of Black nationalism, from the mid-1960s to the early 1970s. The last chapter introduces Baraka's most recent shift toward Maoism. The book concludes with excerpts from a conversation with Baraka.

I am especially indebted to three of my teachers: to Charles Nichols, for my initiation into Afro-American literature, for the initial suggestion of the subject, and for encouragement during the writing process; to Robert Bone, for invaluable discussions, critical guidance, and many specific suggestions which became crucial to my understanding of Baraka as a Black modernist; and to Jules Chametzky who, with his vast knowledge and profound understanding of American ethnic literature, provided me with constructive support and challenging criticism at every stage of the work, and who patiently read, reread, and helped me revise the manuscript. The completion of the work was greatly facilitated by grants from Deutscher Akademischer Austauschdienst and the American Council of Learned Societies; and I am especially grateful to Dr. Franz Eschbach and to Dr. Richard Downar.

The library of the John F. Kennedy-Institut in Berlin, and especially Dr. Hans Kolligs, assisted me in many practical ways. I am further indebted to Dr. Donald Gallup and Joseph Fuchs at Beinecke Library, Yale University; to Dr. Ernest Kaiser at the Schomburg Collection, New York Public Library; and to the staffs of the Library of Congress, Butler Library at Columbia University, Howard University Library, the Library of SUNY at Stony Brook, and the Theater Collection at Lincoln Center. The help extended to me as a student and as a teacher by the Freie Universität Berlin and by Columbia University is especially appreciated.

Amiri Baraka provided his help in innumerable ways. Hettie Cohen Jones and George Stade gave me valuable background information on literary life in the Village. Nathan Huggins and Lawrence Levine read earlier versions of the manuscript and gave me extensive commentaries. Letitia Dace, Diane Dippold, and Theodore Hudson kindly sent me copies of fugitive sources. Frederick Hellman collected newspaper clippings and taped radio and television programs with or about Baraka. Columbia University Press has been supportive of my efforts from the moment I hesitatingly brought my manuscript to the office; and I would hereby like to express my thanks to William F. Bernhardt and David Diefendorf.

Parts of this book were first presented as lectures at the University of Maryland at Heidelberg and at the College Language Association Convention at Savannah. A German version of my reading of "The Screamers" first appeared in *Die amerikanische Short Story der Gegenwart,* ed. Peter Freese (Erich Schmidt-Verlag Berlin, 1976); and excerpts from my interpretations of Baraka's poetry were first published, in a slightly different form, in *Boundary 2.*

WERNER SOLLORS

Cambridge, Mass.
January 1978

Amiri Baraka / LeRoi Jones:
The Quest for a "Populist Modernism"

*"We must untiringly strive to fight
those things in us which are a contradiction to the choice we have made."*
—TOURÉ

*"Was I to have made this far journey,
only to find the very thing which I
had fled?"*
—PAUL GAUGUIN

Introduction

*"Who is this man, why are we here,
will we survive?"*
—*Norman Mailer*

Amiri Baraka was once better known as LeRoi Jones. His public image is that of an angry man, a Black artist given to violence, a writer who has yet to learn "how to transform anger into art."[1] Baraka, the Black agitator, represents the violence and spontaneity of the radical 1960s, when he was at the very core of literature, culture, and politics. When he received his name "Amiri Baraka" ('blessed prince')[2] from the same orthodox Muslim who had buried Malcolm X, Baraka became the symbolic heir to Malcolm, the "Malcolm X of literature."[3] Baraka's stature as a people's hero and rebellious outlaw was affirmed, at various points in the 1960s, by such public figures as Huey Newton, Eldridge Cleaver, Rap Brown, and Stokely Carmichael. More than any other American writer, white or black, Baraka is the committed artist *par excellence*.[4] His line of ancestors might include Zola, Malraux, and Richard Wright, Nat Turner and John Brown, Thoreau and Karl Marx.

On the other hand, Baraka is a subtle and innovative poet whose achievements were praised by Allen Ginsberg and Charles Olson, as well as by many poetic successors. He is the author of *Dutchman*, according to Norman Mailer "the best play in America";[5] and his contributions to a transformation of the American stage are crucial.[6] Baraka is also an important modernist fiction writer. Like a character in one of his plays, Baraka may be seen as a "Black Baudelaire," a highly accomplished, visionary, postromantic writer, whose literary ancestors are different from those of Baraka the

rebel and might include Jakob Boehme, Rimbaud, Mallarmé, Kier-
kegaard, Joyce, Kafka, Strindberg, Ionesco, Genet, and André
Breton, as well as Melville, Whitman, Mark Twain, Eliot, Lorca,
Williams, Pound, Toomer, Cummings, and Yeats.

Although the metaphor of "avant-gardism" is political *and* artistic, the images of a "Malcolm X of literature" and of a "Black
Baudelaire," of a practical man and of a visionary, of an Afro-
American leader and of a Western modernist do not merge easily.[7]
Baraka felt the dichotomy between "The psychological and the
social. The spiritual and the practical" (T 37). In his development
as a writer, he offered different solutions to the problem of fusing
"populism" and "modernism" (M xvi).

In its vaguest sense, the unity Baraka aspires to is a romantic
unity of life and art, which must be wrested from "bourgeois" systems of classification and separation of realms. This accounts for the
constancy with which Baraka has attacked the bourgeois aesthetic
of "new criticism," of declaring "art" an "object" unrelated to author, reader, society, or history. Baraka's quest for a populist modernism began with a rejection of the *"objective"* [8] aesthetic and artifact fetishism which he sensed in the particular bourgeoisie from
which he emerged.

Amiri Baraka was born Everett LeRoi Jones in Newark, New
Jersey, on October 7, 1934. He is the son of Coyette LeRoy Jones,
a postal supervisor, and Anna Lois Russ Jones, a social worker and
Tuskegee graduate; the grandson of Thomas Everett Russ, a man
active in trade, politics, and religion; and the descendant of Baptist
preachers and teachers.[9] Baraka attended Newark's Central Avenue School and Barringer High School, then nominally "integrated" by the token presence of a few Black students. As a student, Baraka was interested in religion and intended to become a
minister. After graduation from high school in 1951, however, he
enrolled at the Newark branch of Rutgers University on a science
scholarship. In 1952, Baraka transferred to Howard University,
where he took courses in philosophy, religion, and German while
concentrating in English literature. Baraka despised Howard and
considered it a "sick" institution which "makes most Negroes who
go there turn out bourgeois conservatives."[10] However, it was at

Howard that Baraka acquired the intellectual tools for such an indictment of "bourgeois conservatives"; he profited especially from
his classes with E. Franklin Frazier, and from the influence of
Sterling A. Brown.

In 1954, Baraka dropped out of Howard and joined the Air
Force. After basic training in South Carolina, he became a

weatherman and gunner on a B-36 stationed at Ramey Field, Puerto Rico.
"We were the Strategic Air Command, right out of 'Dr. Strangelove.' I
spent most of my time reading, in the air and on the ground."[11]

After his return to civilian life, in January 1957, Baraka moved to
New York's Beat community on the Lower East Side. What was
blocked off by the Black bourgeoisie seemed open and accessible in
Bohemia. In his very important first phase of rebellion against the
separation of life and art, his Beat period, Baraka voiced aesthetic
protest against his background. His first strategy of defying the
concept of art as an "object" was to articulate an *expressive* aesthetic and to define art as an expression and extension of the artist.

In New York, Baraka worked for the *Record Changer* magazine
and for the Phoenix bookstore, where he met Hettie Roberta
Cohen, with whom he coedited the avant-garde literary magazine
Yugen (meaning "elegance, beauty, grace, transcendence of these
things, and also nothing at all"). In the eight issues that were to appear from 1958 to 1962, Baraka and Hettie Cohen published works
by William Burroughs, Gregory Corso, Diane DiPrima, Allen
Ginsberg, Jack Kerouac, Tuli Kupferberg, Ron Loewinsohn, Michael McClure, Frank O'Hara, Charles Olson, Peter Orlovsky,
Tom Postell, Gilbert Sorrentino, A. B. Spellman and many other
illustrious and less illustrious friends and associates from Black
Mountain, the New York School, and the "Beat Scene." *Yugen* 1
and 2 also contained Baraka's own first proper literary publications.

In 1958, Hettie Cohen, of Jewish-American descent, and Baraka
were married in a Buddhist temple on New York's Upper West
Side; in the following years they had two daughters, Kellie Elisabeth and Lisa Victoria Chapman Jones. Hettie Cohen Jones, who
had become an editor at *Partisan Review*, encouraged Baraka to
publish his first essay, a defense of the Beat Generation, in the cor-

respondence section of that magazine. Beginning in 1958, Baraka wrote more and more prolifically, and little magazines such as *Naked Ear, Birth, Epos, Quicksilver, Hearse, Odyssey, Jazz Review, Big Table, Evergreen Review, White Dove Review, Kulchur, Nomad,* and *Metronome,* published his poems, essays, letters to the editor, and book, movie and record reviews. In 1959, Baraka began his own series of literary broadsides, Totem Press, a name suggested by George Stade. In this series, Baraka edited Michael McClure's *For Artaud,* and Charles Olson's *Projective Verse.* Totem Press published Baraka's first collection of poems, entitled *Preface to a Twenty Volume Suicide Note.* One of Baraka's own contributions to Totem Press books was a poem, "For You," which was included in an anthology entitled *Jan 1st 1959: Fidel Castro.* Partly as a result of this poem, Baraka was invited to Cuba in 1960. Baraka's "Cuba libre," the account of this trip, became the first of a series of political essays, later collected in *Home: Social Essays,* which document his increasingly explicit social commitments.

Accepting some tenets of the emerging New Left, Baraka moved toward a *mimetic* definition of the function of art. The unity of life and art was no longer limited to the inwardness of the artist, but was supposed to take place "inside" and "outside" at the same time. The opposition began to take the shape of individual vs. society.

At this point Baraka turned toward drama. His first extant play, "The Eighth Ditch (Is Drama)," included in the small literary journal *The Floating Bear,* which Baraka coedited with Diane DiPrima, was confiscated by the post office for alleged obscenity. His next plays were *The Baptism,* a satirical and blasphemous indictment of religious philistinism, and the most famous of his protest drama, *The Toilet, Dutchman,* and *The Slave.* With the acclaimed productions of these plays, Baraka became a famous playwright and social figure. He accepted offers to teach poetry and drama at Columbia University and the New School for Social Research; as a visiting lecturer, he went to the University of Buffalo; he travelled to France and Germany to attend openings of *Dutchman.* Back in New York, he received several literary awards. Baraka also edited *The Moderns,* an anthology of contemporary prose writers, and published a social history of Black music in America, *Blues People,* his first book to appear with an established publishing house in which he held no editorial position. In 1964 he published a second volume of poems, *The Dead Lecturer.* His novel, *The System of Dante's Hell,* appeared in 1965 and a short story collection, *Tales,* in 1967.

In the mid-1960s, in the more and more ethnocentric phase of Black cultural nationalism, Baraka came to see art predominantly as a "weapon"; and he adhered to this *pragmatic* concept of literature even as the politics of his commitment changed. His antibourgeois opposition was now rephrased as a black-white antagonism. In 1965, the year of the assassination of Malcolm X and the ghetto revolt of Watts, Baraka withdrew from the literary avant-garde that had been his—second—home, left his family and moved to Harlem. There he started the Black Arts Repertory Theatre/School, employing only Black actors and catering exclusively to Black audiences. The Harlem theatre project, although short-lived, was an innovation that revolutionized Black theater in America: it provided a model that was quickly followed throughout urban Black America. The Black Arts Repertory Theatre, which was financed with federal money through the HARYOU Act and the Office of Economic Opportunity, was closed when the police claimed to have discovered a weapons arsenal in the building. By that time, however, Baraka had left the project and returned, disappointed, to his native Newark.

Back home, he utilized his experiences as writer, editor, essayist, and theater director, and founded or helped to organize in quick succession several groups: an unsubsidized Black cultural center, "Spirit House," with a dramatic troupe, "The Spirit House Movers and Players"; a campaign group for local politics, "Committee for a Unified Newark," and a community organization, "United Brothers"; a cultural-nationalist, quasireligious group, "Black Community Defense and Development," influenced by the Nation of Islam, orthodox Islam, and by the Kawaida-teachings of Maulana Ron Karenga, chairman of the California organization, US. He followed with a publishing house, "Jihad" (i.e., "Holy War," or "Striving Toward Righteousness") Productions, an "Afrikan Free

School," a cooperative book and record store, "Nyumba Ya Uja-maa," and a controversial, still unfinished, housing project, "Kawaida Towers."

In August 1966, Baraka married a Black woman, Sylvia Robinson, now Amina Baraka, director of the New Ark[12] Afrikan Free School. Their children are Obalaji Malik Ali, Ras Jua Al Aziz, Shani Isis Makeda, Amiri Seku Musa, and Ahi Mwenge.

During the Newark ghetto revolt of 1967, Baraka was injured, arrested by the police, and indicted for unlawfully carrying firearms. An all-white jury convicted him, and after the judge read Baraka's poem "Black people!" (B 225) to the court, the poet was sentenced to 2–2½ years in jail without parole. Baraka won a retrial motion and was later acquitted. Also in 1967, Baraka helped organize a National Black Power Conference in Newark.

Jihad Productions, which had published a small collection of Baraka's poems, *Black Art* in 1966, brought out two Baraka plays in 1967, *Arm Yourself or Harm Yourself* and *Slave Ship*. Jihad also printed young Black writers such as Ben Caldwell, Yusef Iman, Clarence Reed, and Marvin X in books and pamphlets which, in format and outlook, resembled the earlier Totem Press series. Many of the Jihad authors were also included in *Black Fire* (1968), an anthology of contemporary Afro-American writing coedited by Baraka and Larry Neal. In the introduction to this anthology, Baraka first used his new name. In the same year, his music criticism was collected under the title *Black Music*.

Upon the assassination of Martin Luther King, who had visited Newark and talked with Baraka just days before,[13] Baraka urged Newarkers not to "riot," and later charged white leftists with inciting unrest in the Black ghetto. This statement, which Baraka made in a nation-wide CBS interview in the presence of Newark's chief of police and of Anthony Imperiale, the leader of a white conservative group, was perhaps dictated by political expedience: at that time, Baraka was beginning to agitate for a Black mayor in Newark and may have used this red-baiting technique to demonstrate his own independence of the New Leftists who had respected him since "Cuba libre." But this gesture also introduced the antileftist tone which characterized Baraka's Black nationalist commitment of the 1960s.

In 1969, Baraka's poetry and drama collections, *Black Magic: Poetry 1961–1967* and *Four Black Revolutionary Plays* appeared. In 1970, Baraka initiated the "first modern" Pan-African Congress in Atlanta, the proceedings of which were published in 1972 under the title *African Congress,* and he campaigned actively and successfully for the election of Kenneth Gibson, the first Black mayor of Newark. Also in 1970, Baraka issued *The Black Value System,* the program of Kawaida (later included in R 133–46). In the same year Third World Press, a Black publishing house in Chicago, published *Jello* and *It's Nation Time,* and Bobbs-Merrill brought out *In Our Terribleness,* an album of photographs of Black life accompanied by Baraka texts. In 1971, Baraka's *Strategy and Tactics of a Pan-African Political Party* and *Raise Race Rays Raze: Essays Since 1965* appeared. In 1972, a new volume of poetry, *Spirit Reach,* followed. In the same year, Baraka was one of the three organizers of the famous Black American Congress in Gary.

In 1974, Baraka made yet another move, away from Black nationalism and toward socialism. As Chairman of the Congress of African People, he has transformed this organization into the Revolutionary Communist League; his monthly newspaper, *Black New Ark,* has become *Unity and Struggle;* and a reinterpretation of the Black situation is under way which refers to economic rather than cultural factors, discards many of Baraka's ideas of the 1960s as chauvinistic, and agitates against cultural nationalism.[14]

Baraka's first works emerging from this new commitment adapt his artistic idiom to agitprop techniques in plays such as "S–1" and "The Motion of History," in the poems collected in *Hard Facts* (1976), and in ubiquitous political essays, from the Congress of African People Ideological Papers to pamphlets like *Crisis in Boston!!!!,* published by "Vita Wa Watu—Peoples War Publishing," the former Jihad Productions.

Obviously, Baraka's literary and political positions have covered much heterogeneous territory. However baffling the range of Baraka's changes may appear, a roughly chronological chart can cautiously be drawn in order to delineate four major phases in his political and aesthetic commitments:

	1958–61	1960–65	1964–74	1974–
COMMITMENT	aesthetic protest	political/ ethnic protest	Black Cultural Nationalism	Marxism Leninism Mao-Tse-Tung-Thought
	Beat Bohemianism	New Left	Kawaida	
AESTHETIC	expressive	mimetic	pragmatic	pragmatic

   This schematic division is helpful to an understanding of the magnitude of Baraka's changes in art and politics, but of course it does not "fit" each and every work he wrote. There are forward-looking and backward-looking elements in all phases, and works which mark "turning points" from one aesthetic-political mode to another. The phases are furthermore linked by Baraka's persistent demand for a populist modernism, a unity of life and art, literature and society, through all his periods and changes. This unified con-cern helps to establish identity and "sameness" in the personal idiom and literary voice of the man who is both the Malcolm X of literature and a Black Baudelaire. The term Baraka applied to a discussion of Rhythm and Blues music is also an appropriately dialectic characterization of the way I would like to present Baraka's own development: as "The Changing Same" (BM 180–211).
   My own approach[15] is located somewhere between American Studies/Black Studies and Comparative Literature: the latter dis-cipline helps to establish and take seriously the *literary* voice of Baraka in the international context of the "Isms" of 19th- and 20th-century literature, from Symbolism to Dadaism, Surrealism, and Absurdism, while the former interdisciplinary orientation sheds light on the *social* dimensions of a Black writer in confrontation with the political and ethnic reality of America and helps us to con-ceptualize Black bourgeois socialization, "Crow-Jimism," and dif-

ferent models of Black nationalism. This double focus may contribute to a new interpretation of Baraka's works and increase our understanding of the cultural climate of contemporary America, black and white.

1 From Black Bourgeoisie to Beat Bohemia

1. "BLACK BOURGEOISIE"

In the early poem, "Consider This," first published in 1959, the speaker describes himself:

> I am wearing a brown flannel suit
> & button down shirt.
> I have degrees from three colleges; & an
> affected french name. I'm well liked (UP 17)

The character projected here experiences a crisis of identity; he is a recurring Barakian persona, developed most fully in the figure of Clay in *Dutchman*. The young man from the Black middle class finds himself defined and confined by externals and becomes alienated from himself as a reflector of bourgeois manners and aspirations, clothes and beliefs. Something inside is "buttoned down," or repressed, by an alien costume and mask. The Black bourgeois's choice of "conservative" suits and shirts signals the larger principle of hidden identity. Baraka parallels the desire of Black people to be merely Americans with that of the Carthaginians to become Romans; therefore the poet sees "Hannibal with his / 8 button Italian armor" (UP 17) in the same way in which he interprets the confinement of his own Black self under button-down shirts and three-button suits. Unbuttoning repressed Christians and acquisitive middle-class citizens in order to lay bare the African emperor under the Western bourgeois masquerade thus becomes a natural task for a writer who searches for truth behind masks and who attempts to cut through religious hypocrisy and false consciousness, through social delusions and sexual repression. One crucial element in Baraka's "Changing Same"-ness is a continuing struggle with Black bourgeois façades, including the poet's own masks and costumes. For Baraka, literature had to be committed to self-liberation, unbuttoning the Hannibal from the Roman armor.

Baraka's Howard professor E. Franklin Frazier depicted the world of the *Black Bourgeoisie* harshly, and it is along the lines of Frazier's indictment of the Black middle class that Baraka's own disaffiliation from his background unfolded. Seen through Frazier's eyes, the Black middle class appears as a small, ridiculous stratum of Afro-America, which has achieved a moderate standard of living at a horrible price. Emulating the white bourgeoisie but denying its own blackness, the Black bourgeoisie has not found a real economic role or a meaningful identity in America. It compensates for its collective inferiority complex by living in a world of make-believe. According to Frazier, middle-class Negroes direct their repressed hostilities

inward toward themselves. This results in self-hatred, which may appear from their behavior to be directed towards the Negro masses but which in reality is directed against themselves. . . . They are insulted if they are identified with Africans. . . . [N]othing pleases them more than to be mistaken for a Puerto Rican, Philippino, Egyptian or Arab or any ethnic group other than Negro.[1]

In conceptualizing his critique of the "sickness" of the world of his father, Baraka relied on Frazier; and one summary of this critique is given in a poem which shares the title of Frazier's study.

> *Black Bourgeoisie,*
>   *has a gold tooth, sits long hours*
>   *on a stool thinking about money.*
>   *sees white skin in a secret room*
>   *rummages his sense for sense*
>   *dreams about Lincoln(s)*
>   *conks his daughter's hair*
>   *sends his coon to school*
>   *works very hard*
>   *grins politely in restaurants*
>   *has a good word to say*
>   *never says it*
>   *does not hate ofays*

hates, instead, him self
him black self (B 111)

Baraka's satiric exegesis of Frazier's thesis is precise; and his pun on "Lincoln(s)" suggests Black bourgeois object fetishism displayed in "fancy" cars as well as false historical consciousness about emancipation. Baraka's relationship to his bourgeois background is not always as unambiguously satirical as in the poem "Black bourgeoisie." As part of a self-questioning attitude, Baraka's antibourgeois commitment is directed against aspects of his own past, against a part of himself.[2] The obsessive recurrence of buttoned-up Black middle-class characters in Baraka's works and his persistent polemic against the "mainstream," "middle-headed," "middle-brow" middle class attest to an intimate attachment to the sensibility of the class from which he struggled so hard to extricate himself; thus, middle-class or petit bourgeois consciousness has a negative centrality for Baraka's world view. Baraka often ridiculed the hypocrisy of the Baptist church, but retained a deep-seated sense of religion and used Christic references and biblical language throughout his writings. He punctured the Black middle class's inflated esteem for educational accomplishments, but found it advisable to maintain that he held several academic degrees, although his friends Allen Ginsberg and Jack Kerouac boasted of being dropouts. He satirized bourgeois sexual mores, but explained, ironically, that he married "as protection against Bohemia."[3] He pitted his artistic "disorder" against petty bourgeois concepts of orderliness, but he dressed neatly among Bohemians, was known "for his impeccable tweeds"[4] and had *office hours* "by appointment only" in his fourth-floor walk-up artist's pad.[5] He criticized middle-class Blacks for betraying other Blacks in their individualistic adherence to the American "economic sensibility," and he cast his own lot, against them, with the opposing "imaginary sensibility." In this opposition, however, he was no less individualistic than his opponents and displayed an exaggerated obsession with his own self in often hermetically privatistic autobiographic literature. Baraka, the self-declared "prodigal" son of the "shabby" Black bourgeoisie, thus protested against his cultural matrix, using patterns that that culture had first conveyed to him.[6] His first form of protest against the middle class was an aesthetic rebellion, formulated as an indictment, not of racism, capitalism, or the Cold War, but of middle-brow taste.

When Baraka, who had been a voracious reader during childhood and adolescence, turned toward writing, he defied the restrictive "philistine" aesthetic of the Black bourgeoisie which defined art as an artifact, an "object,"[7] and a credit to the race. When Baraka broke into print in the "placid" decade of the 1950s,[8] Afro-American literature had reached the peak of its integrationist universalism, middle-class orientation, sexual inhibition, and naturalistic conventionality. Lorraine Hansberry's Broadway and Hollywood success *A Raisin in the Sun* (1959) epitomized this literature; and it was an anathema to later Black writers that Hansberry insisted on interpreting the characters of her play as "honest-to-God, believable, many-sided people who *happened* to be Negroes," and herself, not as a "Negro playwright," but as a writer who "happens to be a Negro."[9] Despite Baraka's own contradictory relationship to his bourgeois background, he never published a work of a similar aesthetic and social orientation, and very early in his career began polemicizing against Christianized, middle-class, middle-brow, integrationist, and naturalist "Negro literature."

Since the world of the Black bourgeoisie was, for Baraka, an *unreal* world of false façades, draperies, and costumes, the world of the imagination had to be more "real" than the empirical one. Committed to reveal the truth behind façades, Baraka's ideal literature could never be that of a "well-made play" or of an accomplished art *object;* for him, art had to be the dynamic *vehicle* of antibourgeois rebellion. Defining his anti*object*ive art as an act of liberation and self-liberation, Baraka embraced contradictory literary prototypes. He opposed the bourgeois notion of art as an object both from "above," in the name of avant-gardism and modernism, and from "below," in the name of people's and popular culture. This antibourgeois cultural strategy which is directed both at bourgeois guilt feelings toward the masses and at a sense of inferiority toward the upper class, is known as Bohemianism.

2. BOHEMIA: "AXEL'S CASTLE"

> *"I have the feeling people*
> *think I'm depraved. A man looked*
> *me in the eye in the subway and he sd,*
> *Bohemian."*
> —*"Consider This" (UP 17)*

An early uncollected poem by Baraka is significantly entitled "Axel's Castle (1958)" (UP 35). Appropriating the title of Edmund Wilson's study in the imaginative literature of 1870–1930, Baraka casts himself in the tradition of European Symbolist writers who have "tended to overemphasize the importance of the individual, . . . have been preoccupied with introspection sometimes almost to the point of insanity," yet have "succeeded in effecting in literature a revolution analogous to that which has taken place in science and philosophy." They "have revealed to the imagination a new flexibility and freedom."[10]

In "Axel's Castle," this imaginative freedom is sought in the interior of an ivory tower. The very existence of this illuminated fortress of the imaginative sensibility transforms and poeticizes the "real world" of the protagonist:

> *The man with the fruit stand*
> *Lives in a castle. A huge rusty thing.*
> > *With a roaring moat*
> > *And red flags strea-*
> > *Ming from its towers.*
> *Each evening, after selling his fruit,*
> *The man dashes out the back door, giggling*
> *Obscenely, and leaps on his white horse.*
> *Rushing across the countryside: Across*
> *Bleecker St. to McDougal, down McDougal*
> *Till the castle can be seen outlined*
> *Against the water, stuttering in some*
> *Effusive glow, like an illuminated trunk.*

Baraka juxtaposes the worlds of economics and of imagination and ironicizes both the economic reality of the Greenwich Village fruit seller (with his white "horse" connection) and the visionary construct of the Wagnerian-Arthurian castle. The titles of Wilson's study and of Baraka's poem refer to the protagonist of Villiers de l'Isle-Adam's lyrical fin-de-siècle drama *Axel* (1890). The decadent hero Axel withdraws completely into his isolated Gothic castle where he achieves a state of perfect separation from reality. Indeed, his separation is so absolute that, after discovering an immense treasure, he prefers suicide in unison with his lover Sara to anything he could do with the money in real life: "Live? our servants will do that for us. . . . Oh, the external world! Let us not be made dupes by the old slave. . . ."[11] Baraka's defense against "reality" is weaker than Axel's. Although the fruit vendor's castle is protected by "Twelve stern guards . . . Armed with pikes and / Twelve foot switchblades" his world is forever defined by the economic realities from which he can secede only symbolically:

> In the mighty halls, the stodgy armor stands clanking
> Silent. And Tintoretto's line the walls like guests.
> In the dining room, Lady fruitseller waits. Her white
> Soft arms flung open in greeting. She wears a jade gown
> And Guinevere's hat, jewels bristling on her flesh like
> Blemishes. They embrace, and squat before the fireplace
> > Which stands, a tunnel, glowering in
> > The great room. Soon the bird is cooked
> > And eaten; its bones tossed to the mangy
> > Cur that graces the Persian rugs.
> After the meal, the man tells the wife of the big world.
> The cold world. The hard indifferent world of the outside.
> The world of inflationary prices and rotting fruit.

Like the fruit vendor, the Barakian artist absorbs reality into the very heart of the house of fiction, because, like the lettuce salesman, the writer is subject to "the risks of unemployment and overproduction."[12] This state of affairs, described by the words "economic and cultural alienation" in Renato Poggioli's *Theory of the Avant-Garde*, is also one source of the artist's antibourgeois rebellion. In "Axel's Castle," Baraka employs an antibourgeois strategy by resorting to the aristocratic dream world of a feudal castle with a

Greenwich Village street address; he fends off the world of the middle class, however weakly and self-doubtingly, from "above," from the aristocratic position of high art, represented by Tintorettos and Guinevere's jewels.

At the same time, the setting of this mock-refuge betrays its roots in the countless Arthurian castles built by the popular culture industry in Hollywood and elsewhere; and the presence of "red flags" and of guards with "switchblades" attests to an antibourgeois threat from "below," represented by mass culture and violence as a premonition of "dangers" to come in the future. "Axel's Castle" thus employs Baraka's Bohemian strategy of combatting the middle world of the bourgeoisie from the merged points of view of prince and pauper, king and beggar, castle and switchblade, symbolism and popular culture, of high art and "trash." This strategy forces the ex-bourgeois renegade to "proletarianize" the aristocrat and to ennoble the lumpen, until the diverse nonbourgeois allies are absorbed into a single visionary consciousness.

The short story, "Round Trip" (UF 2), published in 1959, further illustrates this process. The plot of this apprenticeship tale is simple. The narrator, a street-sweeper, encounters a Bohemian arch-hero and outsider *par excellence,* a mythic philosopher/prophet/singer/bum. This modern-day Diogenes lives, not in a barrel, but in cardboard boxes; he eats what he finds in the trash and invites the narrator to join him for "dinner," during which the quasi-saint sings for his guest. One day, the narrator finds him dead.

His face was caked with blood and his eyes were still open, staring straight up. Somebody had stabbed him in the side and God knows where else. I ran for the cops. They came and carried him away . . . said he was a bum and that he was probably in a brawl. Stupid bastards, what do they know? They never heard him sing. (UF 2, p. 81)

Through his martyrdom, the singer assumes Christic stature and becomes a saint of the imagination, slaughtered by an unfeeling society:[13] "Even his feet and hands had stab marks in 'em. Can you imagine?" In "Round Trip," the bum is sanctified, just as in "Axel's Castle" the aristocratic ivory tower is "popularized." "Can you imagine?" becomes a question with an intended larger meaning; and the nonbourgeois people who *can* use their imaginations are the new chosen people, the Bohemians.

The concept of Bohemianism, despite its evident centrality to the Beat Scene, has been largely ignored by critics of Beat literature. On the other hand, studies of Bohemianism and avant-gardism have generally included the American Beat movement, seeing it as part of a historical tradition. Baraka interpreted his own artistic departure from the middle class as a *Bohemian* gesture. He emerged as a writer in the Bohemian milieu of the Beat Generation and has retained Bohemian traits throughout much of his career. He placed himself, as we observed in "Axel's Castle," in the tradition of symbolism, and, as his first essays document, in the international camp of aesthetic protest and antibourgeois Bohemianism, from Dada and Surrealism to Beat, from avant-gardist music and painting to Bebop and modern jazz. At one point, Baraka planned a book entitled "The Black Bohemian: A Study of the Contemporary Negro Intellectual,"[14] and his continuous concern with Bohemianism is expressed in the very terminology used by European and American observers of the phenomenon. It is therefore essential to this study to delineate the politics and aesthetics of Bohemianism in order to more fully comprehend Baraka's first, and perhaps most pervasive, form of cultural commitment.

The tradition of Bohemianism is of comparatively recent origin. Bohemian tendencies "began with Edgar Allan Poe"[15] (who was also seen as a "prophet of symbolism" by Edmund Wilson) and first became prevalent in those industrialized societies of the 19th and 20th centuries which granted sufficient individual liberties to permit symbolic aggression. In liberal democracies, Bohemians are complementary to the middle classes. According to Helmut Kreuzer, at the core of Bohemia is an emotional identification with, and sympathy for, "such peoples and races, social classes, castes, strata, and groups . . . which are suppressed and persecuted . . . or simply discriminated against socially."[16] Indeed, the very name "bohème" goes back to a French word for Gypsies, an etymological connection of which Baraka was aware. While sympathy for out-

casts and oppressed minorities is crucial to Bohemianism, the definition of what constitutes oppressed outsiders is generous enough
to include anybody who is in conflict with the middle class, from
the proletariat to deposed kings, from criminals and lunatics to artists and Bohemians themselves. Characteristic of Bohemian literature is a listing of the downtrodden, who may range from "suf-
fragettes, Negroes, Jews, whores and fairies," to "wage-slaves,"
"intimidated soldiers," and, of course, to "ridiculed cubist
painters."[17]

While the Bohemian empathizes with the victims of bourgeois
societies, he is likely to perceive their plight in aesthetic, rather
than in political terms. The Bohemian's sympathies for socialism
are often nourished by a facile equation of the "revolutions" of
modern art with the social upheavals of subbourgeois classes, of the
"avant-gardism" of the cubists and futurists with that of the Lenin-
ists. Taking the metaphor of "avant-gardism" literally, Bohemians
may not merely consider aesthetic and political revolutions as part
of the same struggle against bourgeois domination, they may also
believe aesthetic avant-gardism to be superior. It is for this reason,
Kreuzer argues, that artists occasionally demand a position of
power and leadership for the "aristocracy of the ingenious ones" in
postrevolutionary societies:

The enthusiasm for the working classes was at least partially an enthusiasm of self-appointed leaders for those masses they intended to lead in the
name of "mind" and in the interest of intellectuals.[18]

In political terms, aesthetic protest is closer to its bourgeois an-
tipode than Bohemians would have it. In their desire to be as anti-
middle-class as possible, Bohemians present no political alternative
to bourgeois rule, but merely invert images of bourgeois *values*. In
their alternating aristocratic and plebeian masquerades, they reject
the bourgeois obsession with money by acting as wasteful dandies
or as penniless oppressed artists, by withdrawing to the ivory
towers of the arts or by agitating for spontaneous violence in the
streets. They are suspect in the eyes of socialist theoreticians and
communist revolutionaries; and Karl Marx viewed Bohemians in

The Eighteenth Brumaire of Louis Bonaparte (1852), in the most
pejorative terms, as "scum, offal, refuse of all classes" and as the
lumpenproletarian base of Bonaparte's ascent to power.[19]

Despite its dubious political role, Bohemianism, as a "culture of
negation," may appear more "radical" than any political commitment. Aesthetic protest may paradoxically hover beyond the extremes of political Left and Right in its determined attempt to be
as far removed as possible from bourgeois, middle-class values,
against which it defines itself, but on the axis of which it remains.[20]
Disgust for the political center makes the Bohemian discard the
conservative and the liberal and embrace the fascist and the communist. In his investigation of "Politics and Literary Imagination,"
David Daiches sees Georges Sorel as a key figure, because he

admired equally Lenin and Mussolini; Sorel, who in his strange career of
political questing came to repudiate not only the principles of 1789 but
those of the Enlightenment, of bourgeois democracy, of humanitarianism
of any kind, to preach violence as "a very beautiful and heroic thing" and
to move from belief in the heroic violence of the proletarian strike to join
forces with the extreme nationalist, royalist Right. Throughout all the
vagaries of Sorel's extraordinary career, one thing remained more or less
constant: his contempt for the bourgeoisie.[21]

In many of his conclusions, Daiches supports Kreuzer's and
Poggioli's observations:

Politically, then, modernist art is Janus-faced, combining a revolutionary
urge to smash the existing system with an ideal vision of order which is
often politically reactionary.

If Bohemian politics is ambiguous and elusive, the imaginative
geography of Bohemia is more easily charted. In 1896, Gelett
Burgess published his own "Map of Bohemia,"[22] which represents
the country of the arts as a land ranging from the Sea of Dreams to
the Hills of Fame, including a Pays de la Jeunesse, The Port of
Peace, The Forest of Arden, Vagabondia, and the capital, Veritas.
At the frontier of unknown territories are Licentia and its center,
Crudelitas. A long, straight borderline separates Bohemia from
Philistia with its Great Philistine Desert, the City of Shams and the
capital, Vanitas. Burgess' ironic, and in itself quite Bohemian,

moral geography of Bohemia posits an artistic cult of youth, beauty, truth and flourishing life against the bourgeois desert of hypocrisy, vanity, and fraudulence. The location and geographic shape of Bohemia, however, also resemble those of the Holy Land; and both the chosen people of Israel and the chosen people of the Bohème were pitted against the neighboring Philistines.[23]

The Beat Generation was an archetypical American Bohemian art movement. Beat poets were constantly at odds with the Philistine excesses of the 1950s: they protested against bourgeois concern with wealth and "progress," against the Cold War and anticommunist witchhunts, against H-bomb tests and defense drills, and against the persistence of racism in American society. Their essentially aesthetic protest, however, was so "total" and "radical" that it did little to further its supposed social ends in the larger society. Kenneth Rexroth's interpretation of "disengagement" thus confirms Kreuzer's and Daiches' observations:

The youngest generation is in a state of revolt so absolute that its elders cannot even recognize it. This disaffiliation, alienation, and rejection of the young has, as far as their elders are concerned, moved out of the visible spectrum altogether.[24]

The Bohemians' point of retreat, their "absolute revolt," turned out to be one of the cornerstones of American liberalism—i.e., uncompromising individualism—which made their protest frequently introverted, oblique, and, from a political point of view, ineffective. According to Hans Magnus Enzensberger, the very name "Beat Generation" gave witness to the rebels' willingness to be accepted, or at least tolerated, by the society they supposedly revolted against;[25] they were prepared to interpret their function, tongue-in-cheek, not as a serious alternative against "America the Moloch," but merely as another injection of fresh generational blood into the otherwise decadent mainstream. This is indicated by the ironic motto of the *Beatitude Anthology,* with its allusion to Hemingway's equally fictional "Lost Generation" in *The Sun Also Rises* (1926):

"You are all a Beat Generation."—Gertrude Stein in conversation with Jack Kerouac.[26]

The Beats' dependence upon the rejected bourgeoisie becomes apparent not only in their willingness to interpret themselves within the American literary mainstream as a new Lost Generation, but also in their desire for publicity in the bourgeois press. Kerouac's frequently quoted *Playboy* article on the origins of the Beat Generation shows that such publicity was, perhaps, a desirable side effect of "disaffiliation." Kerouac reports that he had just returned to San Francisco from a two-month stay in the mountains; he was about to get washed when

my friend Gregory Corso opened his shirt and took out a silver crucifix that was hanging from a chain and said "Wear this and wear it outside your shirt and don't comb your hair!" so I spent several days around San Francisco going around with him and others like that . . . and finally on the third day *Mademoiselle* magazine wanted to take pictures of us all so I posed just like that, wild hair, crucifix, and all, with Gregory Corso, Allen Ginsberg and Phil Whalen . . . and the only publication which later did not erase the crucifix from my breast . . . was *The New York Times*, therefore *The New York Times* is as beat as I am and I'm glad I've got a friend.[27]

In the definition of what it was they protested against, there was hopeless confusion; and a rambling dualism evolved of what was good (beat, hip) and bad (square) that left only the individual creative act intact as an unchallenged goal. From one day to another, newspapers, philosophers, even words like "beat" or "Bohemian" could fall into disgrace and be considered "square," depending on the spontaneous creative impulse of individuals. Thus, Norman Mailer disagrees with Kerouac's flippant assessment of the *New York Times*, labelling it "square," as opposed to the "hipper" *New York Herald Tribune*. Other examples from Mailer's two-page list of opposites are:

HIP	SQUARE
romantic	classic
instinct	logic
Negro	white
spontaneous	orderly

associative	sequential
Catholic	Protestant
Heidegger	Sartre
Trotsky	Lenin
Nixon	Dulles
Churchill	Clement Attlee
hipster	beatnik
anarchists	socialists
barbarians	bohemians
to listen to the sound of the voice and take one's meaning from there	to listen to the meaning of the words and obey no other meaning.[28]

The arbitrariness of the pros and cons chosen is immediately apparent and, indeed, part of the aesthetic program. There is no political meaning in Mailer's opposites, merely the intention to thwart expectations. Although Bohemian literature of the 1950s was occasionally measured by a political yardstick, the antibourgeois yet individualist values Mailer calls "hip," "romantic," "spontaneous," and "associative" contained only a latent reservoir of prepolitical resistance, upon which the New Left could consciously draw in the 1960s. The notion of "hipness" constituted the self-oriented position of Bohemianism and aesthetic protest which assigned a quasisacral function to works such as Allen Ginsberg's *Howl* (1956), Jack Kerouac's *On the Road* (1957), and William Burroughs' *Naked Lunch* (1959). The emotional center of the spontaneous aesthetic and of hipness was in the symbolic identification of the artist with the Black man, since, according to Mailer, "the source of Hip is the Negro."

3. CROW-JIMISM

> *Wipes*
> *her nose*
> *on the draperies. Spills drinks*
> *fondles another man's*
> *life. She is looking*
> *for alternatives.*
> —*"Crow Jane in High Society"* (DL 51)

The European Bohème identified emotionally with Gypsies and their music; the American Beat community emulated Black Americans, and especially the subculture of Bebop musicians. As an avant-gardist art movement, the Beat Generation cherished the notion of an American "art of alienation." Therefore, Baraka argues in *Blues People,*

the life of the Negro in America and his subsequent production of a high art which took its shape directly from the nature and meaning of his own alienation . . . reshaped certain crucial elements of the American art of the last two decades, and gave a deeply native reference to the direction of American Bohemianism, or artist's life, of the fifties. (BP 231)

This "native reference" was used, in a characteristically Bohemian way, as a negation of bourgeois attitudes. While the Bohemians' impulse was sympathetic to Blacks, their perception was tainted by those misconceptions which, according to Gunnar Myrdal, white Americans generally cherished. Although hoping to transcend racist discrimination, if not in America at large then at least in the world of Bohemia, Beat writers approached the problem in the "white man's rank order," and then inverted that order. Sexual integration, most abhorred by Myrdal's sample of whites and of least concern to Blacks, became a most desirable Bohemian goal; whereas discrimination in the world of the "economic sensibility," perceived as the most oppressive form of discrimination by Blacks, did not concern the Bohemians very much.[29] Baraka discussed this strategy of inversion critically in the 1965 essay "American Sexual Reference: Black Male" and observed that in the various bohemias and nearbohemias . . . such normally hidden or reversed image of the black man as superstud for white women . . . is not only given large currency, but taken literally by both black and white. (H 227)

A psychological survey of a Beat community conducted by Francis J. Rigney confirms Baraka's observations. Rigney concludes that in the Bohemians' sexual relations

in sharp contrast to the usual American pattern (mostly Southern) of exploitative relations between Caucasian men and Negro women, the sexual relationships are almost exclusively between Negro men and Caucasian women. (This reversal has been called "Crow-Jimism.")[30]

The term "Crow-Jimism," attributed to Kenneth Rexroth, elucidates the inversion of white segregationist Jim Crow society in the Bohemian subculture. If "Jim Crow" sexual politics meant predominantly white male oppression which tabooed relationships between Black men and white women, "Crow-Jimism" stood for the positive acceptance of such relations, in which (in another inversion) the white woman frequently appeared as the dominant partner. It is in this context that Baraka's "Crow Jane" poems must be seen. Alluding to Yeats's "Crazy Jane" and drawing on a blues piece by Mississippi Joe Williams, Baraka makes Crow Jane an incorporation of the aggressive white female Bohemian and "body missionary" who is looking for "alternatives." She is a Bohemian who defies bourgeois draperies and façades, and rebels against "straight" America by ironically reaching "High Society," or by having affairs with Black lumpenproletarians: "Young gigolo's / of the 3rd estate. Young ruffians / without no homes" (DL 49). This sexual aspect of American Bohemianism recurs in Baraka's works, culminating perhaps in the figure of Lula in *Dutchman*.

Even outside the narrower sexual implications of Crow-Janeism, Crow-Jimism remains a form of "reverse patronization" (BM 13), and the strategy of viewing the outcasts of society (in the familiar catalogue from Blacks to junkies and homosexuals) as *heroes* is another characteristically Bohemian inversion. When beats and hipsters symbolically try to "become" Blacks, they seek to explore, as Mailer's seminal essay, "The White Negro" illustrates, "all those moral wildernesses of civilized life which the Square automatically condemns as delinquent or evil or immature or morbid or self-destructive or corrupt."[31] An offspring of a *ménage-à-trois* of bohemian, juvenile delinquent, and Negro, the hipster imbibes Black life-styles as his model of conduct. Among the distinctively Black cultural traits Mailer enumerates are "psychopathy," keeping "the art of the primitive," living "in the enormous present" and for the "pleasures of the body," and giving voice, in Black music, to "rage and the infinite variations of joy, lust, languor, growl, cramp, pinch, scream and despair of . . . orgasm. For jazz is orgasm. . . ."

What Mailer presents as "Negro" is, of course, what Bohemians imagined, or needed, to be Negro, a composite of antibourgeois stereotypes, some of which emerged in the earlier aesthetic protest movement of the Harlem Renaissance. Whether imagined as a noble savage, an exotic primitive, or a violent psychopath, the Beats' "Negro" remained a projection, an inversion of earlier, square, racist versions of the brute Negro,[32] as Charles Nichols' criticism of Mailer points out:

It is clear that Mailer's tone is sympathetic to the Negro, that he feels the psychopathic state caused by oppression, but it would be difficult to find a more vicious debasement of the Negro character in the works of Thomas Dixon.[33]

Mailer's essay initiated a critical controversy in *Dissent* which continued with a longer review essay by Norman Podhoretz in *Partisan Review*. Podhoretz calls the Beats "know-nothing Bohemians" and criticizes their image of Blacks as "idyllic."

Kerouac's love for Negroes and other dark-skinned groups [in *On the Road* and *The Subterraneans*] is tied up with his worship of primitivism, not with any radical social attitudes. . . .[34]

Reminding the readers of the *Dissent* debate of Mailer's thesis, Podhoretz argues that "to see the Negro as more elemental than the white man . . . is 'an inverted form of keeping the nigger in his place.' "

The Bohemian identification with Blacks was hardly more than an attempt to reconcile the repressed qualities of the Bohemian's own Id. For the sake of convenience, the Bohemian might call "Negro" everything he thought white America unjustly repressed: sexuality, aesthetic creativity, spontaneity, political resistance, love for violence, psychopathy, aristocratic elegance of an old nobility, and lower-class assault on bourgeois rule.

Leslie Fiedler noted the emergence of Black Bohemians who were trying to act the part "Crow-Jimism" has assigned to them:

it scarcely matters whether the Negro whom the hipster becomes in his imagination ever really existed at all; for it is with the rejected self which we have called "Negro" that we must be reconciled. Moreover, a new generation of Negroes is presently learning in Greenwich Village, or in Harvard College, to be what the hipster imagines it to be, imitating its would-be imitators.[35]

But for Baraka and his generation, the concept of a specifically Black Bohemianism was real and could be readily experienced in the musical culture since the emergence of Bebop and Rhythm and Blues. Far from being a "white" invention, Black Bohemianism and symbolic protest grew out of the musical rebellion against the softness of "white" commercial Swing. When psychiatrists Aaron H. Esman and Norman M. Margolis analyzed the jazz culture of the 1940s and 1950s, they reported that contemporary "Hot Jazz" which symbolically transgressed artistic, social and sexual taboos, attracted audiences predominantly from three social groups: intellectuals, Negroes, and adolescents. While other groups reacted with anxiety toward modern jazz—an anxiety that "accompanies many advances in art, and is, superficially, ascribed the impact of something new, unknown, untried"—jazz fans sought liberation and individuality in the new music. Their cultural gesture was no overt social protest, but, in the view of these psychiatrists, an indulgence in "regressive narcissistic gratification," which allowed them to experience the "dissolution of barriers between self and outside world."[36] At the height of the Bebop craze, Baraka was an adolescent Negro intellectual and thus triply attracted to jazz. It is thus safe to assume that this first exposure to avant-gardism was reinforced when Baraka became affiliated with the Beat scene, where Black Bohemians, in part because of "Crow-Jimism," assumed a position of absolute centrality.

Whereas the inversion of an identity of social pariah (in the society at large) to that of Bohemian messiah (in the Beat subculture) often left the Black Bohemian with a sense of ambiguity about any social role, the suggestion to follow Bebop impulses and to symbolically incorporate antibourgeois rebellion, superior creativity, as well as all the *Id*-qualities customarily repressed in western societies, often met the Black Bohemian's own wishes for an antibourgeois identity. Moreover, Bohemia, for many of its white affiliates a place of refuge from a secure middle-class background, offered some of its Black members exactly what many whites were apparently trying to escape: a job with a modest income.[37]

If "square" society seems to ask Black people the question "How does it feel to be a problem?" (DuBois' famous formula which Baraka chose as the motto of *Kulchur* 12), the Black Bohemian has to learn how to be viewed as a "solution." The position of Black Bohemians is complexly ironical, and Baraka experienced this situation not only as an object of Crow-Jimism, but also as an extremely conscious observer and, a few years afterwards, as a sharp critic of Bohemian ethnic politics.

In the poem "tele/vision" (1965), Baraka viewed his own role disparagingly as that of a "sammy davis for allen ginsbergs frank sinatra" (B 207); yet Baraka's Bohemianism, which was fed by the impulses from Black music and Beat poetry, remained a persistent aesthetic force in his work.

4. BEAT AESTHETIC: "HOW YOU SOUND??"

Baraka's first published essay was a reply to Norman Podhoretz's "Know-Nothing Bohemians" in *Partisan Review* (1958), which placed Baraka directly in the middle of the Bohemianism debate. Baraka echoes Georges Sorel with the threatening notion that "violence *is* just fine" (UN 1, p. 472), and is Dadaist enough to ironically concede "the obvious immaturity and ingenuous quality of a good bit of the literature" by Beat and Dada writers. Interpreting Beat as "less a movement than a reaction" against "*New Yorker* suburban intellectual types of the late 40s and early 50s" and against "fifteen years of sterile, unreadable magazine poetry," Baraka attacks Podhoretz as part of what the Beat Generation reacted against. In the characteristic polarization of Bohemianism, Baraka sides with the artistic innovations of Ginsberg and Kerouac and with the present generation of runaways from the bourgeoisie against Podhoretz's "rather early-30s middle class assumption(s)" (473). Baraka specifically resents Podhoretz's notion that Bohemia is, for the Negro, "a means of entry into the world of whites" and maintains instead that

Harlem is today the veritable capitol city of the Black Bourgeoisie. The Negro Bohemian's flight from Harlem is not a flight from the world of color but the flight of any would-be Bohemian from . . . "the provinciality, philistinism and moral hypocrisy of American life." (UN 1, p. 473)

In an inversion of Claude McKay's Bohemian movement *Home to Harlem* (1928), Baraka thus argues that there is no essential difference between the Black Bohemian's "flight from Harlem" and any other Bohemian's departure from "square" America. As he writes later in *Blues People*, the

young Negro intellectuals and artists in most cases are fleeing the same "classic" bourgeois situations as their white counterparts—whether the clutches of an actual black bourgeoisie or their drab philosophical reflectors who are not even to be considered a middle class economically. (BP 231)

Baraka's early essays rarely emphasize the implications of his ethnicity and attribute greater importance to the contradictions between bourgeois and Bohemian than between white and Black. He polemicizes against "addlebrained individuals" (UN 1, p, 472), the poetry of the "academies," and the "simplemindedness &/or immaturity of the official literary hierarchy" (UN 15, p. 4). As a gesture toward cultural politics, and as an elitist expression of his better taste, Baraka derides the awarding of the National Book Award to Robert Lowell and of the Pulitzer Prize to W. D. Snodgrass. Honoring two "academic" poets in the same year exposes to Baraka a "methodology . . . of actual *filth*": "I.e., 'he got *one* . . . let's give ol' Snod the other' " (UN 15, p. 4).

In these literary battles, Baraka comes to equate academic intellectual sterility with political and cultural Liberalism: "Peripatetic academism, is certainly another name for, like, American Liberalism" (UN 11, p. 7). Baraka's "Liberal" of this period is characterized by a desire to keep literature separate from life, by poor taste, power in the literary hierarchies, lack of understanding of Beat and other modern writers, and belief in ideas stemming from the 1940s, the 1930s, or even the 1920s. He is, in other words, the Philistine *par excellence*.

Baraka's few direct references to the condition of Afro-Americans in his nonfiction writings from 1958 to 1961 usually occur in the context of polemics against the Liberal *literati*. A pattern begins to emerge: Baraka the essayist invokes the possibility of Black violence as a threat against Liberal writers and critics. While this is not an unusual configuration and, in fact, became commonplace in Black *political* rhetoric of the mid-1960s, it is noteworthy that Baraka resorts to this strategy in discussions of the reception of a poetry anthology or the literary qualities of certain Beat writers. Obviously, the invocation of Black violence against Liberals is, in such a context, the result not of a political gesture of a committed Afro-American writer, but rather of the traditional identification of the Bohemian with the down-trodden of a given society against its mainstream center. As we have seen, this "plebeian" strategy complements the "aristocratic" attack (from the point of view of taste) as the totally antibourgeois stance of Bohemianism.

Thus, in the 1961 essay "Revue," Baraka deplores the *Hudson Review*'s negative reception of Donald Allen's anthology, *The New American Poetry* (which contained several contributions by Baraka) and argues against Liberals who believe that

Negroes in the south cannot utilize violence to achieve their ends. . . .
But if you don't want another man to *handle your life* . . . you *might*, just
might, mind you, have to kill him. (UN 11, p. 7)

The Bohemian quality of this brief interlude is underscored by the
subsequent statement that the Negroes' "wants" do not proceed
"from the demands of some abstract social situation," but are formulated by a few individuals, "intrepid souls," who follow "some
personal ethics" (UN 11, p. 7). In "Revue," Baraka equates the
struggle in the arts with that in civil rights politics and maintains
that Black goals should be defined by self-appointed poetic leaders.
The reference to the "Negroes in the south" remains without a
function in the literary argument; however, it does add to the
harshness of the critique and supports the violent tone of the concluding sentence: "O, Christ, why not for once shoot standing
still?" (UN 11, p. 8).

Baraka employs the same pattern in a brief satire in *Yugen*. In a
"Public Notice," representatives of Baraka's Liberal academicians,
among them James Dickey, Mr. & Mrs. Lionel Trilling, John Updike, and The Yale Series of Recorded Poets, are informed that
they

will kindly report to Pier 9 New York City, on or about March 5, 1961, for
the purpose of being shipped directly to the dark continent (in order that
you might help those yng countries who are under-developed literarily
. . .). Kindly report to the gentleman pictured above. (UN 16).

The photograph under which the "Public Notice" appears is one
of Black nationalist Marcus Garvey in uniform. Black nationalism is
invoked as an ironic threat in an essentially literary battle.

Some additional representatives of academic Liberalism are as-
sembled in the brief satiric piece, "Hafaz Fellowships." Agitating
for a Whitman-conscious American Independence from a colonial
status in poetry,[38] Baraka ironically awards the nonexistent fellowships with the Muslim name "for outstanding achievement in 19th
century English verse"

to Wm. Meredith, John Hollander, Pack-Simpson & Co., Stan Kunitz,
May Swenson, W. D. Snodgrass, David Galler & all the professors

who've ever waxed (& for outstanding work in psycholeptic criticism) Alfred Alvarez, Norman Podhoretz (and for staying as sweet as he is) Truman Capote. (UN 4)

In Baraka's Bohemian world picture, the "Liberal" assumes the very position of the philistine bourgeoisie against which Bohemian rebels define themselves as an antipodal force, both from above and from below. In the role of the oppressed underdog, Baraka threatens his opponents with violence and enlists Blacks to fight for the cause of avant-gardist modernism. In the role of the antibourgeois "King of the East Village,"[39] Baraka passes judgment with "some personal aesthetic" and formulates an extremely privatistic, individualistic, and elitist theory of art.

Baraka's Beat aesthetic, while striving for a unity of life and art, all but ignores the social implications of poetry. The effect of the poem on the reader and its relationship to reality are subordinated to the primary demand that a poem be an "honest" expression of its author. Baraka echoes his contemporaries in "How You Sound??" (1959):

MY POETRY is whatever I think I am. . . . I CAN BE ANYTHING I CAN. . . . I *must* be completely free to do just what I want, in the poem. "All is permitted". . . . There cannot be anything I must *fit* the poem into. Everything must be made to fit into the poem. There must not be any preconceived notion or *design* for what the poem *ought* to be. (UN 6).

The desired freedom of the omnipresent "I" is at the same time a limitation of the scope of literature. Thus, the social aspect of literature is totally secondary to the "expressive" elements of art. The literary tradition is utilized eclectically to feed the needs of the writer. Since the bourgeoisie remains associated with artifact worship, the Bohemian aesthetic is antiobjective: artifacts are secondary; art takes place in the creative process. (This notion was developed further in later years and will be discussed under Baraka's term "art-ing" in the third chapter.) The artistic process is viewed, in an analogy to modern jazz, as the art of spontaneous improvisation. This cliché of much Beat literature was explicitly affirmed by Baraka in his 1961 "Paterson Society Statement." In this aesthetic *homage à* William Carlos Williams, Baraka rejects "object"-

oriented aesthetics, since "no amount of attention to craft will make anybody write beautiful (or whatever) poems" and instead asserts the power of "*the sweep of the mind.* To trust what 'notes' come under the fingers (as an improvising musician)" (UN 10).

In his emphasis on a spontaneous aesthetic and in his selection of literary prototypes (Lorca, Williams, Cummings, as well as the traditional favorites Eliot, Pound, and Yeats) Baraka differs little from other Beat writers. He is, indeed, in an avant-gardist tradition for which Renato Poggioli uses the terms "cerebralism and voluntarism." The unity of life and art is established only in the arbitrariness of the poet's mind.

For Baraka, the most influential specific aesthetic inspirations come from Charles Olson and Jack Kerouac. Olson's important essay, "Projective Verse"—which Baraka edited in his Totem Press series and which he invoked on many occasions—defines the poem as a "high-energy-construct," a dynamic, "OPEN" work in which "ONE PERCEPTION MUST IMMEDIATELY AND DIRECTLY LEAD TO A FURTHER PERCEPTION."[40] Since "FORM" for Olson, "IS NEVER MORE THAN AN EXTENSION OF CONTENT," the most successful modern poetry had to abdicate rhymed, metered forms and concentrate instead on syllable and line. Emphasizing the importance of the immediate creative process for poetry, in a manner which became Baraka's guideline for many years, Olson stated apodictically that the line comes.

from the breathing of the man who writes, at the moment that he writes, and thus is, it is here that, the daily work, the WORK, gets in . . . (389–90)

Olson therefore saw the typewriter as a major asset in the composition of projective verse, since

due to its rigidity and its space precisions, it can, for a poet, indicate exactly the breath, the pauses, the suspensions even of syllables, the juxtapositions even of parts of phrases, which he intends. For the first time the poet has the stave and the bar a musician has had. (393)

Jack Kerouac's essay, "Essentials of Spontaneous Prose," which Baraka also edited as an appendix to *The Moderns,* returns the analogy of poet and musician to the familiar Beat notion of the spontaneous poet as improvising jazz musician. Kerouac sees literary creation as an "undisturbed flow from the minds of personal secret idea-words, *blowing* (as per jazz musician) on subject of image" (M 343). This improvisational process begins "not from preconceived idea of what to say about image but from jewel center of interest in subject *at moment* of writing" (M 344). While pauses, afterthoughts, revisions, improvements, and even corrections ("except obvious rational mistakes") are considered violations of the spontaneous method, writing " ' without consciousness' in semi-trance" or "with writing-or-typing-cramps" (M 344) is thoroughly recommended.

Throughout his early book reviews, Baraka draws on these aesthetic definitions. In his essentially positive reviews of Creeley, McClure, and Wieners, he measures the works against their authors' (and his own) aesthetic. He invokes Olson, Williams, Ginsberg, "EP" (Ezra Pound) and Whitman, in order to more fully admire Creeley's *A Form of Women* (UN 18). In McClure's *Hymns to St. Geryon*, Baraka is happy to find that McClure "is concerned not with THE POEM, THE ARTIFACT . . . but with the complete purity and honesty of what he is saying. What he is thinking" (UN 18, p. 85). And, reading Wieners' *The Hotel Wentley Poems* in 1960, Baraka is intrigued by the sense the poems "make for us that we are watching the poet; disposed as he is at the moment of the poem's emergence" (UN 9, p. 94). In less enthusiastic reviews, as in his criticism of George Stanley's "twelve poems," Baraka cautiously rejects poems because "the very object-ness of which they are possessed makes them completely unimportant from the point of view of 'creation' " (UN 13). The adherence to an antiobjective, expressive aesthetic is self-evident here; but the most "radical" (in the Bohemian sense) aesthetic statements occur in the context of a defense of Jack Kerouac.

In 1959, a few months after siding with Kerouac against Podhoretz in *Partisan Review*, Baraka wrote a letter to *Evergreen Review*, in which he extolled Kerouac's "Essentials of Spontaneous Prose" and applied Kerouac's very own categories in performing the praise.

(I)t is more than just an *apologia pro* his writing, it has genuine *creative* as well as literary value. . . . Kerouac is at his best when he adheres strictly to his outline (which I believe was also largely spontaneous, and therefore quite 'honest'). (UN 2, p. 253)

Not only poetry and prose, but even the definition and formulation of art theory is supposed to be arrived at "honestly" and spontaneously. This aesthetic stance is an avant-gardist radicalization of romantic demands for an expressive and spontaneous art.[41] Logically, Baraka's only criticism of Kerouac had to originate in the consistent application of Kerouac's own principles to his prose.

I, personally, favor short stories as opposed to the novel, especially in the case of a writer like Jack Kerouac, whose highest poetic force is usually not sustained for long periods. (UN 2, p. 255)

Baraka also takes the romantic assumption that poetry is "of the nature of a soliloquy," untinged by "that desire of making an impression upon another mind,"[42] to its avant-gardist extreme, at which only the author can fully understand and enjoy a poem. Elaborating Kerouac's reference to Wilhelm Reich (with the suggestion that writers have to *come*), Baraka develops a significant parallel between the joys of the creative and of the procreative act.

(T)he pure ecstatic power of the creative climax can never be the reader's; even though he has traced and followed frantically the writer's steps, to that final 'race to the wire of time.' The *actual* experience of this 'race' is experienced *only* by the writer. (UN 2, pp. 255–56)

It is interesting to compare Baraka's espousal of hermetic art with a *transition* manifesto discussed by Poggioli: "The writer expresses. He does not communicate. The plain reader be damned."[43] While both statements close off poetry from the reader's understanding, the *transition* manifesto is hostile and antagonistic to the audience, whereas Baraka's statement is narcissistic in its self-centered obsession with the "ecstatic power" of the author's own "creative climax" at the time of composition. It is hard to imagine an aesthetic more remote from the concept of a socially committed art; yet, as we shall see, elements of this narcissistic notion of hermetic art are more than marginal in Baraka's later formulations of a Black aesthetic.

2 Preface to a Twenty Volume Suicide Note: Early Poetry and Prose

". . . Eliot, earlier . . ."
—Baraka on literary influences (UN 6)

1. THE ELIOT SHELL

Baraka's early works are thoroughly "expressive." The poems written from 1958 to 1961 and included in *Preface to a Twenty Volume Suicide Note* and the uncollected poems and stories of the same period are written in free forms and printed with striking graphic and orthographic peculiarities, among them CAPITALS, *italics*, and abbreviations (yr, sez, wd, cd, sd, tho, thot, &, &c.) suggestive of Olson's typewriter. Baraka echoes those writers who are mentioned most frequently in his early works, or at least in the dedications: the familiar group of Creeley, Ginsberg, Kerouac, McClure, O'Hara, Olson, Snyder, Whalen, Wieners, and Williams. Among Baraka's own specific and distinguishing qualities are not only name-dropping and abundant literary allusions, but also an associative speed which drives his poems at a great acceleration, away from frequently enigmatic, sometimes apparently unrelated titles, through fragmentary or incomplete thoughts, images, quotations, imaginary soliloquies and reflections, into continually new and occasionally quite surprising situations, considerations, puns, or observations, and toward frequently strong, occasionally even harshly abrupt endings.

The effect of rapidly progressing montages approaches an "avalanche of words" (P 15), which Baraka unleashes, sometimes spontaneously, in much of his early poetry.[1] As "projective verse," the poetry works through a connection of poetic turns, modes, lyrical situations, and imaginative and associative lines with perceived and recreated "reality," frequently suggested by names of places, streets, and cities, of poets, friends, politicians, and relatives, and even of commercial goods and brands. In "Axel's Castle," the location of the world of romance within a few blocks of Bleecker and McDougal Streets in Greenwich Village illustrates this technique. The opposition of literature and reality is also reflected in Baraka's poetic idiom. In his Wieners review, Baraka expressed his awareness that any kind of "colloquial usage is 'dangerous' in poetry, since if it is not done extremely well, it is most easily vanquished, or at least, made ridiculous" (UN 9, p. 95). In many of his own poems, Baraka was willing to face this danger, and contrasted traditional poetic moods (love, loneliness, suicidal feelings, seasonal changes, or artistic creation), which are often expressed in a "high" modernist diction, with sudden flashes of "low" street language, jargon, or colloquialisms, usually without achieving a ridiculous or destructive effect.[2]

The early poems are collages of several recurring thematic elements. In most of the poems an omnipresent "I/eye"[3] remains in the center of consciousness. Often the poet probes into the realms of autobiography and identity, high art and avant-gardist artists, Black music, American popular culture, and the heroes and anti-heroes of the Western world. Or he expresses himself as an outsider in protest against "others," while exorcising his own past and indulging without inhibitions in provocative sexual themes.[4]

The invocations of poetic peers and elders are numerous, as Baraka appropriates modern poetry to his own uses. The allusions are frequently playful and ironic, and occasionally hostile and iconoclastic; but at all times, Baraka employs his strategy of "popularizing," i.e. of playing the "high" against the vernacular. In the title of an early poem, Baraka continues the word play that led from the cliché "spring and fall" to William Carlos Williams' "Spring and All"; the poem "Spring & Soforth" (UP 12), published in 1960, develops a Melvillean concern for the "equinoctial," which is, significantly, awakened by the poet's *visionary* possession of a woman. He characteristically compares himself to a ray ("an arm of the sun") lying quietly

between your legs
like my bright
equinoctial eye. (UP 12)

Baraka's wide reading is reflected in his poetry, but it is the struggle between the formal demands of the Eliot tradition and the free-verse "local" sense of Williams' poetry which shapes Baraka's own struggle for a poetic idiom. Baraka's affinities to Williams are pervasive; and more than once Baraka explained that he learned from Williams "how to write the way I *speak* rather than the way I *think* a poem ought to be written"[5] or, in other words, how to achieve the freedom of his expressive aesthetic. In contrast to Williams, T. S. Eliot represented, for Baraka, an objective art of structural containment and tight aesthetic control. It is therefore not surprising that Baraka referred to his "earlier" "Eliot period" as a "shell" (UI 1) which he had to break out of, since Eliotic "rhetoric can be so lovely, for a time . . . but only remains so for the rhetorician" (UN 6, p. 425). Allusions to Eliot, whom Baraka later calls "the Missouri lad who wishes himself into a Saville [sic] Row funeral" (R 21), the American who buttons himself up in an English suit, and thus chooses an English death, are plentiful throughout Baraka's writings, and especially striking in *Preface,* as the following examples may illustrate:[6]

the evening	*the evening is spread*
spread against the windows	*out against the sky*
("Duke Mantee" P 35)	*("Prufrock")*
Respect the season	*But at my back in a cold*
and dance to the rattle	*blast I hear*
of its bones	*The rattle of the bones*
. . .	. . .
Winter rattles	
like the throat	*I do not find*
of the hanged man.	*The Hanged Man*
("From an Almanac 2" P 43–44)	*("Waste Land")*

Eliot is certainly present in Baraka's works, even if Eliot's "objective," "academic" art is what Baraka struggles away from. In an unpublished poem, "The Shadow Waltz," Baraka answers the question "what kinds of books there were" with a partial list of his own favorites, reserving a question mark for Eliot.

> *There were Creeley books and Olson books Lorca*
> *books and Pound books. Are there Eliot books?* (UP 14)

In 1959, in the poem "The Plumed Serpent" (a D. H. Lawrence title), Baraka apparently offers an account of his relationship to Eliot. In a world of "old Anglos dying" the poet demands "a glass of water for the speaker who is English." Later in the poem, Baraka invokes Olson and accepts the necessity for "the destruction of the old temple." If this temple refers to the shell of Eliot's rhetoric, the strategy of overcoming Eliot is expressed in Eliotic terms, in a phrasing close to Eliot's "The Hippopotamus": "On this church I build my rock" ("The Plumed Serpent" UP 16). Baraka constructs his poetry on, and out of, the ruins of his Eliot shell. "March" (1959), a seasonal poem about dejection in early spring in New York City, discusses Shelley and Melville at length; Eliot, to whose "April is the cruelest month" the poem obviously alludes, merely receives a curt and parenthetical comment: "(Eliot, you fraud!)" (UP 26). The Eliot shell is stubborn, however, and necessary even in the formulation of its own destruction. Baraka's poetry often expresses the agony of "old Anglos dying in commercials," of Eliot's impersonal art under the onslaught of Baraka's self-centered voice, which defines itself as American against the English tradition, and as commercial and popular against the academies. Baraka sees his struggle for the destruction of Eliot's temple as a personal and a national affair, fought in the name of the Bohemian self against the academies and in the name of Whitman's America against the "Colonial School" (UN 25). The "new American poetry" of Baraka attempts to continue the tradition of Williams, Pound, Lorca, and the French Symbolists in order to

restore American poetry to the mainstream of modern poetry after it had been cut off from that tradition by the Anglo-Eliotic domination of the academies. (M xi)

Baraka mocks Eliot's use of footnotes in poetry.

> *There is some German word*
> *that could say the thing: (with a footnote)*
> *but I am on W. 20 st. &*
> *must have it my way. ("March" UP 26)*

Committing himself against Eliot to the "I" on the "street," however, is as "suicidal" as walking

> *out for beer without yr coat.*
> *A wind will suddenly whip up off the Hudson &*
> *like a spear pinion you to an old Puerto Rican.*
> *One must become involved in so much bullshit*
> *to remain a pure romantic. (UP 26)*

Refusing to don the Eliot coat, Baraka is forced, by a poetic animus of his river god, to embrace a romantic commitment to self and street, to autobiography and ethnic marginality. Characteristically, Baraka justifies his anti-Eliotic ways with Eliotic references. He defends the unfootnoted use of the "Seagram's Building" in Frank O'Hara's "Personal Poem" and maintains that there is as little need to know that building for an understanding of this poem as there is to read Jessie Weston in order

to find out what whole sections of THE WASTE LAND mean. The Seagram's building is certainly less obscure than certain Celtic rites. And I do not see why it is any less valid because it comes from a person's life, rather than, say, from his academic life. (UI 1, p. 21)

On the one hand, this emphasis on the personal permits a full poetic development of the drama of the alienated and narcissistic self. On the other hand, this procedure allows for the inclusion of casual references to real places and names, for the uninhibited use of any level of language, and for a persistent interest in popular culture in Baraka's poetic collages.

2. GENEALOGY AND IDENTITY

The "difficult" character of much Baraka poetry originates in this anti-Eliotic stance. Many poems are informed by Baraka's tenet that the creative "climax" can never be the reader's. In "Look for You Yesterday, Here You Come Today," the poet asks cryptically

Was James Karolis a great sage??
Why did I let Ora Matthews beat him up
in the bathroom? Haven't I learned my lesson. (P 15)

The references are only understandable in the light of Baraka's later publications: they are school friends whose names recur throughout his works (e.g., SD 28, 31, 37, 44, 54, and 65ff) and whose story is finally told in *The Toilet*.

This example illustrates how expressive poetry may lead Baraka toward *his* pressing themes, regardless of their impact on, or even their intelligibility to, contemporary readers. The freedom of "How You Sound??" is the freedom of the creator and *only* the creator, who may poetically explore street language and bathroom settings and who has no responsibility to convey "reality" to audiences. Thus, Baraka states quite "correctly" in a later poem:

I am what I think I am. You are what
I think you are. ("Audubon, Drafted" DL 56)

"Reality" is an extension of the "I": there are no "standards." So conceived, the "I" is not only the omnipresent speaker, but also the truest subject for poetry. Only rarely does Baraka create another consciousness, from whose point of view the poem develops; and when he does, as in "Duke Mantee" (P 35), the "other" is really part of the self. Having absorbed "Duke Mantee" poetically, Baraka can use the name as a *nom de plume* in a later essay (UN 23).

The narcissistic poet may question himself as a lover and see love-making as a form of masturbation[7] with somebody who probably never "really remembered my name" ("Love Poem" UP 37). Or he may scrutinize his roles as a husband ("For Hettie in Her

Fifth Month" P 14), as a not yet "suicided" father ("Preface . . ." P 5), and, again and again, as a tormented poet ("Vice" P 27) who is locked in with "dull memories & self hate, & the terrible disorder / of a young man" ("The Turncoat" P 26).

There are many moments of lightness, of irony, and humor, especially as the poet plays with the ambiguities of his alienation or with the process of verbal creation. "In Memory of Radio" inverts the word "love":

> ↺ *Love is an evil word.*
> *Turn it backwards / see, see what I mean?*
> *An evol word. ↺ besides*
> *who understands it? (P 12)*

Baraka's first published poem, "Slice of Life" (UP 1), is set in the railroad station of segregated Hartsville, South Carolina, the home town of Baraka's grandparents. There the angel-poet encounters three toilets, "one marked MEN, one / Marked WOMEN, and the third marked OTHERS." Metaphorically identifying racial discrimination and secret sexual otherness,[8] the humorous poem concludes: " 'I wonder, could they have known?' " (UP 1). The tone of the poem, published in 1958, may be characterized by Poggioli's term "humorism"; the apparent lightness points to a deep-seated and serious sense of alienation. All God's Chillun may have wings, but those who are *aware* of their angelic quality become outsiders.

In "The Gift of the Unicorn" (UP 5), published later in 1958, Baraka links the angel metaphor with that of another spiritual outsider, the "unicorn," a Yeatsian image of the writer "Caught up in his own corny fictions."[9] "Central Park in Winter" (UP 6) uses the antagonism of a poetic "I" against "white and irrational" signs that read "No parking," "No littering," and "No picnicking," and likens the alienated self to "exiled statues" in the park. The Beat poet perceives the "square" New York skyline as a "herd of symmetrical gangsters" and is beset by "those fears all spies must feel." "The Last Roundup" (UP 7) develops the theme of alienation out of a confrontation between the sensitive poet and the object of his rejected love, a "blonde" fellow student and fighter. The poet admits to "inhaling" the blonde one's "sensual eyes" although the visionary is rejected and treated as a "traitor."

The poet's early tendency to explore the theme of alienation takes the form of an identification with spiritual and visionary outsiders (angels, unicorns, "spies") against a square, white or blonde opponent. The symbolic association of whiteness and evil is a literary strategy which subtly reflects both Baraka's sense of racial alienation and his literary debt to Melville. In his 1959 short story, "The man who sold pictures of god" (UF 3), Baraka alludes to the *Moby-Dick* chapter "The Whiteness of the Whale." A canvas salesman is apparently mistaken for an avant-gardist nihilist who sells paintings with "absolutely nothing on them": "The whiteness of the canvas was purely symbolic."

Baraka maintains an ironically alienated relationship to himself as a Black man and a Bohemian in one of the best *Preface* poems, "Hymn for Lanie Poo." In the fourth part of this poem, reprinted separately in Langston Hughes's anthology *New Negro Poets, U.S.A.*, Baraka immerses himself into his specific New York locale in order to create a Whitmanesque cosmic genealogy for himself. Like Langston Hughes, Baraka speaks of rivers; and when the author of "Lanie Poo" stares at the Hudson, he, too, imagines more than his prosaic "place of origin," his "step mother" city Newark on the other side. The rising horizon, the sun itself, becomes a father image for the alienated poet who is thus elevated to a son of sun.

> *Each morning*
> *I go down*
> *to Gansevoort St.*
> *and stand on the docks.*
> *I stare out*
> *at the horizon*
> *until it gets up*
> *and comes to embrace*
> *me. I*
> *make believe*
> *it is my father.*
> *This is known*
> *as genealogy. (P 9)*

The poet's elevation to cosmic origins is a source of strength, but a social liability in America, where racist folklore assigns a quality of "evil" to the sun: "Beware the evil sun . . . turn you black" (P

6). In a parallel passage in *Blues People*, Baraka explains this corre-
lation of sun and blackness:

"You are black . . . which means you lived too close to the sun. Black is
evil." "You are white . . . which means you lived too far from the sun.
You have no color . . . no soul." These are equally logical arguments. (BP
10)

The relationship toward the sun becomes a central metaphor for
the attitudes of Black Americans toward their own blackness and
their African heritage. This sun, which can "turn your hair / crawl
your eyeballs / rot your teeth" (P 6), is using this country as a "com-
mode" (P 9). The square "firemasons," the staunch civic, and more
conservative civil rights organizations of the Black middle class, organize parades which have no recognizable connection with Black
identity; they wear hats with brims and "beware the sun"—just as
Baraka's sister Sandra Elaine[10] (whose childhood nickname, "Lanie
Poo," appears prominently in the title of the poem) evades her
Blackness: she "doesn't like to teach in Newark / because there are
too many colored / in her classes" (P 11).

> *O, generation of ficticious*
> *Ofays*
> > *I revere you . . .*
> > *You are all so beautiful* (P 11)

Baraka ridicules the attitude of the Black bourgeoisie because
its self-evaluation is based essentially on a self-hating reverence
for "ofays" (which, translated back from pig Latin is really the
plural of "a foe") and a desire to become this enemy, by turning
white. These "faux Nègres," having lost their own group identity,
are characterless,

> *Smiling & glad / in*
> *the huge & loveless*
> *white-anglo sun / of*
> *benevolent step*
> *mother America.* (P 12)

"Lanie Poo" sounds the familiar theme of aesthetic opposition to
the Black bourgeois past; and it is therefore not surprising to hear

Baraka's recorded introduction to the poem on the Library of Congress tape of 1959:

It's about what E. Franklin Frazier called the *Black Bourgeoisie.* It tries to equate modern life, modern Negro life in America, with the life . . . in some unknown African tribe.

Against the middle-class fear of the "evil" sun, Baraka posits his "genealogy" as a conscious negation of Black middle-class self-denial. He evokes scenes of a wild, Bohemian, imaginary Afro-America. Physical pleasures, wild hunting scenes [11] and feasts dominate his exotic countervisions, as he enjoys the "uncivilized" and the obscene, everything the "firemasons" would reject.

Baraka's exoticism remained recognizably indebted to the Bohemian cult of the exotic primitive, of "Crow-Jimism," of "The White Negro."

> *All afternoon*
> *we sit around*
> *near the edge of the city*
>> *hacking open*
>> *crocodile skulls*
>> *sharpening our teeth.* (P 6)

Baraka's poetic montage ironically contrasts images of urban America and Tarzanlike, exotic notions of an "Africa" in the Bohemian mind.

> *I wobble out to*
> *the edge of the water*
> *give my horny yell*
> *& 24 elephants*
> ~ *stomp out of the subway*
> *with consecrated hardons.*
> .   .   .
> *She had her coming out party*
> *with 3000 guests*
> *from all parts of the country.*
> *Queens, Richmond, Togoland, The Cameroons . . . (P 7)*

Reminiscent of Eliot's lists of cities, this latter passage creates a fantasy setting combining New York boroughs [12] with West African nations from which many Afro-Americans originally came, and a New York subway (one of Baraka's obsessive literary settings) with identifiably male elephants which are, like Ionesco's *Rhinocéros,* stomping through the cities. Among the party guests are Hulan Jack, Tarzan,[13] and John Coltrane. During the feast, the poet yokes Eliot's "Phoenician" in "The Burial of the Dead" with the American ritual of the burger cookout and yells cannibalistically:

> *"Throw on another goddamned Phoenecian."*

> *We got so drunk (Hulan Jack*
> *brought his bottle of Thunderbird),*
> *nobody went hunting*
> *the next morning. (P 7)*

After this communion with cheap wine, the poet spends a week in a fantasy land of genesis, reminiscent of popular accounts of the seven days of the creation of the earth. The activities range from gulping down monkey foreskins to trying to get some sculpting done, from watching television to catching a 600-pound ape. Baraka alludes to William Empson's *Seven Types of Ambiguity* with the lines

> *Read Garmanda's book, "14 Tribes of*
> *Ambiguity," didn't like it. (P 8)*

The creative vision, intended to negate Black middle-class attitudes, reaches its zenith with the figure of a "wild-assed" (P 6) Black goddess, who is seen through the filter of a Bohemian imagination of Black wildness:

> *The god I pray to*
> *got black boobies*
> *got steatopygia.*[14]

It is this filter which again and again reconstitutes the imaginary character of the world created, and which ultimately leaves the poem resigned and unresolved. The poet regrets that Africans and Afro-Americans are "civilized;" they are "wild-assed trees" (P 6) who have been transformed, under the spell of the Western world, into "charming / wicker baskets" (P 6). Baraka's Bohemian fantasy negates this metamorphosis and envisions Black self-liberation through inversion and re-creation:

we all know
these wicker baskets
would make wild-assed trees. (P 8)

The poem thus plays "wrong" ways of being Black against each other and utilizes as well as criticizes the ambivalence of white prejudices without arriving at a suggestion for a "correct" Black consciousness. Baraka sides with his unrepressed Black goddess and with a masturbatory self-affirmation against the ridiculous Black Christians in the "silly little church" who allow a preacher with "conning eyes" to trick them into some supposedly "real" happiness (P 9–10).[15] But there is also self-criticism of what Baraka calls, in German/Yiddish, "die schwartze Bohemien" (P 10). Black Bohemians are not depicted as a pioneer group on the road to a true Black identity; they lack any kind of meaningful connection with people and with Black communities, e.g. Harlem, "uptown" (P 11). The Black Bohemian may have a secret Black goddess with Black breasts and a big bottom, but is taken breathless by any white woman who passes the coffee shop. Despite his belief that "white cats can't swing" (P 11), the Black Bohemian interrupts his conversation to exclaim "Man Lookatthatblonde / whewee!" (P 10) He talks about Zen, Gandhi, and "Mr. Lincun" and retains so little of his own cultural identity as a Black man that even his French coffee seems symbolic of his Bohemian integrationism, "Cafe Olay."[16] The memory of white Bohemians who became racists in their later careers adds seriousness, and the section ends on a sad note with the Black Bohemian's rationalization:

It's just that it's such a drag to go
Way uptown for Bar B Cue,
                    By God . . .
How Much? (P 11)

In "Lanie Poo," Baraka reflected his own alienation and questioned Bohemian self-definitions, however, he did not transcend an ironic criticism of various possibilities of "false" blackness. The poem's motto, "vous êtes des faux Négres," taken from Arthur Rimbaud's "Une Saison en Enfer" (1873), is appropriate. Rimbaud was one of the cultural heroes of the Beat Generation, and Baraka first published Kerouac's famous "Rimbaud" poem in *Yugen*. In Rimbaud's "Saison," the white-Black value scale is inverted so that whites can be criticized as "false Negroes." The decisive Rimbaud passage was translated by Edmund Wilson in *Axel's Castle*.

I have never been a Christian; I am of the race who sang in torture; I do not understand the laws; I haven't the moral sense, I am a brute; you are doing wrong. Yes, my eyes are closed to your light. I am a nigger, a beast. But I may be saved. You yourselves are false niggers, savage and grasping madmen. Tradesman, you are a nigger; magistrate, you are a nigger; general, you are a nigger; emperor, old itching palm, you are a nigger: you have drunk of a contraband liquor from Satan's distillery.[17]

This comes close to the ambivalent concept of the noble savage[18] who can criticize bourgeois, Western civilization (merchants, bureaucrats, generals, emperors) for being *truly* savage in the pursuit of hypocrisy, war, profit, and Christian order. Similarly, Rimbaud wrote to his family about "nègres blanc des pays dits civilisés."[19] "Lanie Poo" shares Rimbaud's Bohemianism and is a comprehensive literary formulation of Baraka's own contradictions. The poem also explores a specifically Barakian imagery which recurs in many other works.

The image of the sun as a Black father and as a touchstone for a Black identity is crucial in Baraka's poetry. "Columbia the Gem of the Ocean" (UP 21) invokes a Hudson-"Landschaft" after sunrise "and though you're uptown, still your black hair does reflect it." "One Night Stand" (P 21–22) can be read as a poem about the migration of Southern Blacks to the cities of the North,[20] adding a historical dimension to the poet's insecure sense of identity:

We are *foreign seeming persons. Hats flopped so the sun*
can't scald our beards; odd shoes, bags of books & chicken.
We have come a long way, & are uncertain which of the masks
is cool. (P 22)

In "For Hettie in Her Fifth Month," the expectation of a "mulatto" child is fictionalized by the image of the Black poet's white wife sitting

in a chair by the window
one finger holding the blind back
so that what sun's left
washes into your womb. (P 14)

"Scenario VI" moves from an initial minstrel act in which the
poet balances his cane "tilting the hat to avoid the sun" (P 22)
through a stream of images to a final sequence which returns to the
tone of "Lanie Poo" in a post-Thoreauvian *Week* on the Sumer and
Indus rivers:

Sylvia has come out in her smashing oranges & jewelry. . . .
   . . . we make it in great swirls out to the terrace,
which overlooks Sumer . . . & the Indus river, where next
week probably all kinds of white trash will ride in
on stolen animals we will be amazed by. (P 23)

"Ostriches & Grandmothers" (P 20–21) employs the sun imagery
to urge a stronger expression of a Black identity beyond all masks
and stances:

All meet with us, finally: the
uptown, way-west, den of inconstant
moralities.
Faces up: all
my faces turned up
to the sun. (P 20)

The connection between bourgeois and Bohemian masks remains a source of tension, which is only occasionally and temporarily resolved in poetic adaptations of Black music. "The Bridge"
leads to a strong affirmation of Blackness through Black music:[21]

The bridge will be behind you, that music you know, that place,
you feel when you look up to say, it is me, & I have forgotten,
all the things, you told me to love, to try to understand, the
bridge will stand, high up in the clouds & the light, & you,

(when you have let the song run out) will be sliding through
unmentionable black. (P 26)

Baraka keeps approaching his Black identity through genealogy.
His short story, "Suppose Sorrow Was A Time Machine" (UF 1),
first published in 1958, pursues Baraka's real genealogy, not an

imaginary one as "son of sun." This story follows the northern migration of his maternal grandparents, from Dothan, Alabama, to Beaver Falls, Pennsylvania, and to Newark, New Jersey. "Slice of Life" approaches its subject metaphorically, using the angel as a symbol of the outsider situation; "Suppose Sorrow Was a Time Machine," however, ventures into family history as part of ethnic history.

In Dothan, Alabama, at the turn of the century, Baraka's grandparents, Thomas Everett and Anna Cherry Brock Russ, owned a general store, which was burned down twice by "unholy bastards"—white racists—and which the grandparents-to-be rebuilt into "the biggest funeral parlor in the country" (UF 1, p. 10): "so fancy, the niggers killing each other so that they can get an excuse to go to it." But the funeral parlor was also burned down, and by 1917, the Russes had moved to Beaver Falls to "sell eggs, produce. Best liquor in the country" (UF 1, p. 10) and, eight years later, to Newark to "Russ Super General Store" which closed its doors during the depression. Possibly, Tom Russ was hit "in the head with a street lamp" and died in "Greystone Sanatorium, 1943" (UF 1, p. 11), when his grandson, the narrator of the story, was nine years old.

The story has the potential for a Black *Buddenbrooks,* yet, although Baraka was so deeply affected by his family history that he incorporated it in *Blues People* (96), included Tom Russ in the gallery of Black heroes in the poem "Black Dada Nihilismus" (DL 64), and dedicated *Dutchman and The Slave* to his grandparents, he never narrated the story in the epic dimensions it would require. Instead, he used H. G. Wells's time machine to reach out for his grandfather's spiritual "vibrations," and wrote an experimental story, an address by the still unborn author to his grandfather.

Say that you are Tom Russ. It is Dothan, Alabama, U.S.A. 1898. You are a Negro who has felt the ground vibrate . . . I know you Tom. You are my grandfather. I am not born yet but I have felt the ground vibrate too. (UF 1, p. 9)

The unborn narrator feels that his grandfather's fate imposes an obligation on him:

I hear they finally hit you in the head with a street lamp, Tom. Is that so? Gave you a cane and a wheelchair, and made you sit by the wood stove nodding and spitting, trying desperately to remember exactly when and where it was the ground vibrated. But do you realize that your unborn grandson has finally got here? Or is it that he's still unborn and only the body managed to make it right now. (UF 1, p. 11)

At the end of the story, the young author claims his inherited sorrows; he seems to be summoning his grandfather's spirit in that ritual of invocation of the dead, which frequently precedes a call for revenge:

Tom, are you listening? Don't stare like that. Tom. Tom. O my god. (UF 1, p. 11)

The early short story is exceptional in its treatment of the author's real past; more characteristic is the 1959 poem "Parthenos" (UP 10), in which the past is remembered in a Ferlinghetti allusion, merely as

> *another street, with more trees . . .*
> *an insipid suburbia of the mind. (UP 10, p. 23)*

In "Parthenos," Baraka pursues an invented maternal genealogy and traces "a straight line . . . backwards till it stops / infinity? (the white sleek thighs of a woman)" and "beyond the straight line / catching the sun in her eyes / the moon in her thighs. / very early / when night was a pickaninny on a pony." The poem then turns into what is characterized as "(chantnow)" and playfully explores the poet's multiethnic American mothers:

> *My chinese mother*
> *is full of compassion*
> > *my japanese mother*
> > *dances all day*
> *I have a white mother*
> *pale as a bone, with*
> *red moons smeared in*
> *her cheeks, who thinks*
> *nothing of vanishing*
> > *trailing leis of orange flame. (UP 10, p. 24)*

And continuing the metaphor of an exotic, multiracial, imagined maternal lineage, "Parthenos" proceeds:

> *My black mother*
> *was a witch doctor*
> *a crazywoman with a red cape*
> > *hucklebucking beneath the pyra-*
> > *mids.*
> > *before beyond the night.*
> *at the end of the straight line. (UP 10, p. 24)*

This Oedipal pursuit of a man's heritage into his fictional mothers' wombs culminates in the laconic remark "(Only the mothers survive)" (UP 10, p. 26). Taken together, "Lanie Poo" and "Parthenos" replace a "real" ancestry (UF 1) with a complete, fictional, cosmic genealogy of the Bohemian visionary, who was, perhaps, created by a sun-ray hitting a virginal "lunar womb" (UP 10, p. 26). But "Parthenos" also expresses the remembrance of yet another womblike home for the young poet-to-be: the world of American popular culture.

> *(when I was young*
> *I'd take the radio*
> *under the covers*
> *and let it play*
> *all night*
> > *and when morning came*
> > *toss it across the room*
> > *staring at it disdainfully) (UP 10, p. 25)*

The radio as a tossed-away lover god is emblematic of Baraka's love-hate relationship with popular culture.

3. POPULAR CULTURE AND PEOPLE'S CULTURE

The central theme of "Look For You Yesterday, Here You Come Today" is the poet's "maudlin nostalgia" (P 17) for the popular culture of his youth: "(When will world war two be over?)" (P 16). Baraka's interest in America's modern mythology amounts to an obsession with comic-book heroes and code words, with radio programs and Hollywood movies, since "what's best in popular culture is really what's strongest in this society" (UI 20).

It has been suggested that Baraka's use of popular culture is limited to an early "clearing" period, at the end of which (approximately at the time of "Look For You Yesterday") the "heroes" were discarded, or that his use of popular culture essentially demonstrates the struggle of the Black poet with the American myth of innocence, against which the concept of "soul" is pitted.[22] But these interpretations do not go far enough in explaining Baraka's pervasive use of popular mythology, both in his early poetry and in his literature of Black nationalism and Maoism.

This mythology possibly constitutes the largest single literary influence on the writer, who, in the short story, "The Screamers," called pulp cowboy magazines "the truest legacy of my spirit" (T 74). Not surprisingly, Baraka's first attempts at writing were a comic strip, "The Crime Wave," and science fiction short stories (none of which are extant) for his high school paper.

"Look For You Yesterday" is, in Baraka's own words on the Library of Congress tape, "about my vision of my childhood, some of the things that have stayed with me and how I used these things to show that I am gradually getting older." The process of aging, the *tempus fugit*-blues of the "cobblestone clock" that commands the author each morning to rise "& rot a little more" (P 16), the "terrible thoughts about death" (P 17) are contrasted with a nostalgic attempt to reach out for his lost childhood:

> All the lovely things I've known have disappeared.
> I have all my pubic hair & am lonely.
> There is probably no such place as Battle Creek, Michigan!
>
> Tom Mix dead in a Boston Nightclub
> before I realized what happened.
>
> People laugh when I tell them about Dickie Dare!
>
> What is one to do in an alien planet
> where the people breath New Ports?

Where is my space helmet, I sent for it
3 lives ago . . . when there were box tops.

What has happened to box tops??

O, God . . . I must have a belt that glows green
in the dark. Where is my Captain Midnight decoder??
I can't understand what Superman is saying!
            THERE MUST BE A LONE RANGER!!! (P 16–17)

The function of popular culture in "Look for You Yesterday" is similar to that of a time machine. Like Proust's "madeleine," Baraka's popular heroes help the author in search of a lost past and take him back "3 lives" to his childhood. But the author's loneliness, the fact that people laugh at his nostalgia, and the doubtful tone of his questions indicate that the popular culture of the poet's youth has been consumed and forgotten by the people, and that he is now one of the few witnesses who remember that it ever existed. What was once culture for the millions has now, in an ironically elitist turn, become a secret password, a code understood only by those few visionaries who are "dumb" enough "to be sentimental about anything" (P 17). At this point, Baraka's poetry shows affinities to "trash" art, which elevates the discarded soup cans of yesterday.

The theme of yesterday's popular culture as today's secret, quasireligious code is developed more fully in the poem "In Memory of Radio" (P 12–13), which starts with an invocation of the invisible crime fighter and popular radio hero, "The Shadow."

Who has ever stopped to think of the divinity of Lamont Cranston?
(Only Jack Kerouac, that I know of: & me.
The rest of you probably had on WCBS and Kate Smith,
Or something equally unattractive.) (P 12)

The Radio is a medium in which God reveals himself through magic and miracles, through hypnotic gestures, coded messages, and transformations, and this epiphany is the legacy for the poet, whose imaginative power of pretending can lead to sudden shocks of awareness, called "satori" in Zen,[23] of the inverted connection between love and evil. In this sense, the initiate to the radio cult has become a "sage": although lacking the "real" power of a German dictator or the governor of California to order executions, he has the power of knowledge, the capacity to understand and use the magic of words:

> *Am I a sage or something?*
> *Mandrake's hypnotic gesture of the week?*
> *(Remember, I do not have the healing powers of Oral Roberts . . .*
> *I cannot, like F. J. Sheen, tell you how to get saved & rich!*
> *I cannot even order you to gaschamber satori like Hitler or Goody*
> *   Knight*
>
> .   .   .
>
> *Saturday mornings we listened to Red Lantern & his undersea folk.*
> *At 11, Let's Pretend/& we did & I, the poet, still do, Thank God!*
>
> *What was it he used to say (after the transformation when he was*
> *   safe*
> *& invisible & the unbelievers couldn't throw stones?) "Heh, heh, heh,*
> *Who knows what evil lurks in the hearts of men? The Shadow*
> *   knows."*
>
> *O. yes he does*
> *O, yes he does. (P 12–13)*

The sacral magic of popular culture is similarly invoked in "Metaphysical Ode to Birth" (UP 19), which celebrates the old radio programs and, "after a hard day turning on the radio," achieves a moment of surprise with the announcement "Ladies and gents, a short talk by God." "The Making of a Poem from a Paint Can" (UP 20), an occasional poem from the year 1959, echoes "In Memory of Radio" and ascribes to "Mandrake's hypnotic gesture of the week" the power of metamorphosis, of "changing Lothar into a Hershey bar." These uses of popular culture correspond to Baraka's antibourgeois and antiobjective strategy; breaking the Eliot shell with the help of narcissism and street language is paralleled by elevating popular art to the level of divine inspiration.

Nonwhite victims and clowns, puppets and villains are central to American popular mythology, and Baraka increasingly identifies with this ethnic dimension. In the early works, this strategy is just beginning to emerge. "Where is Mu?" (UP 13), a "satirical poem dedicated to Kenneth Koch," resembles the spirit of "Look for You

. . ." in the poet's lament for his "seven years of hired education washed away by the cold breath of art," and in his nostalgic invocation of Mu as a "childhood vision of an adventurer" and as a savior. "Save me, MU. Collect me in your outrageous bosom" is the desparate invocation of Mu, the poet's "gentle boy-god" and "illegal celestial connection." The figure of Mu, however, is also the son of Ra in Egyptian mythology, which fascinated Baraka, and thus introduces an Egyptian, pre-Western point of refuge from "this idle posturing." This Bohemian-Gypsy-Egyptian opposition to the West is strengthened by Baraka's uses of Black music and by his strategy of inverting the stereotypical roles assigned to non-whites in American popular culture. It is thus significant to note that the poem with the blues title "Look for You Yesterday, Here You Come Today" ends when the Lone Ranger's silver bullets are gone

> *& Tonto way off in the hills*
> *moaning like Bessie Smith. (P 18)*

The spirit of Mu may well be seen looming behind Baraka's concern for popular culture and opposing the mood of pure nostalgia. The persistence of ethnic victims as buffoons poses the question of whether or not mass culture is contradictory to a true people's culture. Lorca, who was also crucial to Baraka's struggle with the Eliot shell, represents a point of departure for a political and ethnic popular art in one of Baraka's earliest poems.

Significantly, "Lines to Garcia Lorca" (UP 2) begins with a Negro Spiritual which serves as a motto and which is linked, in the end, to Lorca's voice, "laughing, laughing / Like a Spanish guitar." "Lines" ascribes a religious importance to music in an oppressive situation. The violent death of the Spanish poet at the hands of Franco's fascists is reenacted by the reader of Lorca's poem, and similarly, we are to assume, Black music can actualize in the listener the memory of Black suffering.[24] The laughter is the laughter of a surviving art, collected by Buddhist, "orange-robed monks." Poetry is thus seen as a people's reservoir of strength against political oppression.

"April 13" (UP 9) brings Lorca's Spanish theme home to a Puerto

Rican neighborhood in New York which is contrasted with the
Andrews Sisters at Radio City Music Hall.[25] The poem uses elements of outsider imagery, e.g., the opposition to "blondes" or
"snow," in order to raise the larger question of the role of oppressed minorities at home and of cultural imperialism abroad; this
is done, however, with the help of the self-consciously trite cliché
of cats and mice.

> *Out the window:*
> > *HIJO DE PUTA!*
> > *HIJO DE PUTA!*
>
> *this is probably a job*
> *for a social worker.*
> *One with blonde stringy hair*
> *& lipstick stains on her mustache.*
>
> *Last night it snowed . . .*
> *today, some old dirty cat*
> *is crouched on the back fence*
> *thinking about the various kinds*
> *of mice.*
>
> > *There was a time*
> > *when Radio City Music Hall*
> > *was really a great place.*
> > *Hot summer, 1942: Everybody sang*
> > *"working for the yonkee dollahhh"*
>
> *& something about Coca-cola.*
> *HIJO DE PUTA*
> *MARDICON, PINDEO, CHOLITO etc.*
>
> *things are happening slowly.*

Among Baraka's early poems, "Lines to Garcia Lorca" and "April
13" are exceptional in their statements on cultural politics. The
dominant concern in this period is less for social action than for an
immersion into a self which is tormented, and often suicidal.

4. SUICIDE AND BEYOND

The poem "The Death of Nick Charles" (P 31–34), an allusion to Dashiell Hammett's detective novel, *The Thin Man*, develops the suicidal theme.

> *Sad*
> *long*
> *motion of air*
> *pushing in my face. Lies,*
> *weakness, hatred*
> *of myself. Of you*
> *for not understanding*
> *this. Or not*
> *despising me*
> *for the right causes . . . (P 32)*

After pessimistic considerations of love and loneliness, the poem ends with oblique references to darkness and blackness and a suicidal sleep, from which there is no *satori*-awakening. The "Glorious death in battle" (P 31) of the beloved popular heroes seems to have been taken literally:

> *Boats & old men*
> *move through the darkness . . .*
> *Sea birds*
> *scalding the blackness . . .*
> *I merely sit*
> *& grow weary, not even watching*
> *the sky lighten with morning.*
>
> *& now*
>
> *I am sleeping*
> *& you will not be able*
> *to wake me. (P 34)*

These suicidal lines correspond to the serious meaning of the bizarre title of the collection (possibly influenced by Langston Hughes's short poem, "Suicide's Note") whereas the title poem,

"Preface to a Twenty Volume Suicide Note" (P 5)—dated "March 1957," but dedicated to Kellie Jones, born 16 May 1959"—corresponds to its ironically contradictory form. As William Fischer says:

To bring so much heavy apparatus to bear—prefaces and volumes—on a mere note, is to mock the ostensible value of the poems themselves.[26]

The title poem elaborates the contrast between the poet's nihilistic ways and his young daughter's unshattered religious faith. For this modern Hamlet "Things have come to that"; and "the broad edged silly music the wind / Makes when I run for a bus . . ." has replaced the songs of his childhood: "Nobody sings any more." The difference in the perspectives of father and daughter is most clearly articulated in their relationship to God, who is very real for the praying daughter, but only an absence, a "no one," for the poet.

> And then last night, I tiptoed up
> To my daughter's room and heard her
> Talking to someone, and when I opened
> The door, there was no one there . . .
> Only she on her knees, peeking into
>
> Her own clasped hands. (P 5)

The recurrence of Baraka's themes and motifs unifies the early poetry; but the playfulness and the nostalgia increasingly give way to a sense of suicidal despair. Baraka's suicidal and agonistic poetry reflects the death of the "Anglo shell," which at times appears like the death of the poet himself. The writer who is almost "suicided" by the cultural dead weight of "objective" art, often doubts whether he can extricate himself from the decline of the West. In "Consider This" (UP 17), Baraka ironically accepts a European tradition, as seen by Henry Adams or Henry James, when he says:

> And those lovely cathedrals at Chartres
> your way of saying it
> I must . . . love them
> I have no other voice left.

But the poet does have another, inner, voice which survives the suicidal temptations to die with the shell. This voice ultimately transforms agonism into antagonism as it is raised to the scream of "Black Dada Nihilismus." The confrontation of inside and outside, of life and death, sharpens. The *Preface* poems occasionally envision a "new turn." "Theory of Art" (P 40–41) vaguely anticipates "a dark singular consciousness" and the terror that will be caused by "the animal sleeping" "when he wakes." "The New Sheriff" (P 42) alludes to Baraka's childhood heroes of the Lone Ranger type and subtly elaborates a contrasting imagery of cruelty/virginity, color/whiteness, and inside/outside that forebodes, in Eliotic terms, more radical changes to come:

> *There is something*
> *in me so cruel, so*
> *silent. It hesitates*
> *to sit on the grass*
> *with the young white*
>
> *virgins (P 42)*

The turning toward "new" things is critically reflected in the last poem of the volume, which departs from *Preface to a Twenty Volume Suicide Note* in its more communicative title, "Notes for a Speech." Instead of the valedictory and suicidal soliloquizing of some earlier poems, there is, in this poem, the strengthening of the gesture of "speech," of finding oneself and others in the verbal process. The theme of the speech, however, is an assessment of the isolation of the Black Bohemian from other Black people, his alienation from Africa and the Black American community. While implying dissatisfaction with this alienation, the poet cannot resolve the fact that "African blues / does not know me" (P 47), a lyrical reminder of Countee Cullen's famous question "What is Africa to me," and ends, instead, on a resigned note:

> *My color*
> *is not theirs. Lighter, white man*
> *talk. They shy away. My own*
> *dead souls, my, so called*
> *people. Africa*
> *is a foreign place. You are*

as any other sad man here
american. (P 47)

A possible reason for this return to resignation may be that the poem was written as the intended end to *Preface;* but it may also be that the poet, who achieved the strongest anticipatory thoughts in his most expressive and most personal poems, assumed a more formal and almost essayistic role in his "Notes for a Speech," the conclusion of which, significantly, resembles the last paragraphs of "Cuba Libre." "Notes for a Speech" contains very little that is cryptic, no obscure personal references, no "names" and almost no Beat peculiarities except in the line arrangement. At the end of *Preface* Baraka, not unlike Ralph Ellison, sees his alienation as a symbol of the estranged situation of "any other sad man" in America.

The Library of Congress recordings of Baraka's early poetry reinforce the impression of an alienated poet who talks to himself. His voice is rarely raised beyond the occasionally ironic emphasis of a point ("THERE MUST BE A LONE RANGER!!!"); and usually, the raised voice is combined with a tone of ironically undercut frustration, as in sending "lewd poems" to Uncle Don's radio program for children and emphasizing: "IF ONLY HE WOULD READ THESE ON THE AIR" (P 19). The poet has fears of being inaudible, or of not being able to communicate, an ironic sadness, since the Beat aesthetic frowned upon communication as something secondary to art. Indeed, the most striking "oral" effects are the frequently ironic references to silence, the antithesis of speech-art.

On the printed page, Baraka could develop his poetic voice without the inhibiting interference of editors; unlike most earlier Afro-American writers, he started his literary career as a writer *and* an editor and could, like Whitman, approach the literary market from a position of relative strength. A writer with "his own offset press in the back room," [27] Baraka was an active editor involved not only in several crucial journals of the New York Beat coterie (*Yugen, The Floating Bear,* and *Kulchur*), but also in the Totem Press and Corinth Books publications of such important writers as Allen Ginsberg, Jack Kerouac, Frank O'Hara, Charles Olson, Gary Snyder, and Philip Whalen.

Despite Baraka's active participation in the literary life of New York's "New Bohemia," the works of his first period of creativity increasingly show signs of a desire to transcend their own limitations and to take the freedom of his aesthetics at face value. The Bohemian's relationship to himself, his art, his subject, and his audience is challenged, and the questions of ethnic identity and the social functions of art remain unanswered. After hardly more than two years with the Beat Generation, Baraka began to tire of his literary milieu, a fatigue expressed implicitly and explicitly in his early works and letters. Thus, he wrote Ron Loewinsohn on November 30, 1959:

I am so goddamned thoroughly tired of this beatnick shit I'm screaming.[28]

This dissatisfaction with the media exploitation of all things beat was so total as to include everything except his writing. He had defined his *ennui* in a previous letter to Loewinsohn in the following striking manner:

I want to get the fuck out of all of it. This fucking city. the goddamn editorpublisher shit. . . . every every fucking thing thats keeping me from writing, from thinking, from even taking a leisurely shit in peace. I can't do all this much longer . . . & I DAMN SURE WONT.
. . .   love roi[29]

Baraka was, of course, not the only Beat writer who wanted to "get out"; by 1960, discontent was spreading among those whom America labelled "beatniks." An article by John Fles in the *Village Voice*, written upon the suicide of a close friend, is indicative of the mood:

. . . the revolution which started with "Howl" in 1956 and "On the Road" in 1957 is ending. . . . The old idols—insanity (Artaud), junk (Burroughs . . .), homosexuality and crime (Genet)—are fast crumbling, i.e., worth questioning seriously. But the old social-consciousness routine, as Ginsberg *et al.* have shown us, is dangerous to literature—the desert of the 30's—and absurd as commitment. The commitment still essentially has to remain romantic, *i.e.*, to ourselves, to our art and to what values we can make. . . . maybe the reality we think we see is different than it seems; maybe it calls for different involvements than the reality of the late 40's and early 50's when the Beat Generation, as a literary fact, came into being. Maybe there is a middle ground between the opportunistic and philistine Pollyana-ism of Henry Luce and, oppositely, suicide: and that this is the role of the committed artist.[30]

Bohemian artists still defined themselves within the intellectual framework of aesthetic protest ("romantic commitment"), but struggled for new roles. The era of "pure" Bohemianism was coming to an end, and Baraka was soon on the barricades "against hipness as such" (UN 17).

3 To "Cuba Libre" and **Home** : From the 1950s to the 1960s

The new yr.; squatting
on the hardwood, polished
floor reading
the new york times.

> *& come the revolution*
> *it will be the same,*
> *Miles Davis &*
> *bourbon. Sunday mornings;*
> *after we have won.*
> *—"For You" (UP 18)*
> *"which is to my wife and Fidel"*

1. "CUBA LIBRE"

Staughton Lynd saw the late 1950s as an "incubation period" for the nascent New Left, during which

the "beat" writings . . . helped young people to take the first groping steps toward a psychological freedom from convention which, in 1960, suddenly found political expression.[1]

The year 1960 appears as a crucial turning point, "crowded so thickly with events that any summary seems arbitrary." Indeed, a glance at New Left chronologies shows that 1960, the year after the Cuban Revolution, brought much radical activity. Early in the year, the sit-ins began in Greensboro, N.C., from where they spread to Woolworth lunch counters throughout the country; in April, the Fair Play for Cuba Committee (FPCC) was founded;[2] in the same month, SNCC, the Student Non-Violent Co-Ordinating Committee was constituted; in June, SDS, Students for a Democratic Society, came into being. The new "Movement"[3] was concerned with the issues of Free Speech and of domestic investigations by government agencies; thus, the Internal Security Subcommittee investigated FPCC in 1961, at the time of the abortive Bay of Pigs invasion. Writers and intellectuals protested against U.S. foreign and domestic politics.

Confronted with the threat of an American invasion of revolutionary Cuba, many Bohemians and students identified strongly with the Cuban rebels of Fidel Castro and believed that there were remarkable "ideological similarities between the Cuban and the Campus revolutions":[4]

Baraka did not share such a naively optimistic identification with foreign rebellions (cf. H 43, 61–62), but his development after 1960 reflects the radicalization of the American intelligentsia as a whole, even in its persistent Bohemianism. Although Baraka's involvement with the New Left in the late 1960s must be called marginal,[5] he participated centrally in the cultural transformation of "pure" aesthetic protest into political and ethnic protest.

The clash between the 1950s and the 1960s is dramatically apparent in "Cuba Libre," Baraka's account of his trip to Cuba in July 1960.[6] He traveled with a group of Black writers and intellectuals at the invitation of Richard Gibson of the FPCC. In Cuba, Baraka met Fidel Castro[7] and other representatives of the new government, as well as Latin American intellectuals. His descriptions of these meetings make "Cuba Libre" one of his best essays and a touchstone for his growing disaffiliation with the American system and with aesthetic protest.

Challenged to explain his politics, Baraka portrays himself as defensive of his aesthetic position.

Look, why jump on me? . . . I'm a poet . . . what can I do? I write, that's all. I'm not even interested in politics. (H 42)

In response, the Mexican intellectual Señora Betancourt called him a "cowardly bourgeois individualist," and Jaime Shelley, the Mexican poet, continued:

You want to cultivate your soul? In that ugliness you live in, you want to cultivate your soul? Well, we've got millions of starving people to feed, and that moves me enough to make poems out of. (H 42–43)

The Cuban experience, of central importance to many contemporary Afro-American radicals,[8] was one cause (and in the view of some critics, *the* cause)[9] of Baraka's transformation from aesthetic to political protest, from a belief in the end of ideology to a new politicized awareness. In terms reminiscent of C. Wright Mills's[10] critique of Western intellectuals, Baraka describes himself before the Cuban trip as a "know-it-all" poet.

Being an American poet, I suppose, I thought my function was simply to talk about everything as if I knew . . . it had never entered my mind that I might really like to find out for once what was actually happening some place else in the world. (H 12)

After Cuba, Baraka concludes that there is little difference between the "unideological" comment of one of his sophisticated friends about Cuba, "I don't trust guys in uniforms" (H 20), and the straightforward anticommunist warning of the cab driver who took him to Idlewild: "Those rotten commies. You'd better watch yourself, mister, that you don't get shot or something. Those guys are mean" (H 20).

To Baraka, aesthetic protest, the Bohemian negation of "square" American attitudes, has become a

so-called rebellion against what is most crass and ugly in our society, but without the slightest thought of, say, any kind of direction or purpose. Certainly, without any knowledge of what could be put up as alternatives. To fight against one kind of dullness with an even more subtle dullness is, I suppose, the highwater mark of social degeneracy. Worse than mere lying. (H 20)

Baraka's development since 1960 may be interpreted as a search for "direction" and "purpose," a real "alternative" to America;[11] but he perceived these new ideas—as well as much of the Cuban trip—within the older framework of aesthetic protest rather than in the context of a political theory or an ethnic ideology. He sees the limitations of the Bohemian approach, but still shares its central assumptions.

Baraka's dissatisfaction with "What I Brought to the Revolution," the title of the first part of "Cuba Libre," is clear, but "What I Brought Back Here," part two of the essay, is merely the beginning of a vague process of rethinking:

The "new" ideas that were being shoved at me, some of which I knew
would be painful when I eventually got to New York. (H 61)

The negative evaluation of the "pre-Cuban" past is unequivocal:

The rebels among us have become merely people like myself who grow
beards and will not participate in politics. (H 61)

But the anticipation of the "post-Cuban" future is pessimistic and
demonstrates the pervasiveness of aesthetic protest even in the act
of criticism; the essay ends not with the prospect of a real "alternative" but with the nihilistic statement that there "is none."

We are an *old* people already. Even the vitality of our art is like bright
flowers growing up through a rotting carcass. But the Cubans, the other
new peoples (in Asia, Africa, South America) don't need us, and we had
better stay out of their way. (H 62)

"Newness," the goal of all modernism, is limited to other,
"younger" nations,[12] and Baraka does not question his Ameri-
canness in the Cuban confrontation. He sees no possibility for an
identification of Black Americans with those "young" peoples of the
Third World and considers himself a member of an "old" society;
(the pronoun "we" in "Cuba Libre" never stands for Afro-
Americans.) Baraka sees the contrast between the "radical human-
ism" of Fidel Castro (H 53) and the world of "the Eisenhowers, the
Nixons, the DuPonts" (H 42) as a conflict between youth and old
age. Perhaps, the attractiveness of the Cuban experience lay less in
its revolutionary egalitarian philosophy than in the youthful vitality of the country and its leaders.[13] Years later Baraka still
cherished the cult of youth as a substitute for political concepts in
discussing Cuba as a Bohemian "Pays de la jeunesse."[14]

The central difficulty Baraka faced with the Cuban inspiration
was how to translate a vaguely political impulse into a new aesthetic that would be meaningful for an "old" country. Harold Cruse
showed that Baraka, because of his literary avant-gardism, could
not possibly work on a common basis with communist Afro-
American writers.[15] Baraka's rejection of their protest literature
was even more explicit than Cruse implies. Thus, "Cuba Libre" is
full of polemical, cutting remarks about the old-fashioned communists in the travel group who ask "embarrassing" questions about

"integration" and want to see pictures of Negroes in Cuban school books. In Baraka's eyes, American communists (white or Black) are about as "old" as one can get. He describes one such couple in the group:

One embarrassingly dull (white) communist, his professional Negro (*i.e.*, unstraightened hair, 1930s bohemian peasant blouses, etc., militant integrationist, etc.) wife who wrote embarrassingly inept social comment-type poems, usually about one or sometimes a group of Negroes being mistreated or suffering in general (usually in Alabama, etc.) (H 13)

Baraka criticized apolitical avant-gardism and "embarrassing" communist writing; yet he believed that his art would be able to combine political contents and avant-gardist forms; that his writing could take a political "turn" which would not seem formally "inept," or embarrassingly old-fashioned.

Baraka's own "bright flowers," the first poems written during and after the Cuban visit, are as ambiguous as his essay. In "Betancourt" (P 36–40), the poem that introduces the theme of Cuba and a new sense of people and movement, Baraka relates to the new challenge not in political, but in aesthetic-erotic terms. Dated "30 July 1960 Habana," the poem asks the important question "What are influences?" (P 36) When Baraka uses the term "El hombre" (P 39), he perhaps refers to Fidel Castro and alludes to William Carlos Williams.[16] The poem "Betancourt" pictures Cuba as a revolutionary pastoral setting

> *Not*
> *in the gardens*
> *of Spain, but some*
> *new greenness* (P 37)

Baraka is shaken by his conversation with Señora Betancourt and other Latin American intellectuals, but appears sexually and politically impotent. He gropes for a point of departure from the identity of a Beat writer to that of a politically and ethnically committed man, who has a new and "un-white" consciousness.

> *Desert man*
> *whose mind is some rotting*

> *country of snow* . . .
> *There is more*
> *underneath.* (P 38–39)

If the poem suggests "dropping" books (P 39) in order to unearth that consciousness "underneath" the mind, it advocates the desired "turn" in Eliot's and Lorca's terms.[17]

> *Think*
> *about it! As even*
> *this, now, a turning*
> *away. (I mean I think*
> *I know now*
> *what a poem*
> *is) A*
> *turning away* . . .
> *from what*
> *it was*
> *had moved*
> *us* . . .
>   *A*
> *madness.*
>   *Looking at the sea. And some*
> *white fast boat.* (P 39–40)

Leaving "America on the first fast boat" (T 74) remains a Bohemian desire for disaffiliation; but the creative "climax" for the narcissistic Bohemian has become an image of sexual as well as, perhaps, political impotence.

> *the cock*
> *flat*
> *on skin*
> *like*
> *a dead*
> *insect.* (P 38)

The American poet does not partake of the new vitality of Che or Fidel, but he does learn how to see again.

Another "Cuban" poem, "The Disguise" (UP 33), is apparently addressed to Sra. Betancourt and shows the poet's turn from "self" to "outside world." In the pre-Cuban poem "Consider This" (1959),

Baraka articulated the difficulties of looking at the "street," since the poet's own mirror image in the window pane is always super-imposed upon the world.

> *You cannot look out the window at the street.*
> *There is nothing there but your own waving. (UP 17, section 1)*

In 1961, in the post-Cuban "The Disguise," Baraka attempts to "open" this window. He begins the poem with what may be the most cogent image for his Bohemian mask and for his desire to move away from an expressive and narcissistic aesthetic.

> *When you spoke to me, I turned, I thought,*
> *away from the grey glass, & into the world. (UP 33)*

The "grey glass" implies both the mirror-window into the poet's self, and his "white," or, in Black English, "grey" identity. Once the window to the world is open, the "blinds" cannot keep the sun and red air out for long.

> *Red air pushed on the blinds & made them clatter,*
> *but nothing happened. (UP 33)*

In a state of unresolved yearning for change, the poet tries to recall the setting of his conversation with Sra. Betancourt, but cannot proceed beyond a repetition of the beginning of the poem:

> *nothing moves . . . (when you spoke to me,*
> *I thought I'd turned & gotten to it,*
> *but a truck moved by*
> *& must have obliterated the rest of*
> *your thot.)*

Baraka cannot formulate a solution to the confusion in his own head, he cannot decode the "indian knots behind my eyes" which have affected his vision. Aware of his old disguises, the poet has not reached a new sense of self or reality.

>   *(I thought*
> *I'd turned)*
>
> *The window hung open, & red air*
> *blew in. (UP 33)*

The Bay of Pigs invasion attempt of April 17, 1961, increased the pressure of "red air" and heightened Baraka's sense of political "reality." Joining other prominent artists and intellectuals, Baraka signed two petitions denouncing U.S. intervention in Cuba. The first was published as a letter to *Evergreen Review* and included such writers as Diane DiPrima, Lawrence Ferlinghetti, Allen Ginsberg, Paul Goodman, and Norman Mailer.[18] The second was published in the *Afro-American* and was cosigned by Black intellectuals such as John Henrik Clarke, Harold Cruse, Ossie Davis, W.E.B. DuBois, Richard Gibson, Julian Mayfield, and Robert F. Williams.[19]

Baraka could now see his own social role as that of a poet-"mediator" between black and white. On the one hand, he organized an interracial "On Guard For Freedom Committee" in Harlem where he maintained that it was not "necessary to restrict whites from participation. . . . More than that, he said he could not understand why Harlem Negroes should hate whites."[20] On the other hand, he translated the attitude of the young nationalist Harlemites to white liberal audiences and maintained in his "Letter to Jules Feiffer" (the cartoonist of the *Village Voice*) that

Afro-Americans (Negroes, spades, shades, boots. woogies, *etc.*) in this country can afford, I believe, the luxury of hate. They certainly have enough to hate. . . . I am in favor of no kind of Negro protest that does not distress the kind of ethical sterility your and Mr. Harrington's liberalism represents. (H 65–66)

This political and ethnic ambivalence is closely related to Baraka's developing theory of art. He uses the example of Robert F. Williams (H 66), not in order to write Third World literature,[21] but in order to attack white liberals and to make them understand that they *cannot* understand. Baraka's ideal audience and target in this period is white.[22] Despite this communicative pattern, Baraka takes a more and more ethnocentric attitude in addressing whites and invokes a Third World consciousness as an opposing force to American liberalism. Thus he couples the rejection of the "Feiffer / Harrington / *Village Voice* liberal" (H 64) with the reminder that the new countries of Asia, Africa, and Latin America are not interested in your shallow conscience-saving slogans and protests of moderation or "political guarantees." (H 65)

But in order to illustrate the interests of the Third World, Baraka resorts to literary modernism:

As a character in Burroughs' *Naked Lunch* says, "You think I am inarrested in contracting your horrible ol' condition? I am not inarrested at all." (H 65)

Baraka advocates, or defends, hatred, violence, and Black nationalist as well as socialist concepts; but he ends his letter in defense of the term "Afro-American" on a curious note of multiethnic harmony:

. . . if perhaps there were more Judeo-Americans, and a few less bland, cultureless, middle-headed AMERICANS, this country might still be a great one. (H 67)[23]

While many of Baraka's statements begin to assume ethnic overtones in the early 1960s, he still defines "the enemy" in essentially aesthetic categories ("bland," "cultureless," "middle-headed") which naturally transcend class and race definitions. When asked about his ambitions, he answers flippantly:

To write beautiful poems full of mystical sociology and abstract politics. To show America it is ugly and full of middle-class toads (black and white). To become a great political agitator and invade Britain.[24]

2. TOWARD A DEFINITION OF "ART-ING"

In Baraka's visionary geography, Harlem moves from Philistia to Bohemia in the early 1960s. Baraka revises his old notion of Harlem as the "capitol city of the Black Bourgeoisie" (UN 1). Using a pattern of hip vs. square, he now elevates Harlem to the status of hipness and describes Black New York as even more Bohemian than an artists' colony.

In a very real sense, Harlem is the capital of Black America (H 87) . . . a community of nonconformists, since any black American, simply by virtue of his blackness, is weird, a nonconformist in this society. A community of nonconformists, not an artists' colony—though blind "ministers" still wander sometimes along 137th Street, whispering along the strings of their guitars—but a colony of old-line Americans, who can hold out . . . against the hypocrisy and sterility of big-time America. (H 93)

The identification of the Black and the hip is made the basis for formulating an art theory, and becomes the precept for a Black literature in the modernist tradition. In *Home, Blues People, Black Music, The Moderns*, and uncollected essays and interviews, Baraka establishes, or reaffirms, the elements of his post-Cuban aesthetic. To Baraka, the true artist must express political, ethnic, and aesthetic commitment in the best modern idiom, informed by Pound and Joyce, Melville and Kafka, but, as a *Black* artist, he must also draw on Black speech and Black music, from folk expression to avant-gardism. He must not yield to bourgeois anality and artifact fetishism and must give priority to the dynamic and improvisational process which Baraka calls "art-ing."

One of the crucial developments in Baraka's artistic self-definition after 1960 is his expansion of the formula given in "How You Sound??": "I must be completely free to do just what I want, in the poem" so that the last three words lose their confining meaning. After Cuba, Baraka is eager to extend the freedom of spontaneous art to include political freedom. In a conscious analogy to the supposed "progress in the arts" (H 77), Baraka states in "Tokenism: 300 Years for Five Cents" that "It is not 'progress' that the majority of Negroes want, but Freedom" (H 70). Making "freedom" a political just as much as an aesthetic demand means asking writers to be socially committed. In his "Brief Reflections on Two Hot Shots," Baraka maintains that, unlike James Baldwin, a writer

must have a point of view, or he cannot be a good writer. He must be standing somewhere in the world, or else he is not one of *us*, and his commentary then is of little value. (H 118)

This is a call for an ethnic rather than a political point of view. Directed as it is at a prominently *Black* writer, the demand for ethnic partisanship is a departure from Baraka's original demand that "The only 'recognizable tradition' a poet need follow is himself. . . . To broaden his *own* voice with. (You have to start and finish there . . . your own voice . . . how you sound.)" Following your "*own* voice," in William Carlos Williams' sense, now comes to mean following Black speech.

In 1960, Baraka still defined his ethnicity in a very limited sense. Asked specifically whether "being a Negro" had influenced his poetry, Baraka referred to the possibility of utilizing "Southern Baptist church rhythms" (UI, p. 81); but he distinguished his own poetic "stance" from Langston Hughes's by explaining:

I'm fully conscious all the time that I am an American Negro, because it's part of my life. But I know also that if I want to say, "I see a bus full of people," I don't have to say, "I am a Negro seeing a bus full of people." I would deal with it when it has to do directly with the poem, and not as a kind of broad generalization . . . it's a new generation now, and people are beset by other kinds of ideas that don't have to do much with sociology, *per se*. (UI 1, p. 81)

By 1964, however, Baraka was telling his students at Columbia:

I don't think I am seeing a bus full of people. I think I am a *Negro* seeing a bus full of people.[25]

Baraka's shift from the nonethnic point-of-view of 1960 to the ethnic consciousness of 1964 is symptomatic of the period in which it occurred. Baraka's specific and personal espousal of "Blackness," and, indeed, his very definition of Blackness, however, grew out of the literary positions he had adopted in the 1950s. Furthermore, his ethnocentric tendencies in the first half of the 1960s were neither systematic, nor did they exclude other literary, philosophical, and political vantage points in his works.

Despite the growing ethnic emphasis in Baraka's discussion of point-of-view and voice of the poet, he is not satisfied with the demand that Black literature merely stress its "Negro-ness," its "Negritude." In "A Dark Bag," a review of non-American Black writers, he discusses the concept of "Negritude" without enthusiasm:

This idea seems to me merely a useful, though ironically Classical, statement that reference determines value, and that for every culture there is a definite set of aesthetic, moral, etc., judgments based quite literally on specifically indigenous emotional and psychological response; although it is usually made to seem by European commentators like the crafts program of the Black Muslims. (H 131)

Most of the Black writers he reviews he considers bad poets, victims of the "Colonial School" who

employ the meta-language and shallow ornament of contemporary academic British poetry with, a great deal of the time, the same dreary results. (H 127)

Baraka's antiacademic, anti-British, and antiliberal stance is stronger here than his "Negritude."

In a 1962 review of two volumes of *The Yale Series of Younger Poets* (Alan Dugan's *Poems* and Jack Gilbert's *Views of Jeopardy*) (UN 24) Baraka reaffirms his affiliation with the avant-garde, which he again opposes to sterile academic poetry. Thus, Dugan's poetry is criticized as a

godsend to those who will not be convinced that Creeley, Olson, Duncan, Ginsberg and the others are doing the real work of our time, but who also realize that Pack, Simpson, Meredith and the rest of the schoolmarms begin to tire. (UN 24, p. 89)

Gilbert's poems, on the other hand, are definitely and "honestly 'non-academic,' " and are therefore praised for their "American idiom":

their rhythms, diction, and line are issued from the Post-Whitman American mind (aware that Whitman *did* live, and did not get C's in poetry from Allen Tate). (UN 24, p. 90)

In other essays from 1961 to 1963, Baraka's ambivalence in describing himself both as a Negro who sees a bus full of people and as an antiacademic writer in the "modern tradition" becomes more and more obvious. While increasingly critical of his fellow-

Bohemians, he still identifies his art as part of the modern movement. The 1961 essay "Milneburg Joys (or, Against 'Hipness As Such')" (UN 17) begins with an elusive discussion of the opposing worlds of "uptown" (Black New York) and "downtown" (the place of Bohemia):

someone (if you work "uptown") will tell you yours is the bird world. "Mine is real." (UN 17, p. 41)

Ostensibly, Baraka still identifies with the quasireligious function of the art of Creeley, Olson, Ginsberg, and Duncan and heads " 'downtown' to our real world. Our real homes . . . our real friends . . . and loves") (UN 17, p. 41).[26] Yet, he is skeptical now of the "reality" of this world, and rejects the cliquish cult of opinion and the lies upon which Bohemian coteries are based:

That we are all, somehow, friends. And there are some pacts, &c., that must be kept. The code words, the cult of the idea. The community of intellects. Where all is admitted; where no standard exists at all . . . (UN 17, p. 42)

The essay ends unresolved, with another reference to violence as a solution to a literary problem.

The word "taste" becomes a bludgeon to crack open your skull. Taste, relativism, opinion, get in on all points. Bullshit. Why did we leave that other world[27] in the first place if the same undifferentiated vagueness is to be canonized once again. (UN 17, p. 43)

In 1962, Baraka published "Voices From the Art World (Or, Bright Sayings)," a collection of 25 brief aphorisms and phrases concerning the contemporary art scene (UN 23). He used the pen name Duke Mantee, assuming the character of the gangster Humphrey Bogart played in *The Petrified Forest*. The "bright sayings" show Baraka's increasingly bitter and sarcastic distancing from "the art world" of Bohemia.

Question: Can you explain why you paint this way?
Answer: Uh—it gets—uh—very complicated
when you—uh—talk about it.—Andy Warhol.

He mocks the ridiculousness of Beat jargon:

Dig man, hip, groovy, swing, baby, junk, pot,
yeah!—Anselm Hollo.

and of political ignorance and the mutual admiration syndrome of
the artistic coterie:

How come all those little countries hate the
United States? —Gregory Corso.

Larry Rivers is one of the finest painters in
America. —Kenneth Koch.
Kenneth Koch is one of the finest poets in
America. —Larry Rivers

(Together) We're—just—a couple of song and
dance men . . . (UN 23)

In *The Petrified Forest*, the gangster Duke Mantee kills the intellectual, Alan Squier; thus Mantee may represent Baraka's ever-
present theme of violence committed against "sensitivity."

The introduction to *The Moderns* (1963) continues the line of
thought expressed in "Milneburg Joys," as Baraka reaffirms that he
is not interested in "another 'establishment' " (M x), but in "writing
that shows a care for deeper involvement beyond the specific instance of its virtues as 'literature' " (M ix). The kind of "involvement" or "commitment" advocated is contradictory. On the one
hand, it is Williams' "local" concern, "and in a broader though
vaguer sense, American" (M xii). Avant-garde writing, in the tradition of Joyce, is not a *vehicle*, even for expressing involvement; it is
not so much "about something" as "an event in itself" (M xv). On
the other hand, it is not *l'art pour l'art* and stands in contradiction
to "the main body of popular American fiction" (M xvi). Still, the
literature Baraka includes in *The Moderns* is "no 'protest' against
that 'stylish' fiction of our time" (M xvi). Baraka sees the solution to
his paradoxical demands in the metaphor of avant-gardism, which
implies a political and an aesthetic revolution. In explaining his
choice of authors and texts for *The Moderns*, Baraka arrives at the
crucial formulation of his demand for a unity of art and politics:

the work in this collection does exist out of a continuing tradition of
populist modernism that has characterized the best of twentieth-century

American writing. [Its] common stance . . . is perhaps one of *self-reliance,* Puddin'head Wilson style. (M xvi)

Modernism and populism are to merge;[28] the elitist and popular conceptions of art are held together by the common opposition to bourgeois, mainstream, or middlebrow art, in the familiar manner of Bohemianism. The invocation of the American principle of self-reliance, from Emerson to Mark Twain, emphasizes the individualist character of the antibourgeois opposition. In other words, the term "populist modernism" is Baraka's rephrasing of the Bohemian assault on the bourgeoisie, from "above" and "below."

Confronted with the choice between the avant-gardist, aesthetic impulses and populist, political ones, Baraka in 1963 still gives priority to modernism over populism. He sides with Dada and Surrealism against the artistic limitations of "political art."

Only march music is political. Only posters can call for volunteers. . . . If everyone was a credit to the community could there still be art? (UN 28, p. 93)

March music and posters are no viable prototypes for Baraka's conceptions of "new" art, but neither is the whole body of Afro-American literature. In his view, the music of Afro-Americans is aesthetically as well as socially more significant than their literature; therefore he attempts to translate the values of Black music into a modern literature. According to Baraka's polemical statements in "The Myth of a Negro Literature," Afro-American literature, as opposed to Black music, had always been addressed to white people, as an expression of the assimilationist tendencies of the Black middle class. In order to be accepted by white America, Black writers denied everything that could connect them and their literature "with the poor black man or the slave" (BP 132); and, to better exhibit their "cultivation," the writers looked to white middlebrow authors as prototypes.

[O]nly Jean Toomer, Richard Wright, Ralph Ellison, and James Baldwin have managed to bring off examples of writing, in this genre, that could succeed in passing themselves off as "serious" writing, in the sense that, say, the work of Somerset Maugham is "serious" writing. That is, serious, if one has never read Herman Melville or James Joyce. And it is part of the tragic naiveté of the middle class (brow) writer, that he has not. (H 107)

For this reason,

the literature of the blues is a much more profound contribution to Western culture than any other literary contribution made by American Negroes. (H 107)

The Black author of the future should integrate the "populist" Black experience as expressed in the "Blues continuum" with the most excellent examples of modernist Western literature. With an awareness of Melville, Joyce, Pound, and Williams, as well as of Charlie Parker, Bebop, and the Blues tradition, the Black writer should utilize

the entire spectrum of the American experience from the point of view of the emotional history of the black man in this country: as its victim and its chronicler. (H 111–12).

Were there really a Negro literature, now it could flower. At this point when the whole of Western society might go up in flames, the Negro remains an integral part of that society, but continually outside it, a figure like Melville's Bartleby. He is an American, capable of identifying emotionally with the fantastic cultural ingredients of this society, but he is also, forever, outside that culture, an invisible strength within it, an observer. If there is ever a Negro literature, it must disengage itself from the weak, heinous elements of the culture that spawned it, and use its very existence as evidence of a more profound America. (H 114–15)

These definitions attempt to balance the elements of aesthetic protest (the emphasis on the modern idiom, the interpretation of Afro-Americans in terms of Bartleby, and the Spenglerian conviction of *The Decline of the West*) with the new impulses of political and ethnic protest. In the essay "Expressive Language," as well as in remarks throughout his nonfiction writings, Baraka illustrates the appropriateness of "Black speech as a poetic reference."[29] His definition in *Blues People* was to become the motto of the first comprehensive scholarly book on *Black English:*

It is absurd to assume, as has been the tendency, among a great many Western anthropologists and sociologists, that all traces of Africa were erased from the Negro's mind because he learned English. The very nature of the English the Negro spoke and still speaks drops the lie on that idea. (BP 9)[30]

Baraka sees this language influenced by political class differences and by historically developed ethnic differences. Thus, money "does not mean the same thing to me it must mean to a rich man" (H 167) and "FREEDOM" is "the most ambiguous term known to man, if Barry Goldwater . . . and Martin Luther King can use it, presumably with a different sense intended" (H 204–5). These differences in language refer to power relationships, and Baraka advises the writer to liberate himself from the "culture of the powerful." He maintains that "To be any kind of 'success' one must be fluent in this culture. Know the words of the users, the semantic rituals of power" (H 169).

In addition to the class differences, which should be identical for poor whites and poor Blacks, there is a specific cultural tradition in Black language, which the Black middle class has attempted to suppress. Thus, Baraka quotes, disparagingly, a professor of English at Howard who thought that a production of James Baldwin's *Amen Corner* "set the speech department back ten years" (H 109). Baraka, of course, identifies with those cultural elements most threatening to the Black middle class and endeavors to salvage the specific form of Black expressiveness in literature.

I heard an old Negro street singer last week, Reverend Pearly Brown, singing, "God don't never change!" This is a precise thing he is singing. He does not mean "God does not ever change!" He means "God don't never change!" The difference, and I said it was crucial, is in the final human reference . . . the form of passage through the world. A man who is rich and famous who sings, "God don't never change," is confirming his hegemony and good fortune . . . or merely calling the bank. A blind hopeless black American is saying something very different. He is telling you about the extraordinary order of the world. . . . The God of the damned cannot know the God of the damner, that is, cannot know he is God. And no Blues person can really believe emotionally in Pascal's God, or Wittgenstein's question, "Can the concept of God exist in a perfectly logical language?" Answer: "God don't never change." (H 171–72)

Through his growing awareness of Black English, Baraka hopes to break the "semantic rituals of power"; through the reference to, and translation into literature of, Black music, he attempts to give the Black writer a historical dimension as victim and chronicler;

and through the use of the modern literary idiom, this new Black literature is to be truly contemporary, not merely an "inept" or academic exercise in "art" as an object.

The central element of Baraka's aesthetic, "art-ing," grew out of his pure expressive phase. Through "art-ing," Baraka attempted to transfer the spiritual, "non-Western" essence of the Black experience into a literature that would defy becoming a "thing." Originally, he developed this aesthetic opposition to reification without any specific reference to Blackness. His 1962 essay "Names & Bodies" (UN 22), published under the pseudonym "Johannes Koenig," an inverted Germanization of "LeRoi Jones," emphasizes, with allusions to mystics and German philosophers from Meister Eckart and Jakob Boehme to Heidegger, the priority of art as a "process," a "verb," over the "purely arbitrary" art product, the "noun."[31] The verb-derived "ing"-form is on the side of "body" and "reality," whereas the "Nominative/Name" represents the reification, "THINGING," of the "hideous artifact."

Baraka upholds "art-ing" over "artifacts;" this is a crucial antibourgeois element of his aesthetic; and his analysis of Black music forms a link in the development of his concept of art as a process. Baraka elaborates this concept in "Names & Bodies" and applies it in *Blues People*. He characterizes the acceptance of some elements of Afro-American music into "the mainstream of American culture" as a reification which necessarily disconnected the product from its roots. In a chapter significantly entitled "Swing—From Verb to Noun," he argues that swing music

ceased to have meaning for a great many Negroes. . . . Swing music, which was the result of arranged big-band jazz, as it developed to a music that had almost nothing to do with blues, had very little to do with Black America, though that is certainly where it had come from. (BP 164–65)

In order to arrive at an art which would be relevant to its creators and faithful to the Blues tradition, Baraka suggests abandoning the notion of art as artifacts and trophies, since "Hunting is Not Those Heads on the Wall." Ironically, then, he advocates a spiritualization in the service of relevance. The dynamic verb character of art is seen as a guarantee against uncommitted *art pour l'art:*

Art is like speech, for instance, in that it is at the end, and a shadowy rep-
lica, of another operation, thought. . . . Art-ing is what makes art, and is
thereby more valuable.

The academic Western mind is the best example of the substitution of
artifact worship for the lightning awareness of the art process. Even the
artist is more valuable than his artifact, because the art process goes on in
his mind. But the process itself is the most important quality because it
can transform and create, and its only form is possibility. The artifact,
because it assumes one form, is only that particular quality or idea. It is,
in this sense, after the fact, and is only important because it remarks on its
source. (H 174)

Baraka's aesthetic demand, expressed in terms of Black music
and of European mysticism, is thus for improvisational "art-ing"
that defies congealing into a worshipped object. He has always
defied definitions (whether they be the label "beatnik" or the naming of sinners in Dante's Hell); and art-ing, as a spontaneous expression of the author, and as an Olsonian "force," an "energy"
that comes from, and returns to, life, has remained an essential of
Baraka's aesthetic outlook.

Baraka's aesthetic and political writing of the early 1960s is full of
contradictory impulses. Yet at the time of his greatest theoretical
confusion he wrote many of his best poems, plays, and fictions.
More than that, the very contradictions within his increasingly
divided self are an important source of his creativity.

4 "Who Substitutes for the Dead Lecturer?": Poetry of the Early 1960s

In many ways, Baraka's second poetry collection, *The Dead Lecturer* (1964), appears strikingly similar to *Preface*. There are, in the new volume, many "pure" Beat poems, concerned with love (DL 9, 17, 36) or the function of poetry (DL 10). Some poems restate the familiar themes of *Preface:* e.g., *"The invention of comics"* (DL 37) returns, as does the motto of *Lecturer,* to the products of American popular culture in Baraka's youth.

> *Its*
> *small dull fires. Its*
> *sun, like a greyness*
> *smeared on the dark. (DL 37)*

In *"The invention of comics"* the poet explores his heritage, as he did in "Lanie Poo;" again, there are strong echoes of Eliot.

> *I am a soul in the world: in*
> *the world of my soul the whirled*
> *light / from the day*
> *the sacked land*
> *of my father. (DL 37)*[1]

Despite the continuity, however, a significant development has taken place from *Preface* to *Lecturer.* While there is no "sudden departure in style,"[2] the poems in *Lecturer* do move away from the playfulness and spontaneity of *Preface;* from solipsism toward a new consciousness of "the People" (DL 10); from soliloquy to direct address with an increase in "volume," until "rage" and "anger" are vocally affirmed.

These changes do not occur in orderly, chronological ways, but hit Baraka in different poetic situations. Sometimes the poet gives a new slant to old images, as in "suns" (DL 47); sometimes he openly rejects previous poetic practices, as in "without preface" (DL 10); and occasionally, he forms new lyric entities that were altogether unthinkable in *Preface*, as in "BLACK DADA NIHILISMUS" (DL 61–64). "Dichtung" (DL 77), one of the last poems in the chronologically arranged *Lecturer*, still resembles the *Preface* poems in tone and imagery, whereas "A contract. (for the destruction and rebuilding of Paterson" (DL 11), one of the first poems in *Lecturer*, already contains many of the "new" elements. Significantly, the transformation of Baraka's poetry from the 1950s to the 1960s can be measured by the way in which the imagery of death is developed.

When a poet's first volume is entitled *Preface to a Twenty Volume Suicide Note* and ends with "Notes for a Speech," and the title of his second collection is *The Dead Lecturer*, we may with some justification assume that the poet's preoccupation with his own agony has reached its terminal point and that the "dead lecturer" of the title is none other than the poet himself. Yet there is a living and increasingly affirmative voice in Baraka's poems of the first half of the 1960s, a voice, moreover, which often alludes to, and sometimes distances itself from, the earlier "suicide note."

"Rhythm & Blues," a poem dedicated to Robert Williams, reflects the post-Cuban spirit, but returns to the themes and Eliotic forms of *Preface:*

> *I am deaf and blind and lost and will not again sing your quiet verse.*
> *I have lost*
> *even the act of poetry, and writhe now for cool horizonless dawn.*
> *(DL 47)*

The poet articulates a poetic death, yet implies that there may be poetry which will not be "quiet verse" and will transcend the limitations of *Preface*.

"Footnote To A Pretentious Book" (DL 42) is harshly critical of *Preface* and its portrait of the artist as a suicided man:

> *you could say of me,*
> *that I was truly*
> *simpleminded. (DL 43)*

There is, then, a dead lecturer who once composed that quiet suicide note, and a new poet of politics, war, and rhythm and blues.

In "Political Poem" (DL 74) Baraka again sides with "self" and "street" and "undoes" a poem by the spontaneous interference of the poetic "I."

> *the poem undone*
> *undone by my station, by my station,*
> *and the bad words of Newark. (DL 74)*

This recalls his earlier poetic strategy, which he now uses to mock his former self: a "dead lecturer / lamenting thru gipsies his fast suicide" (DL 74). The association with Gypsies implies a critique of Bohemianism; and the poem "Riding & Shooting" (UP 42) depicts the poet

> *in black, the*
> *gypsy whore, sprawled*
> *across a field. (UP 42)*

The thrust of the poet's post-Cuban self-criticism is directed at what Poggioli calls "agonism." In "The Liar" (DL 79), the new voice distances itself from the agony announced in *Preface* and reflected in *Dead Lecturer*.

> *When they say, "It is Roi*
> *who is dead?" I wonder*
> *who will they mean? (DL 79)*

A dramatic opposition of "Roi" and "I" against the background of an audience, "they," is beginning to emerge. This opposition of someone older and now "dead" and of someone else who is younger, vital, and ready to "Substitute For The Dead Lecturer" (DL 59) gives the poems an increasingly dynamic quality. The poems often cast this opposition in the familiar terms of a suffering inner self, soul and heart, obscured and oppressed by outward masks, shells, clothes, even "buttons" (DL 29). In the 1959 poem "Consider This" (UP 17), Hannibal struggled under the "8 button Italian armor;" the poems of the early 1960s record the process of *creation* out of this struggle.

In "Riding & Shooting" (UP 42), the poet is a "raw spirit" creating poems despite, and against, "Iron bands / around my body."

> *Blackest heart is blackest, a basic*
> *machine. It fails when I lose*
> *my straightness for craft*
> *or whatever pulls back. Steel bands.*
>
> > The Mind. (UP 42)

"*An Agony. As Now*" (DL 15–16) continues just this struggle within the poet as a creative but nearly lethal confrontation between lively, suffering inside and metallic, deadly outside which affects the very eye of poetic vision.

> *I am inside someone*
> *who hates me. I look*
> *out from his eyes. Smell*
> *what fouled tunes come in*
> *to his breath. Love his*
> *wretched women. (DL 15)*

The "enclosure" of "white hot metal" is the composite image of artistic reification and alienation, political confinement, and ethnic masquerade. It is an expanded version of the "Eliot shell" as rhetorical form and of Hannibal's Roman armor as a bourgeois costume. "In Wyoming Territory (a story" (UP 45) suggests that Baraka, in his opposition to this shell, negated "whiteness" to such an extent that even his wife Hettie, seen as a "left-handed" fellow-outsider in *Preface*, becomes part of the enclosure.

> *Hettie.*
> > *Of what use darkness. Hands, steel bands*
> *around the head. (UP 45)*

This association also gives the beginning of "*An Agony. As Now*" a sense of an inimical sexual and racial encounter.

Abandoning the "quiet verse" of *Preface*, Baraka lets "the thing inside" *scream*, as it is being scorched black by the white hot metal. This image is emblematic of the art of *The Dead Lecturer*, wrested from the unbearable pressures and frictions of iron body masks. It is the scream of pain and feeling, flesh and soul, of ethnic and political suffering and it is the dada scream which annihilates the "withered yellow flowers" of "Western poetry" from Joyce Kilmer's trees to Eliot's hollow men and Baudelaire's *Fleurs du Mal.*

The victim of the hot metal arises from the ashes as the victor of this poetic suicide; and the "killed is the killer," as Baraka states in "Green Lantern's Solo" (DL 69). What is being killed in *"An Agony. As Now"* is the poet's past; and after the "old Anglos" are dead, the poetic imagery may become activist, ethnic, and full of a new sense of selfhood. A new poetic "I" may, indeed, "substitute" for the *Dead Lecturer.*

The process of birth in death, of the phoenixlike emergence of a new poet from an old shell is crucial to Baraka's poetry. A visionary, descended from cosmic sun-rays, razes old Western conceptions in order to raise new race-conscious ones: this is the verbal strategy which remained with Baraka through the essays of *Raise Race Rays Raze.* The first comprehensive poetic statement of this process is made in "A contract. (For the destruction and rebuilding of Paterson" (DL 11), which locates the conflict of *"An Agony. As Now"* not merely in the self, but in "society," in the dismal urban environment of William Carlos Williams' Paterson, New Jersey.

> *Flesh, and cars, tar, dug holes beneath stone*
> *a rude hierarchy of money, band saws cross out*
> *music, feeling. Even speech, corrodes. (DL 11)*

The continued exploration of the antithesis of inside and outside in "flesh and cars," "music" and "band saws" is immediately apparent. "Speech" is, of course, the poet's notion of "art-ing" in confrontation with the definitions of "nouns," associated here with the "rude hierarchy of money." In "cold fear" "at the death of men, the death of learning . . . at my own," the poet tries to face up to his antagonist. His goal is a poetic inversion of the semantic rituals of power. The struggle for a new poetic voice has become a battle for the oppressed of society, a fulfillment of an old Bohemian dream. It is important that the struggle is acted out with the rhetorical help of William Carlos Williams; as Allen Ginsberg observed, it was Williams' influence which tended to bring Baraka "back home to his own speech and to his own soul and to his own body and to his own color and to his own town."³ The emergence of Baraka's *Black* voice is linked with the Eliot-Williams controversy.

As people move into the foreground of the poetry, they are often seen as not-yet-conscious bourgeoisified *potential* revolutionaries, in need of the artist to tell them what to do. The artistic process, if it is to escape "corrosion," must cut through the veil of lies, in the language, which help the powerful "to control the world," and which are "so marvelous" as to be presented under oath—"Cross my heart and hope to die." Taking Green Lantern's stance against those "who worship evil's might" (DL 8), Baraka suggests that Blacks and Puerto Ricans take this oath literally and give up non-violence:

> *So complete, their mastery, of these*
> *stupid niggers. Loud spics kill each other, and will not*
>
> *make the simple trip to Tiffany's. Will not smash their stainless*
> *heads, against the simpler effrontery of so callous a code as gain.* (DL
> *11*)

This early poetic advocacy of counterviolence is formulated as an externalization of a psychic drama. However, Baraka does address his next lines to the Black bourgeoisie which shares responsibility for oppression as repression.

> *You are no brothers, dirty woogies, dying under dried rinds, in*
> *massa's*
> *droopy tuxedos. Cab Calloways of the soul, at the soul's juncture, a*
> *music, they think, will save them from our eyes.* (DL 11)

The Black middle class is here seen as an accomplice in the attempt to petrify the status quo and to silence the oppressed, at the price of giving up its own "life" and memory of history. The rape of Africa has become "unintelligible," and the life force of the Black bourgeoisie has been extinguished with the memory of the African past: "Killed in white fedora hats, they stand so mute / at what / whiter slaves did to my fathers."

In its poetically unresolved expression of violence, "A contract . . ." is an interesting step toward Baraka's more political and ethnic art. The title illustrates the process from drama of self to social statement and makes the poem Baraka's specific application of William Carlos Williams' idea "that a man himself is a city, beginning, seeking, achieving and concluding his life in ways which the various aspects of a city may embody."[4] The meaning of the "destruction and rebuilding," the razing and raising, of Williams' *Paterson* is thus twofold: on the one hand, it is the violent destruction of "abstract prisons," petrified city structures of oppression, and the rebuilding of a new life, free of the rude hierarchy of money; and, on the other hand, it is the transformation of "speech"—as Williams' legacy to art-ing—to an anti-Eliotic aesthetic that would allow expression of the "boiling in my veins," and would make this new poetry impervious to "corrosion." This definition gives the oral performance of increasingly committed poems a life of its own which soon begins to supersede the versions on the printed page.

At this point, Baraka experiments with methods of destroying and rebuilding language. He ventures into the communicative extremes of "silence" and "screaming"; and he makes the "bad words of Newark" part of his poetry. Silence was prominent in much of the low-keyed "quiet verse" of *Preface*, and is still prevalent in *Lecturer*. It is now, however, a much more aggressive version of silence, as "SHORT SPEECH TO MY FRIENDS" suggests:

> *A compromise*
> *would be silence. To shut up, even such risk*
> *as the proper placement*
> *of verbs and nouns. To freeze the spit*
> *in mid-air, as it aims itself*
> *at some valiant intellectual's face.* (DL 30)

The other poetic speech-extreme, the scream, appears only faintly in the earlier poems, but comes to a fuller life in Baraka's poetry of the early 1960s, beginning, perhaps, with *"An Agony. As Now."* The scream functions in a "populist" as well as in a "modernist" context: it is the scream of the oppressed and of the expressionist painting by Edvard Munch, the scream of political anger and artistic rebellion.

The process of "razing and raising" is intimately linked with Baraka's development of a Black voice, with his use of Black speech as a reference to a culture that "does not 'speak proper,' or is not fluent with the terms of social strength" (H 171). Only by reconstructing his personal and collective voice can Baraka avoid the fate of disembodied, clowning Black entertainers:

> *The face sings, alone*
> *at the top*
> > *of the body. (DL 18)*

The scream merges the aesthetic and the ethnic reference and becomes, in "Rhythm & Blues" (DL 44–47) and in the more fully developed short story "The Screamers" (T 71–87), the rebellious act of "the dozens, the razor, the cloth, the sheen" that "unfinished cathedrals tremble with." (DL 46) In Black music, in the "roaring harmonies of need" (DL 46), is the jewel center of inspiration for Baraka's poetry of populist modernism.

In "BLACK DADA NIHILISMUS" (DL 61–64), Baraka develops the Black scream as the heart of his aesthetic;[5] and the visions of vengeful racial violence are a touchstone of the distance Baraka travelled since *Preface*. The first part of the poem forcefully rejects the culture of the powerful: its life-sucking deadness, its Christian façade, its assimilationist and genocidal minority politics. Against the murderous hypocrisy of the oppressors, however, Baraka posits no working-class-conscious vision of liberation, but only the lumpenproletarian gesture of sanctified and self-gratifying violence.

> > *Murder, the cleansed*
>
> *purpose, frail, against*
> *God, if they bring him*
> > *bleeding, I would not*
>
> *forgive, or even call him*
> *black dada nihilismus. (DL 61)*

Baraka refers to Jewish assimilation in the harsh and puzzling image of the

> *ugly silent deaths of jews under*
>
> *the surgeon's knife. (To awake on*
> *69th street with money and a hip*
> *nose. (DL 61–62)*

Despite what appear to be anti-semitic overtones in this passage, the thrust of Baraka's argument is still an expression of his wish for a retention of ethnic identity. Plastic surgery is seen as a self-deceptive acceptance of the beauty ideal of the oppressive culture, a middle-class gesture of ethnic betrayal. At this point, Baraka sees other ethnic groups, and especially Jews, as a metaphoric extension of Blacks. In a parallel argument in *Home*, Baraka holds up the fate of German middle-class Jews (who "believed that it was only the poor Jews, who, perhaps rightly so, would suffer") in order to criticize the Black middle class:

Like these unfortunate Jews the middle-class Negro has no real program of rebellion against the *status quo* . . . because he believes he is pretty well off. The blatant cultural assassination, and the social and economic exploitation of most Negroes in this society, does not really impress him. The middle-class Negro's goal . . . is to be ignorant comfortably. (H 149–50)[6]

The middle-class Black appears as an "umbrella'd jesus," shielded from the revelatory waters of rain,[7] and hypnotized by Gandhi's nonviolence and the gold fetishism of the acquisitive bourgeoisie. He has no voice of his own, but is instead mesmerized by the Svengali-like powers of American popular culture.[8] Baraka here opposes what he sees as a white-oriented living death, and his "program of rebellion" aims at uprooting both the "comfortable ignorance" of the Black middle class and the faith in the supposed rationality of the West.

The vehicle for Baraka's critique of reason is alchemy, the "black art" taken from the Egyptian god Thoth, whose Greek name, Hermes Trismegistos, is invoked in the poem. His name suggests the Egyptian theme in Baraka's poetry and summons up the memory of "pre-Western" Hermetic cults; in this tradition, Baraka writes "hermetic" poetry. Baraka's Egyptian theme, strengthened by the etymological link from Bohemians to Gypsies to Egypt as the supposed land of origin of Gypsies, implies a cyclical view of history, a Black parallel to the notion of the westward course of empires. Baraka clarifies this theme in a later essay:

Study the history of ancient Egypt. The move from Black to white. Reversed is the story of America. America who always (secretly) patterned her self after Egypt. Because she was so influenced by the sons and daughters of the ancient Egyptians. (R 109)[9]

Part two of "BLACK DADA NIHILISMUS" carries this identification of "black art" as an alchemistic concept and as a vehicle for ethnic upheaval to its frightening end as an irrational counterimage to the bourgeoisie, Black and white. Baraka embraces Egyptian astrology and medieval alchemy, not to find gold, but to initiate the victims of the West, that "grey and hideous space," into the "blacker art" which will lead to rebellion: "from stone / to bleeding pearl, from lead to burning / looting." At the end of the path is the screaming incitement to rape and murder. Baraka is in love with racial violence as a means to exorcise the middle-class Negro's "cultivated" complicity with oppression. "BLACK DADA NIHILISMUS" is Baraka's negation of his middle-class background; but the poem had a very real appeal to readers who, like Eldridge Cleaver, identified with Baraka's deification of the criminality of the young Black lumpenproletarian male.[10]

> *Come up, black dada*
>
> *nihilismus. Rape the white girls. Rape*
> *their fathers. Cut the mothers' throats. (DL 63).*

The description of a bankrupt Western civilization ("From Sartre, a white man, it gave / the last breath") and the invocation of rape and murder as antidotes are presented with a stark horrifying clarity and a nihilist joy. The Black scream is a victorious "hollering" to the bloody Weltgeist of "B.D.N.":

> *Black scream*
> *and chant, scream,*
> *and dull, un*
> *earthly*
> *hollering. (DL 63–64)*

To legitimize the argument for violence and revenge, Baraka invokes victims of the moral code of the West, "so cruel / it destroyed Byzantium, Tenochtitlan, Commanch / (got it, Baby!" (DL 64; cf. BP 8). In an attempt to "blacken" the reference system of victims of Western culture, the poem which begins with a period

ends with a dedication (another inversion) to Black rebels Denmark
Vesey, Toussaint L'Ouverture, Patrice Lumumba, and W.E.B.
DuBois; to minstrels and stereotyped entertainers Tambo, Willie
Best, Mantan Moreland, Buckwheat, The Bronze Buckaroos;[11] to
boxer Jack Johnson and blues singer Billie Holiday, who are all,
Baraka says, "secret murderers" under the masks imposed upon
them; and to Baraka's own grandfather, Tom Russ.

The poem ends with a prayer to a "kind" African god, Damballah:

> (*may a lost god damballah, rest or save us*
> *against the murders we intend*
> *against his lost white children*
> *black dada nihilismus. (DL 64)*

Damballah, a Voodoo God originally from Dahomey, may appear
in the shape of a snake that makes people "hiss," but he is also the
incorporation of fertility, associated with the cult of the rainbow,
the snake of heaven.[12] In Voodoo rites observed in New Orleans

the two ministers of the serpent god—the king and queen, . . . or papa
and mama—communicated the will of the sacred serpent.[13]

The "papa" who transmits the will of Danh-gbi, or Damballah, a
god who never demands human sacrifice, is implied in the "black
dada" addressed by the poem. The "nihilismus," both as an outcome of Western philosophy and as an attitude of the genocidal
Nazi killers, gives the dada priest, who is essentially friendly in
Voodoo, a new function in a "cult of death."

Baraka, who has pursued this dada element as the spontaneous
eruption of "craziness" and of "surrealist" violence in Black
America in many of his works, saw in this concept a true possibility
for literary modernity and political liberation. In *Home,* he offers
an explanation for the "program of rebellion" advocated in
"BLACK DADA NIHILISMUS":

Something else I aspire to is the craziness of all honest men. (And as an
. . . aside: one way Negroes could force this institutionalized dishonesty
to crumble and its apologizers to break and run even faster than they are
now would be to turn crazy, to bring out a little American dada, Ornette

Coleman style, and chase these perverts into the ocean, where they belong. (H 183)

This political message shows its Bohemian roots in the omnipresent identification of the "crazy" artist with the violence of the oppressed. The poem is, of course, not addressed to "people," but to an emanation, a principle, an aestheticization; and the Weltgeist of surrealism remains at the center of Baraka's art.

Baraka's poetry in the first half of the 1960's reflects the transposition of the struggle between "literature" and "life" from the "inside" of the poet's consciousness to the "outside" of American political and ethnic reality. In this process, the expressive elements of aesthetic protest confront the demands of political and ethnic protest. This dramatic conflict, more than any explicitly *political* statement,[14] is the source of Baraka's dynamics in the poetry of *The Dead Lecturer*. The new tensions lend themselves to new forms; and Baraka turns toward drama and prose fiction in order to respond artistically to the felt pressures.

5 From Off-Bowery to Off-Broadway: "The Eighth Ditch (Is Drama," The Baptism, and The Toilet

1. "THE EIGHTH DITCH"

Proceeding from an expressive aesthetic which preferred short forms of poetry, Baraka was only one step away from short plays, from "lyrical drama." To move from poetry to drama, Baraka had to radicalize his introspective stance to the point at which lyrical monologue becomes lyrical dialogue. In this sense, Baraka turned "into the world" not by turning "away from the grey glass" as he states in "The Disguise" (UP 33), but by turning *toward* his own mirror image with great intensity. The division of a narcissistic self into two personae, a literary motif occasionally linked with homosexuality, is the central dramatic element of "The Eighth Ditch (Is Drama" (SD 79–91)[1] and, at the same time, a continuation of his poetry of the divided self.

"The Eighth Ditch" is set in 1947 in a Black boy scout camp. After the narrator's introduction, the first scene shows the gradual seduction of "46," a "middle class Negro" boy scout by "64," a somewhat older "underprivileged negro [sic] youth now in the boy scouts," (SD 85) who introduces himself with the Melvillean salute "Call me Herman."[2] In a lyrical dialogue interspersed with the vernacular and the vulgar, 64, who seems to know everything about 46's past and future, and 46, who is reading a book, exchange memories of childhood and school, and talk about writers and jazz musicians. During their conversation, 64 is moving physically closer and closer to 46 until 64 finally *"moves his body onto the prone 46"* (SD 84). This movement is temporarily interrupted by the narrator's second comment: "The mind is strange. Everything *must* make sense, must *mean* something some way . . . This is a foetus drama. Yr hero is a foetus. Or if we remain academic . . . he is a man dying" (SD 84). The action continues where it left off; 64 slowly undresses both 46 and himself, accompanied by longer, more and more ecstatic addresses to 46 with the recurring word "blues." Soon, 64 establishes a sexual union with the slightly reluctant 46. Then, in what is probably the second scene, "62," or Otis, another boy scout, enters the tent and "wants some too" but is rebuffed by both 46 and 64.

The third comment of the narrator—"The past / is passd. But you come back & see for yourself" (SD 88)—is followed by a "FIRST SCENE AGAIN," a condensed repetition of the previous scene at night, toward the end of which two other boy scouts, Wattley and Cookie, discover 64 on top of 46. When 64 realizes this, he begins laughing, *now making loud sounds for the others' benefit"* (SD 90). While Wattley and Cookie *"crowd around the bed harassing* 64 *and screaming with anticipation,"* 64 indicates that he'll let them "get some too." 46's repeated question, "What other blues do you have, Herman? How many others?" (SD 90), is answered by a laughing 64: "all kinds, baby. Yes, indeed, as you will soon see" (SD 90). Then Otis-62 comes running in, and in the ensuing "melee" the play ends with 64's ecstatic command directed at 46: "Oooh, baby, just keep throwin it up like that. Just keep throwin it up" (SD 91).

This short play, which has elicited very little serious criticism,[3] illustrates Baraka's development from Beat poetry to a groping for social commitment, which remains, however, entrapped in the old sense of self. Depending on whether we focus on the contradiction between 64 and 46, or between them and the other boy scouts, the play invites two interpretive approaches, both of which elucidate the transformation from poetry to drama.

Seen as actors in a drama of the self, neither "64" nor "46" are realistic characters: they both indulge in lyrical prose which reveals, in amazingly similar language patterns, aspects of Baraka's life:

> 46: I'm stronger than people think . . . Ha, I'll bet you wdn't play
> the dozen with me. (SD 83)
> 64: I had the Kafka blues . . . and give it up. So much I give up.

> Chicago, Shreveport, puerto rico, lower east side, comeon like
> new days. (SD 87)

The "conversation" between 46 and 64 resembles more the shifts
from "I" to "you" in Baraka's novel *The System of Dante's Hell* than
dramatic dialogues: "I hid out all night with some italians. . . .
You've done everything you said you wdn't" (SD 12–13). As the
epic center of consciousness absorbs all pronouns, the dramatic
personae are aspects of the same self; "I" is also "you," and 64 and
46 are mirror images of each other; not two different "characters,"
but rather two different stages of the "author's" development. The
play, written in 1960 when Baraka was 26 years old, is set in 1947,
and, as 64 tells 46, "there are at least 13 years before anything falls
right for you" (SD 84). Seen this way, "The Eighth Ditch" marks
the very center of Baraka's life and of his novel *Dante;* the play
recreates the fictitious visit of the author as a Bohemian and Bebop
fan, as a "bellyrub man" (SD 84) who easily unbuttons and takes off
his shirt (SD 82), with himself as a younger middle-class school
boy. The line of self-division, the contradiction between 46 and 64,
is one of class affiliation (bourgeois vs. working class), age, and consciousness, but not one of race or sex.[4] At the root of this temporal
self-division and self-encounter is perhaps the creator's wish that
experiences acquired later should have already "impregnated" him
then, removing the "inferno of . . . frustration" (SD 154) by showing him a world that is "clearer" and "more easily definable" than
the "hell" of his early misguided "definitions."
    Seen this way, many otherwise cryptic lines of 46, 64, and the
narrator make sense:

> 64: I want you to remember me . . . forever. (SD 82)
>   I want to sit inside yr head & scream obscenities into your
>   speech. I want my life forever wrought up with yours! (SD 82)
>   I will spread over you like heaven & push black clouds thru your
>   eyes. (SD 82)
>   You're not even out of high school yet. Paintings to see. Spend
>   time in college. Spend money for abortions. Music to hear. (SD
>   83)
>   I'll be a . . . foil! (SD 84)

> I know names that control your life that you don't even know
> exist. Whole families of definitions. Memories. (SD 84)
> All these blues are things you'll come into. I just got visions and
> words & shadows. I just got your life in my fingers. Everything
> you think sits here. (SD 86)
> 46: I mean, you don't lie about who you are. I don't recognize you as
> anything. Just dust, as it must be thrown into the air. You'll
> disappear so fast (SD 80)
> You know you cd turn up years later in a park studying *drama*.
> (SD 82)
> NARRATOR: . . . slant the scene towards its hero's life. His black
> trusts. Together, we look in. (SD 79)
> It comes back. What you saw . . . of your own life. The past/is
> passd. But you come back & see for yourself. (SD 88)

"The Eighth Ditch" constitutes an exorcism of the author's age of
hellish innocence with the help of his acquired experience; this experience is denounced as "fraudulent counsel"—the sin that was
punished in the eighth *bolgia* of the eighth circle of Dante's *Inferno*—possibly because the author cannot rid himself completely
of all hellish definitions. Thus, 64 tells 46:

What do you know? You sit right now on the surface of your life. I have,
at least, all the black arts. The smell of deepest loneliness . . . I know
things that will split your face & send you wild-eyed to your own meek
thoughts. (SD 83)

For the others' benefit, 64 makes loud sounds while "loving" 46;
and when the others want their share, he asks only for a little more
time: "Ok, Ok, don't rush me. This is just gettin good" (SD 90). 64
both liberates and corrupts 46; he is a mentor and a traitor, playing
not only the part of Dante's Virgil, but also of *Everyman's* Devil.
But despite 64's Janus-faced role, and despite the author's nostalgic
wish for an earlier release from Dante's hell, it remains clear that
there is no time machine out of hell, that 46 will have to make all
his experiences for himself and will have to remain—for years to
come—in "a wilderness" (SD 84). In this aspect, "The Eighth
Ditch" echoes *The System of Dante's Hell*, of which it was to
become a part; the play also repeats the novel's structure and
progression from loosely associative memories toward more
straightforward action.

One yardstick against which the movement away from the inferno of false consciousness is measured in "The Eighth Ditch"
(and throughout much of Baraka's works) is the awareness of Black
music and "Black arts":

64: Who's yr favorite jazz musician?
46: Jazz at the Philharmonic, Flip Phillips. Nat Cole.
64: Ha Ha . . . OK, sporty, you go on! Jazz at the Philharmonic,
    eh?
46: Yeh, that's right. I bet you like R & B & those quartets.
64: You goddam right . . . and I probably will all my life. (SD
    83–84)

Afro-Americans are seen as "Blues People"; however, at this junc-
ture, the blues is an ambivalent metaphor, denoting both a leading
toward, and a leading away from, a positive acceptance of identity:

64: Talkin bout blues. There's a bunch. I mean, the 3 button suit
    blues. White buck blues (short short blues, go thru me like
    wind, I mean, pure wind). I'm pure expression. White friend
    blues. Adultery blues. . . . I had the Kafka blues . . . and
    give it up . . . Sun everywhere in your eyes. Blues, comeon,
    like yr beautiful self. (SD 86–87)

As a drama of a "beautiful self," "The Eighth Ditch" is a direct
continuation of narcissistic tendencies in Baraka's poetry. But the
little play also anticipates central structural elements of Baraka's
later drama. Viewed on the literal level, the drama represents the
two protagonists' inability to achieve a truly intimate sexual relationship, since they are confronted with the threatening presence
of "others." At the end of the play, 46 is no longer a lover; but, for
the benefit of Wattley, Cookie, and Otis-62, he has been reduced
to a commodity, a male whore. As in the later plays, *The Toilet* and
Dutchman, the dramatic conflict originates with the assumed hostility of the not very well characterized "others" (boy scouts, classmates, or subway riders) toward generally more sensitive and perceptive protagonists, a hostility which perverts love into abuse,
into violence, or into the very act of killing.[5]
    In "The Eighth Ditch," as in *Dutchman*, a division separates a
more intimate scene, in which only the protagonists are on stage,
from a more hostile scene in which the infringement of "others"

changes the private interaction into a public performance. This transformation is only possible, however, because the original interaction of the "loving" protagonists already contained the latent possibility of aggressiveness: 64's seductiveness as well as Lula's flirting are suggestive of aggression. Still, only the presence of "others" brings about the actual change. In Baraka's terms, these others reify the verb-process of intimate communication into a "noun," a defining power associated with hell. At this point, even the "social" reading of the play refers us back to Baraka's Beat poetic, which compares the act of creation with orgasm and views others, critics, readers, or listeners, with hostility. Whether we focus on the division of the self into a 64 and a 46, or on the confrontation between 46/64 and the "others," "The Eighth Ditch" remains a drama of the lyrical self.

The play is suggestive of a reaching out for the "social," while assigning to a divided self the source of "drama." "The Eighth Ditch" also reflects the private fears of an expressive artist whose self-revelations are leading him to an increasingly "public" career. In that aspect, too, "The Eighth Ditch" is a case study for the conflict between private artist and public authorities. "The Eighth Ditch" was first published in the June 1961 issue of *The Floating Bear*, a literary newsletter edited by Baraka and Diane DiPrima. It was with this issue that the newsletter, which was distributed by mail and whose circulation totaled about 300, first encountered difficulties with the police. Issue # 9 (which contained "The Eighth Ditch"; a satire, "ROUTINE: Roosevelt after Inauguration," by William Burroughs; a poem by Philip Whalen; and an excerpt from an 18th-century slave song) was intercepted by the authorities of Rahway prison in New Jersey, on its way to an imprisoned Beat poet. Nothing was done about the complaint until a week before the New York Poets Theatre scheduled its first performance of "The Eighth Ditch." Then, on October 26, 1961, the *Village Voice* reported:

Bright and early on Wednesday morning, U.S. Marshal Joseph Caffery, an F.B.I. agent, and another government officer showed up at the Jones residence with a warrant. Jones and his wife Hettie were routed out of bed while the men searched the apartment. When Mrs. Jones enjoined them to be quiet and not to wake the children, one of the arresting officers reportedly said: "Shut up or we'll arrest you too."

Jones was charged with sending obscenity through the mail and taken to the Federal Courthouse. . . . Miss DiPrima surrendered voluntarily later in the day, and the two were released on their own recognizance after the arraignment.[6]

Baraka commented that "the Post Office should hire people who can judge this kind of writing if they're going to arrest people,"[7] and confidently reminded the *Voice* reporter of *Tropic of Cancer* and the argument that has become standard in anticensorship trials: both works contained old Anglo-Saxon words which were necessary for the literary effect.

Because of the publicity that this affair attracted to "The Eighth Ditch," the Poets Theatre was drawn into another lawsuit, and at the end of 1961 the theatre was charged with failing to obtain "the required $100 license for special entertainment and sporting events" and was fined $25.[8] Baraka's tactic in the *Floating Bear* case proved successful; after a closed hearing, "not even Jones's lawyer was allowed in," the Federal grand jury dismissed charges of obscenity. Baraka's account shows how he defended himself and began to develop a strategy against comparatively harmless obscenity charges that proved useful to him when his commitments became more political and ethnic:

Luckily . . . the prosecutor . . . was so sure that he had the case that he let me talk, and I gave a Barrymore-type speech. . . . I brought out letters from people all over the world. I read all the filthy parts of 'Ulysses' and Catullus aloud. I read the Judge Woolsey's decision (on 'Ulysses' in 1933). The key argument . . . was the phrase in the Woolsey decision which describes obscene literature as that which is arousing to "the normal person."[9]

With the help of the Woolsey decision, Baraka could address the jury with the persuasive argument: "I'm sure none of you people were aroused."

"The Eighth Ditch" is an interesting early attempt at drama, or, in Baraka's own words, a "foetus drama" (SD 84). It anticipates many crucial structural elements of Baraka's later plays as well as of the novel of which it became a part. Its interest and focus are still primarily lyrical and expressive, but Baraka's expressive aesthetic is close to its breaking point. As Baraka's artistic interest in the social grew, his drama continued these rather introspective concerns in the development of a theater of political and ethnic protest. At the same time, the conflicts with censorship that "The Eighth Ditch" provoked were the prelude to Baraka's manifold controversies with judges and editors, policemen and teachers, media managers and editors in the 1960s.

2. THE BAPTISM

Baraka's fame as a playwright rests on his plays *The Baptism, The Toilet, Dutchman,* and *The Slave.* All four plays deal with a confrontation between sensitive protagonists, whose speeches frequently resemble Baraka's own writings, and a hostile "world," which bans those qualities most cherished by the protagonists (honesty and free self-expression), and which turns even "love" into hatred and violence. Baraka is, however, not always sympathetic to his protagonists and increasingly criticizes their central weakness: their lack of group identification is viewed as alienation from ethnic roots. Having established this confrontation between protagonists and "world" as the basic structure of his drama in "The Eighth Ditch," Baraka developed the dramatic conflict in different ways and with varying degrees of success in the plays of the early 1960s.

The Baptism[10] seems to defy any consistent reading. A Bohemian drama of opposition, *The Baptism* pits a masturbatory Christ figure and a homosexual devil-hero against a hypocritical minister and his sexually repressed and commercially exploited congregation. All the characters in *The Baptism* are nameless.

The play begins with a lyrical interchange between the minister, who is the philistine representative of the established Baptist

church, and the homosexual, who is a sophisticated Bohemian protagonist associated with the eternal adversary, the devil. Then "the
boy . . . in a black robe, with a bag on his back," enters the "almost well-to-do" church, which carries its commercialism openly
on the "plaque that says WHBI RADIO," placed under the inscription "IHS" on the speaker's stand, and asks forgiveness for his sin.
The precise nature of his sin, repeated masturbation while praying,
is revealed by an old woman who denounces the boy to the minister and describes the sin in lavish and affectionate detail; the
woman has repressed her own sexuality and replaced it with philistine indignation and religious ecstasy. In the words of the homosexual—who has computed with respect that the boy sinned 1095
times in the course of one year—the old woman "takes flesh, just
like you did son, but she makes it abstract and useless. So it is holy
and harmless" (BT 18). As the homosexual and the minister exchange insults, "a procession of WOMEN, perhaps six, young girls
. . . march slowly" into the church. These women believe the boy
to be the "Christ child come back . . . Our Lord Jesus Christ" of a
popular culture denomination.

He is the Son of Man. The big stroker of the universe. It was he who
popped us. (*They all moan ecstatically, sinking to their knees, praying.*)
God bless mommy and daddy, and Rochester, and Uncle Don. And
please God bring me a new baby sister. (BT 24)

But the boy, who supposedly "popped" the women "in those
various hallways of love," denies being "the Christ"; he claims that
he had only "thought I might save the girls by telling them I was
related to God. I didn't say Son. They only assumed" (BT 25).
With this gesture into the direction of the theatre of the absurd,
the play turns comic book.[11]
    With the exception of the homosexual, all characters are pro-
fessedly shocked by the boy's deeds—a "second coming" not in the
sense they had anticipated.[12] Not satisfied with prayers that wish
the boy dead or castrated, the women and the minister move toward him menacingly, knocking down the homosexual who is trying to protect him. As the congregated Christians prepare to kill
him without forgiveness, the boy picks up his bag and, with the

words "You have no charity! No humanity. No love," pulls out a "long silver sword"—a familiar comic-book penis symbol. He fights back, killing the women and the minister with his sword, and utters the words which identify him with Christ and express the "moral" of the short play:

It is not right that youth should die to cleanse your stinking hearts! I *am* the Son of God. The Christ. . . . There will be no second crucifixion! (BT 29)

The movement of the play has come to an end, but *The Baptism* continues, on the premise that the boy really *is* the Son of God. A messenger, who "can be Spanish or resemble Lee Marvin," and has the words "The Man" stenciled on the back of his leather jacket, enters the church with his motorcycle. He has come to fetch the boy, whom he calls "Percy"; he tells the boy, whose mission it apparently was to bring salvation to the world, that "The man. Your father . . . says you just blew your gig." The boy is ordered to return to his father, who is going to destroy the world with a grenade that very night "as soon as the bars let out." When the boy refuses to go along, he is hit "over the head with a tire iron" and carted away on the motorcycle. In the final action of the play, as the light in the church is beginning to dim, the homosexual frees himself from the "pile of bodies" and speaks the concluding lines to himself and the audience:

Good Christ, what's happened in this place? (*Turns Minister's body over with his toe.*) Serves him right for catering to rough trade. All out like lights. I better get out of here before somebody comes in and asks me to help clean the place up. Damn, looks like some really uninteresting kind of orgy went on in here. (*Looks at watch.*) Hmmmm. 1:30. I got about an hour before the bars close. Think I'll drift on up to 42nd Street and cruise Bickford's. (*Starts to leave.*) Wonder what happened to that cute little religious fanatic? (*Does his ballet step. Starts to sing his song.*) God, Go-od, God, etc. (BT 32)

The characters of the play are not individualized; they lack motivation and show their indebtedness to the absurdist tradition in the uninhibited, and frequently unrelated, jokes that pass as dialogue. The criticism of the Christian church, which is willing to sacrifice youth, honesty, self-expression, love, and sexuality in order to serve commercial and hypocritical ends is carried through with a freewheeling sarcasm. One may conclude from the end of the play that, even after the physical destruction of the congregation, the concept of a wrathful father-god prevents a new positive beginning for religion and spirituality.

The criticism of sexually repressive Christianity is not new; but beyond its excoriation of hypocritical Christians, the play lacks a clear focus. In making the dramatic move from the narcissism of "The Eighth Ditch" to social criticism (however interrelated with Baraka's own past in the Black Baptist church), Baraka has entered new territory. *The Baptism* is an attempt to open up to the social implications of drama, but, in too many ways, it does not go far enough.

The boy remains an abstract victim who is neither developed as a protagonist nor as an absurd antihero, though he has elements of both. In his confrontation with the hostile "world," he lacks a real counterpart. The boy is supported, if not overshadowed, by the figure of the homosexual who, despite all that Baraka adds to make him ridiculous, is the true spokesman of the drama. Although occasionally motivated by lewd self-interest, the homosexual remains the only character with common sense. The minister never develops into a figure worth attacking and killing, and the women, old and young, are constructed as shallow allegories of all that is reprehensible about sexual repression and as true comic book projections of a male imagination. Their characterizations are traditionally negative stereotypes of women: from the loud old woman, "Strong from years of the American Matriarchy" (BT 9), who denounces the boy's autoerotic practices but succumbs to quasireligious ecstasy and performs a ludicrously "seductive" striptease, which appals even the minister, to the "Young sleek 'Village' types" who—supposedly Christ's virginal cheerleaders—are distressed, in their whorelike materialism, because they "fucked for nothing" (BT 26).

At moments, the play does highlight the beginnings of a tentative move toward political art. The politics of the play, however, remain the politics of Bohemia. The homosexual, as the spokesman of aesthetic protest, demands Bohemian "politics" from the minister, who represents bourgeois repression.

> HOMOSEXUAL: . . . Let it be politics or shut up.
> MINISTER: Fascist!
> HOMOSEXUAL: Liberal! (BT 19)

Thus, the homosexual assumes the furthest political distance from his despised enemy whom he identifies with the most derogatory of Baraka's epithets, "liberal." The very inappropriateness of this interchange—the political labels could easily be reversed—attests to the fact that Baraka's political terminology grew out of a Bohemian opposition to the middle class.

The play is disappointing in its neglect of the ethnic dimensions of the criticism of the church. Although the congregation is probably meant to be Black, as the references to Marcus Garvey as a false savior, and to Willie Mays and Thelonius Monk suggest, *The Baptism* lacks Baraka's specific critique of the function of Christianity for Blacks (cf. BP 38–39 and BM 191). Instead of exploring the precise meaning of the title the play contents itself with the expected shock effect of inconsequential blasphemies. *The Baptism* is no more than a dramatic exercise on the way to Baraka's committed theatre.

Despite the obvious abundance in *The Baptism* of at least rudimentary elements familiar from Baraka's poetry—the theme of realization of self against a code, the references to Tarzan and radios, the "hip" and sexually frank idiom, the Bohemian cult of youth—critics who have attempted to interpret the play concretely as social criticism have encountered *The Baptism*'s limitations and noted its contradictions.[13] Gerald Weales concludes that *The Baptism* "is no cousin to *Dutchman*," since the "casual references to Negro personalities . . . and the ambiguous 'the man' do not seem to add up to much." He writes: "No more than a cute idea, it still has an ostensibly serious point: that the world is not worth saving."[14] Donald P. Costello read *The Baptism* as an attempt at "comedy-of-cruelty," in which Baraka "strains to be shocking; and the play ends up incoherent and adolescent, with scatter-shot fury. In his racial plays, his fury finds its target."[15] It is noteworthy, however, that those critics who reviewed the play on the day between its first presentation and the opening of *Dutchman* and who could not approach *The Baptism* in the context of *Dutchman,* enjoyed the play's elements of absurdist playfulness, its "unrestrained blasphemous travesty . . . on . . . sacred subjects"[16] or the young author's "freshness, flair, originality, disrespectfulness."[17] Taylor Mead, who played the homosexual in the Writers' Stage Theater Production, praised these qualities as late as 1969: "It was a good play. It was a paean to life and grooving."[18] The occasion of the statement, however, was a letter to the editor of the *New York Times* attacking Baraka's previously published essay "To Survive the Reign of the Beasts"[19] (which had denounced absurd white comedy and Warhol). Mead held up the old Baraka against the new by reaffirming that no

mention was made in the play of turgid unfathomable racial irreconcilabilities. No mention was made [i]f you are black or white, and I like to think we all worked together so well that more was said for racial equality than all the right-wing black utterances of Jones and his buddies since.[20]

The Baptism was Baraka's swan song to a theater without "racial irreconcilabilities;" in his next play, *The Toilet,* it mattered very much which parts were given to Black or white actors.

3. *THE TOILET*

The Toilet, as a direct continuation of the dramatic exercises in "The Eighth Ditch" and *The Baptism,* presents another confrontation of sensitive individuals with a group of others, this time against the background of a gang in an urban high school. *The Toilet* seems closer to "The Eighth Ditch" than to *The Baptism,* since it not only deals with self-expression in terms of homosexuality, but also contrasts the homosexual relationship of two protagonists with the hostile and threatening, all-male outside world. Again, homosexuality is viewed positively by Baraka both as an outsider-situation analogous to, though now also in conflict with, that of Blackness, and as a possibility for the realization of "love" and "beauty" against the racial gang code of a hostile society. But there is a new element of race struggle in the play, an aspect of a different aesthetic which would challenge all other readings.

The one-act play is set during the last period of a school day in the dirty and foul-smelling latrine of a boys' high school; the urinals and commodes are used throughout the drama, and the language of the play matches the setting. As the play opens, the Black students slowly congregate in the toilet, constantly insulting each other and each other's mothers in the style of dozens and signifying. "Short, ugly, crude, and loud" (BT 35) Ora, the motherless, and therefore less vulnerable, "Big Shot," emerges as the meanest of the kids. From the boys' violent interchanges the information emerges that they are cutting Miss Powell's class in order to watch a fight in the bathroom; Ray Foots, their "popeyed" (BT 39) "short, intelligent, manic" (BT 35) gang leader who, in contrast, *does* attend class is supposed to confront the white student James Karolis, a "muthafuckin' " (BT 41) "sonofabitch" (BT 38) whose crime is that he allegedly sent Foots a love letter "telling him he thought he was 'beautiful' . . . and that he wanted to blow him" (BT 56). While waiting for Foots, Ora socks the only other white boy, Donald Farrell, in the stomach, and roughs up Karolis, who has been brutally "persuaded" to come into the toilet. When Foots, who has been talking with the principal Van Ness after class, finally shows up, his ambivalence about the fight into which he has been forced by the gang is obvious to the audience, but not to his fellow students.

Ray almost succeeds in getting out of the fight by arguing that Karolis is knocked out already; then applause from the wrong side—white student Farrell's comment that "somebody's got some sense here" (BT 54)—forces Foots to take a harder line. Farrell doubts the validity of the cause of the fight and indicates with his remark, "Oh, Ray, come on. Why don't you come off it?" (BT 56), that Karolis' love letter may have been a response to a first move by Ray; at this point, Farrell is hit by Ora and violently thrown out of the toilet by Knowles. As Foots is trying, for the second time, to persuade everybody to forget about the fight, Karolis comes to and challenges Foots:

You have to fight me, I sent you a note, remember. That note saying I loved you . . . The note saying you were beautiful . . . You remember that note, Ray? (BT 58–59)

Karolis gets the upper hand in the ensuing fight, and yells out the true story, ignored by the Black students:

Are you Ray or Foots, huh? . . . I'll fight you. Right here in this same place where you said your name was Ray. . . . You put your hand on me and said Ray! (BT 59–60)

Ora, Knowles, and the whole crowd come to the aid of Foots and punch the fallen Karolis in the face until he stops moving. Then they pick up Foots and leave Karolis motionless in the latrine. The play ends with the following stage directions:

After a minute or so KAROLIS *moves his hand. Then his head moves and he tries to look up. He draws his legs up under him and pushes his head off the floor. Finally he manages to get to his hands and knees. He crawls over to one of the commodes, pulls himself up, then falls backward awkwardly and heavily. At this point, the door is pushed open slightly, then it opens completely and* FOOTS *comes in. He stares at Karolis' body for a second, looks quickly over his shoulder, then runs and kneels before the body, weeping and cradling the head in his arms.* (BT 61–62)

The play functions forcefully as an extension of Baraka's vision of a more and more insoluble conflict between individual outsider and society, but also between Black and white. In *The Toilet*, the Black protagonist, "possessor of a threatened empire" (BT 35), has to choose between his generic identity as "Foots" and his individual peculiarity as "Ray." While Foots denotes a "lower" kind of "plebeian" existence, that is closer to the ethnic roots and the soil, "Ray" suggests a more spiritual personality with a cosmic genealogy familiar from Baraka's poetry.

The protagonist is one of Baraka's frequent biographic projections; Baraka used the name "Ray" (close enough to his appellation "Roi") in his prose fiction,[21] and his obsession with the theme of

The Toilet in his poetry and prose offers insights into the degree of his identification with Ray Foots. *The Toilet,* supposedly written in 1961 in one night's session of six hours, came, according to Baraka, "out of my memory, so exact";[22] these same memories haunt his associative prose:

> That was a wide street where James Karolis lived. He died in a bathroom of old age & segregation. His nose was stopped up and he could pee all over anybody's floor . . .
> Does the word "foots" mean anything to you?
> (SD 28, 37; cf. also SD 31, 44, 54, 62, 65ff. and P 15)

The recurring references to the characters of *The Toilet* create the impression that if Baraka wrote the play "just like I was a radio,"[23] then the broadcasting of two signals must have interfered with each other. Baraka maintained that he "didn't have to do any rewriting," but the different versions indicate a less spontaneous mode of production.[24] The duality of Ray Foots and the ambivalence of *The Toilet* originate in the strong identification of the author with the play and its protagonist and are reflected again in Baraka's own subsequent interpretations.

The "Introduction by the Playwright," which accompanies the condensed and somewhat expurgated version of *The Toilet* in *The Best Plays of 1964–65,* is indicative of the two directions that interpretations of the play can take.

> *The Toilet* is about the lives of black people. White people tell me it is not. They have no way of knowing, but they insist they do. They try to deny my version (and any black man's version) of American reality, on the stage, just as they do in the street. They insist that there is no reality except the poisonous numbness they are stuck with (which they insist, yes they do, is beautiful).
> *The Toilet* is also a play about love. And a boy's inability (because he is a victim) to explain that he is something stranger than the rest, even though the blood and soul of him is as theirs. It is a play about social order, and what it can mean, i.e.: the brutality its insistence will demand, if it is not an order which can admit of any man's beauty.[25]

Seen as a play about love, *The Toilet* is the affirmation of individual self-expression—of a person different from that majority which defines his reality negatively. *The Toilet* contrasts the possibility of the free expression of homosexual love, as admission of "any man's beauty," not only with the repression of this freedom of the protagonists through a "social order," but, more than that, with a total inversion of the positive metaphor of homosexuality into the perversion of sadism. There is an important interrelationship between Ora's repressed homosexuality and his sadistic urges, between the group's obsession with calling each other names like "cock sucker," or "dick licker" and their violence against the white homosexual as an identifiable outsider. Willie Love, one of the less cruel boys, who "should have been sensitive" (BT 35) with that telling surname, spells out this interpretation when Ora nudges beat-up Karolis:

> ORA: . . . Hey, baby, why don't you get up? I gotta nice fat sausage here for you. . .
> LOVE: . . . You know that's his [Ora's] stick. That's what he does *(laughing)* for his kicks . . . rub up against half-dead white boys.
> *All laugh* (BT 50).

Willie repeats this view of Ora's brutality as a perverted outlet for repressed sexuality, when Foots tries to get out of the fight:

> FOOTS: . . . He [Karolis] sure don't look like he's in any way to fight anybody.
> ORA *(laughing)*: No, but, he might be able to suck you off. Hee, hee.
> LOVE: Shit. You the one that look like you want that, Big Shot. (BT 52–53)

As a play about love, *The Toilet* is undoubtedly an indictment of a brutal social order, depicted fittingly against the background of a filthy latrine. If the primary concern is perceived to be love, race becomes secondary. Otis L. Guernsey emphasized that there are "no racial designations for the characters in the script";[26] Michael Smith sees the play as a "rather obvious story about the odds against love," which uses "race for clarification, as boxers wear black and white trunks";[27] the reviewer of *Kulchur* sees an "essentially meaningless" "minor semblance of race-conflict" in the play's violence, which would have happened to James Karolis "just as surely had he been Negro";[28] and Langston Hughes made the suggestion "for the sake of today's sensitive Negroes and battered white liberals" to "double cast" *The Toilet* and

alternate performances racially. Every other night, let all the present Negro characters be played by white actors, and vice versa. Four times a week I would like to see *white* school boys in "The Toilet" beating up a *colored* boy and sticking his head into a urinal. . . . Black would then be white—and white, black—which alternatively would cancel out each other.[29]

These comments reflect only the "love story" reading of the play. Even without Baraka's contradictory "Introduction by the playwright," the configuration of *The Toilet* makes unconvincing the reading of the play as merely a love story in which race is incidental. This time, in Baraka's familiar confrontation of outsiders with the group, the representatives of the "social order" are male Black youngsters, the kind of group Baraka increasingly attempted to speak *for*, and with whom he tried to identify, in opposition to "Liberals."

The psychological approach to the play as a "love story" is contradicted by a sociological interpretation of the majority-minority relations that inform *The Toilet*. With this approach, the function of homosexuality and the roles of Ray Foots, Ora Matthews, and James Karolis appear in a different light. Instead of representing love and the situation of the outsider, homosexuality now becomes a metaphor for "acceptance in the white world,"[30] and of the "dictates of the suprasociety."[31] In other words, homosexuality becomes the gesture of individual assimilation, of trying to rise above the peer group, of "liberal" betrayal. As a consequence, the identity of a down-to-earth "Foots" would now seem more desirable than that of the lofty "Ray," who has removed himself from his ethnic reality. For, if the "love story" is a sentimentalization of "Ray," the "black-and-white story" is a bitter acceptance of Foots. And this acceptance, which implies a painful exorcism of interracial and homosexual love, is necessary if the Black intellectual wants to cast off what Eldridge Cleaver called a sophisticated "racial death-wish."[32]

The process of cultivating Ray's individuality can only succeed at the expense of Foots' soul: a "whitening" and "weakening," as Baraka would call it a few years later, "through contact with a beatified decadence." (H 226) In this context, the larger setting of the play, an "integrated" high school, becomes a symbol for the organized attempts at "brainwashing" Black children, controlling them by "cultivating" a few and criminalizing the rest. Ray, who has "transcended his social history, and entered a world of pure light" (H 226) is designated to play a crucial role in this game of oppression:

> FOOTS: That goddamn Van Ness had me in his office. He said I'm a credit to my race. (*Laughs and all follow.*) He said I'm smart-as-a-whip (*imitating Van Ness*) and should help him to keep all you unsavory (*again imitating*) elements in line. (BT 51)

Although Foots rebels against his supposed role as an agent of oppression, and parodies the principal for the benefit of the "unsavory elements," his performance cannot eradicate his attitude of betrayal: he attends classes, accepts the praise of the principal and has white friends.

If Ray's homosexuality comes to mean "sell-out integrationism" in a racial reading of the play, then Ora "Big Shot" 's violent repression of homosexuality is a positive, almost heroic step toward affirming Black manhood.[33] Conversely, James Karolis' function also changes in this context: for if, in the "love story," Karolis is the pure, poor victim of "mob violence," in the "race story," he becomes, with teacher, principal, and Donald Farrell, identifiable with the white power structure. It is therefore not surprising that the Blacks in *The Toilet* can remain completely impervious to Karolis' version of the background of his relationship with Ray; in the process of violently exorcising the "white devil," they must not listen to his persuasive lies.

The interpretation of *The Toilet* as simply "a play about Black people" is ultimately as insufficient as was its reading as a "love story." The characterization of James Karolis and the ending of the play impede such a reading. If Karolis is really supposed to be seen as a white agent, then why is he sentimentalized in an almost maudlin manner as a noble, honest, and brave victim? Can *he* be the "devil?"[34]

The ending of the play, and its subsequent reinterpretations by Baraka, underscore once again the ambivalence that was characteristic of Baraka's writing of this period. As it appears in the stage directions quoted earlier—and even more emphasized by Leo Garen's changes in the abridged version[35]—the ending of *The Toilet* affirms the triumph of "Ray" over "Foots." Baraka's later interpretations, however, side with "Foots" and seek to disavow the ending altogether. On one occasion, Baraka ascribed the structure of the ending to the influence of Leo Garen:

Actually the embrace was put in there by the director. [The] way I wrote it I had the Negro physically picking up the white, bringing him back to life, and that would be valid only if all brothers decided to do that, not any one individual brother.[36]

More recently, Baraka explained away the ending as a concession to the integrationist milieu:

When I first wrote the play, it ended with everybody leaving. I tacked the other ending on; the kind of social milieu that I was in, dictated that kind of rapprochement. It actually did not evolve from the pure spirit of the play. I've never changed it, of course, because I feel now that would only be cute. I think you should admit where you were even if it's painful . . .[37]

The ambivalence between the "love story" and the "race story" remains unresolved in the text, and is open to interpretations with different emphases by directors, critics, and audiences.[38] Both readings were controversial enough to alert the authorities; and *The Toilet* met with several, mostly muffled attempts at censoring by law enforcement agencies.

In New York, License Department investigator Herbert Ruhe, a prosecution witness in the Lenny Bruce case, saw *The Toilet* very shortly after it opened at St. Marks Playhouse, since Police Commissioner Murphy had initiated an investigation for possible obscenity charges.[39] Despite Ruhe's seven-page report, perhaps the longest single piece of criticism of *The Toilet*, that there was no gratuitous obscenity in the play, his superiors requested obscenity prosecution. This request was turned down by the District Attorney's office. In Los Angeles, where *The Toilet* shared a double bill with *Dutchman*, the plays were closed by the police on charges of obscenity one day after they had opened on March 24, 1965: "Vice Squad members revealed that they had taken tape recordings of the plays to demonstrate their obscenity."[40] After reopening, the plays were pressured out of business by the police and the newspapers:

The owner of the Warner playhouse charged that the police had "suggested" that he banish the Jones plays before they granted his theatre a permanent license. *The Los Angeles Times* and the *Hollywood Citizen-News* both decided they would no longer accept ads for the plays.[41]

The Toilet reflects Baraka's increasing ethnic commitments in his literary exploration of Black ghetto speech, the psychology of repressed Black male [homo]sexuality as a source of violence, and the sociology of the gang. *The Toilet* is Baraka's first attempt to integrate "the bad words of Newark" (DL 74), replete with obscenities, dozens and signifying into the formal structure of a play. His psychological and sociological view of growing up male in the ghetto makes the Black gang in the play more important and interesting than the sentimental love story that Baraka may have intended to write. The characterization of the male Black youngsters and their playful-tough interaction was generally interpreted as an innovation, for better or worse, on the American stage.[42] The majority of the dialogue is given to the Black gang, and James Karolis and Ray Foots, who carry the weight of the "love story," are present on stage for less than half the play. Although the Black gang is not unambiguously idealized, and is depicted, in fact, as destructive of love and beauty, its very presence on stage is a theatrical event, comparable in effect to the impact of gangster movies; even a negative characterization may lend itself to identification.

The Toilet is not a purely social, political play; it never completely transcends the individualistic "love story" reading. It is an unresolved fusion of aesthetic protest (as the abstract sentimentalized affirmation of individual beauty against the brutal social order) and emerging ethnic protest (in the depiction of the Black gang and the implications of the reading as a "race story"). If Baraka's art is moving toward liberation, then *The Toilet* is primarily self-liberation, because Baraka, through his projection into the character of Ray Foots, whom he describes as "victim" in "The Revolutionary Theatre" (H 211), exposes his own nightmarish duality. By writing a personal play, however, Baraka makes a public statement. As a "priest of the unconscious" (T 76), he explores the repressed "nether regions of America" as well as of his own private condition. But, as the readings of *The Toilet* as "love story" and "race story" have made so evident, the gesture of aesthetic protest and that of political/ethnic protest do not merge easily. It was just such a fusion that Baraka attempted to achieve in the plays, *Dutchman* and *The Slave*.

6 Dutchman, and The Slave

> . . . the idea of Surrealism aims quite simply
> at the total recovery of our psychic force by
> a means which is nothing other than the dizzying
> descent into ourselves, the systematic illumination
> of hidden places and the progressive darkening
> of other places, the perpetual excursion into
> the midst of forbidden territory . . .
> —André Breton, Second Manifesto of Surrealism

> O brothers mine, take care! Take care!
> The great white witch rides out tonight.
> —James Weldon Johnson, "The White Witch"

1. *DUTCHMAN* AS DRAMA

The play *Dutchman* is synonymous with Baraka's fame as a "protest writer" in the 1960s. With the successful production of *Dutchman* at the Cherry Lane Theater on March 24, 1964, Baraka became the nationally and internationally known "fierce and blazing talent" who shocked fascinated audiences with his "murderous rage" and the "black man's bitter gall." *Dutchman* made Baraka famous as "one of America's angrier young men."[1] Frequently reprinted and performed, filmed in England under the direction of Anthony Harvey, and adapted in France for Jean-Luc Godard's movie *Masculine–Féminine*, *Dutchman* is Baraka's most familiar as well as his most intensely analyzed and highly praised play.

A continuation of "The Eighth Ditch" and *The Toilet*, *Dutchman* is a "social" drama of lyrical introspection. It is a play from the theater of the absurd which effectively integrates social myths with private themes, literary surrealism and political ethnocentrism.

In *Dutchman,* the dramatic encounter of a 20-year-old middle-class Negro and a 30-year-old white Bohemian woman takes place as an absurdist ritual on the New York subway. The woman, Lula, flirts with the young man, Clay; her aggressive hipness makes Lula the dominant partner in their interchange. In the presence of other subway passengers, her attacks become harsher and more and more provocative; and when the Black man responds with a rhetorical tirade, he is stabbed to death by the aggressive white woman who, at the end of the play, prepares for her next victim, another young Black man.

The "realistic" elements of *Dutchman* are outweighed by absurdist drama techniques,[2] which make the play provocative and unsettling. The introductory stage directions suggest that the protagonists are not fully individualized "characters" in the sense of realistic drama, but reified types whose encounter takes place in a dreamlike, Kafkaesque setting that is both specific and vague.

Opening scene is a man sitting in a subway seat, holding a magazine but looking vacantly just above its wilting pages. . . . The train slows after a time, pulling to a brief stop at one of the stations. The man looks idly up, until he sees a woman's face staring at him through the window; when it realizes that the man has noticed the face, it begins very premeditatedly to smile. The man smiles too, for a moment, without a trace of self-consciousness. Almost an instinctive though undesirable response. (DS 3–4)

The stage directions refer to "a man" (not to his name, Clay) and reify the woman, Lula, by making her *face* the subject of her action: not "the woman" smiles, but her face, "it," does it "premeditatedly," whereupon "the man" makes an "instinctive" response. As in many plays of the absurd, the characters are objects of an external situation and of internal instincts, puppets rather than persons, body parts rather than full personalities. There is a difference between "the woman's face," which brings about the initial action, and "the man," who only responds, but both figures are involved in a ritualistic situation.[3] It is essential, and very Barakian, that initially, the woman's face takes *visual* possession of the man by staring at him. It is also a shift in visual perspective which underlines the victimization of "characters" by environment. In the first scene, "the man"

is sitting alone. That is, only his seat is visible, though the rest of the car is outfitted as a complete subway car. But only his seat is shown. (DS 4)

In the beginning of the second scene, the setting

is the same as before, though now there are other seats visible in the car. And throughout the scene other people get on the subway. (DS 22)

This slight change in perspective makes other seats and, very soon, other passengers, visible to audience and protagonists. Seeing, and being seen by, others becomes a necessary part of Clay's and Lula's drama. When Lula is closest to Clay, at the "groovy" end of the first scene, she says, significantly:

And we'll pretend the people cannot see you. That is, the citizens. And that you are free of your own history. And I am free of my history. We'll pretend that we are both anonymous beauties smashing along through the city's entrails. (DS 21)

But Baraka asserts, and reminds us of it with the presence of "others" in scene II, that this liberation from one's own history is only a kind of make-believe and superficial at best (H 223). When Lula first becomes aware of the presence of other "riders of the coach, white and black" (DS 3), the stage directions describe her as suffering a

mild depression, but she still makes her description [of a night with Clay to be spent in her "tenement"] *triumphant and increasingly direct.* (DS 24)

Clay's reaction to the presence of others is more naive:

Notices another person entering, looks quickly, almost involuntarily up and down the car, seeing other people in the car.
Hey, I didn't even notice when those people got on. (DS 25)

Clay and Lula desired "invisibility" as an escape from history into a transracial sexual encounter in a Bohemian "groove." The hostility between them is at its lowest point in the play when the other passengers appear. The presence of these "citizens" increases Lula's aggressiveness and helps to reveal that her idyllic description was an illusion, that her and Clay's *situation* does not leave them this "liberated" alternative. Lula acts as if obsessed, and Clay responds, in a gesture reminiscent of the opening scene, "almost involuntarily." As more and more people board the train and move closer and closer to the two main figures, the private dialogue between Clay and Lula assumes, increasingly, the character of public address expressed in more and more aggressively obscene language. Only when the others laugh with Lula at Clay does Clay raise his voice and address the passengers directly; and only after Lula has reached an agreement with the "citizens"—"All right! *The others respond*" (DS 37)—does she stab Clay (whose body is, fittingly, disposed of collectively by the group of train riders).

Just as the hostile closeness of Otis-62 and the group of boy scouts in "The Eighth Ditch" transformed the relationship of 64 and 46, and Ora's gang code inverted Ray Foots's love for James Karolis into violence, the mere presence of the Black and white riders of the coach illustrates that the world turns what might have been a harmless flirtation or a loving relationship into plain aggressiveness and murder.

Philip Roth criticized *Dutchman*, charging that the silent acquiescence of the other passengers to the murder was "not a truth anyway; it is a fact we already know from the newspapers." What *Dutchman*

might have revealed was not simply that such atrocities are practiced in this country, as of course they are, but what it is to be a Negro man and a white woman meeting in a country where these possibilities constantly impinge upon the consciousness, and so cannot but distort every encounter between the two angry races.[4]

Because Roth measures *Dutchman* with the yardstick of the realistic theater, and consequently decries the lack of "character development," he fails to see that *Dutchman* does indeed fulfill his own demand. Of course, there is no psychological character transformation caused by the physical presence of the "citizens": for *Dutchman* does not show the infringement of others upon Clay's and

Lula's consciousness as a "realistic" *process* which changes their attitudes gradually, but rather posits this infringement of social and historical forces upon the "instinctive" responses of "characters"—fatalistically and in the absurdist tradition—as having started long before Lula and Clay ever met. If *Dutchman* is a play about the "Fall of Man,"[5] then the expulsion out of Eden is complete before the play starts.

The absurdist situation of *Dutchman* is a two-fold inversion of *The Toilet*. On the one hand, the physical victims have changed: instead of the white Karolis, who could be comforted by Ray Foots in the end, the Black Clay has irrevocably become the victim of Lula's (and America's) violent racism. On the other hand, the sequence of action elements has been inverted, and thereby the statement of *Dutchman* has become much less ambiguous: the conciliatory ending of *The Toilet* corresponds to the ostensibly harmless idyll at the end of scene I in *Dutchman*, and the violence in the course of *The Toilet* is paralleled by the murder at the end of *Dutchman*. These changes allow no hope for a solution to the race problem through "love," as at least one reading of *The Toilet* suggested.

The ending of the play finally and irrefutably demonstrates that Lula's desire for Clay was not for him as an object of love but as an object of racism. In a forceful adaptation of a common absurd drama technique, Baraka leads his play to a circular ending:

LULA *busies herself straightening her things. Getting everything in order. She takes out a notebook and makes a quick scribbling note. Drops it in her bag. The train apparently stops and all the others get off, leaving her alone in the coach. Very soon a young Negro of about twenty comes into the coach, with a couple of books under his arm. He sits a few seats in back of LULA.* (DS 37)

The full circle, which makes the play end the way it began and therefore allows for an eternal repetition of the same plot, is achieved in slightly different ways in the two authoritative *Dutchman* editions.[6] Both versions make clear that Lula will repeat her murderous acts after the formal end of the play; however, the Morrow version parallels the circular motion with the introduction of the theme of Black brotherhood, represented by the old conductor with the Uncle Tom mask;[7] the Parone version limits itself to an unambiguous emphasis on the circular structure by ending the play just as Lula is biting into an apple, an exact repetition of the beginning of scene I.

The absurdist circular ending of *Dutchman* is part of a conscious literary strategy which demonstrates that Lula is caught in a situation of compulsive repetition. At times, she is even aware of her affliction: "But it's always gentle when it starts" (DS 13); "A gray hair for each year and type I've come through" (DS 13); or "how could things go on like that forever? Huh? . . . Except I do go on as I do. Apples and long walks with deathless intelligent lovers" (DS 28).

The ending underlines those elements of the play which make it the portrayal of a hopeless situation in which the Clays and Lulas, as social masks rather than "individuals," are trapped. It is not, the ending suggests, a unique occurrence but a *rule* that *Dutchman* presents.

In this respect, *Dutchman* is more "European absurdist" than, for example, Jack Gelber's *The Connection*, which employs the circular structure to convey the hopelessness of the drug addict scene, or Albee's *Zoo Story*, which shows a deadly confrontation between two men who represent the different worlds of New York's East Side and Upper West Side. Eugene Ionesco's *The Lesson*, though more mathematical and humorously detached than *Dutchman*, uses reified role players (professor and student) in order to demonstrate the "rule" that education is a continuous form of rape and murder. After the pupil has been stabbed by the professor, and her body disposed of, the doorbell rings, and the professor prepares for his next victim. The interrelationship of power and sexuality and the obsession with language as a form of possible communication which turns into a tool of domination further link *The Lesson* with *Dutchman*.

Baraka's play also shows certain affinities to preabsurdist European theater. Thus, *Dutchman* parallels Strindberg's *Miss Julie* in theme and plot structure. In both plays, there is a confrontation between a man and a woman separated by social barriers—class structure or color line; and the protagonists' mutual attraction is possibly a result of that very barrier. Strindberg's Jean and Baraka's Clay imitate the males of the dominant class/race, whereas the women in both plays are attracted by the very otherness (working class/black) in the men they tempt. Julie drinks beer and dances to the fiddle at Midsummer Eve; Lula tries to lure Clay into a Black dance, wears sunglasses, and uses a "hip" Bebop language; and in both *Miss Julie* and in *Dutchman*, the women are the aggressors. Both plays have a brief intermission (rare in the one-act play) suggestive of physical closeness or sexual union, which marks the beginning of the inevitable end of the relationship. While this parallel may not be extended to the *tone* of the plays, it illustrates the statement of *Dutchman* as a social drama: the protagonists cannot transcend their backgrounds; there is no hope for an *individual* rapprochement; the social chasm cannot be bridged. To adhere exclusively to such an interpretation, however, is to ignore many passages of the dialogue and to overlook the connections which link *Dutchman* to Baraka's earlier works.

2. *DUTCHMAN* AS DRAMA OF THE SELF

Like "The Eighth Ditch," *Dutchman* is a drama of the self.[8] While it is generally accepted that Clay is a Baraka-projection and -spokesman, Lula, too, expresses many of Baraka's ideas in Baraka's own language. Clay and Lula are not merely depersonalized, absurd, two-faced *social* symbols, but are also endowed with elements of their creator's self. Like "64" and "46," they represent different temporal aspects of an artistic consciousness which has divided itself into opposing forces.

Lula first becomes visible to Clay as he looks "blankly toward the window" of the train; this suggests the genesis of the woman out of the Adam's rib of Clay's mirror image. Seen this way, the beginning of *Dutchman* is an elaboration of Baraka's narcissistic mirror-window images in the early poetry (e.g., UP 17, UP 33). Again, the dark window is a "grey glass" and reveals, at first, only an image of a "white Negro."

In the first scene of *Dutchman*, Clay represents those familiar Black bourgeois hang-ups which Baraka criticizes in poetry and prose. Like "46," Clay is the "buttoned down" Negro *par excellence*, the incorporation of Baraka's own rejected New Jersey Black middle-class background. Clay is a "type" from the "dead" world of unconditional assimilationism, of "lukewarm sugarless tea" (DS 8) and tall skinny black boys with phoney English accents (DS 10), of "hopeless colored names," like Baraka's own baptismal name "Everett," "creeping out of New Jersey" (DS 15), of "three-button suits" (DS 18), social-worker mothers and would-be Christians (DS 31).

In her taunting of this "Black Baudelaire" (DS 19–20), Lula resembles "64." She attacks Clay's middle-class mask from the point of view of Bohemianism and thus represents a later stage of the writer's development. Ten years older than Clay, she is perceptive to the point of omniscience. She knows everything about Clay's life, his place of origin, his destination on the train, and his friends' names; she is even aware of Clay's most intimate incestuous memories or fantasies (DS 9), and she knows all about Black manhood, which Clay so energetically represses. In Baraka's own words, Lula is a "better critic" than Bosley Crowther (who reviewed *Dutchman* for the *New York Times*) and says "essentially true things" to Clay.[9] More than that, Lula is perhaps everything Clay does not permit himself to become. "64," having overcome the "3 button suit blues" (SD 86) which Clay and "46" are still singing, casts himself as the "belly rub man" (SD 84); Lula mocks Clay's three-button suit (DS 18) and entices him, more and more aggressively, to "Rub bellies. Rub bellies" (DS 30). Lula's technique of arousing what Clay has buttoned up is familiar from Baraka's poetic strategy of freeing the Hannibal under the Roman armor (UP 17); and her suggestions for a sexual, racial, political, and aesthetic self-liberation are largely those of Baraka's poetry:

LULA: . . . Come on, Clay. Let's rub bellies on the train. . . . Clay! You middle-class black bastard. Forget your social-working mother for a few seconds and let's knock stomachs. Clay, you liver-lipped white man. You would-be Christian. You ain't no nigger, you're just a dirty white man. Get up, Clay. Dance with me, Clay.

CLAY: Lula! Sit down, now. Be cool.

LULA: (*Mocking him, in wild dance*) Be cool. Be cool. That's all you know . . . shaking that wildroot cream-oil on your knotty head, jackets buttoning up to your chin, so full of white man's words. Christ. God. Get up and scream at these people. (DS 31)

The scream Lula wants Clay to express so that he can "break out" of his shell of false consciousness is of course, the scream of the "thing" inside, in "*An Agony. As Now*" (DL 15), and the scream of "Black Dada Nihilismus." At this point, the Parone edition is even more explicit in making that connection; here, Lula continues her invective with an allusion to the title of the play:

LULA: Get up and scream at these people. A dada man. Like scream meaningless shit in these hopeless faces. . . . Clay, you got to break out. Don't sit there dying the way they want you to die. Get up.[10]

Baraka's familiar aesthetic strategy of escaping from a middle-class "death" by becoming a "dada man" is expressed, in *Dutchman,* by a white female persona; consequently, the opposing Black male part of the divided self is at first reluctant to adopt this program of artistic rebellion. Confronted with Lula's harsher insults, with her Uncle Tom invective, and with her dozens against his mother, Clay finally does "get up"; he grabs Lula and slaps her "as hard as he can, across the mouth" (DS 33).

This gesture brings the interaction between "Black Bourgeoisie" and "Bohemia" to an abrupt end. Virtually without any "development," the protagonists change their functions to themselves, to each other, to the other train riders, and as artistic self-projections. The other sides of their Janus-faces suddenly emerge. If until this point, Lula was the protagonist of the play Clay now becomes the hero. As he drops the bourgeois masquerade, he assumes the role of Baraka's more contemporary mouthpiece. In his three-page address, the most famous section of *Dutchman,* he vents his aggression and pent-up violence and posits a Black mystique, an inner identity of repressed murderous instincts held back forcefully by masks and sublimated by artistic expression:

The belly rub? You wanted to do the belly rub? . . . Belly rub is not Queens. Belly rub is dark places, with big hats and overcoats held up with one arm. Belly rub hates you. Old bald-headed four-eyed ofays popping their fingers . . . and don't know yet what they're doing. They say, "I love Bessie Smith." And don't even understand that Bessie Smith is saying, "Kiss my ass, kiss my black unruly ass." Before love, suffering, desire, anything you can explain, she's saying, and very plainly, "Kiss my black ass." And if you don't know that, it's you that's doing the kissing. Charlie Parker? Charlie Parker. All the hip white boys scream for Bird. And Bird saying, "Up your ass, feeble-minded ofay! Up your ass." And they sit there talking about the tortured genius of Charlie Parker. Bird would've played not a note of music if he just walked up to East Sixty-seventh Street and killed the first ten white people he saw. Not a note! And I'm the great would-be poet. Some kind of bastard literature . . . all it needs is a simple knife thrust. Just let me bleed you, you loud whore, and one poem vanished. A whole people of neurotics, struggling to keep from being sane. And the only thing that would cure the neurosis would be your murder. Simple as that. I mean if I murdered you, the other white people would begin to understand me. You understand? (DS 34–35)[11]

Clay's address is often cited as the pumping Black heart of the New Black Aesthetic and of the Black Arts Movement of the 1960s, and hailed as an act of political liberation or deplored as a dangerous advocacy of violence. While it is true that Clay becomes, at this point in *Dutchman,* a Black nationalist spokesman who rejects his middle-class background to affirm a restoration of sanity for the wretched of the earth, he articulates, at the same time, what Lula asked of him. He fulfills Lula's and Baraka's conception of dadaism as established by Baraka in "Black Dada Nihilismus" and paraphrased by Lula's demand for "a dada man." However, Baraka advances Clay one step further by subjecting him to the surrealist exaggeration of dadaism. In the central scene of *Dutchman,* Clay, who once thought of himself as a Black Baudelaire, has become a Black Breton; and his address is not merely a racial address in the tradition of Frantz Fanon, but also shows strong affinities to André Breton's "Second Manifesto of Surrealism" (1930) which claims a surrealist tenet of "total revolt, complete insubordination, of sabotage according to rule" and "expects nothing save from violence."

The simplest Surrealist act consists of dashing down into the street, pistol in hand, and firing blindly, as fast as you can pull the trigger, into the crowd. Anyone who, at least once in his life, has not dreamed of thus putting an end to the petty system of debasement and cretinization in effect has a well-defined place in that crowd, with his belly at barrel level.[12]

The way in which Clay adapts Breton's "simple" act of anti-art is, of course, Barakian and ethnic, and transforms, once again, an example of European surrealism into American racial "realism" (UI 21). (Perhaps it is interesting that Godard's movie version of this *Dutchman* scene restored Breton's pistol shot in lieu of Lula's knife thrust.)[13] Baraka-Clay's concept of Black surrealism leaves the arbitrariness of the "simplest Surrealist act" only partly intact, directed as it is against the first ten—*white* men. This racial dimension places Clay's speech also in the tradition of Richard Wright's *Native Son*. Seen in this context, Clay represents an inversion of Bigger Thomas: whereas Bigger sees the "act" of murder (if only by accident) as a perverted form of creativity, as the only "artistic" endeavor his society leaves open for him, Clay sees art as a neurotic perversion of violence, and violence as the only act which would restore the Black man's sanity. Clay may thus be seen "surrealizing" Black nationalism and "ethnicizing" surrealism. This fusion of aesthetic and racial avant-gardism makes Clay's speech a forceful example of Baraka's strategy of populist modernism and a key passage for the avant-gardist Black Arts Movement of the 1960s.

Significantly, Clay advocates racial violence in the course of formulating an answer to an *artistic* dilemma, and the aesthetic quality of his argument seems to outweigh his concern for the political implications of Black creativity. If murdering whites is "the simplest Surrealist act" for Black Bretons, Clays, dada men, then Clay shies away from surrealism, except as a shocking aesthetic theory, and concludes his statement with characteristic lyricisms. No matter what he says, he seems more concerned with being understood than with taking his Surrealist solution as literally as does Lula. Clay hopes to escape into the shelter of artistic sublimations that was Baraka's own abode: "Safe with my words, and no deaths, and clean, hard thoughts, urging me to new conquests" (DS 35).[14] At the end of his speech, Clay the artist reaches for his books; Lula silently and businesslike gets out her knife.

For Lula, too, has been transformed, from the omniscient Bohemian into an incorporation of everything that is murderous in white Western society; and the Black dance she tried to entice Clay into, is now, as George Knox pointed out, a white *Danse macabre*.[15] An agent of repression, Lula must crucify Christ, must silence Clay in order to bring the *Dutchman* ritual to an end. Before Clay's speech, Lula represented aesthetic protest as a challenge to Clay's middle-class mask; now, Clay symbolizes the surrealist-realist threat of Black nationalism to Lula as white America. Like the secretary in Camus' *State of Siege*, Lula is a bookkeeper of murder, who keeps a record in her notebook of the "contracts" she has fulfilled. However, she can quickly retransform herself into the aggressively flirtatious hipster when she senses new prey. The dramatic strategy of self-division has led Baraka, in *Dutchman*, to the creation of two opposing forces who are again divided in themselves. The play's "corporate Godhead" (DS 24) consists of a double Clay and a double Lula.

The mirror image of the white-oriented poet changes as the train moves on. The self-total's identity is increasingly polarized along racial lines; and the black part of the self is being killed by the white mirror image. As the black writer stares through a glass darkly, he sees a white woman with sunglasses who becomes a witch with a knife; she is a deadly metallic enclosure, Baraka's familiar "shell." This agonistic confrontation yields a scream and a formulation of a defiant aesthetic as the legacy of the sacrificed inner self.

3. *DUTCHMAN:* "MYTH," TITLE, RELATED POEMS

Dutchman is powerful as a drama because it functions as a social construct, as an absurdist play, as a drama of the self and as a "modern myth" (DS 3).[16] The mythical dimensions extend from the frequently observed Edenic connotations to American popular culture and to the African and Afro-American archetype of a white witch; from the names of the protagonists to setting and meaning of title. Clay, who is also identified with Christ, Uncle Tom, and Bigger Thomas, denotes an Adamic quality as well as moldability; he is, at the same time, the "original man" out of whose mirror image Lula is created, and the sacrificial lamb whose blood must be spilled to seal a new covenant. Lula is the apple-eating Eve, but is also associated with Juliet, Tal*lula*h Bankhead, and "Lena the Hyena," the ugliest woman in a L'il Abner contest (with the connotation of the animal that preys on carcasses); "Lula" summons up a line of associations ranging from Frank Wedekind's Lulu to the biblical seductress Lilith and even to a lullaby. Her function as a compulsive manhunter and mankiller, a *femme fatale* on a "dutchman" mission,[17] also evokes the association with furies, witches, and vampires.

As the white woman imagined and feared by a Black man, Lula also is reminiscent of the West African goddess Erzulie, depicted as a white woman who "strolls slowly along, swings her hips, throws seductive glances at the men." Among her lovers is, interestingly, Damballah, the serpent god of "Crow Jane" and "Black Dada Nihilismus."[18] But more fear-inspiring than the white goddess in Africa is the white witch in Black America, of whom James Weldon Johnson warned his brothers. Johnson's portrait recalls Baraka's Lula: despite her youthful appearance, "Unnumbered centuries are hers," and she pursues her eternal manhunt behind a luring mask.

> *And back behind those smiling lips,*
> *And down within those laughing eyes,*
>
> . . .
>
> *The shadow of the panther lurks,*
> *The spirit of the vampire lies.*[19]

The immortality of Lula the vampire and the infinite repetition of the action suggested by the circular ending give some weight to a reading of the title of the play as a version of The Flying Dutchman. Baraka's first stage directions strengthen that connection:

In the flying underbelly of the city. Steaming hot, and summer on top, outside. Underground. The subway heaped in modern myth. (DS 3)

This description of the setting places *Dutchman* both in the real and concrete location of the New York subway and in a nightmarishly mythical "nether-land" of the unconscious; and the surrealistic "excursion into the midst of forbidden territory" is undertaken in a vague eternal present. How does the Flying Dutchman myth fit into this absurdist time and place? Critics have linked this myth to Lula, Clay, or the subway, compared the libretto of Richard Wagner's opera with the text of Baraka's play, and searched for other direct and oblique connections. Hugh Nelson interprets the subway as the Flying Dutchman ship (as the French translator implicitly did when he called the play *Métro fantôme*, alluding to *Vaisseau fantôme*, the French version of *The Flying Dutchman*), and casts Lula as captain and the other passengers as crew; in his view, however, Clay lacks association with the Dutchman myth and is therefore more "natural" in his reactions.[20]

In a more historical reading, Sherley Anne Williams has suggested that while Lula "is likened to a ghost ship" in *Dutchman*, the title of the play is equally significant against the background of the slave trade,

for it was a Dutchman, a Dutch man-of-war, which brought the first Black slaves to North America. America symbolically comes full circle through Lula's—the *Dutchman's*—murderous action. . . . What the Dutchman has given, the *Dutchman* also takes away.[21]

These two dimensions of the play's title[22] are not as unrelated as they may seem. The connection between the Flying Dutchman legend and the slave trade is actually older than the motif of redemption through love, which was added to the myth by Heinrich Heine and Richard Wagner. In 1811, the Scottish poet and collector of folklore, Dr. John Leyden, imputed the Flying Dutchman curse to "the first ship which commenced the slave trade," in what is probably the first printed occurrence of the word "Flying Dutchman" in the English language. Leyden's verses about the "spectreship, denominated the Flying Dutchman," are included in his *Scenes of Infancy: Descriptive of Teviotdale.*

> *Stout was the ship, from Benin's palmy shore*
> *That first the freight of bartered captives bore:*
> *Bedimmed with blood, and sun, with shrinking beams,*
> *Beheld her bounding o'er the ocean streams;*
> *But, ere the moon her silver horn had reared,*
> *Amid the crew the speckled plague appeared.*
> *Faint and despairing, on their watery bier,*
> *To every friendly shore the sailors steer;*
> *Repelled from port to port, they sue in vain,*
> *And track, with slow unsteady sail, the main. . . .*
> *The spectre ship, in livid glimpsing light,*
> *Glares baleful on the shuddering watch at night,*
> *Unblest of God and man!—Til time shall end,*
> *Its view strange horror to the storm shall lend.* [23]

Baraka's view of the slave trade as an original sin, and of the legacy of slavery as a curse upon America, makes plausible the relationship of *Dutchman* to the Flying Dutchman. The analogy between Baraka's play and the myth is most specific in the hopeless *situation* of the play, rather than in the characters. [24] The allusions to The Flying Dutchman strengthen the absurdist character of the play.

Dutchman is a complex attempt to merge narcissistic mirror art and growing ethnocentric consciousness in a communicative gesture that is truly an Olsonian "high energy construct." The play is Lula's and aesthetic protest's last stand. She is only the physical victor in the end of the play; spiritually, she has been exorcised. *Dutchman* indicates the direction Baraka's art would take: toward Clay's speech, into the contradictions of surrealism, artistic sublimation and "real" action, into the *Slave Ship* dimension of the play's title, and away from whiteness, femininity, and absurdism, which would become the unambivalent stigmata of decadence in his later work.

Dutchman is central to Baraka's literary development; and his poetry has been haunted by the imagery of the play, by subway settings and the "simple knife thrust," by Crow Jane Lulas and middle-class/surrealist Clays (e.g., B 37, 40). "Look For You Yesterday, Here You Come Today" (P 15–18), for example, yokes the notion of a Black Baudelaire with the subway motif in a way which anticipates *Dutchman:*

> *All these thots*
> *are Flowers Of Evil*
> *cold & lifeless*
> *as subway rails (P 16)*

Several poems support an interpretation of *Dutchman* as an exorcism of Lula and aesthetic protest; and there may well be an "Ur-*Dutchman*" in which Lula dies at the hands of a young Black man. (This would also constitute a link from James Karolis to the new killer-Lula.) "Vice," (P 27–28), a poem which struggles hard with an understanding of rage and anger, shows the female part of the divided self as the physical victim of the self-confrontation:

> *years after, you stand in subways watching your invincible hand*
> *bring the metal to bear again & again, when you are old & the lady,*
> *(o, fond memories we hide in our money belts, & will not spend)*
> *the lady, you young bandits who have not yet stolen your first purse*
>
> *the lady will be dead.*
>
> *And if you are alone (if there is something in you so cruel)*
>
> *You will wonder at the extravagance*
>
> *of youth. (P 28)*

The uncollected poem with the Dostoevskian title "Note from the Underground" (UP 38) is perhaps the only Baraka poem written from the point of view of a female persona, who is also very much like Lula.

> *Something incredulously ludicrous*
> *Is grasping me by the throat*
> *Shouting:*
> *SUBWAY UGLY*

BLONDE WOMBFED
What have you created today?
I answer:
JOLLY, JOLLY, DYING
JOLLY, JOLLY, DYING
THOUSANDS OF WRINKLES HAVE MADE ME A SAINT (UP 38)

After a dialogue with a man, the poem concludes with the woman's request:

save me save me save me save me save me save me
you're not worth it
he whispers. (UP 38)[25]

As the agony of the divided artistic self became a less pressing theme for Baraka, he used his *Dutchman* myth in a more political way. In the recent poem "Clay" (HF 13), Baraka returns to his *Dutchman* persona as an ironic vehicle for antibourgeois satire: Clay's "death" has become connected with the success of the Black middle class.

Killed
by a white woman
on a subway
in 1964,
he rose
to be the first negro congressman
from missouri.
we're not saying
that being dead
is the pre
requisite
for this honor
but it certainly helped make him
what he is
today. (HF 13)

4. THE SLAVE

The Slave, another short play concerned with the relationship of a Black man and a white woman, did not achieve a successful integration of Baraka's diverging artistic and political energies. Even with the addition of the figure of Baraka's old literary archenemy, the liberal professor, to complete a triangular situation, The Slave is a less convincing, more conventional play than Dutchman. Many critics agree that this follow-up to Dutchman is "dull," "neither arresting nor, ultimately, very interesting," that it "never ascends to the level of ritual drama," and that it "fails in plot and character and exists only for its central idea, which Jones expressed more vividly in his essays."[26]

Indeed, in its over-explanation of an obsessively autobiographical nightmare, The Slave has a counterproductive heaviness that comes as a disappointment after the structure of Dutchman. The sentimental motif of screaming babies in a Black-white race war in America, and the portrayal of the self-absorbed protagonist not only as a poet and military leader, but also as a drunkard,[27] divorced from his white wife, are elements of the play which obstruct access to its message.

The play was written after Dutchman—according to one source, after the very first presentation of Dutchman in 1964[28]—and it remains a distinctly secondary, "Son-of-Dutchman" kind of work.

The Slave takes place in the future, during a race war, in the course of which the Black leader Walker Vessels pays a seminostalgic visit to the house of his ex-wife Grace, married now to Walker's former professor Bradford Easley. Walker's relationship to his ex-wife, with whom he has had two daughters,[29] is characterized by a stage direction, which also establishes the connection with Dutchman: "WALKER. (Looks over slowly at GRACE and waves as from a passing train . . .)." (DS 47). Like passing trains, Walker and Grace had moved in different directions. And under the pressure of Walker's increasing Black nationalist commitments, which Grace could no longer understand, they had separated.

GRACE: Walker, you were preaching the murder of all white people. Walker, I was, am, white. What do you think was going through my mind every time you were at some rally or meeting whose sole purpose was to bring about the destruction of white people?

WALKER: Oh, goddamn it, Grace, are you so stupid? You were my wife . . . I loved you. You mean because I loved you and was married to you . . . had had children by you, I wasn't supposed to say the things I felt. I was crying out against three hundred years of oppression; not against individuals. (DS 72)

Walker Vessels, the sensitive former poet, cannot cope with racial polarization, which conflicts with his personal inclinations. One the one hand, he is the rebel *par excellence*, leader of a race war with world-wide dimensions (DS 49). Larger than his prototypes, David Walker and Denmark Vesey, he represents not only militant Afro-Americans, but also, by allegorical extension, other victims of white racism such as Indians (DS 56) and Asians (DS 58). Likened to Bigger Thomas and Othello, Walker Vessels is in the military vanguard of the universal liberation struggle of nonwhites.

On the other hand, Walker is a sentimental individual whose private life grotesquely contradicts his public role. Instead of remaining with his troops for a crucial battle, he crosses lines and ventures into enemy territory in order to "visit" Grace and Bradford Easley, supposedly to "rescue" his mulatto daughters. He seems to doubt not only that victory is imminent, but also that, should this victory come, the future will be any better. "Antiracist racism" (which required hatred of whites as a necessary transitory stage) has developed a dynamic of its own which reduces the struggle from a confrontation between "good, useful life forces and those which are ugly and exploitive"[30] to a more conventional, bloody fight for power. Thus Walker tells Easley and, by extension, all whites: "The point is that you had your chance, darling, now these other folks have theirs" (DS 73). In such a world, Vessels prefers to drink and remain a cynically detached observer. As Sherley Anne Williams has observed, Walker's "world seems to be divided into They (the Blacks), Them (the whites) and Me."[31] His gesture is a movement away from the Blacks in order to address "Them" and to deliver the message of what "They" want. In a curious paradox he is locked in an aggressive relationship with the white characters, a result of his desire to communicate this aggressiveness. Walker Vessels cannot resolve these contradictions and assumes the role of the individualist escapist who "spites" everything, except his sentimental attachment to his daughters:

I still love those girls. . . . In spite of all the people I've killed. No, better, in spite of the fact that I, Walker Vessels, single-handedly, and with no other adviser except my own ego, promoted a bloody situation where white and black people are killing each other; despite the fact that I know that this is at best a war that will only change, ha, the complexion of tyranny . . . despite the fact that I am being killed in my head each day and by now have no soul or heart or warmth, even in my long killer fingers. . . . O Damballah, chief of all the dead religions of pseudo-nigger patriots hoping to open big restaurants after de wah . . . despite, the resistance in the large cities and the small towns, where we have taken, yes, dragged piles of darkies out of their beds and shot them for being in Rheingold ads, despite the fact that all of my officers are ignorant motherfuckers who have never read any book in their lives, despite the fact that I would rather argue politics, or literature, or boxing, or anything, with you, dear Easley, with you . . .

Head slumps, weeping.

despite all these things and in spite of all the drunken noises I'm making . . . I want those girls, very, very much. And I will take them out of here with me. (DS 66–67)

Despite persistent talk of violence and revolution, Walker's rebellion lacks *any* social vision beyond that of a change in the "complexion of tyranny." Instead of developing a political concept of Black liberation, Vessels merely follows the impulses of his own love-hate emotions, which he expresses with an insistent *larmoyance*. This flaw reduces Vessels' political potential to a nihilistic form of action-for-action's-sake. However, although Walker has no hopeful vision for a revolutionary future, he is fully aware of the mistakes of the liberals in the present. Walker's criticism of Grace and Easley, reminiscent of Baraka's critique of Feiffer and Harrington, is "proven" correct in the course of the play:

You never did anything concrete to avoid what's going on now. Your sick liberal lip service to whatever was the least filth. You high aesthetic disapproval of the political. (DS 74)

The confrontation with the Liberal ends when Easley attacks Walker. Walker kills Easley in an act which the play depicts as necessary self-defense. Grace, who is hit across the chest by a falling beam, also dies on stage. The fate of Grace's and Walker's children is left unclear: Walker declares that they are dead, but at the end of the play, the sound of a child *"crying and screaming as loud as it can"* (DS 88) is heard. The circular ending, linked to the prologue, shows Walker Vessels as an old field slave. He remains the eternal entertainer, the poet, the "slave" unable to liberate either himself or others.

Baraka's famous programmatic essay, "The Revolutionary Theater,"[32] attempts to interpret *The Slave* as a revolutionary play. Although Walker is, like Clay and Ray, a "victim," the play is said to present what the Revolutionary Theatre is supposed to show: "the missionaries and wiggly Liberals dying under blasts of concrete" (H 211). The subject of the race war makes the play, which was written just before the great urban rebellions of the 1960s, prophetic in more than its private aspect; but it is hardly "revolutionary theatre." *The Slave* posits an unresolvable dilemma dramatized with a sentimental theatricality. It is unresolvable not because of a complicated dramatic collision but because of contradictions within the protagonist. Baraka expressed a severe criticism of Walker in a later interview:

Walker Vessels suffers from an ego-worship. He's hung up in his own ego syndrome, his individualism. That's why I call the play "The Slave," because if he is the general, the commander of this revolutionary army, he has no business being in that white man's house: He has no business there talking to these people. He is supposed to be out leading his brothers. He is supposed to be fighting, he's not supposed to be sitting there bullshitting with white people. And this is why, essentially, Walker is a weak man. But his intentions are close to the reality that I believe in. That is, he believes if an equitable social structure is going to be reared in America, it will probably be by force. (UI 6, p. 19)

The Slave argues the case for Black militancy, but ultimately denounces its fictive realization as an absurd, circular, and enslaving situation. No longer predominantly a drama of self[33] in the tradition of "The Eighth Ditch," *The Slave* suffers severely from the cardboard characters who are offered as opposing forces to a contradictory protagonist.

In one single respect, Walker Vessels has reached what Baraka was still striving for: after ridding himself of aesthetic protest, Vessels has begun to "act":

The aesthete came long after all the things that really formed me. It was the easiest weight to shed. And I couldn't be merely a journalist . . . a social critic. No social protest . . . right is in the act! And the act itself has some place in the world . . . it makes some place for itself. (DS 75)

But in another way, Vessels is enslaved by his blind adherence to race concepts. One of Baraka's recent essays contains an ironic allusion to the nationalist sentiment in *The Slave:* in "The National Black Assembly and the Black Liberation Movement" Baraka criticizes the "neocolonial development of the late Sixties and Seventies" during which the Black bourgeoisie took the road of "nationalism" without consideration for the Black masses:

In exchange for a flag and a national anthem, maybe a few niggers in some Mercedes Benzes, the same poverty, exploitation, and oppression! The only thing that has changed is "the complexion of Tyranny." (UN 117, p. 23)

This ironic use of the phrase "the complexion of Tyranny," so important as a characterization of Walker Vessels' position in *The Slave,* in this new context again shows how Baraka came to understand the limitations of his own views.

7 The System of Dante's Hell and Tales: From "Memory Epic" to "Theories of Government or Prose"

*I close, I open, I spit. Beware! This
is the time to tell you that I have lied.
If there is a system in the lack of system—
that of my proportions—I never apply it.
Which is to say that I lie.*
—*Tristan Tzara*, Sept Manifestes dada (*trans. Ihab Hassan*)

*That night I found myself hearing not only
in time, but in space as well. I not only entered
the music but descended, like Dante, into its
depths.*
—*Ralph Ellison*, Invisible Man

1. DANTE

"The Eighth Ditch" marks Baraka's turning point from poetry to lyrical drama; at the same time it functions strategically as the centerpiece of Baraka's first novel. The self-division into a "46" and a "64" provided a dramatic model which Baraka could apply in his best plays, *The Toilet* and *Dutchman*. This same division also brought an epic element into Baraka's works; and the distance between narrating writer and narrated experience, between "subject matter" and "tale" becomes of central concern as Baraka turns toward prose fiction as a genre.

In *The System of Dante's Hell* (1965), Baraka moves from what he calls "association complexes" to "fast narrative" (SD 153), from a long prose poem to recognizable units of prose fiction; and it is "The Eighth Ditch" which, in the very center of the book, encourages the transition from one mode to the other. The long prose poem "narrated" in the most fragmentary and staccato manner, was

written in the late 1950s and first printed in John Fles's collection
The Trembling Lamb (1959),[1] and in Baraka's own collection *The
Moderns* (1963). It is, in many ways, a compendium of themes and
images which are more concisely developed in Baraka's poetry:
parallel passages to *Dante* are to be found in *Preface, Dead Lecturer,* and the uncollected early poetry. Thus, the second para-
graph of "Gluttony" (SD 27) echoes "Central Park in Winter" (UP
6), "The man turned away cranes toward his beginnings" (SD 31)
parallels "Hymn for Lanie Poo" (P 6), and "SEVEN (The Destruction of America" (SD 36) resembles "A contract. (for the destruction and rebuilding of Paterson" (DL 11). The sensitive reader of
Baraka's poetry will recognize the imagery of sun and darkness, of
Mandrake's magic (SD 48) and radio heroes, of Black musicians and
burning metal (SD 41), although the "walls of words" (SD 24) may
be even more hermetic in *Dante* than in the poems.

The prose poem's narrator, hero, and subject matter is an introspective self in a "hell" which Baraka defines elsewhere as a

place of naming. But the mere fact that the naming does get in makes it a
hell. Lecher Glutton Flatterer Seducer &c. Forever. But not a receptacle
at all. That is the fallacy. HELL any positivist can tell you "does not
exist." There is no such *place.* But I feel there is an area of art that is hell.
A process of hellishness. Of being Hell. Hell-ing. (UN 22, p. 8)

The use of Dantean subdivisions for the process of art-ing becomes a strategy which itself represents "hell" to the artist's process of "hell-ing," a shell to the writer's association complexes.
Each ditch of each circle of Dante's Hell permits the writer "to
drag out some corresponding horror in [his] own soul."[2] Despite
the abundance of place names, especially of Newark streets, from
Belmont Avenue to Spruce, from the Krueger Brewery to the tall
brown brick Baptist church, the "hell" of *Dante* is "Hell in the
head" (SD 153), the "system" an adopted "shell" of Western art.
What Richard Poirier observed about American Literature is true
for Baraka's *Dante:*

American literature does offer the most persistent, the most poignantly
heroic example of a recurrent literary compulsion, . . . to believe in the
possibilities of a new style. The new American style was meant to release

hitherto unexpressed dimensions of the self into space where it would encounter none of the antagonistic social systems which stifle it in the more
enclosed and cultivated spaces of England and of English books . . .³

Baraka tried to create the "place" of his hell-ing by illuminating
"all the elements of myself against the backdrop of European form"
in order to find the new style of his own voice (UI 17, p. 26). This
struggle again parallels Baraka's poetic opposition to the Eliot shell.

In the first pages of the book, Baraka stakes out the territory of
the self, and the style does not mediate between self and society,
but emanates from the self and tends to displace existing environ-
ments. He is building *A World Elsewhere*, out of himself:

Nothing to interest me but myself. Disappeared, even the thin moan of
ideas that once slipped through the pan of my head. The night is colder
than the day. Two seconds lost in that observation. (SD 15)

My own ego, expanded like the street, ran under a bridge, to the river.
(SD 94–95)

The writer is painfully self-conscious in the process of creating
the place of the self; again, the *visual* appropriation of the "real,"
i.e. nonverbal, world of others and of the landscape is accomplished by an omnipresent poetic I/eye.

But Dante's hell is heaven. Look at things in another light. Not always the
smarting blue glare pressing through the glass. Another light, or darkness.
(SD 9)

The world was in their eyes. (SD 10)

The mind fastens past landscapes. Invisible agents. The secret trusts. My
own elliptical. (SD 10)

The world. Inside the sealed eyes of obscure relatives. The whole world.
(SD 12)

Each man his own place. (SD 12)

As this poetic act intensifies, Baraka invokes visionary company,
from Ishmael to Beckett, Olson, Ginsberg, Eliot, Pound, Cummings, and Apollinaire, and reaches a state of "transparency" which
places *Dante* in the tradition of Emerson's "Nature."⁴

The first sun is already lost. The house breathes slowly beside the river under a steel turn of bridge. Myself, again, looking out across at shapes formed in space. My face hangs out the window. Air scoops in my head. To form more objects, fashioned from my speech. Trees in the other state. More objects, room sags under light. My skin glistens like glass. Metal beads on the pavement. Eyes on mine. Slick young men with glass skin. (SD 19)

The big-eyed visionary remembers his telling childhood nickname, "Bubbles," and wonders, "does that mean anything" (SD 38). He circles narcissistically around the cosmic orbit of his life, his "own elliptical," into the dizzying vision of his self which is, ironically, organized according to the well-charted circles of Dante's Hell. The principle of an organized maelstrom, of a paradoxical fusion of stasis and motion, is borrowed from music:

Pieces from *The System of Dante's Hell* are all part of musical-literary scheme. And all the stories after *Dante* use much of the same technique. *Dante* 'stories' are from later part of the work, and have, literally come together as narrative after the accretion of single images, silences, and what I called 'association complexes.' These are the individual sounded notes and phrases that build to form motifs that are jammed together to make straighter narrative. But all the writing is 'variations' on whatever abstract concrete themes (or pictures or memory epics) come readily to me. So the image and the catalyst form the phrase, and the 'sense' is what the variation is played against. This, I hope, provides different thicknesses of meaning, that finally solidify, to the kind of narrative that 'The Heretics' represents. Where earlier, single images and associations are strung together or are heard together, and give an extended sense of the whole. My influences have been Joyce, Dante, Burroughs, Ginsberg, Olson, Heidegger, Mao Tze-tung, and Negro music. As, listen to the beginning of Sonny Rollins' *Oleo*, new version, to get a sense of the first part of *Dante*, or Cecil Taylor's *Of What* to discover the total rhythm form I collect my words around. Also *Risk* is something I need, a 'romantic' to my liberal/fascist friends.[5]

The term "memory epic" is fortuitous, as it describes the exact manner in which *Dante* unfolds from lyrical motifs to more strictly narrated units. In "The Eighth Ditch," the thematic elements, which have been thickening in "Hypocrite(s)" and "Thieves" "solidify" into an "event" and "characters." This allows a dramatic reading of the play as the starting point of oppositions and collisions pursued in Baraka's theatre and an epic reading as the incorporation of a temporal division between narrator *now* and hero *then*. The characteristic gesture of Baraka's memory epic is the concern to create fiction out of a temporally divided self, not out of any "realistic" portraiture of life.

"If anyone ever lived in a closet, it was me" (SD 50). Coming out of the "closet" and claiming space, the "total area of existence," is what Baraka endeavors to achieve in his fiction and, later on, in "reality." He views his artistic goal as analogous to the goal of Black musicians, and argues that Sonny Rollins' "Oleo," for example,

becomes not merely a set of chords fixed under a set of changes, but a growing and constantly changing work based on the total musical shape of the piece. In a sense the music depends for its form on the same references as primitive blues forms. It considers the *total area* of its existence as a means to evolve, i.e. to move, as an intelligently shaped musical concept, from its beginning to its end. The total area is not merely constantly stated chords, but the *more* musical considerations of rhythm, pitch, timbre and melody. All these shaped by the emotional requirements of the player, i.e., the improvising soloist (or improvising group). (BM 53–54)

Analogously, *Dante* aims at the creation of the *total area* of consciousness in the act of verbal creation.

In Baraka's plays of the early 1960s, we observed a dramatic splitting of the artistic self into conflicting agents. In the novel, there is an epic splitting of the narrator's personality into the remembering subject and the remembered object, and also into different aspects of remembering and being remembered. In itself, this procedure becomes the subject of many passages in the novel, which confounds the division of personae even more by the writer's repeatedly articulated awareness that in recreating memories and aspects of himself he is also creating, and being bound by, confining "systems" of language and perception:

I am myself. Insert the word disgust. A verb. Get rid of the "am." Break out. Kill it. Rip the thing to shreds. . . . Now say something intelligent! (SD 15)

The writer's self-consciousness remains painfully in the foreground; and even Baraka's frequent references to literary predecessors are not literary discussions-within-fiction (in the tradition of Goethe or Joyce), but vague suggestions of the ultimate impossibility of a fusion of life and art; the names of writers appear as representatives of ivory towers which cannot grant the writer of *Dante* sufficient protection from his remembered reality:

The first guy (he spoke to me grinning and I said my name was Stephen Dedalus. And I read Proust and mathematics and loved Eliot for his tears. Towers, like Yeats (I didn't know him then, or only a little because of the Second Coming and Leda. (SD 58)

The ineffective and dubious character of literature is demonstrated when the Black girl Peaches (whose name appears several times in the novel) is trying, in an act of aggression and salvation, to get the narrator to go to bed with her; when she threatens him with the words

Goddam punk, you gonna fuck me tonight or I'm gonna pull your fuckin dick aloose (SD 140),

the narrator is crying and imagines this defense:

Or say to Peaches: "Please, you don't know me. Not what's in my head. I'm beautiful. Stephen Dedalus . . ." (SD 140)

This gesture of helplessness corresponds to an escape through air (which the mythic Daedalus once ventured): literature becomes, for the "black man unfocused on blackness" (SD 153), a means of escape from reality. ("White") literature therefore appears as yet another inadequate response to ("Black") reality, which is deformed into the metaphoric deadness and vacuity of Black middle-class, middle-brow life:

Eliot, Pound, Cummings, Apollinaire were living across from Kresges. I was erudite and talked to light-skinned women. (SD 31)

I loved the middleclass & they wd thrust pikes at me thru my shadows. (SD 96)

The specific dichotomy of the Black intellectual, torn between writing "about" his own Black life and, in the *embourgeoisement* resulting from the writing process, being alienated from his "subject," is one of Baraka's central prose themes. This conflict is a crucial source of tension in his fiction; and the "fast narratives" or short stories which follow "The Eighth Ditch" in *Dante* show the hero-author, like 64/46, "caught between the working class and the aspiring bourgeois" (UI 20).

In "The Rape," a story reminiscent of Hubert Selby, the relationship of the middle class to an "actual damned soul" (SD 116), a syphilitic whore from the "3rd ward" (SD 110) is seen as "Treachery To Kindred" and as a murderous rapaciousness. Five Black middle-class youths, under the leadership of the narrator, pick up the "skinny, dark and drunk" (SD 109) girl, offering to drive her to "Jones St." They see her merely as a sexual object as they drive through middle-class neighborhoods. When she tells the boys of her disease, they literally discard her, throwing her out of the moving car. Throughout the story, Baraka reflects upon the Black middle class and his "leadership" in such an inhuman setting:

THE BEAUTIFUL MIDDLECLASS HAD FORMED AND I WAS TO BE A GREAT FIGURE, A GIANT AMONG THEM. (SD 107)

I would see the woman squatting in the street, under the fake gasoline lamp as we turned the corner, everybody screaming in the car, some insane allegiance to me. (SD 117)

The relationship of sensitive leader and violent gang is seen as ambivalently in *Dante* as in *The Toilet*. The last section of the novel, "The Heretics" is reminiscent of Ralph Ellison's "Flying Home" and exposes the alienation of the narrator and Air Force flyer from "The Bottom," a southern ghetto not unlike "Spruce & Belmont (the ward) in Nwk. A culture of violence and foodsmells" (SD 123–24). In this environment, the narrator is an "imitation white boy" (SD 128), and despite the partial bridging of the gulf that separates him from Black folk—a bridging achieved in "The Cotton Club" through "dancing like a rite no one knew" (SD 129)—he remains something "weird" in the eyes of the Black people he encounters: a representative of the white-oriented middle class, a "slick city nigger" (SD 151) who deserves the insult "Mr. Halfwhite muthafucka" (SD 151) and the beating by three tall "strong black boys with plenty of teeth."

Since literature is held responsible for alienating the writer from his Black identity, it is not surprising that literature, though not Black music, is ultimately rejected as a form of masturbatory narcissism in a world demanding social commitment.

Thomas, Joyce, Eliot, Pound, all gone by & I thot agony at how beautiful I was. And sat many times in latrines fingering my joint. (SD 119)

2. *TALES*

Baraka's uneasiness with literature did not lead him to an immediate or total abdication of modernist prose. Baraka continued to struggle with the creation of himself in space in some of his best prose writings collected in *Tales* (1967). If *Dante* is a logbook of Baraka's immersion into a memory epic out of lyrical association complexes which establish the *area* of self, then *Tales* is the record of a movement from fiction to life, and from fantasy to reality.

The first story in *Tales*, "A Chase (Alighieri's Dream),"[6] is very closely related to *Dante* in theme, staccato association, and setting; like *Dante*, it is concerned with memories of "hell-ing" in Newark.

4 corners, the entire world visible from there. Even to the lower regions. (T 4)

The fast association of streets and images, people and buildings in Newark is part of a vivid and loosely associative account of a nightmarish chase, which gives the *Dante*-like jazz style of writing an additional metaphoric function. The second story, "The Alternative" also contains material reminiscent of *Dante:*

Or in the dull windows of Chicago, an unread volume of Joyce. Some black woman who will never hear the word *Negress* or remember your name. Or a thin preacher who thinks your name is Stephen. (T 20)

"The Alternative" analyzes Howard University from the perspective Baraka had applied to the high school in *The Toilet*. As narrator and outsider-hero ("leader"), Baraka affirms individual beauty in the manner of aesthetic protest, against the shallow representatives of the Black middle-class educational process:

The 3rd floor of Park Hall, an old 19th-century philanthropy, gone to seed. The missionaries' words dead & hung useless in the air. "Be clean, thrifty, and responsible. Show the anti-Christs you're ready for freedom and God's true word." Peasants among the mulattoes, and the postman's son squats in his glasses shivering at his crimes. (T 22–23)

Although, on a superficial level, the students seem to reject the spirit of the school motto, they are, to the autobiographic projection of the "leader without cause or place" (T 18), revealed as perfect examples of "citizenship":

And at the top of the stairs, the leader stops, the whole hall full of citizens. Doctors, judges, first negro directors of welfare chains, morticians, chemists, ad men, fighters for civil rights, all admirable, useful men. (T 27–28)

Baraka describes the scene with the most disparaging irony: these "citizens," representatives of the future middle class, have just revealed their essential inhumanity by venting their aggression not against the institution, but against an outsider. The quoted section is incorporated into a passage in which these admirable, useful men are trying to break down a door and "get in on" one of their fellow students who is in the room with a homosexual.

"YEH, YEH. WE SAW WHAT YOU WAS DOIN' HUTCHENS. OPEN THE DOOR AND LET US GET IN ON IT."
　　　　　　　"WHEEEEEEE! HIT THE FUCKING DOOR, RICK! HIT IT!" (T 27)

The dramatic tension is similar to the conflict in "The Eighth Ditch," only the narrator, "Ray" casts himself as "leader" of the others, not as involved in the homosexual outsider situation. This Ray, like his namesake in *The Toilet*, loses his position of leadership on the issue of how to "deal with" homosexuals; as in the high school latrine, the gang code in the college dorm provides only one solution: violence against outsiders, against homosexuals as well as against those who, like Ray, speak out against violence. The story ends with the narrator-leader beaten and lying, in a typological identification with Christ,[7] with his face "pushed hard against the floor. And the wood, old, and protestant" (T 29). There is the suggestion of imminent violence against the student and against the homosexual who is literally hiding in the closet. In a situation of helplessness the narrator, ironically using a phallic image, affirms his own individual beauty:

I am a poet . . . I am the man who paints the gold balls on the tops of flagpoles. I am, no matter, more beautiful than anyone else. (T 29)

This archetypical statement of Baraka's aesthetic protest is given further substance by the last lines of the short story, which summarize his criticism of the reified inhumanity of the group of "others":

And their voices, all these other selves screaming for blood. For blood, or whatever it is fills their noble lives. (T 29)

"The Alternative" is a prose approximation of the tension which Baraka expressed in his plays between the individual outsider and the group; in the prose formulation of this conflict, Baraka again invokes the references familiar from his poetry in order to elucidate the mind of the "individual." "The Alternative" therefore contains much oblique and evocative material ranging from references to Popular Culture—"Radio City" (T 6); Black heroes and musicians—"Willie Mays" (T 17), "King Cole" (T 19); writers like Garcia Lorca—"Verde, que te quiero verde" (T 19 and 22), or an inverted Albert Camus—"Trebla Sumac"[8] (T 26); to a constant verbalization of the creative process in which the narrator becomes the *maker* of the world he supposedly only describes:

And it's me making a portrait of them all. That was the leader's job. (T 8)

That you exist alone, as I make you. (T 9)

Except they sit now, for this portrait . . . in which they will be portrayed as losers. Only the leader wins. (T 11)

The narrator plays with words, his area of power, both as a character of the story and as its creator:

The leader loses . . . but is still the leader because he said some words no one had heard before. (T 9)

Wall. Even to move, impossible. I sit, now, forever where I am. No further. No farther. Father, who am I to hide myself? And brew a world of soft lies. (T 21)

This involvement in the process of art-ing further underlines the difference between the narrator-leader and the characters. In his role as a figure in his own story, the narrator is an object of his characters' insensitivity and proclivity to violence, in his role as a creator he can see *them* as objects, "floating empty nouns" (T 11) in sentences he can construct at will.

"The Alternative" thus transcends the situation it describes through a thematization of the prose narrator's dual function as participant and creator, or, as Baraka said elsewhere, as "victim and chronicler" (H 112). The separation of the artist from society is depicted as an affirmation of beauty and sensitivity, but also as alienation:

> *You're much too sensitive for a place like this.* (T 24)

> *But my*
> *country. My people. These dead souls, I call my people.*
> *Flesh of my flesh.* (T 22)

In "The Alternative," the concept of literature as a cause of alienation includes even the narrator in the process of telling a tale, "with the covers of books turned toward the audience" (T 11). Similarly, a character uses books as a shield from reality—in a manner resembling "The Eighth Ditch"—"Man, I'm trying to read" (T 13). Rather than serving as means of communication among people, words have become "walls." Despite the title, there is no alternative envisioned by Baraka, and the Camus references underscore the wall-image of existentialist futility.

The stories following "The Largest Ocean in the World" (another short piece of experimental Beat prose) further sound the problem of communication. "Uncle Tom's Cabin: Alternate Ending" poses the problem within the American Black and white situation and explores the confrontation of Eddie McGhee, a Black grade school student and autobiographic projection,[9] with the white educational system. Four communicative gestures show the separation of what Baraka calls "The psychological and the social. The spiritual and the practical" (T 37) and thus become milestones on the "road to the commonest of Hells. The one we westerners love to try to make art out of" (T 37). With this affinity to *Dante*, "Uncle Tom's Cabin: Alternative Ending" investigates how stereotypes (going back to pro-slavery as well as to the type of abolitionist fiction alluded to in the title of the story) distort Black-white and even Black-Black communication in America. The four examples given by Baraka in capsule fashion effectively illustrate the impediments to communication. In the beginning of the story, McGhee says "6 ½" in response to Miss Orbach's (the white teacher's) question; and although the answer is apparently correct (we never learn the question), the teacher is irritated by the fact that the answer "should be there, and in such loose possession. 'OH who is he to know such a thing? . . .' " (T 35).

"6 ½" had wrenched her unwillingly to exactly where she was. Teaching the 5th grade, in a grim industrial complex of northeastern America; about 1942. (T 36)[10]

The narrator returns a second time to the beginning of the story and ventures his suggestion to the intelligent boy:

"6 ½" the boy said. After the fidgeting and awkward silence. One little black boy, raised his hand, and looking at the tip of Miss Orbach's nose said 6 ½. And then he smiled, very embarrassed and very sure of being wrong.

I would have said "No, boy, shut up and sit down. You are wrong. You don't know anything. Get out of here and be very quick. Have you no idea what you're getting involved in? . . ." But those people had already been convinced. Read Booker T. Washington one day, when there's time. What that led to. The 6 ½'s moved for power . . . and there seemed no other way. (T 37)

The boy's answer, then, is the expression of two communicative situations: on the surface level, it is the "right answer to the woman's question" (T 37) and should entail no reaction beyond a statement to that effect; but, in the context of America's racial hierarchies, the answer "6 ½" represents a challenge and becomes a symbol of an oppressed minority's move for power. Eddie is simply not supposed to know the answer. The conflicting readings of

"6 ½" are expressed perfectly in the last sentence of the passage just quoted, in which Blacks have become menacing "6 ½'s."

Miss Orbach replies to the surface level, after an investigative "How do you get that answer?" (T 37), with a repeated "Well, it's right" (T 37). His classmates, responding to the teacher's tone, react in two ways: a Negro boy pinches him, and a little white girl touches his hand—from which he tries to pull away "with his brain" (T 38). This third level of communication implied by "6 ½," signals an involuntary movement away from Black manhood and toward white effeminateness, a movement the hero tries to control "with his brain" and regrets. Miss Orbach is unaware of that dimension of the boy's answer, but she perceives the threat of "6 ½" very clearly, although her reaction is delayed.

Later on in the day . . . Miss Orbach became convinced that the little boy's eyes were too large . . . Also, his head was much too large for the rest of the scrawny body. And he talked too much, and caused too many disturbances. (T 38)

This reaction constitutes the second communicative gesture Baraka explores in the story:

She wrote a note to Miss Janone, the school nurse, and gave it to the boy, McGhee, to take to her. The note read: "Are the large eyes a sign of ————?" (T 38)

The "long word" that the dash stands for is never spelled out in the story, although the narrator tells us that it was misspelled in Miss Orbach's note to the nurse. The enigmatic long word thus becomes part of the "semantic rituals of power" (H 169), a second example of failing communication. Instead of verbalizing the threat Miss Orbach senses in the boy's reply (which, of course, she cannot), she resorts to an erroneous diagnosis of a supposed illness she ascribes, significantly, to the boy's *eyes*. Although the boy forgets the word and the doctor discards the teacher's suspicion immediately, Mrs. McGhee feels obliged to

speak to Miss Orbach about the long word which she suspected might be injurious to her son and maybe to Negroes In General. (T 39)

The boy's parents respond to the vague insult with a general suspicion of Miss Orbach, and the never-mentioned "long word" she had used gains a new racial dimension.

This suspicion had been bolstered a great deal by what Eddie Jr. had told her about Miss Orbach, and also equally by what Eddie Sr. had long maintained about the nature of White People In General. (T 39–40)

As Baraka's third model for the use of words shows, Eddie's mother's philosophy is far removed from Black nationalism; she resents her son's "mispronunciation" of a word just as much as she does the teacher's antidote against Black slang:

> "Is Miss Orbach the woman who told you to say sangwich instead of sammich," Louise McGhee giggled.
> "No, that was Miss Columbe."
> "Sangwich, my christ. That's worse than sammich. Though you better not let me hear you saying sammich either . . . like those Davises."
> "I don't say sammich, mamma."
> "What's the word then?"
> "Sandwich."
> "That's right. And don't let anyone tell you anything else. Teacher or otherwise." (T 39)

This is a detailed example of the humorously depicted socialization process of the "thriving children of the thriving urban lower middle classes . . . Making a great run for America . . ." (T 36) by striving for a distinction from the Black lower classes, the Davises of this quotation.

The inadequacy of the communicative models is driven home to the point of absurdity by the end of the story which presents "love" as a nonverbal, yet equally inadequate attempt at Black-white communication; in these last lines of "Uncle Tom's Cabin . . ." Baraka touches lightly upon a theme dealt with seriously in his plays *The Toilet* and *Dutchman.*

When Miss Orbach got to the principal's office and pushed open the door she looked directly into Louise McGhee's large brown eyes, and fell deeply and hopelessly in love. (T 40)

"The Death of Horatio Alger"[11] examines the code of Black-Black communication and the changes it undergoes in the presence of whites. The story describes how what might have been a simple "dozens" exchange is transformed into an ugly insult and a real fight, in the course of which the narrator cannot communicate with his counterpart, "J.":

I called to him, for help really. But the words rang full of dead venom. I screamed his mother a purple nigger with alligator titties. His father a bilious white man with sores on his jowls. I was screaming for help in my hatred and loss, and only the hatred would show. (T 47)

In a striking departure from the Afro-American tradition of "laughing to keep from crying"[12] Baraka suggests the following substitution:

And to keep from breaking down I wheeled and hid the weeping by screaming at that boy. (T 48)

Antagonism among Blacks is thus seen as a failure in communication, caused by the lack of a common code that would resist class hierarchies and bridge social and regional divisions.

J. was looking at me hard, like country boys do, when their language, or the new tone they need to take on once they come to this cold climate (1940's New Jersey) fails, and they are left with only the old Southern tongue, which cruel farts like me used to deride their lack of interest in America. (T 47)

As a faint hope for a Black code, impervious to outside interference, Baraka suggests the pronunciation nuances of Dey Street in Newark, "pronounced *die* by the natives, *day* by the teachers, or any non-resident whites (T 41)." But until such beginnings of a meaningful communication are further developed and intensified, violence will be committed by Black people against each other.

"Going Down Slow" returns to a color-blind viewpoint, from which the creation of reality out of imagination is scrutinized. On the surface, this story is an indictment of the hypocrisies fostered by the institution of marriage. Different from *The Baptism*, which criticizes antilibidinal hypocrisies of the Baptist church as an institution, "Going Down Slow" is a precisely focused literary form for such an attack.

At the beginning of the story, Lew Crosby—from whose center of consciousness the story develops—is on his way home. It is 2:30 A.M., and Lew has spent the last hours with his mistress Leah Purcell. When she asked him, this time, whether he would mind if Rachel, his wife, was having an affair with somebody else, "like you do" (T 51), he got dressed quickly and left Leah. After the long walk home, Lew discovers that his wife is, indeed, out, just as Leah had predicted, and a college friend who is sleeping in their apartment confirms Lew's suspicion that his wife must be with Mauro, a Japanese painter living in the neighborhood. On his way to Mauro's, Lew reinterprets many occasions upon which his wife went out "for a walk" (T 54). Reaching Mauro's, he discovers Rachel and drags her back home; he refrains from hitting Mauro only because he is afraid of the painter's knowledge of judo. Back at home, Lew keeps shouting profanities at Rachel, repeatedly calling her a "stupid mediocre bitch" (T 57). When Rachel mentions Leah Purcell, Lew denies ever having slept with Leah, starts kicking chairs and tables against the wall until her screaming makes him stop; after she hits him, "he slapped her once, across her face, and caught her before she fell. Then they stood holding each other for about thirty minutes" (T 58). In a second section, Lew leaves his wife, grabs a metal pipe, goes to Mauro's place, and hits Rachel's lover several times on the head, wondering "whether the guy was dead" (T 59). Next, he is running toward Leah Purcell's house. In the third section, fifteen minutes later, Lew bypasses Leah's place and goes instead to see Bob Long, to whom he tells everything. Bob is a painter of people in all colors, "always working out . . . They made it from behind. Standing on horses. All ways. Girls and girls, men and horses. Girls and horses" (T 60). He has two "nodding bohemians" in his house, and the story ends—quite "unresolved"—when Bob shows Lew how to shoot up with heroin ("horse") and Lew gets high, "so far away from anything you can name . . . just out of everybody's reach" (T 61; cf. B 7).

Quite obviously, the story is a criticism of Lew's consciousness entrapped in social conceptions of marriage as a form of possession allowing for a dual standard of conduct. But "Going Down Slow" is equally critical of "getting high," of the Bohemian "counterculture" which evades personal responsibility by envisioning free love merely as a mechanical, Kama-Sutra-like variety of positions and partners on the basis of drugs. What the characters lack is, again, understanding communication, in the absence of which they cannot deal with their own problems.

On a deeper level, "Going Down Slow" is a criticism of Lew's consciousness as a writer. Read this way, the story exposes a man narcissistically absorbed in a "conversation with himself" (T 49), to whom "reality"—as opposed to the creation of his imagination and fantasy—has become a secondary concern.

He got days mixed up and dates, and stories. Fantasies replaced each other. Fantasies replaced realities. Realities did not replace anything. They were the least of anybody's worries. (T 53)

Indeed, most of the interior monologue that forms the story is concerned with Lew's *perception* of past, present, and future events rather than with the happenings themselves; the story begins, significantly, with this statement:

In his mind Lew Crosby was already at Mauro's loft. But the soft neon rain and long wet city streets caused the separation. (T 49)

The words of the other characters—reduced to simple phrases like Mauro's repeated pleading, "have a drink. We civilized people" (T 55–56)—have no chance against the verbose workings of Lew's mind. Lew goes into a page of rambling reflections upon his wife's infidelity perceived, in a literary context, as "Brook Farm" (T 54), and as an infringement upon his cherished Melville-reading-time: "How can you read *Pierre* if you think your wife's doing something weird? Then you got to take time out to think about *her*. . . . How much time can you waste like that?" (T 54).

He achieves a self-definition that can be a defense against this intrusion:

I am Lew Crosby, a writer. I want to write what I'm about, which is profound shit. Don't ask me anything. Just sit there if you want to." (T 55)

At this point, we realize that while this interior monologue was going on, Rachel must have asked Lew questions which never even reached his consciousness (so absorbed was he with himself): "Lew, Lew, answer me. Lew? Say, don't you ever listen to what I'm saying?" (T 55). "Going Down Slow" thus provides yet another illustration of the process of alienation, of separation from others, from reality, and, ultimately, from conscious life itself, that the self-oriented writer goes through. As the title suggests, this process is a decadent one, and, as in many other existentialist tales, no viable alternative emerges.

Two stories, "Heroes Are Gang Leaders" and "Salute," take the theme of alienation and lack of communication as well as the representation of the center of consciousness in contrast with "reality" to such extremes that they may well be interpreted as breaking-points of Baraka's "fast narrative" prose, suggestive of new modes of prose writing or of the abandonment of fiction.

In "Heroes Are Gang Leaders" a Polish tramp from the Bowery who swallowed paint remover and whose speech is reduced to a gurgle is harassed by the police. But it is as much a story about an incident in a New York hospital as it is an essay about the futility of prose writing. The common denominators of the two strains are the strong presence of the narrator and the concept of "heroism." And Baraka is dissatisfied both by posing as narrator and by creating a hero in the tradition of Ford Madox Ford's *No More Parades*. The concern with concepts rather than with people, with the tradition of narrative prose writing rather than with a useful message to a real audience, seems so hopelessly literary to Baraka at this point, that he questions both the subject and the form of prose writing. The story begins with a thesis statement of self-criticism:

My concerns are not centered on people. But in reflection, people cause the ironic tone they take. If I think through theories of government or prose, the words are sound, the feelings real, but useless unless people can carry them. (T 63)

The yearning for a functional and pragmatic theory of government *and* prose remains unfulfilled; and the tale unwinds as an illustration of the uselessness of literature separated from real people. The

Bohemian narrator discovers the humanity of a post-Tennessee-Williams-Kowalski, a speechless Bowery bum.

Bums have the same qualifications as any of us to run for president, and it is the measure of a society that they refuse to. . . . Bums know at least as much about the world as Senator Fulbright. (T 66)

In the Bowery hospital, the narrator is "not like the rest of these guys. They're just tramps. But I'm a tramp with connections" (T 66). The connections are, of course, literary and appear profound enough to influence not only his awareness of a coterie, an artists' colony, he is writing for, but also his very perception of "reality," of which he has become most skeptical:

But one day two men came into our ward. . . . When I looked up from my book at them, I thought immediately what a stupid thing to think about people that they were cops. Although, of course, that is just what they were: cops. (T 66)

The narrator projects a similar type of perception on Kowalski:

I'm sure he'd never expected to see cops in a place the Geneva Convention states very specifically is cool. In fact he wiped his eyes convinced, I'm certain, that the two police officers were only bad fairies, or at worst, products of a very casual case of delirium tremens. But, for sure, the two men persisted, past any idea of giggling fantasy. (T 67)

The story takes the narrator, who is reading about Ford Madox Ford's hero Christopher Tietjens, who believed that life failed because of the lack of good communication, to the point at which he can no longer escape reality, represented by the rough treatment the policemen give to the Polish patient in the next bed. At this moment, the narrative mode changes from the fictional to the essayistic and the narrator becomes part of the story rather than only a literary observer.

And here is the essay part of the story. Like they say, my *point of view*. I had the book, *No More Parades*, all about the pursuit of heroism. . . . Big Man in the Derelict Ward. The book held up in front of my eyes, to shield what was going on from slopping over into my life. Though, goddamn, it was there already. The response. The image. The total hold I had, and made. Crisscrossed and redirected for my own use (which now sits between the covers of a book to be misunderstood as *literature*. . . .

Till finally I said, "That man can't speak. His voice is gone." (T 68–69)

This brief venture into "reality" remains without consequences for the story; after one policeman brushes the narrator's comment aside with a brusque "And who the fuck asked you?" (T 69), the narrator, now with increased discontent, returns to literature as a shield:

It is the measure of my dwindling life that I returned to the book to rub out their image, and studied very closely another doomed man's life. (T 69)

If "Heroes Are Gang Leaders" denounces literature as a shield from, or misunderstanding of, reality and demands the development of an "essay part" of a story, "Salute" takes the complication of prose fiction to another, equally unsettling, extreme: since literature is only a form of covering "the real world with words" (T 83) and words are "dangerous" (T 84), there are infinitesimal literary strategies, none of which will be able to really represent reality, "duller, less flashy than any kind of fancy, and finally a lot grimmer" (T 83). Instead of pursuing, within the "house of fiction," a theory of the short story as an "epiphany"[13] Baraka arrives at the frustrating conclusion that "there are hundreds of halfway houses to any revelation, and the simplest fact of vision needs probably hundreds of seeings" (T 83).

In "Salute" Baraka demonstrates that the approximation of "realistic" prose is a Kafkaesque task which requires an exact recording of the hundreds of halfway houses, of apparently irrelevant origins of specific emotions, a procedure which ultimately overwhelms the "subject matter" (nonexistent outside the dangerous words). The proper "plot" makes up hardly a third of this seven-page story; the "rest" consists of the narrator's reflections, possible reactions which never became reality, and speculations about the function of reading and the nature of fiction. While in the Air Force—"where I did all my reading, or a great deal of it" (T 82)—and stationed in Puerto Rico, the young sergeant and narrator, whose consciousness is explored throughout the story, is suddenly confronted by a white Southern lieutenant's question: "Don't you know you're supposed to salute officers?" (T 87). The lieutenant is introduced by Baraka in two variations: one version emphasizing the Black-white aspect of their encounter (and its historical dimension through the memory of the Russ family's grocery store); the other version elaborates the Bohemian-square confrontation. Both variants begin with the three sentences:

But now there was a thin blond man standing directly in front of me. He didn't know me. He'd never even seen me, before. (T 86)

Version one continues:

(Maybe his mother got fucked by an escaped mad coon sex deviate who resembled the perspiration of my ideas. Or the father! I mean, there could have been some wild connection . . . did his wife buy a broom in my grandfather's grocery store? No. In the South or the North? Ahhh. No she never been there. (T 86)

Version two reads:

(Maybe . . . but he recognized the clothes I wore, though he didn't like their style. He wdn't now, with what I've got on this minute, yellow corduroy pants, and a beard, so no progress finally. (T 86)

The answer to the lieutenant's question is left completely in the range of possibility by the narrator:

When the focus returned. (Mine) I don't know what that means. Focus, returned . . . . that's not precise enough. Uh . . . I meant, when I could finally say something to this guy . . . I didn't have anything to say. But I knew that in the first place. I said, "Yes sir, I know all about it." No, I didn't say any such shit as that. I sd, "Well, if the airplanes blow up, Chinese with huge habits will drop out of the sky, riding motorized niggers." You know I didn't say that. But I said something, you know, the kind of shit you'd say, you know. (T 87)

Baraka's story-telling technique has become extremely self-conscious, and romantic irony has been exaggerated to the point at which the narrator interferes in a plot, not to propel it into the desired direction, but to show the problems of any fictionalization

In an attempt to grasp reality, the last sentences ask the reader for the answer to the lieutenant's question. The writer of modernist fiction has given up pretending to be able to organize reality or to present "focused" stories. This is a reversal of the process in *Dante.*

"The Screamers," one of Baraka's last attempts at writing "fast narrative," indicates a way out of the writer's dilemma and advocates a solution to the problem of alienation and lack of communication. By turning to a Black audience and following the example of Black popular music, Baraka envisions a coded ritualization of art which would both liberate the artist from his narcissistic isolation and help to destroy the oppressive conditions of the ghetto. From Baraka's special vantage point, this meant an identification of his own Bohemian outsider consciousness with a new Black consciousness—facilitated through opposition to the common enemy of a square and white dominant culture. In other words, the two versions (the Black and the Beat) of a self-definition against the Southern white lieutenant in "Salute" merge in "The Screamers."

The narrator of "The Screamers" remembers and recreates a summer night in Newark in the late '40s or early '50s, when Lynn Hope played the saxophone at the Graham for a Black audience whose hopes and desires are apparently fulfilled by the screamingly wild music which sets out to overshadow all previous music. With his provocatively displayed Blackness (turban and wild rhythmic gesturing) and with the Rhythm & Blues style of his band (in the course of the evening, they play *Night Train* and *Harlem Nocturne,* as well as the sexually stimulating dances with the telling names, *The Grind, The Rub,* and *The Slow Drag*), Lynn lures the audience, which consists of light and dark Blacks, of urban Newarkers and of country folk with big hats who have only recently come north, into more and more extreme forms of self-expression. After screaming, howling, and stomping, the band gets into the repetition of a riff, and finally into one honking note, at the sound of which more than 500 dancers line up behind Lynn and move, with him, around the dance hall and finally out onto Belmont Avenue. From there, the strange procession goes on to Spruce Street, through the traffic of "dazed white men who sat behind the wheels" (T 79). People from the late show join the line, and almost immediately, police and firemen, equipped with clubs and water cannons, move in, and "America's responsible immigrants were doing her light work again" (T 79). Before the streetfighting reaches its climax, however, Lynn, some of his musicians, a few dancers and the narrator—all still screaming the same note—move back across Belmont Avenue into the lobby of the Graham, "halfway up the stairs, then we all broke our different ways, to save whatever it was each of us thought we loved" (T 80).

Like Baraka's earlier short stories, "The Screamers" is concerned both with the event and with the narrative creation of it from the point of view of a narrator who is, this time, drawn, through the ritual of the action, from his original position of a distanced observer into the very center of the collective happening. In the "dada" scream, unbearable social oppression and individual repression reveal themselves to the narrator, who becomes physically aware of the necessity for political and emotional liberation. The first glimpses of this struggle for liberation become visible in the "nihilistic" though creative expressiveness of music and through the anarchist gesture of the street battle. Lynn Hope's "one scary note" (T 78) erases false consciousness and brings about individual and collective self-awareness, which may force the *status quo* to dance. Lynn's music is, thus, revolutionary art, whose effect Baraka tries to translate into prose, so that "The Screamers" becomes a poetic reflection on the function of art, and especially of Afro-American art, against the background of political oppression.

Lynn Hope's technique, described in detail in the story, places the artist in the group of "honkers" and "contortionists," whose most famous representatives, Eddie "Lockjaw" Davis, Illinois Jacquet, Willis "Gatortail" Jackson, and Big Jay McNeely, are either mentioned in the story or discussed in *Blues People*. These musicians have pushed the quality of the saxophone to create a "warm, sometimes even hot, living and human tone"[14] to the extreme of the human scream, as a reaction against the softness of Black instrumental music since the advent of swing (BP 172).

In their attempts to produce the very antithesis of the popular music white America could accept, the honkers tried to surpass each other by their showmanship. They would leap and twist their heads, strut up and down the stage, shake their hair in their faces and coolly mop it back, fall on their knees and on their backs, "with both feet stuck up high in the air" (T 76–77) and thus achieve, through the ritual character of their performance, a form of "Black Dada Nihilismus." The musical result, informed by the avant-gardist logic of Marcel Duchamp's or Salvadore Dali's "Mona Lisa with the mustache, as crude and simple" (T 77), is, on the aesthetic level, a frontal attack against traditional "western" concepts of art and music, and in its political implications, a "social form for the poor" (T 77) in which those Black bourgeois illusions which distract from a clear self-image for the Black minority and from the abolition of the "flaw of that society" (T 74) are "erased" (T 75) by spat-out "enraged sociologies" (T 77): "the sound itself became a basis for thought" (T 76). Through their radical artistic avant-gardism, "pushed in its insistence past music" (T 76), and through their ability to express their "personal evaluation of the world" (T 78) in one honked note, the screamers become "ethnic historians, actors, priests of the unconscious" (T 76) who can raise the political consciousness of their audiences in an ecstatic ritual.

In an attempt to outdo his predecessors, Lynn Hope "thought further, and made to destroy the ghetto" (T 79). Lynn's music and performance, according to Robert Bone "the exact equivalent of 'Burn, Baby, Burn,' "[15] release the repressed violence of the oppressed, their "hatred and frustration, secrecy and despair" (T 76), and lead, in a perfect harmony of art and political action, to the street battle between Blacks and whites. The Blacks (called "Biggers" in an allusion to Wright's *Native Son*) battle the machinery of white "civil servants" (T 80), who, themselves descendants of poor immigrants, are members of the police force and fire brigade and only symbolically represent the "real oppressors" to the even poorer Blacks.

Even if this Black surrealist act fails, Baraka is convinced that it is still important for Blacks to vent their aggression against whites rather than to misdirect it within the Black community. Accordingly, Baraka's interest in the "enraged sociologies" of Black revolutionary music is primarily psychological in nature; and Lynn, who "made to destroy the ghetto," leaves the street battle and the "maddened crowd" (T 80) at the end of the story and returns, together with some musicians and the narrator, to the dance hall. The function of art remains limited to that of a catalyst, which may, in certain historical and social situations, release energies; the effects of this energy impulse, however, rapidly emancipate themselves from their origin and ultimately make art superfluous. What Baraka says of Big Jay McNeely's music during a contortionist performance is true, in a figurative sense, of Lynn Hope viewed from the perspective of a street-fighter: "there was still music, though none of us needed it now" (T 76). Like Clay in *Dutchman* the narrator of "The Screamers" sides with art and utilizes Black violence as a subject of literature. Thus, he describes the effect of Lynn's music:

We screamed and screamed at the clear image of ourselves as we should always be. Ecstatic, completed, involved in a secret communal expression. It would be the form of the sweetest revolution, to hucklebuck[16] into the fallen capital, and let the oppressors lindy hop out. (T 79)

The process of the Black revolution in dance steps is expressed (and remains) in the subjunctive; and the most important real result of the music of the screamers is the "clear image," based on an inversion of white-orientedness. The main emphasis of Lynn's agitation and of Baraka's art theory and production is thus on the creation of Black consciousness, to be formed by the creation of new and the inversion of old, negative "images." Ultimately, the cultural revolutionizing of the narrator through the influence of Lynn's Black aesthetic and through the street battle seem more significant than the outcome of that battle itself, from which the end of the story moves away. "The Screamers" is told not from the perspective of a streetfighter, but from the point of view of yet another autobiographic projection of its author: the narrator is an intelligent, sensitive son of the Black petite bourgeoisie, who, with the help of the intensive reception of Black Rhythm & Blues music, "an anathema to the Negro middle class" (BP 172), turns his back on his milieu and defines himself in a conscious contradiction to all "middle class" values.

In the course of the story the contrast between the narrator's origins and new self-definition is fully developed. The element of time distance—there is roughly a decade between narrated time and time of narration—so important in many previous tales, allows the narrator to reflect upon the limitations experienced by the youthful "I" and to interpret—from a perspective of omniscience—the total situation and even the meaning of the story.

Baraka juxtaposes the autobiographic "social-worker mothers and postman fathers" (T 71) with Lynn's pimping—"macking with any biglipped Esther" (T 71). Further contrasts between the worlds of the Black bourgeoisie—"our camp" (T 71)—and of Lynn Hope appear throughout "The Screamers." The internalization of a white ego-ideal, visible in "lightskinned projects" (T 71) and the narrator's " 'good' hair" (T 73) which, however, is "not straight enough" (T 73) for one of the girls in the story, is characteristic of Black middle-class self-negation, whereas Lynn makes an exhibition of his *Negritude* with a "black turban / on red string conked hair" (T 71). The following juxtaposition of key words shows the systematic antagonism developed in "The Screamers":

soft voices (T 72)	The singers shouted, the musicians stomped and howled (T 75)
mute bass players (T 74)	
important Negroes (T 73)	niggers (T 72)
'good colored friends' (T 75)	hopped-up woogies (T 79)
Baptists . . . praying in their 'faboulous' churches (T 74)	gritty Muslims (T 77), black cults of emotion (T 76), priests of the unconscious (T 76)
sit still for hours under popular songs (T 74)	dancers ground each other past passion or moved so fast it blurred intelligence (T 75)
join the Urban League (T 74)	destroy the ghetto (T 79)
mediocrity (T 73)	elegance (T 76)
my father never learned how to drink (T 73)	wine blotches on four-dollar shirts (T 71), a wino's daughter (T 72–73) so high we all envied him for his connection (T 76)

The contrast is between white-oriented and Black conscious, but also between "square" and "Beat." "The Screamers" thus exemplifies Baraka's artistic strategy of merging the structure of aesthetic protest with elements of ethnic and political protest; the story is also representative of Baraka's inclination to emphasize the psychological and individual (usually autobiographical) aspect of social commitments. The narrator of "The Screamers" interprets his decision against the straight world ultimately as *personal* partisanship for the Black lower classes: "I disappeared into the slums, and fell in love with violence" (T 74). This commitment is brought about by an attempt at personal self-realization—"desiring everything I felt" (T 74)—against the middle-class fate that had been prepared for him: "Willing for any experience, any image, any further separation from where my good grades were sure to lead" (T 74). The means of escaping his fate—frequently associated with metaphors of death, e.g., "deaths of clean politicians" (T 74), "advertising cemeteries" (T 75), or "they had a son . . . they killed because he was crazy" (T 73)—is the notorious Black music of the dance halls, the true vehicle for his casual remark: "You see, I left America on the first fast boat" (T 74). Once the narrator has entered the dance hall of "pure emotion" (T 74), he experiences himself at first as an agent of that oppression which the Black middle class represents to poor Blacks, "a naked display of America" (T 73). But soon he is initiated into Lynn Hope's communal ritual. "Lynn was trying to move us, and even I did the one step I knew, safe at the back of the hall" (T 78). After the "communion" through the cup of wine "a murderer friend of mine made me drink" (T 78) the narrator gives up this safety and becomes one of the first dancers to fall in line behind Lynn's wild horn men, "strutting like the rest of them" (T 78). From now on, the narrator remains in the "jewel"[17] center of energy, in Lynn's immediate vicinity, until the screaming "fools," upon returning to the Graham from the streets, go their different ways, "to save whatever it was each of us thought we loved" (T 80). These last words of the story allude to the narrator's love for violence as well as to his adolescent sexuality which, with the help of Lynn's music, has begun to emancipate itself from petty bourgeois fetters. More than that, the end of "The Screamers" affirms Baraka's decision to "save" Lynn's revolutionary message by translating it from music into literature.

In a collection which abounds with examples of lack of communication and of the writer's essential alienation, "The Screamers" offers a model of communication and of overcoming alienation through the power of Black music. Baraka has been praised for the accomplished representation of young urban Blacks whose specific culture is portrayed accurately, and distinguished from that of other groups, in "The Screamers." "I've been to a lot of local Brooklyn dances in my day," Beat poet Gilbert Sorrentino writes, "with the same sort of youth attending, but they were white; the dances were not like this one, although the probability of violence often became real."[18]

Baraka achieves the specificity of "The Screamers" through a rendition of elements of the Black ghetto idiom in diction and vocabulary. The language of the story, however, is not "Black English," since Baraka was far more concerned with fusing the impulse of Black music and the ethnic milieu with the prose language of *The Moderns*, with merging Beat writing and Rhythm & Blues, and with combining the theme of violent struggle against oppression and the literary model of dadaism. In "The Screamers" Baraka successfully manages to utilize all these heterogeneous elements in a literary gesture of Bohemian anarchism. Identifying the "hip" and the "Black," he is able to project his painfully felt individual outsider situation upon the Black minority as a whole. Conforming to the aesthetic of "populist modernism," "The Screamers" explores Blacks as outcasts of America:

Selby's hoodlums, Rechy's homosexuals, Burroughs' addicts, Kerouac's mobile young voyeurs, my own Negroes, are literally not included in the mainstream of American life. These characters are people . . . no character in a John Updike novel would be happy to meet. (M xiv)

While this literary strategy represents a conscious romanticization of Blacks, it magnifies Baraka's outsider situation from the previous *Tales* and brings his conception close to its breaking point: if Black communication exists and offers a solution to the Black writer's problem of alienation, then an inversion must be possible, in which the difficulties articulated in his previous prose fiction will be understood increasingly as "white" problems. In a Black context, literature may again have a meaningful function.

The second part of *Tales* reflects this transition to the new "Black" prose. Beginning with "Words," the last seven tales are different from the first nine stories of the collection in form and content. "Words," the only story which specifically mentions the place and date of composition, *"Harlem, 1965"* (T 91), reflects the somewhat Camusian leap into the belief that

The dialogue exists. Magic and ghosts are a dialogue, and the body bodies of material, invisible sound vibrations, humming in emptyness . . . (T 91)

Different from the narrator's concern with the rendition of past events in the first nine stories, the last seven—sometimes more like diary entries than short stories—deal with the present and the future. Significantly, "Words" begins with the word "Now" (T 89) and other stories carry this concern in their very titles—"New-Sense" (T 93), "Unfinished" (T 99), "New Spirit" (T 107), and "Now and Then" (T 117). The end of "New-Sense" is the incorporation of the present-orientedness of Baraka's new prose: "NOW NOW NOW NOW NOW NOW" (T 96–97).

The last tales reject story-telling, which is denounced as a form of lying—"The tales people will tell even to this day, of shit that simply did not happen" (T 99) or "They told tales about themselves. One was short and one was tall" (T 119)—or simply discarded as "bullshit twisted from another time" (T 105). Correspondingly, what was called the "essay part of the story" in "Heroes Are Gang Leaders" (T 68), gains in volume and importance in the second part of *Tales,* and overshadows even "Salute" in its absence of a "plot." The new tales are generally shorter and more tentatively and "openly" constructed than the old ones.

"Words" is a short sketch of the continued struggle with alienation, even in Harlem. "When I walk in the streets, the streets don't claim me, and people look at me, knowing the strangeness of my manner, and the objective stance from which I attempt to 'love' them" (T 89). The intellectual's "jivey books," his visionary disposition to "be always looking, and thinking" (T 90) make him "an old hermit," who expresses himself still in "the alien language of another tribe." His dissatisfaction with his own verbal creations is painfully clear:

I wanted something, want it now. But don't know what it is, except words. I cd say anything. But what would be left, what would I have made? (T 90)

The writer asks, "Why does everyone live in a closet . . . ?" yet resorts to even more intensive introspection as a method of overcoming alienation. Loyal to his "need to reach into myself" (T 91) the narrator envisions himself in the familiar process of building *A World Elsewhere:* "we build our emotions into blank invisible structures which never exist, and are not there, and are illusion and pain and madness." The sketch characterizes this gesture, however, as "Dead whiteness" and ends with a series of new demands, such as

We need to look at trees more closely.
We need to listen. (T 91)

"New-Sense" approaches the opposition of "reality" and "fantasy" as the characteristic contradiction within the writer.

I lived in big mansions that were small shacks huddled against the screams of the poor. I lived fantasies in the center of ugly reality. And reality was the feeling I wanted, and escaped to, from a fantasy world, where I cd have everything. Where I cd be everything. (T 93)

Escaping from the Bohemian world of fantasy freedom and realizing that "romance is dream" (T 94) is only a point of departure, not a program; and even with his "new-sense" the writer remains a *writer* who prefers the irreality of the typewriter to the reality of love.

I could go make love to somebody right now, instead of hacking at this machine. Right now, lost second, I could. (T 95)

But writing also gives the Black intellectual a "new sense" of a literary tradition. He interprets the "grey romance" of his past in the vein of Jean Toomer's "Bona and Paul," in which Toomer artic-

ulated Paul's sense of being "apart from the people around him.
Apart from the pain which they had unconsciously caused. Suddenly he knew that people saw, not attractiveness in his dark skin,
but difference."[19] Similarly, Baraka's narrator of "New-Sense" remembers a night with "a white girl, and then going for that difference it made" (T 94, cf. B 222).

If Toomer provides Baraka with formulations of alienation,
McKay allows him a new sense of libidinal affirmation as part of a
Black strategy in white America. Baraka's self-division into Ray and
Foots in *The Toilet* resembled McKay's into Ray and Jake in *Home
to Harlem*. In "New-Sense," however, Baraka mocks Ray and sides
with Jake.

Like Jake and Ray in my man's book. Jake moved straight and hard and
survived with a fox in Chicago, probably, where he'd come home tired
and drunk at nights after work and work this happiness over (her name
was Felice). And Ray, a name I'd already saved for my self, sailing around
the stupid seas with a "wistful" little brown girl waiting for him while he
masturbated among pirates . . . dying from his education. Shit. It's too
stupid to go into. (T 96)

Baraka now sides with Blackness as libidinal freedom, struggles
away from a Toomerian sense of alienation, and outdoes even
McKay's Bohemianism in facing the opposition of "the reflective
vs. the expressive" (T 96). "Because reflect never did shit for any of
us. Express would" (T 96–97).

"Unfinished" is a Black continuation of "Heroes Are Gang
Leaders." A Black cripple, capable of extreme emotions as his "Inside flowed on out" (T 106), and able to dream of an "actual kingdom of kings and queens," is Baraka's projection of an agonistic artist and visionary. Against this foil, the world of a Harlem barroom
proves to be a sinister sphere of false consciousness. Hypocrisy extends not only to middle-class "Knee Grows" (T 101), but to the
"fool / coward cartel" (T 101) which the poet / narrator detects and
sets out to combat. The images the writer summons to help him in
the battle go back to his older struggles with Philistines. "WHITE
PHILANTHROPY RUNS AMUCK AGAIN" (T 100), and the poet

must reject Christian love and nonviolence in the image of "piles of dead fish being broken in half by a jew to feed niggers at the seashore" (T 105) in order to liberate "Hannibal's mulattoes," who are "still passing for White" (T 105) under the Roman armor of "Consider This" (UP 17). As in previous tales, the distance between narrator and experiencing subject creates a self-conscious story of story-telling itself. "But it wasn't me anyway. I'm here writing, this never happened to this person. It was somebody else" (T 102).

The last stories return the circle to the association complexes of *Dante*. More explicitly connected with Black music, these stories are often cryptic. "New Spirit" is the eulogy for Olabumi, a close friend of Baraka's (cf. B 193–194, 196); and the address to the dead girl is a moving invocation of her "new spirit." "No Body No Place" is another sketch of the narrator's painful and tormented division in his struggle "to be myself. . . . This man whose life I watched. Whose soul is mine, and another's" (T 112). "Now and Then" evokes the "Screamers" theme of Black music as it "razes" whole civilizations. Baraka follows a more spontaneous writing procedure which tries to make the story part of a Sun Ra and Ornette Coleman flow even as it lashes out against the Beatles' *Revolver* album "which has long hair and kills. Even in song" (T 121). The final story, "Answers in Progress" is another jazz tale with a Burroughs touch of science fiction. *Tales* ends with a reference to *Genesis* in the vein of "Lanie Poo" (P 8): "That's the way the fifth day ended" (C 132).[20]

Despite the development out of "straight narrative" back into associative prose, there is a continuity in *Tales* which is most noticeable in the imagery throughout the stories. This unity of imagery extends to much of Baraka's fiction and nonfiction prose, as well as to his poetry and drama, and supports the dynamics of his literary works. A tentative attempt to systematize Baraka's imagery yields the following chart: on the left, in column one, images of the undesirable world of names (hell), and on the right, in column four, aspects of a possible paradise are listed; the second and the third columns contain impeding and supporting elements on the necessary way from left to right.

white	guilt	music, dance	Black
noun	words	scream	verb
reflect	metal	turning	express
lies, fantasies, tales, masks, guises, poses	shield	cold, hot, red air	reality, truth
names	raincoat, umbrella	rain	bodies
jungle	wall	sun	ocean
death		revelation (satori, epiphany)	life, peace, spirit, God

The stories in *Tales* move increasingly from the image clusters on the left to those on the right; in the last pages of the book, Baraka has moved into his desired direction. This direction leads from white to Black, but also from fiction to reality. Baraka has not published prose fiction in the ten years since *Tales;* and *Tales* may be considered the logbook of a fiction writer who, under the social pressures of the 1960s, catapulted himself out of writing fictions while writing a swan-song to telling tales. Baraka's concern for "theories of government or prose" yielded to a predominant interest in government at the expense of prose fiction. As the voice of Baraka the story-teller retreated,[21] the scream of the agitating poet-playwright-essayist of Black cultural nationalism reached its peak.

8 Black Cultural Nationalism and the Black Aesthetic

> *If we have mad animals full of time to haunt us, to haunt us, who are in possession of all knowledge, then we have done something to make them exist.*
> —"A Black Mass" (F 22)

1. BLACK NATIONALISM, BLACK POWER, AND THE BLACK VALUE SYSTEM

The last essays in *Home*, the collection *Raise Race Rays Raze: Essays Since 1965*, and the uncollected nonfiction writings from the mid-1960s to the mid-1970s, reflect Baraka's immersion in Black nationalism, from Black Power to Pan-Africanism. This process, in the course of which Baraka abandoned political protest elements in favor of ethnocentric ones, and came to ascribe racism and oppression to "whites in general," was brought about by an internal dynamic within his works; the sudden and militant appearance of nationalism as the "resolution" to all his contradictions, however, was triggered by social and political events of 1964 and 1965—by the Black urban rebellions, by the murder of the Black children in the church bombing in Birmingham, and especially by the assassination of Malcolm X on February 21, 1965.

The new Black ethnicity to which Baraka increasingly aspired threatened his relationship to literary prototypes (Western moderns) and audiences (predominantly white). He felt that even a literature which openly provokes censors and critics by violating sex, race, and class taboos, could become absorbed in the cultural apparatus. Despite his theory of "art-ing," Baraka could do little to keep his works from becoming reified objects, ineffective as committed art. Harold Cruse observed that "even a LeRoi Jones can be absorbed and tolerated, for the sake of being abused as a threat."[1] A detailed account of Baraka's rise to fame as a Black protest writer who addresses white audiences further elaborates this contradiction:

In 1965, LeRoi Jones was a young, black, literary lion. . . . The more he attacked white society, the more white society patronized him. Who'd have suspected that there was so much money to be made from flagellation?[2]

Baraka was on the road to an American success story. Showered with fellowships, awards, and teaching engagements, Baraka might have "made it," might have pushed his career from Off-Broadway to Broadway and Hollywood.[3] He thought, however, that literary rebelliousness without a parallel commitment in "real life" was

nothing but the establishment flexing its muscles. If they didn't have some so-called rebels running around, they would fall apart quicker.[4]

Baraka's contemporary critics focused their attention on his obvious contradictions. Baraka was especially vulnerable to criticism which ridiculed the incongruity of his theoretical advocacy of Black violence, and his *de facto* integration—by marriage, residence, and fame—into the white cultural scene of New York. Stanley Kauffmann accused Baraka of posturing, and placed him in "The Tradition of the Fake," which consists of writers who

appeared at protest meetings, sometimes visited Gastonia or Cuba, signed manifestoes, but were all busily bucking for the book club, Broadway, or Hollywood.[5]

While supporting Black lumpenproletarian violence in panel discussions, Baraka also taught a class at The New School about modern poetry, and edited anthologies of contemporary prose. But the most blatant contradiction was seen in Baraka's private life: how could he write lines like "Rape the white girls. . . . Cut the mothers' throats" and remain married to a white woman?

When he is given his pistol and his signal, will he do his self-declared duty and begin the slaughter with his wife and children?[6]

A series of letters to the *Village Voice* in January 1965 dealt with Baraka's contradictions in literature and politics,[7] and *The Realist* "exposed" Baraka's dual existence in a satirical comic strip about "Leroy Baldlose" who becomes "Superiorman" when he utters the magic shazam-word, "Muthafuckerrr!" Married to a white woman, he is depicted as a chauvinist agitator and poet who recites the line: "Who was that ofay I saw you with last night? That was no ofay, that was my wife!"[8]

Baraka was forced to make decisions. Was he a Bohemian or a Black spokesman, a political writer or a "priest of the unconscious?" By 1965, he had taken the first step in the direction of an answer; he exaggerated his attacks on white "liberals" to such a degree as to finally convince himself that "whites in general" were not worth attacking, that he should address himself exclusively to Black people. But first, Baraka pursued his strategy of "white-baiting" in notorious "Speak-Outs" in Greenwich Village, and he became synonymous with his emotional antiwhite tirades. This prompted critics to hold up Baraka's private life against his public views; in fact, several of the quoted references to Baraka's contradictions were responses to Baraka's own diatribes. By telling his predominantly white and overwhelmingly liberal Village audiences that "our enemies" include "most of you who are listening," Baraka was posturing in order to exorcise his own association with devil-whiteness; increasingly he felt that "I should not be speaking here. . . . I should be speaking to Black people."[9] The next years showed that Baraka meant this literally: in the phase of Black cultural nationalism, he tried to escape what he felt was a neutralization and absorption process by speaking to Black people. It was a new way of rescuing the verb quality of art-ing from the noun of definitions.

Baraka's essays from the mid-1960s to the early 1970s are documents of an ethnic radicalization in Baraka's position, which developed more and more rapidly toward a total "Black" orientation: "By the time this book appears, I will be even blacker" (H 10). One suspects that much of the momentum of his dynamic development originated in a need to exorcise a feeling of guilt about having been "less black" earlier. The new ethnicity emerged from Baraka's *personal* perception: "if I point out a bird, a black man has pointed out that bird" (UN 36, p. 562). This formula, reminiscent of the earlier description of himself as a *"Negro* seeing a bus full of people," shows the individualist and visionary roots of Baraka's new group consciousness, from which he could now reevaluate his politics and aesthetics.

The emphasis on Blackness as a biological and ontological category appears as a continuation of Baraka's essays, of Clay's monologue in *Dutchman,* and of Walker's position in *The Slave.* Although perceived by Baraka as a synthesis of his earlier confusions and contradictions, the movement toward total Black cultural nationalism was achieved only at the expense of a truly political radicalization, with which it coincided for a short while. At the same time, Baraka did not need to exorcise his aesthetic protest elements to the degree that he rejected his political protest elements; art and culture, occasionally defined in terms not altogether different from his Beat aesthetic, retained a key role in Baraka's version of Black nationalism.

While Black nationalism constitutes a constant undercurrent of Black sensibility in the United States, it becomes a response of larger social dimensions in times of sharpened economic, political, or cultural oppression. The mobilization of race solidarity adds momentum to the agitation against economic exploitation, political underrepresentation, or cultural defamation. In its "pure" form, Black nationalism represents a collective alternative for the collectively discriminated-against Black minority.[10]

The central element of any Black nationalism is the concept of a Black nation, in which the oppression of Blacks as a minority would come to an end. The first, most obvious, strategy toward such a goal would be a literal, physical escape from the oppressive political structure—"back to Africa." With Marcus Garvey's "Universal Negro Improvement Association" as its most famous representative, this concept of a remigration to Africa has been espoused by many Blacks; at present, three-and-a-half centuries after the first slaves were deported from Africa to North America, the real-ization of a back-to-Africa movement seems unlikely; and, since W. E. B. DuBois's criticism of Garveyism, politically dubious: "Back-to-Africa" may easily come to mean suppression of Africans by Afro-Americans, whereas "Africa-to-the-Africans" gives the Black struggle in America an international dimension.[11]

The second strategy of Black nationalism aims at a Black nation in America. Depending on the assessment of the all-important land question, three variants of this concept have been advocated in recent years. The "Republic of New Africa" demands a separate Black nation in the states of Louisiana, Mississippi, Alabama, Georgia, and South Carolina. The "Nation of Islam," popularly re-ferred to as the "Black Muslims" (a religious organization with a vast membership, centered around the recently deceased prophet Elijah Muhammad), wants separation of Blacks from whites, but is ambivalent as to whether this move requires a literal nationhood, or whether a separation within the American nation is sufficient; upon different occasions, Elijah Muhammad advocated the es-tablishment of a Black nation in America, or in Africa, or was con-tent to demand separatism within the United States.[12] The third variant, Black cultural nationalism, as defined by Maulana Ron Karenga, advocates *values* which would govern the lives of Black Americans as a symbolically separate group within the United States; thus, "nationhood" becomes a metaphor for spiritual and cultural separation.[13]

All variations of nationalism are ultimately based on an analysis which ascribes the roots of Black oppression to "whites in general," and not to economics or class; nationalist strategies are therefore based on racial, prepolitical tenets, and require further definitions of "white" or "Black" qualities. Thus, Black nationalists may be ad-vocates of capitalism and may agree to preserve the economic structure of America in the Black nation, in Africa or in America. Or they may reject labor unions as a "white" conception. The defi-nition of what is positive and what is negative about Black and white social reality is crucial for assessing any form of Black nation-alism.

The program of the Black Panther Party, in many ways a secularized version of the platform of the Nation of Islam, attempts to politicize the Black nationalist impulse by defining the "enemy" not simply as *the* white man, but as the capitalist system. Correspondingly, the party's strategy, called "Black revolutionary nationalism," aims at a revolution which would overthrow the economic rulers of America and lead to a liberation of all Americans, Black and white. In this liberation policy, nationalism has been transcended.

Baraka's form of Black cultural nationalism hovered between the religious and the metaphorical, and was soon in sharp contradiction to the revolutionary nationalism of the Black Panther Party. Baraka's response to the oppression of Blacks was primarily cultural, and his precepts toward overcoming the status quo were directed at the cultural level. Social change was to come about through Black consciousness, new images, and the minds of the people. In 1962, Baraka formulated the prototype for metaphorical nationalism in the title of his essay, " 'Black' is a Country." And as late as 1974, an inscription prominently displayed over the stage at Baraka's Newark cultural center on Belmont Avenue read: "The minds of the people are the most important factor of any movement; without them you have nothing else."

Because Baraka used the word "Nation" metaphorically, he defined it in terms of race *consciousness*. He was attracted by the impact of the religious framework of the Nation of Islam upon the racial consciousness of its members and adapted some of their tenets to his own works. In his negation of the oppressive white racist culture, Baraka resorted to biological and even chauvinist arguments in order to reach "the minds of the people":

Nations are races. (In America, white people have become a nation, an identity, a race.) Political integration in America will not work because the Black Man is played on by special forces. His life, from his organs, *i.e.*, the life of the body, what it needs, what it wants, to become, is different—and for this reason racial is biological, finally. (H 246)

This general sentiment which, in rhetoric, can be traced to Baraka's distinctions between "names" and "bodies," is made frighteningly specific by words such as *Lebensraum*, by blatant anti-Semitism, illiberal antihomosexual agitation, reactionary antifeminism, and expedient antileftism. The Bohemian pendulum took a right-wing swing in its shifting antibourgeois opposition.

As a first step toward active Black nationalism, Baraka rejected white participation in the civil rights struggle. At the Village Vanguard Speak-Out, Baraka and Archie Shepp attacked fellow panelists and the audience for being white, and therefore guilty, whether they were committed to social change or not: "All whites are equally guilty—ALL—of the unforgiveable crime of attempting to destroy my humanity."[14]

In order to arrive at this conclusion, Baraka had to view the Village audience as part of that original sin; furthermore, even whites like Michael Schwerner and Andrew Goodman, murdered for their civil rights activities in Mississippi, had to be considered "artifacts," not human victims (i.e., "names," and not "bodies") by Baraka. Indeed, Schwerner and Goodman appeared to Baraka as part of the "homogeneous American soul," essentially different from Black victims like James Chaney, who was murdered along with his two white fellow-fighters. Baraka later regretted this narrow and inhuman view, and scenes of his play "The Motion of History" appear like an apology for the remarks on Goodman and Schwerner. The tendency to exclude even progressive whites and fellow victims from humanistic concern triumphed after the assassination of Malcolm X. In "The Legacy of Malcolm X, and the Coming of the Black Nation" (H 238–50), Baraka cast himself as the cultural executor of Malcolm's will and claimed Malcolm as a proponent of cultural nationalism. Baraka was more metaphorical in his formulation of nationalism than Malcolm; and for 9 years, he ignored the developments of Malcolm's last year, in the course of which Malcolm espoused internationalist conceptions and abandoned nationalism in the sense of the Nation of Islam. For Baraka, it is most important

that Malcolm had begun to call for a Black National Consciousness. And moved this consciousness into the broadest possible arena. . . . We do not want a Nation, we are a Nation. (H 239)

Since Blacks, by virtue of their consciousness, already *are* a nation, the land question becomes secondary for Baraka and can be ap-

1. *Clay (Robert Hooks) and Lula (Jennifer West) at the Cherry Lane production of* Dutchman *(1964).*

Picture: *Alix Jeffry*

2. Dutchman *in West Berlin, 1965.*
Pictures: Renate von Mangoldt

3. *Author LeRoi Jones/Amiri Baraka, director Edward Parone and cast on the set of* Dutchman. *As in the 1967 movie version, Al Freeman, Jr., is Clay.*

Picture: Alix Jeffry

4. *The cast of* The Toilet *on the stage set by Larry Rivers (1964).*

5. *Ray Foots (Hampton Clanton) and James Karolis (Jaime Sanchez) at the end of* The Toilet.

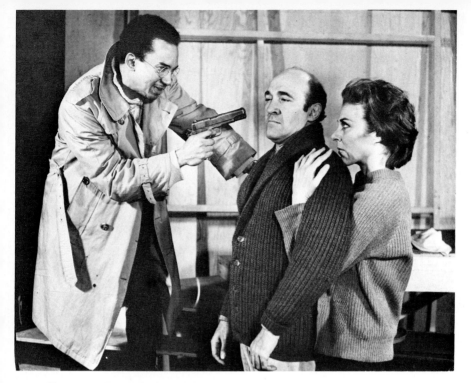

6. *Walker Vessels* (*Al Freeman, Jr.*), *Bradford Easley* (*Jerome Raphel*), *and Grace* (*Nan Martin*) *in* The Slave (1964).

Picture: Bert Andrews

. Slave Ship, *directed by Gilbert Moses (1969).* Lalu, Plantation
om (Garrett Morris) *and other members of cast.*

cture: Bert Andrews

8. "Madheart," directed by Ernie McClintock (1972). Sister (Joan Bailey), Mother (Barbara Landers), and Devil Lady (Marilyn Berry).

Picture: Bill Doll

9. *Portrait by Leroy McLucas (c. 1963) which appeared on the jackets of* Blues People, The Dead Lecturer, The System of Dante's Hell, *and* Tales.

10. *Amiri Baraka and wife Amina at auditions for* The Motion of History *(1977), directed by Baraka.*

Picture: Bill May

11. *Black Power Conference, Newark, N.J., 1967. Baraka is seated at microphone. Seated to his right are Maulana Ron Karenga and Brother Gaida (R.N.A.). Seated to his left are H. Rap Brown*

proached with visionary quips and puns on "abstract" and "concrete" instead of serious answers:

The landscape should belong to the people who see it all the time. . . .
What the Black Man must do now is look down at the ground upon which
he stands, and claim it as his own. It is not abstract. Look down! Pick up
the earth, or jab your fingernails into the concrete. It is real and it is
yours, if you want it. (H 240, 244)[15]

Baraka tried to translate the impulse of Black political radicalism
in the 1960s into a cultural form; and this process continued
Baraka's Bohemianism, which equated revolutions in art and consciousness with those in political history. In his relationship to people, Baraka tended to overemphasize the one aspect of cultural
"de-brainwashing." "We are all John Coltranes ruled by Lawrence
Welk" is a formula indicative of the aestheticization of politics. The
reason for Black oppression is seen in a comparison which illustrates Baraka's monocausal interpretation of politics as a result of
(racial) consciousness:

You can sit on that chair out there, because that chair is less conscious
than you. . . . If that chair were conscious it certainly would debate with
you about sitting on it.[16]

The difference in consciousness between white and Black Americans is ultimately perceived by Baraka as an absolute one, defying
mediation and communication. His new "communication projects"
were all-Black affairs, attempts to reach Black audiences in order to
make them more Black-conscious. These activities, although cultural in origin and scope, moved Baraka into more visibly political
arenas, from Black Power conferences to Pan-African congresses.

The first important influence after Baraka's Malcolm X adaptation was his contact with the Black Power movement. Although the
term "Black Power" is of an older origin and had been used by
Richard Wright as the title of a book about Africa, Stokely Carmichael popularized the term when he used it during the Meredith
march of 1966 as a slogan which was meant to express a variety of
Black political, economic, social, and cultural demands. One reason
for the strength and attractiveness of the term "Black Power" may
have been its vagueness, which appealed to many different political

tendencies, organizations, and individuals, who came together in order to discuss what, in their various opinions, the term *should* mean.

A National Planning Committee grew out of the 1966 Labor Day weekend planning session concerned with defining Black Power and prepared a National Conference on Black Power for over 400 delegates from all over the United States. Baraka attended the conference, which took place in Newark on July 20–23, 1967, just after the Newark ghetto rebellion. A great variety of resolutions were passed which reflected many conflicting strategies among the delegates, who did not share a common political program. Five distinct interpretations of Black Power emerged:

1. BLACK CAPITALISM:
   Black-controlled financial institutions—banks, insurance companies, savings and loan associations—to provide funds for credit unions, housing, loans, etc.
2. MORE BLACK POLITICIANS:
   Election of 12 Black Congressmen.
3. GROUP INTEGRATION (ETHNIC POLITICS):
   Selective buying to force job upgrading, and a nationwide "buy-Black" move. Boycott of magazines that carry ads for hair straighteners and skin bleachers.
4. BLACK CONTROL OF BLACK COMMUNITIES:
   A school for Black political organizers.
5. BLACK LIBERATION within the context of a U.S. revolution:
   Paramilitary training for Black youths.[17]

Baraka's interpretation of Black Power oscillated among several of these alternatives, and his confusion reflected that of many delegates at large. For him, the most decisive element of any Black movement had to be its cultural unity. Baraka thus sympathized with the Nation of Islam, but for a while also with the Black Panthers, and met even with Dr. Martin Luther King in order to discuss possibilities of a Black united front. In order to categorize Baraka in terms of the resolutions of the Black Power Conference, one must resort to at least three of the alternative interpretations offered; Baraka was most interested in Black Power as Black Liberation, but increasingly believed in all the other concepts except Black Capitalism as means toward liberation. This vague definition allowed Baraka a wide range of participation in Black nationalist activities.

The most important influence on Baraka's Black cultural nationalism was exerted by Maulana Ron Karenga, who participated in the Black Power Conference. Baraka had already met with, and was fascinated by, Karenga, and tried to integrate Karenga's precepts into his works, and imitate Karenga's California organization "US" in Newark as "BCD" ("Black Community Defense and Development"). In 1967, Karenga collected his aphorisms in a small volume, entitled *The Quotable Karenga*. Baraka read this manifesto avidly, quoted from it frequently, and attempted to apply the maxims to his private and public activities.

In his aphorisms, Karenga emphasizes *values* which he places "superior to reason."[18] He preaches the primacy of culture and race over economics and politics. Like Baraka, Karenga hates Liberals, and indulges in apocalyptic, religious-revolutionary rhetoric; he denies the concept of equality, and demands that women be "submissive" as a natural expression of their femininity.

Baraka adopted Karenga's demagogic eclecticism, and wrote poems, plays, and essays on the basis of *The Quotable Karenga*, which was also distributed through Jihad Productions. The most interesting document which reflects Baraka's immersion into Karenga's world is the schooling material for the use by Congress of African People cadres edited by Baraka, *10 Phases Of The Kawaida Doctrine of Maulana Karenga*. This inventory of points to be made in order to convert Black people to Kawaida is thoroughly based on Karenga. The sections of the different phases are entitled, e.g., "3 Criteria for Being a Nationalist," "7 Criteria of a Culture," or "3 Functions of a Value System;" and in the last phase, the neophyte learns among the "7 Things A Good Advocate Should Do:"

We must first move to reconvert ourselves to the acceptance and practice in accordance with the ideology. Then we must move to help others to be converted.

Under Karenga's influence, Baraka discarded his traditional advocacy of anarchist violence, and dedicated his political essays to the task of cultural "nation-building," to the transformation of Black consciousness through positive self-images. By accepting this priority, he also arrived at the conclusion that it was the "ballot, not the bullet"[19] which would free Black people; he became an active organizer in the area of electoral politics, instrumental in getting Kenneth Gibson elected as the first Black mayor of Newark in 1970. At the same time, Baraka's agitation against the Black middle class reached its lowest point, since he believed that only a unified Black group could achieve any political gains in America (approaching the third interpretation of Black Power given earlier). At the Black Congress in Gary in 1972, Baraka attempted to practice Karenga's concept of "operational unity" and appeared in the role of a conciliator[20] who tried to keep conservatives and revolutionaries together. Like Karenga, he believed that the lack of Black unity was due to a lack of Black values, and that the Black intellectual had to provide "direction" and "purpose" (Baraka's key words since "Cuba Libre") through the intensive propagation of "A Black Value System" among all strata of the Black community. The practical, moral, religious system of Kawaida was to serve just that function.

Baraka's "7 Principles of US Maulana Karenga & The Need for a Black Value System" is therefore the most important essay in the period of Black nationalism. Originally published in the first issue of *The Black Scholar*, this essay was reprinted widely, distributed as a separate pamphlet by Jihad Productions, and included in *Raise Race Rays Raze*. In many of his later essays, speeches, poems, and plays, Baraka referred to, or quoted from, the seven principles called, in Swahili, the "Nguzo Saba," "the '10 commandments' yet more profound to us."

UMOJA (Unity)—To strive for and maintain unity in the family, community, nation, and race.

KUJICHAGULIA (Self-Determination)—To define ourselves, name ourselves, and speak for ourselves, instead of being defined, and spoken for by others.

UJIMA (Collective Work and Responsibility)—To build and maintain our community together and to make our brothers and sisters problems our problems and solve them together.

UJAMAA (Cooperative Economics)—To build and maintain our own stores, shops and other businesses and to profit together from them.

NIA (Purpose)—To make as our collective vocation the building and developing of our community in order to restore our people to their traditional greatness.

KUUMBA (Creativity)—To do always as much as we can, in the way we can in order to leave our community more beautiful and beneficial than when we inherited it.

IMANI (Faith)—To believe with all our heart in our parents, our teachers, our leaders, our people and the righteousness and victory of our struggle. (R 133–34)

Baraka specifically rejects the term "struggle against capitalism"; he believes that the fight is one against a foreign oppressor.

When you speak of capitalism you speak of the European mind. We do not want to be Europeans. . . . (A)re not Marx, Engels and Lafargue just another list of "great" men . . . but great white men. . . . Another group of white men might give you another list . . . like say Washington, Jefferson, Lincoln, Kennedy, &c. But it is, either way, still a commitment to Euro-American values, to whiteness. (R 138)

Baraka denied the validity of any "white" idea, and his equation of white and diabolic led him to a position from which he no longer distinguished between Jefferson and John Brown, or between Lenin and Henry Ford. This attitude is characteristic of the volume *Raise* as a whole. The book is a collection of very heterogeneous essays and prose pieces that take up where *Home* left off. The essays on nonviolence and liberalism, on Black and white writers included in *Home*, seem decades removed from the affirmatively Black chants of *Raise*. The new themes range from Baraka's traditional fascination with, and contempt for, American popular culture, an intense awareness of the social brutality of Black urban life, and an indictment of the white power machinery responsible for the social condition of Black people, to a contempt for all Afro-Americans who, in Baraka's eyes, are still under the influence of sick devil-whiteness, and to descriptions of alternatives for the Black man through the Nguzo Saba of Kawaida. The tone is often hymnic,[21] and some pieces seem to follow a spontaneous procedure.

Of the strongest and most convincing essays, one deals with Blacks as subjects of an insane system of "justice," "Newark Courthouse—'66 Wreck (Nigger Rec Room)," and another deals with urban politicking ("Newark—Before Black Men Conquered," an essay rejected by "Atlantic & several other periodicals"). Also effective are the sections recounting Baraka's own experiences as an ex-Beat writer and as a defendant following the Newark rebellion. For a while, Baraka was involved in serious attacks on a wide spectrum of Afro-American literati and politicians.

In many of his essays he mocks Eldridge Cleaver, Huey Newton, Bobby Seale, Bayard Rustin, the NAACP, Jim Brown, Charles Gordone, Douglas Turner Ward, and others. Thus, Baraka merges the doctrine of Yacub (from the Nation of Islam)[22] with Bela Lugosi's Dracula in order to attack Eldridge Cleaver as a modern-day vampire who resuscitates Marx and Lenin:

. . . the beasts and devils try to crawl back into the light of day, redefining our lives in 1930s dracula style led by the modern day Yacub, Eldridge Cleaver, who cleaved the movement. . . . And the corpses of Marx Lenin get raised out of the tomb again. (R 111)[23]

After much sharp and authoritarian criticism of "white-oriented Blacks," the last essays of *Raise* and Baraka's politics at the Gary Convention suggest the principle of "operational unity" among all Blacks, unifying diverse and even "white-oriented" Black groups on a broad basis that admits all approaches from the Urban League and NAACP to "athletic and social clubs," churches, and diverse other organizations, in order to achieve pragmatic social advances for the Black masses, rather than a theoretical system: it is better for Black nationalists to "join with the NAACP . . . to bring about real change, where possible, than discussing theoretical nationalism in coffee shops" (R 162). It was this impulse, underscored by the Black success in the Newark mayoralty election of 1970, that showed Baraka's political and social force in the period of cultural nationalism much more clearly than many of the frequently contradictory and overly rhetorical essays included in *Raise Race Rays Raze*.

Baraka's move toward an all-Black unity ultimately included Africa as well as the United States; Baraka expanded his narrower concept of US Black cultural nationalism into a new Black internationalism, "PanAfrikanism." This change in perspective, as well as disappointing experiences with the bourgeois politics of Black elected officials, provided a basis for Baraka's recent shift to socialist concepts, with which he was confronted through the writings of African socialists such as Kwame Nkrumah, Sekou Touré, and Amilcar Cabral. Until that turning point, Baraka's writings remained a "Target Study" (B 45, UP 53) of a white devil enemy image, whose emanations often bore little semblance to capitalism, or to the DuPonts, Rockefellers, Nixons and Eisenhowers, against whom Baraka had defined himself in "Cuba Libre." Baraka's devil is white, but carries in his whiteness fewer emblems of the American ruling class than stigmata of groups discriminated against by "white society."

Baraka's Black cultural nationalist essays incorporated the prejudices of the society at large and directed much of their aggression against traditional outcasts of bourgeois society; in Baraka's works, the image of the devil-enemy appears in the shape of bums, policemen, immigrants, homosexuals, Jews, and women, whereas white Anglo-Saxon entrepreneurs are underrepresented. This observation reveals the Bohemian character of Baraka's Black Cultural Nationalism, which, even in the process of negation, retains middle-class traits and prejudices.[24]

It is this Bohemianism which makes Baraka's expression of nationalism dubious as a counterstrategy that could mobilize effective solidarity among the oppressed. As both Baraka and Karenga would criticize themselves in later years, their fiercely pursued Black cultural nationalism was an "exaggerated exoticism" brought about by their "tendency to talk revolution from the *partial perception* of culture, instead of from lessons learned from global history and struggle."[25] While it is, perhaps, important as a phase of negation which every nonwhite intellectual had to go through in order to "decolonize" himself, Black cultural nationalism does not provide a strategy to "unite the many to defeat the few."

2. THE BLACK AESTHETIC

Baraka's propagation of a "Black Aesthetic" was not a sudden act, but the result of a gradual radicalization of his earlier views. His espousal of Black consciousness, Black Power, and Karenga's Black Value System was paralleled by an increasingly ethnocentric definition of the function of art. Under the pressures of aestheticized Black cultural nationalism, Baraka advocated a politicized art. The "pragmatic" value of a work of art, its effect on audiences, and especially Black audiences, was to be more important than its expressive or mimetic qualities. In Baraka's concept of a Black Aesthetic, the transmission of a message (often, Karenga's "values") from a teaching Black author to a learning Black audience is the touchstone of literary achievement; other considerations are of secondary importance. In order to move from fiction to reality, from "white" literature to "Black" life, Baraka endorsed the strategy of extreme literary functionalism.

This is, on the surface, a total reversal of his earlier Beat aesthetic, which could be characterized by such terms as "spontaneous, individual, and purpose-free." Karenga's and Baraka's Black Aesthetic, however, demands an art that is "functional, collective, and committing."[26] In an essay characteristically entitled "Black (Art) Drama is the Same as Black Life," Baraka argues that

Black Art tries to force consciousness on Black People. It is moral and political, but, if it is to be effective, it must come at us with more form and more feeling than sociology statistics. It must be the actual life of the streets and our minds on those streets. Pictures of black reality and black theater should be able to be exchanged easily as is shown here from stage to street without great disparity. The only difference must be the clarity and directness of the art. . . . (UN 55, p. 76)

The Black Aesthetic still attempts to pursue Baraka's old goal of bridging art and life; but the Karenga paraphrases add a new element. Baraka writes in *10 Phases,* the schooling material for Black nationalist cadres:

Revolutionary Art

1. Collective—must be created out of the context of the people. (In Afrika, art was done by all for all. The art object was not as important as the Soul force behind the creation.)
2. Functional—must possess a relevant and meaningful social message. It can not be art for arts sake, it must be art for the sake of a purpose.
3. Committing—when you see it, it should commit you to some feeling of action and realize the need to move, change and create within the framework of Revolution.

The new aesthetic guidelines required a redefinition of Baraka's literary prototypes. He no longer rejected tne Black literary tradition as middle-class, middle-brow, imitative, and second-rate. In "Philistinism and the Negro Writer," he praised DuBois, Wright, Hughes, Toomer, Ellison, Himes, and Baldwin for having given "top-level performances in the areas in which each functioned" (UN 36, pp. 58–59). Without much analysis of the works of his Black literary predecessors, Baraka felt that "Negro literature has always been, in America, direct social response, which is, I think, the best kind of literature" (UN 36, p. 57).

This wholesale reappraisal of Black literature was accompanied by a very detailed denunciation of Baraka's white exprototypes and literary friends. In "Poetry and Karma," Baraka distances himself from "White Christian Poetry" in general, since it lacks "fire music" and follows " 'academic' rhythms, passed across desks like canceled stamps" (R 18, 19). Although this generalization is still part of Baraka's traditional dislike for *academic* poetry, the essay becomes more specific and attempts to discard *white* poetry as part of white America. In this process, Baraka rids himself not only of the "McKinley age poets" (R 20), but also strikes at the center of his own artistic socialization:

White poetry is like white music (for the most part, and even taking into account those "imitations" I said, which are all as valid as W C Williams writing about Bunk Johnson's band. Hear the axles turn, the rust churned and repositioned. The death more subtly or more openly longed for.

Creeley's black box, Olson's revivification of the dead, Ginsberg's screams at his own shadowy races. . . . my god, they got a buncha ideas, and really horrible crap between them and anything meaningful. They probably belch without feeling. (R 23)

Directing his works at Black audiences, Baraka rejects "white," accepts his version of "Black" values, and defines his artistic intentions with visions of doomsday, with the racist rhetoric of hatred and violence and with the millennial expectation of a Black future beyond Black-white contradictions. In 1965, Baraka wrote to the *Amsterdam News:*

If my words seem full of hate, they are. For too long we have been instructed to Love Our Enemies. But I will love them only when they are safe in Hell where they belong. Until then, the only thing that will flow from my pen, or give me any peace at all will be a violent uncontainable hatred for the white man and his hellish vision of the world. And I would like to see all Black People filled with such hatred that flames would leap from their eyes. A cleansing Black Fire that would again make the earth a sanitary beautiful place. (UN 34)

The apocalyptic rhetoric is sustained throughout many works produced in this period, e.g. in the title of an essay, "The Fire Must Be Permitted To Burn Full Up" (R 117). The new Black world can rise, like a Phoenix, from the ashes of the razed West, or like a New Ark from the conflagration that was prophesied after the deluge; and Black Art shall bring about the ascent of the "post-American form" of "afterwhiteness" (R 34). In this vision, art and life form a sacral, fiery union, in which plays "break heads, and tear down buildings" (R 34). Committed art is not merely a supportive element for revolutionary politics; it is, in Baraka's Black Aesthetic, *in itself* a forceful agent of social change. In this aspect, Baraka goes far beyond Karenga's maxim that "Black art must expose the enemy, praise the people and support the revolution."[27] For the Black modernist Baraka, literature must not only be committed and supportive, it must be activist, or else it is of little value. Using the example of the theater, Baraka explained that showing

the lives of "Negroes" doesn't have anything to do with my definition of Black Theater. Black Theater has to be making a dynamic statement and be of itself an act of liberation. (UI 16, p. 32)

Only the artist involved in such dynamically revolutionary creation can overcome alienation from Black people and become an "organic part of the community," the works of "the uncommitted artist" always remain outside the community as "an alien kind of thing" (UI 16, p. 33). In terms of Baraka's earlier framework, this is a continuation of the distinction between dynamic "art-ing" and uncommitted "trophies," between "names" and "bodies;" to be revolutionary and totally in tune with "the people themselves" in the creative act is to be "art-ing;" to use Black literature as a commercial product, a thing, is to "pimp" (R 111–15). The demand for the creation of a "space" through style, which informed the writing of *Dante,* now becomes an appeal for the creation of a Black nation through a Black aesthetic.

For the conscious "artist of the people," the "idea of the so-called educated intellectual being isolated from communities is Western European alienation" (UI 9). The Black artist has a revolutionary function "right in the center of the community." More important than a lawyer or another specialized professional, the artist performs a crucial function in response to the people's most basic needs:

Art is supposed to be a part of a whole life of the community. Like, scholars are supposed to be a part of the community. A person who has trouble should walk across the street to a scholar, who'll be the heaviest person in that vicinity on that subject, and ask about that. Art is to decorate people's houses, their skin, their clothes, to make them expand their minds, and it's supposed to be right in the community. (UI 7,p. 53)

Using a commercial metaphor (which, in a Bohemian context often denotes the *épicier,* the philistine antagonist to the world of the arts), Baraka asserts that art is "supposed to be as essential as a grocery store" (UI 7,p. 53). This functionalism in Baraka's Black Aesthetic also affects his preference of genres: poetry and drama are seen as better means of pragmatic art than prose fiction. "Black 'Revolutionary' Poets Should Also Be Playwrights" (UN 60), but not necessarily novelists. Prose fiction finds no mention in Baraka's systematic "Communications Project" (UN 45). Since Baraka's Black Aesthetic advocates pragmatic art, the touchstone of evaluation has to be *effect*. The goal is to write "successful" art in the sense of art that reaches and changes its intended audience. For this purpose, simplicity and popularity may become the marks of excellence:

The mass, the body, must be moved. . . . The art must be common expression of the people. The political striving given an aspect that will make it easier to learn. Not MORE DIFFICULT . . . BROTHER JONES!!!, but simpler, faster, stronger, harder, more humbling, more uplifting. Work on directness and simplicity. Work on MASS MOVE-MENT. Create reality larger so it makes more impact isolated. Feed programs into the political reality of Black people. (UN 55, p. 82)

The emphasis on the *impact* of literature of the Black Aesthetic necessarily limits artistic freedom; indeed, the Black Aesthetic is, in that respect, a reversal of the earlier Beat demand that "I *must* be completely free to do just what I want, in the poem" (UN 6, p. 424). Now, the artist's "commitment to certain goals" is of primary importance; and only after accepting this commitment can the artist espouse artistic freedom as "the right to express those goals in any way your personality . . . conceives of it" (UI 9).

The Black collectivism of the Black Aesthetic, however, appears to be more of an outgrowth than a negation of Baraka's earlier notions of art. The attempt to reach Black audiences forced Baraka to deny the validity of "white" criticism and, occasionally, to exclude whites from attending readings or performances, since "You all have enough theaters without this one" (UI 7,p. 53). Baraka gives his cadres "4 Reasons Why We Don't Allow Whites In Soul Session":

1. SPACE—Hospital of a sort, not enough room for Blacks.
2. SECURITY—Protection of whites from Blacks who discover how they've been tricked.
3. SOUL—Whites cramp soul. Blacks try to justify themselves in front of whites.
4. SINCERITY—If whites are sincere, they can help in their absence, by their absence.

When expressed in those terms, the Black Aesthetic may be seen as a radical solution to problems with biracial audiences as dis-

cussed, e.g., by James Weldon Johnson in "The Dilemma of the
Negro Author."[28] Not infrequently, however, this argument is presented in conjunction with a concept of a Black mystique, a quasireligious element inscrutable to outsiders, when Baraka celebrates
the term "soul," "our connection, our relation with the infinite," as
"the power of Kuumba" (R 142). This irrational exclusivism in
Baraka's Black Aesthetic is, perhaps, not as unrelated to the Beat
aesthetic as it may appear.

According to Baraka's narcissistic Beat aesthetic, the "creative
climax can never be the reader's" since the "*actual* experience . . .
is experienced only by the writer" (UN 2, p. 255). This quite obviously exclusivist formulation of 1959 referred to the artistic experience of the Bohemian as an *individual* outsider, whereas the
exclusivism of the Black Aesthetic of the 1960s was based on the
category of a separate *Black* experience. This new view of Black
people *as a whole* as creative outsiders, as a "community of nonconformists" (H 93), whose experience is available and intelligible
only to other Blacks and whose art appreciation therefore can
never be the white reader's, poses the question whether Baraka's
individualism has been "collectivized" or whether the Black collectivity has merely been "individualized," bohemianized, and
usurped for artistic ends.

Some prominent critics like Richard Gilman have accepted Black
exclusivism at face value and declared a "moratorium on the public
act of judgment"[29] of the new Black literature. But while it is
indeed very difficult to evaluate any literature which defines itself
exclusivistically and its function pragmatically, the new Black literature of the cultural nationalist movement of the 1960s remains a
part of the tradition of politically and aesthetically avant-gardist literature. For those readers of Baraka who are hesitant to accept that
exclusivism is, after all, a widespread avant-gardist strategy and not
an absolute reality, it may be useful to compare Baraka's narcissistic Beat aesthetic with his definition of an emerging Black aesthetic.

On December 29, 1965, Baraka participated in a panel on "Jazz
and Revolutionary Black Nationalism," which set the tone for many
similar rituals to come. Baraka declared that, given the situation of

Black-white enmity in America, a white listener could never "like" or understand the music of Archie Shepp, Ornette Coleman, or Albert Ayler: ". . . even in the kind of casual processes that your aesthetic tastes dictate—that is, 'I like this, I don't like that'— you're still defining what you want your world to be, what your culture is, and you're projecting your culture and your domination on the world." When socialist music critic Frank Kofsky replied that he could hear a "revolutionary consciousness" in Shepp's and Ayler's music and that the line should be drawn between people who share this consciousness and people who do not, Baraka gave an answer which illuminates the transformation from Beat exclusivism to Black exclusivism. Insisting on a white-Black opposition, Baraka parallels the difference between white listeners like Kofsky and Black musicians like Shepp with the "difference between a man watching someone have an orgasm and someone having an orgasm."[30] The sexual metaphor which Baraka once used in order to separate any artist's experience from that of any audience now is introduced to separate the Black experience (shared by Black performers *and* audience) from white audiences. The persistence of the orgasmic formula, familiar from Mailer and Kerouac, attests to the Bohemian roots of Baraka's ethnocentric Black aesthetic.

The validity of the demand for a functional, collective, and committing art to serve an oppressed minority is self-evident. However, the Bohemian elements in Baraka's Black Aesthetic provide some paradoxical interference with this demand. Baraka's attempt to build a "New Ark" for Black survival is affected by his Bohemianism, which always moves from art, and from the elitism of the artist, to life, from mind to matter, from consciousness to reality. Therefore, Baraka could subjugate art to politics and, at the same time, overestimate the importance of art. His "assassin poems," "plays that break heads," and music that sets out "to destroy the ghetto" can very easily become substitutes for real political action; and his belief that "art will create politics and politics will create art" (UN 55, p. 82) must remain wishful thinking as long as politics is seen as determined exclusively by culture and race. The Black Arts Movement may now be seen as an *Arts* Movement, which was often less than supportive of the *political* movements of the 1960s.[31]

Perhaps the most persistent aesthetic goal of the movement which Baraka helped to shape was a revolutionary modernization of Black literature. In order to terminate the colonial status[32] of Afro-American writing, it was necessary for Black writers to argue against "white" prototypes, friends, and critics. At the very same time, however, not only Black speech and music, but also large areas of the modernist tradition (which, in itself, often had been influenced by African art and Afro-American music) were, in the course of the Black Arts Movement and with the help of the Black Aesthetic, appropriated and adapted by more Black writers than ever before. The new Black literature of the 1960s was thus often characterized by an overtly ethnocentric content expressed in dadaist, surrealist, expressionist, and Beat forms. Baraka's substitution of Black people's expressive soul for the Beat artist's spontaneous self allowed him and his followers to exoticize *themselves*, to embrace modern literary forms and to end the predominance of naturalism in Black literature.

Despite Baraka's insistence that he was concerned with Black culture as Black people live it, his cultural nationalism never allowed much room for Black culture and Black consciousness as it actually existed; instead, he tended to view Black culture as something Black people could *learn*, or even as something that might have to be forced on people by intellectuals who had renounced their own backgrounds. Thus, being "Black" in the sense of Baraka's nationalism may mean being immersed in a disciplined acceptance of certain codes, may mean being "modernized." It seems doubtful that people generally, or Black people in particular, have to be de-brainwashed against "l'art pour l'art" or "New Criticism." Baraka's strategies often reveal that he is really thinking of his own past when he attempts to exorcise absurd drama, or that he silently equates people's consciousness with popular culture, which convinces him that de-brainwashing is necessary. While rhetorically people-oriented, tradition-conscious, and folk-directed, Baraka may be a modernizer who attempts to impose new synthetic religious-

cultural constructions which he calls Black. Thus it is at least paradoxical that Karenga propagated a Napoleonic military organization
as very Black, while denouncing the blues as "invalid," since they
teach resignation. And it is equally puzzling that many writers of
the Black Arts Movement were formally Western avant-gardists,
although they expressed strong ethnic exhortation. The demand for
a "collective" art was often a camouflage for individualistic, mod-
ernizing artists who feigned collectivity. Despite all the invocation
of "the people," despite the claims that alienation has been transcended in Black cultural nationalism, there remains a struggle between the elitist writer and the people who are to learn the right
Black consciousness from him. Writing "for the people" may mask
a deep-seated opposition to the people. In this context, the elements of opposition to other groups of people—women, Jews, homosexuals—are indicative of a larger opposition between artist and
people.

9 The Blacker Arts: Poetry and Drama of Black Cultural Nationalism

1. THE BROKEN SHELL: *BLACK MAGIC* AND OTHER POETRY

> *"Harlem is vicious*
> *modernism"*
> —"Return of the Native" (B 108)

In the poetry after *The Dead Lecturer*, many of Baraka's traditional themes and structural elements are continued; his new poems include autobiographical pieces, are concerned with grandparents ("The Scholar," UP 59) and mother ("leroy," B 217), and deal with the themes of love ("The World Is Full of Remarkable Things," B 193), alienation ("Citizen Cain," B 8), and amply with American popular culture (B 44, 76, 81, 89–90, 207–8 and, especially, "Three Movements and a Coda," B 103–4). Yet the poetic voice is new and different, indicative of great changes which have taken place since *"An Agony. As Now."* The "thing inside" that was almost "suicided" by a confining shell liberates itself in Baraka's poetry of the mid-1960s.

In the poem "The Evolver" (UP 69), Baraka illustrates this struggle of the "inside" against the enclosure; and the poetic formula is both a continuation of the struggle for self-liberation under bourgeois façades (and Eliot shell) and an expression of the new ethnic polarization:

> *listen to the somber deepness of black singing soul*
> *the emptiness and silence of absolute stillness . . . manifest*

John Coltrane

*the emptiness and stillness in the middle of the wrapped around
flailing*

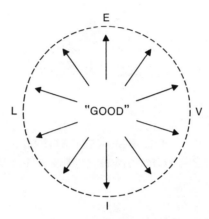

Limit to the expanding whole (UP 69)

The expanding inner identity ("GOOD") is to break through the
shell ("EVIL" or "VILE," but, once inverted: "LIVE") in order to
become one with Black people through the example of Black
music. This configuration allows a poetic consciousness which originated in a narcissistic, symbolic rebellion to claim a collective ethnic identity.

The celebration of self-liberation from the "white" literary shell
tended to move the poetic "I" away from any shaping influences
whatsoever; several poems are "screams," dadaist games with
sounds or keys on the typewriter, or free expressions of everything
that was once repressed, from political anger to violent anti-
Semitism, from self-tormenting introspection to a harsh exorcism of
the "devils" in the poet's own past. Once the shell was broken, the
poetry tended to be self-consciously formless.

In *Black Magic* (1969), the explosions of the inner self outweigh
and outnumber the serious attempts at a new Black poetry.
Baraka's struggles with his emerging new voice often take place in
close proximity to Dadaist and Surrealist prototypes; but much of
this poetry of the Id is poetically inferior to his earlier works.

"Vowels 2" (B 189–91) celebrates the explosion of the inner self
in terms reminiscent of Kurt Schwitters' sonnets in original sounds:

Freeeeeeeeeeeeeeeeeeeee
Freeeeeeeeeeeeeeeeeeeee
Freeeeeeeeeeeeeeeeeeeee
> *EEE EEE EEE*
> *EEE EEE EEE*
> *EEE EEE EEE*
> *EEE EEE EEE*

Freeeeeeeeeeeeeeeeeeeee
> *BURST* (B 189)

The scream, so often invoked in Baraka's earlier poetry, now moves into the foreground of the poems. "Trespass Into Spirit" (B 151–52) is even more "abstract" than the shouting of free! and burst! in "Vowels 2."

> *aaaaaaaaaaaaaaaaaaaahahaaha ahahaaneene*
> > *neeeeneeaahaaahneeeahhh*

> . . .

> *dehhhhh dehhhh dadadadadad ehhhhhehehehehehe*
> *dededededededededededededeed aaaaaaaaaaaaa*
> > *—A Chant to rise with all*
> *with all rising thru and let the scope*
> *diry jsolekks eoo fjoel fjkks ei OO*
> > *dkkle;pspekl'melks;;a;;sll*
> *a;; ,ome. tje rpse. asmd;;e; rwodespimd;;s kek½w ½½*
> *k;;;;a ;;;dkp*
> > *the machines head is gone* (B 151–52)

The poem's way of trespassing into spirit is merely a transcription of a dada scream and the dissatisfaction with the typewriter as (Olson's) Bohemian toy (cf. R 156); the result is sufficiently exclusivist, but demonstrates the difficulties of modernist writers who are trying to break away from form and intelligibility into arbitrariness. "When will the arbitrary be given the position it deserves in the formation of works and ideas?"[1] André Breton once asked. Baraka attempts to give an answer in *Black Magic* by assigning aesthetic arbitrariness a supportive position in a Black revolution; in other words, by making spontaneity a specifically *Black* quality which supposedly moves poems such as "Vowels 2" and "Trespass Into Spirit" out of the realm of white Western poetry. In "Gatsby's

Theory of Aesthetics" Baraka affirms that arbitrariness "is the only thing worth living for" (B 41; for more F. Scott Fitzgerald, B 159). His poems of arbitrariness may thus reveal that "Form Is Emptiness" (B 155) and indulge in often repulsive images of anti-Semitic violence:

> *Smile, jew. Dance, jew. Tell me you love me, jew. I got*
> *something for you now though. I got something for you, like you dig,*
> *I got. I got this thing, goes pulsating through black everything*
> *universal meaning. I got the extermination blues, jewboys. I got*
> *the hitler syndrome figured. . . .* (*B 154*)

The recurrence of such images is all the more frightening since they are accompanied by a new tone of militaristic dogmatism in a "holy" warfare of racial revenge.

> *All greys must be terminated immediately*
> *Project cutoff date moved up Fifty Years*
> *End of species must be assured.*
> (*"Attention Attention," B 135*)

The new poetry seems torn between anarchistic spontaneity and militaristically ordered aggression. After the "Eliot shell" was broken, Baraka's most abstract modernist phase coincided with his most inhumane and reactionary works.

One of Baraka's most typical nationalist poems, "Black Art" (B 116–17),[2] is an expression of his Black Aesthetic, but is striking for its venomous language and for its rhetorical violence. The poem characteristically casts the "negro-leader," the "Liberal," the "jew-lady," or the Eliotic "owner-jews" as the enemies. The "abstract" and arbitrary sounds "rrrrrrrrrrrrrr . . . tuhtuhtuhtuhtuhtuh tuhtuhtuh" are now the volley-shot sounds of "poems that kill" these enemies. The poem itself is to commit the violence that Baraka considers the prerequisite for the establishment of a Black world. By becoming an "assassin" the poem becomes political; and art merges with life by leaving its artfulness behind. Only this process makes an art that is as organic as a "tree."[3] Admittedly, the poem

must abandon poetry in order to perform this function. "Black Art"
implies that poetry must die so that the poem can kill.

But why does Baraka's poem kill Jews—who had once been his
metaphor for Blacks? Precisely for this reason. In Baraka's nationalist world view, Jews remain images of *assimilated* Negroes (who
are not spared Baraka's poetic violence, either). Baraka now regrets
and renounces his own anti-Semitic phase and sees it as a "reactionary thing," an aberration suggested by bourgeois Black nationalism. (The Nation of Islam, e.g., distributed revised versions of
Czarist anti-Semitic propaganda.) As a reaction to the success of the
Black-Jewish alliance in the civil rights movement, anti-Semitism
became, perhaps, even a matter of radical chic among Black nationalists of the late 1960s. Furthermore, if we follow the para-
digms of Bohemianism and avant-gardism for an understanding of
Baraka's development, we may see the period of anti-Semitism as a
reactionary swing on the antibourgeois pendulum. As Harrison's
study of Yeats, Lewis, Pound, Eliot, and Lawrence, significantly
entitled *The Reactionaries*, shows, and as the arguments by Daiches, Kreuzer, and Poggioli explain, such outbursts of right-wing
chauvinism are not infrequent among modernists. But more than
the result of abstract Black nationalist influence, or a version of the
reactionary side of Bohemianism, Baraka's anti-Semitism was also
an intensely personal exorcism of his own past; and his anti-Semitic
references included his former wife and literary milieu in New
York.

Perhaps the most extreme example of Baraka's "pragmatic" and
functional·poetry of this period is "Black People!"

> What about that bad short you saw last week
> on Frelinghuysen, or those stoves and refrigerators, record players,
>   shotguns,
> in Sears, Bambergers, Klein's, Hahnes', Chase, and the smaller joosh
> enterprises? What about that bad jewelry, on Washington Street, and
> those couple of shops on Springfield? You know how to get it, you
>   can
> get it, no money down, no money never, money don't grow on trees
>   no
> way, only whitey's got it, makes it with a machine, to control you

you cant steal nothin from a white man, he's already stole it he owes
you anything you want, even his life. All the stores will open if you
will say the magic words. The magic words are: Up against the wall
    mother
fucker this is a stick up! Or: Smash the window at night (these are
    magic
actions) smash the windows daytime, anytime, together, let's smash
    the
window drag the shit from in there. No money down. No time to
    pay. Just
take what you want. The magic dance in the street. Run up and
    down Broad
Street niggers, take the shit you want. Take their lives if need be,
    but
get what you want what you need. Dance up and down the streets,
    turn all
the music up, run through the streets with music, beautiful radios on
Market Street, they are brought here especially for you. Our
    brothers
are moving all over, smashing at jellywhite faces. We must make our
    own
World, man, our own world, and we can not do this unless the white
    man
is dead. Let's get together and killhim my man, let's get to gather the
    fruit
of the sun, let's make a world we want black children to grow and
    learn in
do not let your children when they grow look in your face and curse
    you by
pitying your tomish ways.[4]

The incendiary poem juxtaposes the sacral and the profane, Biblical and street language, in order to launch its attack on the old
Newark and to prophesy a Black utopia after a Holy War against
whites (and, again specifically, Jews). One could imagine this sermon spoken by a Clay who decides to address Black people.
Baraka's poetic vision of an apocalypse and of a Black future life is
likely to be his most widely known work. It was printed in innumerable newspapers and journals; not, however, in the poetry sec-

tions, but on front pages, as part of the reporting of Baraka's Newark trial. Baraka first read the poem on October 3, 1966, at the
Village Theater in New York. In the newspaper reports, the poem
was interpreted as a direct, agitational "lecture" which exhorted
Blacks to smash the "jellywhite faces."[5] When Baraka became involved with the Newark ghetto rebellion of 1967, the poem was
used as evidence of his "evil" intentions.

On July 14, 1967, during the Newark "riots," Baraka was injured, and arrested by the police for alleged illegal possession of
firearms; in the course of the trial, Judge Leon Kapp read the entire, though expurgated, text of "Black People!" Addressing Baraka
and his codefendents, Judge Kapp explained:

You, Mr. Jones, were tried by a jury and found guilty on November 6,
1967, for the unlawful possession of two revolvers. Now, a person's intentions may be inferred from acts or conduct. . . . Proof of a person's intention may be inferred from all that he did or said. . . .[6]

Kapp applied this principle to the trial by reading the poem in
court, and interpreting it, against Baraka's objections, as legal evidence.

THE COURT: This diabolical prescription to commit murder and to
steal and plunder and other similar evidences—
DEFENDANT JONES: I'm being sentenced for the poem. Is that what
you're saying?
THE COURT: —causes one to suspect that you were a participant in
formulating a plot to ignite the spark on the night of July 13,
1967, to burn the City of Newark and that—
DEFENDANT JONES: You mean, you don't like the poem, in other
words.[7]

This striking use of literature was widely reported under bold head-
lines such as "Poetic Justice," "The Magic Word was 'Prison,'" or
"Curtains for LeRoi."[8] A wave of protest followed the unusually
harsh sentence—two-and-a-half to three years in prison and a
fine of $1,000. A group of writers argued that Baraka was "a con-
spicuous American artist imprisoned for his poetry during a
crisis of authoritarianism in these States." P.E.N. and A.C.L.U.

criticized the violation of the principle of freedom of speech. And Black intellectuals and civil rights leaders saw the sentence as proof "that any black man that expresses the anger of an oppressed people is going to be treated as a political prisoner." The sentence was later reversed, and Baraka was acquitted by a higher court.[9]

In poems such as "Black People!," Baraka established his position as poet-agitator-leader; after 1967, however, he came to deplore the political effects of this art. He felt that the rhetoric of violence appealed to the lumpenproletariat, but did not lead the way to meaningful change for most Black people. The poems were primarily destructive and nihilistic, not yet part of the nation-building process. They were involved in "razing," not in "raising." But how could Baraka's poetic Paterson be rebuilt?

The new "form" that could rescue Baraka from "Form Is Emptiness" had to be Black; and in some poems of *Black Magic* as well as in *Nation Time* and *Spirit Reach*, Baraka experiments with new formal prototypes. Despite Baraka's new appreciation of Black literature in the poem "The Mighty Flight" (B 161), and despite certain affinities to the tone of some of Langston Hughes's poems of the 1930s, the poetic form does not come from Black literature, but, not surprisingly for Baraka, from Black speech and music.

Baraka's poetry attempts to approximate, emulate, and incorporate Black street English, folk forms such as "the dozens" and "signifying," the oratory tradition of the Black sermon, religious and secular, and other Black rhetorical devices.[10] The poem "It's Nation Time" appears, on the printed page, as an unpretentious sermon to Black readers to "get together" and "nationfy." Despite a few cryptic references, the preaching rhetoric holds the poem together as an appeal to cultural nationalism, to move from the clowning mask of "Rastus," to the revolutionary spirit of Ellison's Ras the Destroyer and the Caribbean movement of the Ras Tafari, from "raze" to "race." When read by Baraka, the poem is highly effective as rhythmic "speech art," and becomes a perfect illustration of the immediate auditory appeal of his new poetry. Before reading this poem at the "First Modern Pan African Congress" in 1970, Baraka explained its background:

In NewArk when we greet each other on the street we say, "What time is it?" We always say, "It's Nation time!" (AC 101)

The poem illustrates the process of "raising," in the concrete sense of getting up and in the sense of Black nation-building.

> *time to get up and*
> *be*
> *come*
> *be*
> *come, time to*
> > *be come*
> > *time to*
> > *get up be come*
>
> .   .   .
>
> *It's nation time eye ime*
> > *it's nation ti eye ime*
> > > *chant with bells and drum*
> > > *its nation time*
> > > *(IN 21, 24)*[11]

In *Spirit Reach* (1972), "Kutoa Umoja" (SR 22) celebrates the striving for unity of "all them bad bad meeeeeees" into "a big big black black weeeeeee." Again, the plain style of the printed poem is merely a "score" of the dramatic complexity of the spoken version. Turning to Black speech, Baraka tries to transcend those limitations he encountered in his earlier poetry. In some cases, however, when Baraka reaches for the rich, subtle, and frequently ironic Black folk traditions, he is hampered by his avant-gardist technique of killing poetry so that poetry may kill. Such poems are usually not successful, unless they remain merely imitative of chosen prototypes.[12] Compared with the poetry of Langston Hughes or Sterling Brown, Baraka's nationalist oeuvre contains few "folk" poems; however, Baraka's adaptation of Black speech models is pervasive. His poetry of the 1960s comes to life in oral performance. Baraka consciously and radically altered his oral style of recitation, emphasizing Black speech patterns and rhythm, preaching intonation and evocation of audience response. "How you sound" now comes to mean how you sound distinctively Black.

This is especially evident in those poems which were designed to be read to music, and, indeed, to reflect that music.[13] The Black musical prototypes of Baraka's nationalist poetry only rarely include traditional Blues forms; much more frequent is the background of a popular, Motown-type music and the avant-gardist sound of modern jazz. The poems Baraka recorded with musical accompaniment are either "simple" popular songs about visions of love and unity, or complex, modernist, private pieces against the jagged music of Archie Shepp.

"SOS" (B 115)[14] becomes, with the accompaniment of the Smokey Robinson sound of Freddie Johnson, a light and memorable appeal for Blacks to "yoo-hoo-nite." "Beautiful Black Women . . ." (B 148)[15] similarly evokes images of love and peace against a "Detroit sound" falsetto.

"Madness" (B 162–65) and "Sacred Chant for the Return of Black Spirit and Power," (B 192) on the other hand, are exemplary of the more difficult, jazzy tendencies in Baraka's poems. They are ritualized "phoenix" poems, in which Baraka kills or exorcises his old self in order to be reborn. "Sacred Chant . . ." takes up Baraka's play with the word "evil"—familiar from *Preface*—and goes through a theatrical death of white evil—"Agggggggg. / MMMMMMMM / OOOOOOOO"—only to arrive at the very Barakian conclusion that "To turn their evil backwards / is to / live" (B 192). These death and rebirth rituals are counterpointed by the "screaming" sounds of modern jazz; and Baraka has read such poems to the music of Archie Shepp, Don Cherry, and Sun Ra. From the poles of Motown to avant-garde jazz, Baraka again seems to be embracing a Black populism and modernism. In the context of Black cultural nationalism, however, the opponent is no longer middle-brow taste or the bourgeois liberal, but "white deadness." The Bohemian strategy has been adapted to Black nationalist ends.

2. FROM BLACK ARTS REPERTORY THEATRE/SCHOOL TO SPIRIT HOUSE: BLACK DRAMA

> *Negro theatre must be: I. ABOUT US.*
> *That is, they must have plots which reveal*
> *Negro life as it is. II. BY US. That is,*
> *they must be written by Negro authors who*
> *understand from birth and continual*
> *association just what it means to be a*
> *Negro today. III. FOR US. That is, the*
> *theatre must cater primarily to Negro*
> *audiences and be supported and sustained*
> *by their entertainment and approval.*
> *IV. NEAR US. The theatre must be in a*
> *Negro neighborhood near the mass of*
> *ordinary Negro people.*
> *—W.E.B. DuBois*
> (Crisis 32, July 1926)

In the transformation of Baraka's drama from his major plays of the early 1960s to the work of the Black Arts Theatre of 1965, Baraka provided a unique example and direction for many young Black playwrights. In Baraka's new Black theatre of the 1960s, several different forms of nationalist drama flourished.

Satires of "white" culture, high and popular, were attempts to reach and "de-brainwash" Black audiences by parodying *Waiting for Godot, The Jack Benny Show*, absurdist dialogue, or *Frankenstein*, from a Black nationalist point of view. Historical and heroic plays established a past dimension to present struggles and confrontations. In plays which deal with culture as the way people live, Black values (often influenced by Kawaida) were confronted by what was seen as the reality of Black life. Agitprop plays tried to convey a moral to Black audiences, a moral often contained in the title; this goal may be accomplished through slapstick or serious characterization. Black rituals were the desired new forms, the ideal expression of the theatre movement; they may celebrate Blackness in mystical, semireligious liturgies, or show affinities to happenings. Baraka's strength in the Black theater appears to be in the semisatirical, semiserious play which intends to "de-brainwash"

Black people, and in a ritualized and often complex agitprop theater which works with music and magic in order to propagate messages.

Baraka's own contributions to the Black Arts Repertory Theatre/School, the all-Black theater he founded in Harlem, were the plays "Experimental Death Unit No. 1" and *Jello*. These plays are pointed examples of a strategy of inversion and of a movement from literature to life by way of rejecting the old literary prototypes, yet continuing to work within them. "Death Unit" was first performed at St. Mark's Playhouse and first published in the Bohemian *East Side Review*, but it is still characteristic of the new, post-*Dutchman*, Black Arts Repertory style.[16] The play is a short "Black" continuation of *Waiting for Godot,* and reflects Baraka's feeling that "Samuel Beckett is a precise white poet" in the sense that he represents "white decadence" against which Black Arts militates (R 22). The white bums from the Theater of the Absurd, Duff, "*Barely high on heroin*" (F 5) and Loco, "*bobbing in his suede shoes*" (F 5), philosophize in Barakian lyricisms about life and art, beauty and intelligence, when a Black prostitute appears on the Third Avenue scene. Duff and Loco make obscene and perverse propositions to the woman "fresh outta idea alley" (F 7) and denounce each other to the "symbolic nigger from the grave" (F 8), who is in need of money and entices Loco and Duff. The two men begin to make love to the woman in a hallway, fighting each other for the chance to "get it" first; at this point, the Black group for which the play is named comes marching in, behind a "*pike on the top of which is a white man's head still dripping blood*" (F 13). The group leader orders Loco, Duff, and the Black woman killed; then the white men's heads are cut off and fitted on two poles. The bodies are pushed into a heap, and the experimental death unit marches off. The play ends with a dozens exchange between two soldiers of the outfit:

> FIRST SOLDIER: Hey man, that bitch look just like your mother!
> SECOND SOLDIER: Man I'll cut your joint off if you start that stuff. I
> don't play them kinda games.
> FIRST SOLDIER: Yeh, but you'll pat your foot! (F 15)[17]

The play contrasts the culture of the Black soldiers with the world of white decadence of which the Black prostitute has become a part. The punishment, execution by shooting, is very clear, but the crime, decadence, is vague; a possible definition of the crime would come close to John Fles's list of the old idols of the Beat Generation:[18] homosexuality, drug addiction, interracial sex, and blasphemy—modes of conduct which Baraka still related positively to the "outsider" role of the Black man in 1963 (M xiv), or could consider parallel "pariah" metaphors—have become capital crimes in the eyes of the leader of the experimental death unit. "Death Unit" seems more concerned with exorcising Baraka's old Bohemian idols than with presenting a "populist" Black nationalist cause; and in this play, the Black military avant-garde kills off what used to be the literary avant-garde. Baraka was apparently moving toward a new definition of avant-gardism.

The difference between the language of the play's decadent victims and that used by their Black executioners is further developed in the later play, "Home on the Range." This short sketch was first performed at Spirit House and subsequently presented at a benefit for the Black Panther Party in 1968. The text is counterpointed by Albert Ayler's improvised speech-music—"black, blackness, blackness, black"[19]—and the plot is simple. A BLACK CRIMINAL climbs through the window into a house of a white middle-class family. After threatening everybody by shooting at a loudspeaker, the criminal directs the family members as they sing "America the Beautiful"·and the Negro National Anthem, "Lift Every Voice and Sing" (UD 1, p. 110). At this moment, a CROWD OF BLACK PEOPLE enters the house, and a party begins. The daughter of the family dances with a middle-class Black, the mother does the jerk with two big Negroes, the son crawls after a "black red-eyed girl with blonde hair and round sunglasses" (a Lula-image), and the father dances around "nude with a young negro in leather jacket who waves his knife in front of him to make the father keep his manly distance" (UD 1, p. 110).

After an orgiastic Black-white party, the whites in the play fall asleep and become a pile of "weird talking grays" (UD 1, p. 111).

Like in "Death Unit," white conduct is decadent; furthermore, white speech is reduced to unintelligible gibberish:

> SON: Gash. Lurch. Crud. Daddoon.
> FATHER, *turns to son:* Yiip. Vachtung. Credool. Conchmack. Vouty.
> MOTHER, *screams suddenly at scene:* Ahhhhyyyyyyy . . . Grench-
> nool crud lurch. *Rushes forward.* SON *restrains her.*
> CRIMINAL. What kind of shit is this? What the fuck is wrong with
> you people? (UD 1, p. 107)

As a negation of the "native languages" spoken by Blacks in Tarzan and King Kong movies, the language of the whites in "Home on the Range" is reduced to meaningless word fragments reminiscent of Ionesco dialogues. As Baraka exercises cultural inversion, all white characters become bald sopranos, while Black people speak a realistic and intelligible English. In "Death Unit," Baraka could resolve the cultural confrontation of white and Black, of literary and political avant-gardism, only with an execution squad; in "Home on the Range," the Black party alone works its voodoo on the decadent whites who merely fall asleep in exhaustion. A BLACK GIRL prophesies a rhetorically traditional new beginning as the play ends: "Hey look, the sun's coming up. *Turns around, greeting the three brothers.* Good Morning, Men. Good Morning" (UD 1, p. 111).

"Death Unit" and "Home on the Range" are attempts at debrainwashing a Black audience, and at exorcising Baraka's literary past, by ridiculing absurdist drama as an expression of white degeneracy. Against this degenerate white world, Baraka poses the orderly military violence of the Black execution squad and the power of Black music and dance. The references to Robin Hood movies (F 10) and to Frankenstein (UD 1, p. 111) as well as the very title of "Home on the Range," are indicative of another familiar technique, which Baraka now uses to reach Black audiences: he continues his adaptations of American popular culture, even in the process of inverting its mythology.

The best-known example of a Black nationalist popular culture play is *Jello,* a drama written for, and performed at, the Black Arts Repertory Theatre/School. *Jello* was excluded by the publisher from Baraka's play collection (cf. F 89) and appeared in 1970 with Third World Press. The play is a parody of the Jack Benny radio and television show;[20] in the course of *Jello*, Eddie "Rochester" Anderson, Benny's chauffeur-servant, appears in a new, revolutionary role. Rochester lets his hair grow long, is "postuncletom" in appearance, and demands his "back pay" from Jack Benny. Although the miserly Benny does, eventually and reluctantly, part with his $300 in petty cash, Rochester still wants more: "I want *everything* you got except the nasty parts" (J 19).

Rochester is about to clean out the safe, and Jack Benny complains that he "worked hard for this money"; but Rochester knows better:

> ROCHESTER: What you own, one of them appliance stores on 125th Street??
> JACK BENNY: Ohh, that's just one of my interests.
> ROCHESTER: Yeh, you own a few butcher stores and stuff too. Price ten cents higher than downtown too.
> JACK BENNY: Look, I'm not there, I don't control the policies. I'm a comedian, an *artist*. You know that. (J 24)

Benny's defense vaguely resembles Baraka's own apolitical insistence on the autonomy of art in "Cuba Libre"; and appropriately, Benny is later accused of advocating "art for art's sake" (J 37).

Rochester knows everything about Benny, but Benny knows nothing about his chauffeur and "friend." In the key speech of the play, Rochester becomes a pop Clay; he voices his moral grievance, which exceeds his demand for back pay, and criticizes the medium which the play parodies, that "evil tube."

And you talking about my shitty li'l life, man I tol' you you don't know nothin' about my life. (*Quick jerk*) What I do, or think. Except you might know a little something about what I really think of you . . . ha ha, now. . . . I know all about your life, my man, and if I was you, or any of them people like you, I'd stick a shot gun in my mouth. (J 25–26)

When the other characters enter the studio to sing and act their parts in the comedy hour, Rochester stops talking like Baraka's mouthpiece and resumes his servile mask. He is so convincing that, despite Benny's warnings, "highvoiced fag" Dennis Day and

"TV/radio-dikey" Mary Livingston fail to see anything wrong. When Dennis realizes the truth, he screeches like an old lady, but Rochester takes his wallet anyway (J 33). Rochester now approaches Mary, who hides her money under her skirt, and the play becomes a satire of Black-white sexual relations. After Mary faints on top of Dennis, Don Wilson enters the scene. At first, he is puzzled by the deviation from the script, but finally he goes into his routine and conveys the word from the sponsor, which gives the play its title:

Ladies and Gentlemen, The Benny Show has been brought to you by J-E-L-L-O, Jello, America's favorite dessert. Remember, it comes in five delicious flavors, Raspberry, Orange, Cherry, Lemon and Lime. Kids adore it. Remember J-E-L-L-O. (*Big dripping voice*) America's FAVOR-ITE DESSERT. YOU'LL LOVE IT! (J 37)

Baraka gives the ritual of the commercial an alternate ending. Rochester knocks out Don Wilson, searches his Jello-filled pockets for money, says "Fuck Jello" (J 38), finally finds Don's wallet tied in a Jello bag and declaims: "Goodbye Mr. Benny. The program's over. I leave you to your horrible lives!" (J 38)

Despite its underlying criticism of art and television, *Jello* does not transcend what Gerald Weales called a "one-gag play."[21] Like most of Baraka's nationalist drama, it cannot be measured with the yardstick of *Dutchman* or *The Toilet*.

"A Black Mass" continues the technique of inverting elements of American popular culture; it parodies *Frankenstein* as one-dimensionally as *Jello* parodied the Jack Benny show. "A Black Mass," however, is also a Black ritual which incorporates the music of Sun Ra and the mythology of the Nation of Islam into a Black nationalist play which questions the functions of art and creativity. The play was written in 1965 and first performed, after the demise of the Black Arts Repertory Theater, at Proctor's Theater in Newark, in May 1966.[22]

The plot of the play is based on Elijah Muhammad's description of the origins of the white "devil" race, a part of the doctrine the Nation of Islam discarded after Elijah Muhammad's death. Muhammad narrated this "manifest truth" in what appear to be very American terms. Only Blacks were living on earth when,

6,600 years ago, as Allah taught me, our nation gave birth to another God whose name was Yacub. He started studying the life germ of man to try to make a new creation.[23]

Yacub was born out of the "30% dissatisfied" among his people; and he was a typical egghead, as suspect in his time as numerous scientists were in American popular culture of the 1950s.

He began school at the age of four. He had an unusual size head. When he had grown up, the others referred to him as the "big head scientist." (112)

Yacub's dissent caused unrest, so that his proposal to leave the country with his 59,999 followers was welcomed by the king; Yacub and his followers finally settled on the island of Patmos, where Yacub began his genetic experiment to whiten his Black race and to artificially create the white race. His method was based on Mendel's laws and on centuries of experimenting; dark-looking Blacks were not allowed to marry each other, but had to choose light-skinned partners, and dark babies were killed at birth.

The mutant "devils" created by Yacub were "really pale white, with really blue eyes," aboriginal Caucasians, intent on ruling the black nation. Not surprisingly, "all of the monkey family are from this 2,000 year history of the white race in Europe" (119).

In "A Black Mass," Baraka takes this obvious inversion of white racist lore, designed to extend a Black race-consciousness into a mythological prehistory, and adapts the story to his aesthetic perceptions in order to transform it into a popular culture parody, a ritual, and a play about art. The scene is a "fantastic chemical laboratory" (F 21) of Faust, Frankenstein, alchemists, and Hermes Trismegistos,[24] the perfect setting for "Black Magic." Baraka's Jacoub is a restless Faustian spirit who brings change into the static world of his Black fellow magicians, Nasafi and Tanzil. At the beginning of the play, they are busily searching for a potion to countereffect Jacoub's last invention, "time, that white madness" (F 22) and try to teach him that "Everything already exists. You cannot really create" (F 25). Jacoub, however, is deaf to their pleas, and works with dedication on his *magnum opus*, the making of a "man like ourselves, yet separate from us. A neutral being" (F 27)—an allusion to *Dante*—a homunculus, a monster, a beast.

His experiment is an act of defiance against nature, and as he outlines his project, the earth trembles, the sea shudders, and the elements are in rebellion. The women Eulalie, Olabumi, and Tiila seek shelter in the laboratory, as Jacoub is mixing his *"final solution"* (sic!; F 28).

The experiment is successful, and the theatrical moment of the "birth" of the monster is also the transsubstantiation of the Black Mass; underlined by unusually shrill Sun Ra-laboratory background music, this scene is in the best tradition of popular Gothic:

A crouched figure is seen covered in red flowing skins like capes. He shoots up, leaping straight off the stage screaming. . . . The figure is absolutely cold white with red lizard-devil mask which covers whole head, and ends up as a lizard spine cape. (F 30)

This comic-book monster of the leaping lizards variety yells "I white. White. White" (F 30), the women scream, and Nasafi and Tanzil warn Jacoub that "THIS THING WILL KILL" (F 31), but Jacoub is not to be convinced. Dr. Frankenstein's feelings in a comparable moment were different:

I had worked for nearly two years, for the sole purpose of infusing life into an inanimate body . . . ; but now that I had finished, the beauty of my dream vanished, and breathless horror and disgust filled my heart.[25]

Jacoub, however, is not horrified by his creation; he attempts to teach the white beast how to speak—a satirical inversion of the Black-white relationship of Robinson Crusoe and Friday:

> JACOUB: (*Approaching*) You . . . are . . .
> BEAST: (*In weird parrotlike fashion*) You . . . You . . . You . . .
> (*Then goes into initial barely intelligible chant*) White! White!
> JACOUB: (*Pointing to himself*) I. Eye. (*At eye, gesturing*) Me!
> BEAST: (*Stroking its own chest; slobbering smile crosses its face*) Me!
> Me! (*A little hop*) Me! . . . White! . . . White! Me! . . .
> White! (F 32)

Despite such visionary instruction, Jacoub's beast, unlike Robinson's Friday, will not be educated any further, and soon attacks the women and "jacobinizes" Tiila, making her the second monster in the play. Whiteness apparently spreads like vampirism.

TANZIL: It has merely to touch something to turn it into itself. Or
  else it sucks out the life juices. Look at our dying sister . . .
  producing its own hideous image. (F 34)

Jacoub's mistake is the flaw of countless scientists in science fiction:

NASAFI: Jacoub, your error . . . the substitution of thought for feeling. A heart full of numbers and cold formulae. A curiosity for
  anti-life, for the yawning voids and gaps in humanity. . . .
TANZIL: Asking God's questions, and giving animal answers. (F 34)

Jacoub, the cold, rational scientist, interfered with nature, and
trusted "the voids of reason" (F 35). Even when the danger ema-
nating from the beast becomes quite obvious, Jacoub wants to
"teach" the monster and restore Tiila to her original identity; and
so he ignores Tanzil's suggestion to "set these things loose in the
cold north" (F 36). Eulalie and Olabumi start singing, and though
their song changes from purring to screams of horror, Jacoub remains optimistic: "I will begin to teach them. I will have Tiila back.
. . . (*Gesturing*) I will prove the power of knowledge. The wis-
dom locked beyond the stars" (F 38).

His gesturing is a signal for the monsters to "spring into anima-
tion, attacking the magicians and women, killing them with fangs
and claws" (F 38). Jacoub, who dies last, condemns the beast, with
his final breath, to the caves of the north: "May you vanish forever
into the evil diseased caves of the cold" (F 38).

The play ends in turmoil, as the white beasts move out into the
audience, "kissing and licking people" and still screaming "Me!"
and "White!" The Black Mass is over, except for the sermon, which
is delivered through a loudspeaker:

NARRATOR: And so Brothers and Sisters, these beasts are still loose
  in the world . . . Let us find them and slay them. Let us lock
  them in their caves. Let us declare the Holy War. The Jihad.
  Or we cannot deserve to live. Izm-el-Azam. (F 39)

Baraka's adaptation of Elijah Muhammad's story places "A Black
Mass" in the literary tradition of popularized Faustian Gothic.
Baraka's Jacoub, an individualized character and spokesman for his

author, makes the monster through a single chemical experiment rather than through a process of selective breeding requiring the collective participation of 59,999 people. While this change from the original story allowed Baraka to avoid the implication that there is an ultimate identity of the Black and the white race before the grafting process, it also forced Baraka to present the plot in individual rather than in collective terms. If Baraka's play, however, was meant to be even more "anti-white" than the story of Yakub, this intention was subverted by the utilization of the *Frankenstein* tradition. Monsters, be they King Kong, Dracula, corpses revivified by Dr. Frankenstein, or beasts concocted in Jacoub's laboratory, evoke not only horror and fear, but also pity; and the beast in "Black Mass" is "evil" only when judged with a set of rules outside of the play. Within the context of the "mass," however, the beast is as pitiable as Frankenstein's creature—who was left companionless by his creator and resorted to sublimatory violence by mistake, by justifiable anger, or by commands from the wrong brain. The shadow of evil ultimately lurks over the creators, and not their creatures; and Dr. Frankenstein, King Kong's promoter, the Mummy's extomber, or Jacoub will receive less sympathy and emotional identification from an audience than the "horrible" monsters they create. "A Black Mass" is, to be sure, a play against white devils; but it is at least as much an indictment of Blacks who create them.[26]

Baraka faced this problem again in the criticism of white-oriented Blacks in "Madheart." The "beast" of this "morality play" is a "zombie" from the "caves" (F 71), called "Devil Lady"—a Black nationalist extension of Lula and Crow Jane. With the help of "White Magic" (F 77), this paradigm of American popular culture has "brainwashed" two Black women ("mother" and "sister") into following the white ego-ideal. "Black Man" and "Black Woman," however, are idealized as a "complementary" couple in the sense of *The Quotable Karenga* and as active representatives of the Black value system. They interrupt the white fantasies of "mother" and "sister"—". . . a white boy's better, daughter . . ." (F 77)—with the diagnosis of the sickness and the Barakian suggestion for a cure:

BLACK MAN: I should turn them over to the Black Arts and get their heads relined.
BLACK WOMAN: They've been tricked and gestured over. They hypnotized, that's all. White Magic. (F 77)

The play itself is just such an endeavor on behalf of the Black intellectual to "reline" the heads of Black audiences.

In an inversion of *Dutchman* (or, perhaps, as a continuation of an earlier *Dutchman* version), Black Man kills the white devil lady. The Black sister in "Madheart" almost dies with her, thinking that "she has to die because that white woman died" (F 78). Mother, too, demonstrates her white orientation in ridiculous invocations of white culture:

MOTHER: Tony Bennett, help us please. Beethoven, Peter Gunn . . . deliver us in our sterling silver headdress. . . . Batman won't love me without my yellowhead daughter. I'm too old for him or Robin (F 83).

The interaction of Black man and Black woman, on the other hand, exemplifies Baraka's narrow vision of an ideal Black consciousness, "liberated" by the espousal of the Black value system:

BLACK WOMAN: I . . . oh love, please stay with me . . .
BLACK MAN: Submit, for love.
BLACK WOMAN: I . . . I submit. (*She goes down, weeping.*) I submit . . . for love . . . please love. (*The* MAN *sinks to his knees and embraces her, draws her with him up again . . .*)
BLACK MAN: You are my woman, now forever. Black woman.
BLACK WOMAN: I am your woman, and you are the strongest of God. Fill me with your seed. (*They embrace . . .*) (F 82–83)

This scene illustrates the limitation of Baraka's (and Karenga's) concept of a Black nationalist consciousness. Perhaps because the devil is portrayed as a white woman, there is agitation against the devil *as a woman;* and this antifeminist sentiment also affects the few positive portrayals of Black women in Baraka's works. Like "Black woman" in "Madheart," these women are characterless, passive, submissive projections of the same male chauvinist imagination that created the image of the white witch. Characteristically, "Madheart" ends with Black man's answer to Black woman's question of whether mother and sister can still be saved and become as "conscious" as Black woman.

> BLACK MAN: They're my flesh. I'll do what I can. (*Looks at her*) We'll both try. All of us, black people. (*Curtain*) (F 87)

Baraka was more successful in the satiric portraiture of the Black middle class than in his creation of characters whose heads had already been "relined" by Black Arts. "The Great Goodness of Life" is another illustration of this problem, concerned as it is with the "relining" of the mind of kinfolk.

After "mother" and "sister" in "Madheart," a projection of a father is at the center of "The Great Goodness of Life."[27] This man, a post office employee named "Court Royal," is shown killing his son in order to be acquitted in a Kafkaesque trial. He yields to the tempting voice which promises him absolution, and with his "soul washed . . . white as snow" (F 62), he becomes the incorporation of the brainwashed traitor to his family and his race. The play works as an inversion of the minstrel tradition—it is called "a coon show"—and as a parody of court room drama; however, like "Madheart," it is dramatically less forceful than those plays in which Baraka aims at a larger group than the family and in which he refrains from a narrow and dogmatic nationalist exegesis.

Slave Ship: A Historical Pageant, one of Baraka's most interesting plays of the Black nationalist period, attempts to raise the political consciousness of Black audiences by first showing historical models of Black oppression and then breaking them on stage and inviting the audience to join in the ritual. Baraka's first endeavor to write a historical play—beyond the mythmaking of "A Black Mass"—interprets Black history, somewhat statically, as a chain of similar oppressive situations, in each of which Blacks are the victimized group. On stage, the lower boat deck of the middle passage is transformed, first into slave market and "quarters," and finally into a contemporary Black ghetto. At the same time, the whites on the upper tier change their functions—from captain and sailors to slave dealers and plantation owners, and finally, to white business men. Between the two groups of white oppressors and Black people is the middle-class Uncle Tom, who is at first a shuffling "knee-grow" aboard ship, later betrays Nat Turner's rebellion to his slave-master, and finally appears in a reverend's suit as a parody of Martin Luther King:

I have a trauma that the gold sewers won't integrate. Present fink. I have an enema . . . a trauma, on the coaster with your wife bird-crap. (SS 12)

This survey of Afro-American history provides political dynamite for the contemporary audience: the Black actors demonstrate that breaking the chain of oppression requires *violence* against white oppressors and Black traitors. As in "The Screamers," Black music is essential to the coming of the revolution; and at the end of the play, actors and audience are united in a chant, dancing to Archie Shepp's music around the traitor's head.[28]

The play is still very much concerned with relining (or chopping) heads, and equates much too easily the decapitation of the Black "traitor" with final victory in the struggle for liberation; still, *Slave Ship* demonstrates the occasional vitality of Baraka's ritualized Black theater, as he transcends the narrow interpretation of Black nationalist family conduct and utilizes Black music, African words, drums and dance in order to include the audience in an aesthetic spectacle.

Baraka also employed elements of ritualistic theater in minor short plays. "Bloodrites" (UD 7) is a rhetorical collage of a chant about Baraka's familiar image cluster Raise, Race, Rays, Raze. "Rockgroup" (UD 5) satirizes the Beatles and the white commercialization of Rhythm and Blues. The long-haired musicians, "THE CRACKERS" carry a "nigger" with them in a big velvet box marked "Hi-Voltage"; they sing, accompanied by their "geetahs": "White shit white shit white shit / hocuspocus in the clouds allright" (UD 5, p. 41). This sketch is no more than a quick dramatization of Baraka's hostility toward white Rock bands in the 1960s.

While most of Baraka's Black nationalist plays contain elements of agitation, many of them concentrate on attitudes and cultural values, and only a few express immediate political propaganda. Among these committed plays, *Arm Yourself, or Harm Yourself* is a prominent, though largely unknown example. Published in an edition of 500 copies by Jihad Productions in 1967, this ten-page "message of self-defense to Black men" is a one-dimensional effort at "pure commitment," and its dramatic form is merely a vehicle.

The New Left conviction that the police force in a capitalist society represented not only the violent arm of an exploitative system, but was, in itself, the enemy of the people *par excellence,* was embraced by various groups, ranging from Weathermen to factions in the Black Panther Party. Policemen were frequently depicted and addressed as "pigs." [29] It is exactly this interpretation of the policeman as a murderous pig that *Arm Yourself* propounds.

In the prelude ("in dark"), policemen knock and kick at the door of a ghetto apartment and finally shoot through the door. When the lights come up, two Black men are arguing; the "First Brother" is in awe of whites and pessimistic about his own chances, while the "Second Brother" displays a spirit of optimism that seems based on the fact that he has a gun. After a renewed round of gunshots, a Black man, Paul, "staggers onto stage" (A 4) and dies. In tears, his wife tells the Brothers that the police shot Paul as he tried to defend her against a policeman who "put his hands . . . on me . . . asked me for identification" (A 5). The two Brothers continue to argue:

> SECOND BROTHER: . . . You don't deserve no woman . . . if you can't protect them.
> FIRST BROTHER: (*Helping Sister up*) How we gonna protect the women . . . we don't have no power . . .
> SECOND BROTHER: And *you* never will . . . (A 7)

Arguing about the protection of the object sister, the brothers begin to insult each other. Reminiscent of Lula's invective against Clay (DS 31), the Second Brother calls his opponent "the true negro of negroes . . . the king of negroes . . . old raghead, sugarlip, heself" (A 8); and soon the brothers are fighting each other. A "copvoice" discovers them, and the police fire guns. The armed brother is struck first, the first brother next and the woman is hit last. The play ends with a reminder of the Nazi genocide.

COPS: Dumb niggers . . . we oughtta send'em all to the goddam gas chamber.

COPS: Don't worry mac. we will we definitely will. (*they laff, kick bodies, go off*) (A 10)

Despite its obvious shortcomings as a play of pure commitment, *Arm Yourself, or Harm Yourself* shows Baraka's idiom in several ways. There is the combination of sex and racism that shaped so many of his dramatic creations: the lecherous policemen provoke the Black man to defend his woman (the passive role assigned to the female is also typical of this period) and the Black man who understands the message of self-defense embraces the gun as a penis symbol of his manhood. There are verbal echoes from *Dutchman*, "A Black Mass," and "Madheart" in *Arm Yourself*. And Baraka works with his familiar method of showing victims rather than heroes: *Arm Yourself* has no Black survivors.

As an extreme form of "political" commitment, *Arm Yourself* reflects an attitude Baraka held only very briefly. We know from Baraka's criticism of the "gun-cultism" of the Black Panther Party that, some time before the end of 1968, he became much more skeptical of an armed rebellion in Black America. After the assassination of Martin Luther King, Baraka told Black citizens of Newark (very much like the First Brother in *Arm Yourself*) to "keep cool" and that picking up the gun was not the right road to liberation.[30]

"Police" (UD 2) is a somewhat more aestheticized continuation of *Arm Yourself*. The phallic image of the gun is carried to the point at which the real gun becomes a "paper penis pistol," which fulfills many of its multiple functions. As a murderous weapon, it is directed by a Black policeman first against his brother and then against himself; and as a sexual tool, it is admired for its size by white policemen. The Black policeman is portrayed therefore as a traitor and a pervert, who kills the Black manhood of others and self in order to be "eaten" by white "pigs," the true savages who are tearing off chunks of the Black policeman's flesh in the last scene. The mixture of Black cultural nationalist sentiment and sexual symbology, of agit-prop and Bohemianism, hardly amounts to a "functional" political play.

One of Baraka's last published Black nationalist plays of agitation, "Junkies Are Full of (SHHH . . .)," is an ethnic-stereotype show which agitates against the drug traffic as an Italian-Jewish business with Black pushers and victims. In the play, there is a drug chain consisting of "Mr. Confetti," the Mafiosi Frankie and Sammy, and the Jews Izzy and Irving, which is busted, not by the police, of course, but by the Black protagonists Chuma and Damu who gain Black pusher Bigtime's confidence when they offer to spread vast amounts of junk among Black militants, "Peddle it as part of the admission at the next black power conference" (UD 6, p. 20). With the help of a group of young Black warriors, Simbas, they shoot the white mobsters; then they force Bigtime to speak the moral of the play: "Please don't take dope . . . It ain't no good, it's shit, and junkies are full of it" (UD 6, p. 22). Finally, Chuma and Damu kill Bigtime—who is still willing to get high right after delivering the play's message—by giving him an enormous overdose of heroin ("shit"). The moral is clear, but the overly ethnic interpretation of the drug business and the anti-Semitic elements spoil what might have been a concrete agitation play with an important social message. Viewed against the "white horse" of "Axel's Castle" and the story "Going Down Slow," "Junkies . . ." represents the culmination of a turnabout in Baraka's position toward heroin and drugs.

Baraka's dramatic output in the period of Black nationalism was hardly homogeneous. Furthermore, his commitments more and more transcended the "walls" of literature he had run against in his earlier works. Perhaps his "extramural" activities and creations may, in the future, appear more significant than much of his formal work in established genres. An analysis of videotapes and movies (not only movie scripts),[31] scenarios of street and protest activities, leaflets, posters, recordings and ritual performances, newspaper work, religious and political organizing and cadre schooling, Afrikan Free School lessons, speeches, radio and television shows and many other untapped sources may contribute to a fuller understanding of Baraka's active political and cultural commitment. When comparing a Baraka play like "Great Goodness" on the one hand and the court transcript of his Newark sentencing on the other, one gets a glimpse of the vitality of these extraliterary sources. It was no longer in the work of art alone that Baraka tried to find the merger of life and art.

3. TOWARD A NEW SHIFT

As a Black cultural nationalist, Baraka gained prominence in America, and his role became more visibly political. In the early 1960s, Baraka's active politics consisted of signing declarations or of joining one-issue organizations such as the Fair Play For Cuba and the On Guard For Freedom Committees; and in 1968, Baraka still characterized himself as "poet, social critic, and dramatist" (BF 664). In 1973, however, the inscription under a postcard with Baraka's picture—for sale at Nyumba Ya Ujamaa, the "house of co-operative economics" in Newark—read "IMAMU AMIRI BARAKA • SPIRITUAL LEADER • COMMITTEE FOR UNIFIED NEWARK • PROGRAM CHAIRMAN • CONGRESS OF AFRICAN PEOPLES • ARCHITECT AND CO-CONVENER • FIRST NATIONAL BLACK POLITICAL CONVENTION AT GARY."

Becoming a political figure did not mean pursuing a consistent revolutionary line. In Baraka's contradictory political moves, in his antileftism, anti-Semitism, and antifeminism, he often seemed to follow a Bohemian, and later ethnocentric, pattern of negation and self-exorcism rather than to develop a political strategy. Thus, his attitude toward violence on the one hand, and his (however inverted) appeal to the Black middle class on the other were contradictory.

It is not surprising that Baraka, in the phase of Black nationalism, was attacked not only by his traditional enemies—government agencies and censors—but also by critics (and by other groups) who regarded themselves as revolutionaries. *The Black Panther* paper and *Ramparts* attacked Baraka for his cultural chauvinism, calling it "bourgeois" or "pork chop" nationalism; in 1969, Baraka was compared with Black dictator Papa Doc Duvalier of Haiti: "Ron Karenga, LeRoi Jones, and their Karengatangs" are, for Huey Newton, cultural nationalists who "turn into Papa Doc's" by replacing "white oppression with Black oppression."[32] "The names and faces are different but the madness being perpetrated is the same."[33] George Jackson saw in Baraka and Karenga the incorporations of the counterrevolutionaries who consciously mislead the Black masses:

Non-persons like Karenga, LeRoi Jones and the other right-wing blacks are intelligent enough to know what they are doing. We cannot excuse them with the ease that we can excuse the average brother who has no opportunity or inclination to search.[34]

In 1973, the National Caucus of Labor Committees published a 30-page pamphlet on *Papa Doc Baraka: Fascism in Newark*, which is a compendium of all political charges levied against Baraka from the Left, in their most acerbic form. The authors denounce Baraka as a fascist, anti-Semitic *Führer*, whose socialism is that "of a Mussolini—impressionistic, schematic, devoid of any content beyond today's 'gut radicalism.' "[35] Baraka felt compelled to publish a rebuttal in the cultural nationalist paper *Black News*, accusing the National Caucus of Labor Committees of an "anti-black, anti-Third World, Rightist tone," which makes them "paternalist reactionaries . . . supported by the oppressive elements of the society."[36] One year later, Baraka renounced cultural nationalism and became a socialist.

As Karenga's influence began to wane, Baraka dug out an older connection, whom he had once listed as a literary influence, along with Joyce and Ginsberg, Heidegger and Negro music: Mao Tse Tung, or, in Baraka's ironic phrase, "the most respected poet in China."[37] In 1972, Michael Mok talked with Baraka about a planned book, *The Building of the New Ark*, which Baraka characterized as "in part evocative of the writings of Mao, in that it is a handbook for political action, but . . . brightened with unexpected flashes of poetry." Baraka explained that this "is because there is a lyric necessity in my own self—but I have tried to balance this with incisive, instructional material."[38] The "lyric necessity" in the poet to write in the manner of China's "most respected poet" had to come to terms with Black reality through a theory which was more than an aestheticized demonology. In his search for a "correct ideology," Baraka returned to Mao, not as a poetic prototype, but as the "Chairman"; not as a "modernist," but as a "populist."

10 Marxism–Leninism–Mao Tse Tung Thought

"We ain't got the Blues
we got the Reds"
—Baraka in performance, 1977

1. THE NEW POLITICS AND AESTHETICS

It is difficult to account for Baraka's sudden shift from cultural nationalism to Maoism with any degree of precision. The reasons Baraka gives are helpful to an understanding of why he gave up nationalism, but are not an equally compelling explanation of why he chose Maoism. If we remember Kreuzer's paradigm we know that any form of "liberal" reform politics is, of course, a "bourgeois" anathema to Bohemians; and that the whole political spectrum—except the extreme right and the extreme left—is usually shunned by avant-gardists. Therefore, we may perhaps see Baraka's latest development in terms of the Bohemian pendulum on its swing back from the reactionary aspects of nationalism (the anti-Semitism, the antifeminism, and the chauvinism) to the most left-wing movement available. Self-critical exorcism of past errors has furthermore been the pattern of Baraka's earlier changes. He has always favored the extreme shift at the expense of the kind of gradual growth that requires a careful pondering of pros and cons at every phase.

Maoism has allowed Baraka to continue creating in an apocalyptic revolutionary mode, to see himself as an advanced leader (chairman instead of Imamu) whose task has been to raise the consciousness of people and prepare them for the violent cataclysms he sees ahead. Most importantly, Baraka again remains out of reach of his most consistent opponent, the Black bourgeoisie, which had virtually caught up with him, and absorbed him, in the Black nationalist period. Changing his ideology allowed him to extricate himself from a new reification process and to come out violently against Black politicians and businessmen, writers and teachers, who had often accepted some tenets of Baraka's Black nationalist message, but were, in Baraka's view, still far from making life any better for the majority of Black Americans.

As the Congress of Afrikan People (CAP) Ideological Papers[1] show, Baraka's most recent shift took place within one single year; in the course of 1974 he became a communist looking at a bus full of people (another variation on the earlier formula.) The essays indicate that Baraka transcended cultural nationalism in two ways: through the African socialist theory of Kwame Nkrumah, Sekou Touré, and Amilcar Cabral, Baraka became acutely aware of the contradictions inherent in US Black cultural nationalism; and through the experience with Black elected officials, and especially with the Black mayor of Newark, he realized the impact of bourgeois politics on oppressed Blacks, whether the policies were carried out by "white-oriented" or by "Black-conscious" middle-class representatives. Two external events precipitated the change: Baraka's participation in the Sixth Pan-African Congress in Dar es Salaam, and the campaign for Gibson's reelection in Newark.

In "Nationalism, Pan-Afrikanism, Ujamaa, Their Future in America," written in late 1973 or early 1974, Baraka still argues essentially in Karenga's framework, although he emphasizes the socialist aspect of the Black Value System—Ujamaa, cooperative economics. Leftists still appear to Baraka as "the most intensely racist group of whites," since they "denounce all black leadership except their own footmen and insist that Blacks must make the leap from slaves to international socialists without passing through a stage frankly most whites are still in . . . nationalism" (UN 89, p. 4). Baraka doubts if the "liberalism," his generously applied old anathema, of "the Castros and Allendes"(!) would suffice to "completely transform a society like America, whose principal contradiction is *not* capitalist versus proletariat but White vs Black" (UN 89, p. 4).

Capitalist vs Proletariat is a secondary contradiction in America. Whether you lefties like it or not, any serious analysis will show you that. Black vs

White influences all other contradictions in America. Rich vs Poor. Educated vs Uneducated. Men vs Women. Polluters vs Ecologists. Homosexuals vs Heterosexuals. Old People vs Young People, Jews vs Gentiles, &c., Black vs White is the most influential, it influences all the others, defines their terminologies, shapes their rhetoric, must be dealt with even after left communists denounce nationalists as reactionaries and talk wildly about the coming hegemony of the proletariat (in spotless university dining rooms) it is still Black vs White, throughout, over and above, undercutting all other talk or movement in America. (UN 89, p. 4)

In his CAP paper, "Revolutionary Party: Revolutionary Ideology," presented on March 31, 1974, Baraka already sounds different, as he establishes a "historical perspective," points out that primitive accumulation of capital was "based directly on the slave trade," and admonishes his audience that Black nationalist opposition to "industrialization, and computerization or scientific progress" may be the result of "petty bourgeois elitism" which "objectively" aids imperialism.

WE MUST STRUGGLE TO DEFEAT PRIEST CRAFT AND META-PHYSICAL ACCOMMODATIONS WITH RACISM AND MONOPOLY CAPITALISM AS OVERTLY AS IS TACTICALLY SOUND! (UN 93, p. 3)

He now denied that one can be revolutionary "merely by dressing in Afrikan clothes and speaking swahili and cultivating superior diet" (UN 93, p. 4). Baraka's syncretism is obvious in the series of demands made on the ideology of the revolutionary party he envisions:

> It will be a *Black Liberation Party*. . . .
> It must be a *Marxist* influenced Party. . . .
> It must be a *Leninist* influenced party. . . .
> It must be a *Maoist* party. . . .
> It must be a *Nkrumahist* party. . . .
> It must be a *Nyerere* influenced party. . . .
> It must be a *Cabral* inspired party. . . .
> It must be a *Maulana Karenga* influenced party. . . . (UN 93, p. 5–6)

When "Partially Evaluating the Legacy of the '60's" (UN 107), Baraka hopes for a synthesis of Black Panthers and Black value system, beyond cultural nationalism and "gun-cultism," yet in "Black People and Imperialism" (UN 100), he considers the breakdown of strict segregation as a *negative* legacy.[2] At this transitory stage, Baraka sets himself the task of fusing these heterogeneous elements, of "Creating a Unified Consciousness" (the title of another CAP ideological paper).

The essay "Toward Ideological Clarity," dated May 24, 1974, opens with a quotation from Lenin instead of Karenga; and in the course of the argument, which is concerned with Afro-American history, Baraka comes to define racism merely as "one aspect of the ideology produced by the slave trade." As racism becomes understandable to Baraka not as an ontological quality, but as a by-product of capitalism, cultural nationalism appears increasingly "chauvinist." Baraka now sides with Cabral's[3] Marxist definition that *"culture has as its material base the level of the productive forces and the mode of production"* (UN 101, p. 7), and attacks the mistake made "by so called cultural nationalists" (including himself): they take "the concept of culture as a static concept" (UN 101, p. 10) instead of understanding it historically.

This self-criticism leads to a reevaluation of plays such as "A Black Mass" as "chauvinist" (UI 20) and to a redefinition of the goals of Black liberation: "The Black liberation movement is the vanguard of struggle within the U.S. not only against racism but for socialism" (UN 101, p. 25).

Another CAP ideological paper, "Revolutionary Culture and Future of Pan-Afrikan Culture," was originally presented at the important 6th Pan-Afrikan Congress in Dar es Salaam, June 19–27, 1974. In this speech, Baraka argues that it is the Black revolutionary writer's task to "transform his culture from an exploited culture to a militant fighting culture" (UN 104, p. 4), which he later calls *"an international anti-imperialist culture"* (UN 104, p. 16). In this transformatory process, nationalism is only one step; and

if nationalism is not merely a form of preparation for true national liberation struggle which should in any progressive guise lead directly to socialist construction or socialist revolution, then nationalism, black or yellow, becomes as reactionary as the European variety. . . . (UN 104, pp. 6–7)

These abstractions go back to Baraka's concrete observations of Black bourgeois politics. Baraka sees the possibility that

the pseudo-powerful American Black bourgeoisie and petty bourgeoisie could, objectively, be the new agents of yet another scramble for Afrika. By saying Black is beautiful or we are an Afrikan people, yet representing the values and designs of U.S. imperialism. (UN 104, p. 7)

Baraka's changed outlook on Black politics can be seen in his growing criticism of Newark's Black mayor Kenneth Gibson. Baraka's Newark CAP paper changed its name from *Black New Ark* to *Unity and Struggle,* and its motto from "Black people must unify" to "Unite the many to oppose the few," and most recently to "Unite the many to defeat the few." While Gibson was certainly part of the "unity" envisioned in the motto of *Black New Ark*, Baraka now would place him closer to the "few" than the "many" of the new motto. In 1970, Baraka had actively campaigned for a Black mayor in Newark. In 1973, he called Gibson a "puppet" of the Prudential Insurance Company, using one of his favorite popular culture images: "It is a Charlie McCarthy-Edgar Bergen relationship with the Negro's mouth flapping but white racist words coming out."[4]

In "NEW ERA IN OUR POLITICS: The Revolutionary Answer To Neo-Colonialism in New Ark Politics," Baraka reassesses the developments in Newark since Gibson's election within a larger context and chastises the "degenerate negro once upon a time leaders who use the position the community has struggled to create, as personal plums for their own self-aggrandizement and individual profit" (UN 106, p. 10).

In the last four years, many promises made, have died still birth or by gradual withdrawal from reality. The promise of the petty bourgeois Nationalists of late 1960's and early 70's to bring meaningful change to this city by electing a black mayor has not come true. (UN 106, p. 11)

Baraka is disillusioned by what happened to the concept of Black Power in practical politics.

Instead of black power, we have seen black faces animated by white desires. We have seen obscure blacks become influential negroes, risen to prominence on the backs of the black community only to become apologists for racism and capitalism. (UN 106, p. 10)

Baraka sees ample evidence for the antipopulist politics of Newark's Black administration:

A four year old rent strike, people crowded into public dungeons, and what is done, some petty bourgeois negro or negress is appointed to the housing commission. What does it mean? Another salary. Another paycheck. Another party. Another handshake. Another grin. . . . Nothing to make real change. (UN 106, p. 13)

Despite his strong criticism, Baraka reluctantly but pragmatically supported Gibson's successful reelection campaign of 1974:

Faced with Anthony Imperialism in the north, our local ethnic pawn of international imperialism, it is difficult to say the present mayor should be opposed. So I will not say it. (UN 106, p. 17)

In Newark, Baraka sees his new function as a nucleus of a forceful socialist opposition to local politics. In the national arena, Baraka also distanced himself critically from the Black Congressional Representatives, whom he now calls "caucus-ians." In "The National Black Assembly and the Black Liberation Movement" Baraka suggests a popular candidate for national elections "to counter the reactionary views, the imperialist propaganda, of both the Democrats and Republicans. . ." (UN 117, p. 25). Such a move would "signal the creation of a true popular alternative to the two parties of Big Business!" (UN 117, p. 26). Baraka emphasizes that "this movement cannot be all Black,"

but we have a situation now where Black people can take the lead in forming this third force, this popular force, in American politics, which we can make sure is not merely white liberal abstraction or Black collaboration with—fantasy. (UN 117, p. 26)

Alluding to the Watergate affair in his popular culture mythology, Baraka maintains that "Imperialism is losing!" and that

Ford cannot save it. Captain Marvel Rockefeller, the ruling class miracle worker, the fiend of Attica, can't do it. . . . Capitalism does not work! It has never worked, and it must be smashed and destroyed! (UN 117, p. 27)

For Baraka, the only way to that end is his version of Mao Tse Tung thought.

Baraka's Bohemian search for the absolute opposition to bourgeois liberalism seems to have come to what he considers a "scientific" stage. After different forms of antibourgeois negation, Baraka now embraces the framework of scientific socialism as the ultimate, un-bourgeois certainty. In "Revolutionary Nationalism = Scientific Socialism" he explains:

Scientific Socialism is the opposite of Bourgeois ideology, yes, and only a reactionary so called nationalism that is in actuality part of bourgeois ideology (like talking Black but trying to get into the system) could seem to be the opposite or opposed to Socialism. (UN 121, p. 12)

In Baraka's harsh attacks on Black cultural nationalism as a reactionary bourgeois ideology, his traditional talent for polemics found a new outlet. His scientific rationalism and his equation of socialism with Newton's laws of gravity do not moderate his temper.

Baraka fiercely attacks many of his former friends, associates, and followers, among them Don Lee (Haki Madhubuti) as a "reactionary petty bourgeois nationalist," Ishmael Reed as a "right wing 'art major,'" and Nikki Giovanni for supporting "movie star penises, Rev. Ike, Black Congressional Caucus, USIA, and, lately, even Gerald Ford."[5] Baraka accuses Muhammad Ali and, by extension, the Nation of Islam, of what he terms "I AM THE GREATEST-ISM," or sectarianism, a sickness he also diagnoses in leftist organizations. Despite his explicit self-criticism in essays such as "On Being Incorrect!," Baraka never really tackles the question of how much dogmatic sectarianism remains in his own contemporary thought.

He is now impatient with Black cultural nationalism, which he occasionally equates with chauvinism or with "reverse racism," a term he resented as "liberal" in the 1960s. He constructs his opposition against narrow nationalism in the tradition of the enlightenment, where truth and science crusade against superstition.

Nationalism, so called, is reactionary when it becomes simply reverse racism, where the same kinds of pseudo-science and charlatanism are used to justify a black super race. When the same kinds of mysticism, spookism, and metaphysical hogwash (or beefwash) is run on us, to justify the rise of small black capitalism with fascist overtones, as happened with whites. (UN 110)

As controversial a writer as ever, Baraka describes reactions to his new politics in the poem "At the National Black Assembly" (HF 26–27).

> "EEK
> *a nigger*
> *communist," the lady democrat*
> *nigrita squeeked (HF 26)*

Interestingly, Baraka still casts his opponent, here a Black woman politician, in his traditional imagery of "Black bourgeoisie," from gold fetishism to hypocrisy.

> *Going to the airport*
> *interviewed by WLIE*
> *She smiled powdering her*
> *conversation*
> > *& caught a plane*
> > *to*
> > > *petit bourgeois*
> > > *negro*
> > > > *heaven. (HF 27)*

Baraka's attacks against Black cultural nationalism have been met by counterattacks from the nationalist camp. In the widely distributed pilot issue of a new Black periodical, *First World,* founded after the demise of *Black World,* Addison Gayle, Jr. openly criticized the "defection of . . . two of the leading Black Aesthetic theoreticians to the Marxist view"[6] and played Baraka the quotable nationalist of the 1960s against Baraka the socialist anathema of the 1970s. Gayle concludes that an "aesthetic based upon economic and class determinism is one which has minimal value to Black people."

Baraka's introduction to the poetry volume *Hard Facts* is an indi-

rect answer to statements like Addison Gayle's. Baraka posits the
need for poetry as a "weapon of revolutionary struggle" (HF) and
thus reaffirms the pragmatic definition of art. Whereas Gayle's
"blueprint" for a Black Aesthetic proposes a "Black definition" of
reality,[7] Baraka's demand goes further: "We need a poetry that directly describes the situation of the people and tells us how we can
change it." Baraka's previous, and Gayle's continuing, emphasis on
white racism as "the sole cause of our disorder + oppression" (HF),
as the "motivating rationale behind the continual suppression of
non-Europeans by Europeans,"[8] is now rejected by Baraka as part
of an irrational outlook on life, as a "subjective mystification" which
leads to "mysticism, metaphysics, spookism, &c. rather than dealing with reality." In *Hard Facts*, Baraka maintains that nationalism
becomes reactionary and merely serves the "newly emerging Black
bureaucratic elite" when it focuses on "White people as the cause
of our oppression rather than the system of monopoly capitalism"
(HF).

The revised aesthetic can still draw on Baraka's traditional concepts. The notion of "art-ing," of art as a process which loses its dynamic once it is transformed into an artifact, a notion we encountered first in the Bohemian period, is retained in his opposition to
an art which is like

"a teacup in Rocky's summer place," a distraction, an ornament the impe-
rialists wear to make a gesture toward humanity. (HF)

Revolutionary art is now seen as the body, the verb, the hunting
process, whereas artifacts congeal to reified names, nouns, trophies, or, in the new terms, to ornaments for the rich. If the
source of opposition to art as an artifact was once the vision of the
individual artist who is willing to express himself honestly, the
visionary quality is now ascribed to the "omnieyed, multinational
mass." In order to "raise the level of the people" the artist first
must learn, not just from one ethnic group, but from *the* people,
those "dynamic working masses." This process amounts to a redefinition of Baraka's term populist modernism.

We want to raise the level of the people, but to do that we must start
where they are which is on a much higher level than the majority of intel-

lectuals and artists. We also want to popularize, to make popular, to make a popular mass art. To take the popular and combine it with the advanced. Not to compromise, but to synthesize. To raise and to popularize. (HF)

Baraka's formulation of his new Marxist aesthetic, then, is part of his "changing same"-ness. The notions of populism and literary avant-gardism have survived, though with great modifications, throughout Baraka's drastic changes.

2. HARD FACTS

Baraka's poetry and drama since 1974 reflect his new shift. He recites the poetry of *Hard Facts* with the mannerisms of the Black nationalist poems; but the omnipresent social statements and political slogans also evoke the prototype of Langston Hughes's socialist poems collected in *Good Morning, Revolution.*

"When We'll Worship Jesus" is a poem in the Whitman-Williams tradition of Baraka's early poetry, in the oral manner of his nationalist phase, and reminiscent of Langston Hughes's anti-Christian "Goodbye, Christ."

> *we'll worship jesus when*
> *he get bad enough to at least scare*
> *somebody—cops not afraid*
> *of jesus*
> *pushers not afraid*
> *of jesus, capitalists racists*
> *imperialists not afraid*
> *of jesus shit they makin money*
> *off jesus. (HF 6)*

Like Hughes, Baraka proclaims a socialist revolution as the apocalyptic alternative to "jesus worship." Since *religion* is viewed as "opiate of the people," Baraka uses Christianity as only one example of a system of superstitions which misdirect social energies, and Islam is no longer a better alternative:

> *jesus aint did nothin for us*
> *but kept us turned toward the*
> *sky (him and his boy allah*
> *too, need to be checkd*
> *out!) (HF 7)*

In the meantime, the poem advocates a form of collective revolutionary self-worship (in lines with Whitman echoes).

. Other poems in *Hard Facts* satirize the new Black middle class and its Black nationalist art. "Niggy the Ho" is an especially malicious polemic against the once militant writer Nikki Giovanni, whom Baraka now sees making a career for herself in America:

> *Hi Ho, lincoln center crummy, wallow on yr tummy, gospel horror*
> *funky,*
> *a mediocre flunky, now she say she really dig President Ford. Yahoo,*
> *what else is new . . . (HF 10–11)*

"History on Wheels" denounces the Black bourgeoisie as the real winner of the struggles of the 1960s.

> *yeh all the 1st*
> *negroes world wide, joined*
> *knees, and shuffled heroically*
> *into congress, city hall, the*
> *anti-p program . . . (HF 12)*

Baraka perceives the new Black politicians as a "class of exploiters, / in black face, collaborators," at best as "black militants in residence." In their fascination with bourgeois nationalism they do not see the "real enemy," and, indeed, become a part of oppression:

> *babbling about*
> *eternal racism, and divine white supremacy*
> *a hundred thousand dollar a year oppression*
> *and now the intellectualization, the militant*
> *resource of the new class, its historical*

valorization. Between them, john johnson
and elijah, david rockefeller rests his
smiling head. (HF 12)

This theme, again reminiscent of Hughes, is continued in
"Clay," "Rockefeller is yo vice president, & yo mamma don't wear
no drawers," "Gibson," and "Today." Other poems are of an occasional nature and satirize Kissinger ("Horatio Alger Uses Scag"),
Teddy Kennedy ("Real Life") or Nixon ("Watergate"). "Pressure to
Grow" and "Literary Statement On Struggle!" are poetological
poems which reflect the new aesthetic and invoke Charlie Parker
against "crazy-lurk / ideal-ism / and all the non-materialist / loony
tunes." (HF 24) This phrasing is indicative of the continued use
Baraka makes of American popular culture. In "A New Reality Is
Better Than A New Movie!" Baraka opposes the vogue of disaster
movies with the theory of surplus, and the Hollywood image of policemen with the persistence of police brutality:

How will it go, crumbling earthquake, towering inferno, juggernaut,
*   volcano, smashup,*
in reality, other than the feverish nearreal fantasy of the capitalist
*   flunky film hacks*
tho they sense its reality breathing a quake inferno scar on their
*   throat even snorts of*
100% pure cocaine cant cancel the cold cut of impending death of
*   this society. On all the*
screens of america, the joint blows up every hour and a half for two
*   dollars an fifty cents.*
They have taken the niggers out to lunch, for a minute, made us
*   partners (nigger charlie) or*
surrogates (boss nigger) for their horror. . . .

If you dont like it, what you gonna do about it. That was the ques-
*   tion we asked each other, &*
still right regularly need to ask. You dont like it? Whatcha gonna do,
*   about it??*
The real terror of nature is humanity enraged, the true technicolor
*   spectacle that hollywood*
cant record. They cant even show you how you look when you go to
*   work, or when you come back.*

> *They cant even show you thinking or demanding the new socialist*
> *reality, its the ultimate tidal*
> *wave. When all over the planet, men and women, with heat in their*
> *hands, demand that society*
> *be planned to include the lives and self determination of all the peo-*
> *ple ever to live. That is*
> *the scalding scenario with a cast of just under two billion that they*
> *dare not even whisper.*
> *Its called, "We Want It All . . . The Whole World!" (HF 29)*

The poem "Das Kapital" similarly fuses the familiar "old song at radio city, working for the yanqui dollarrrrr" (HF 33, cf. UP 9) with the haunting spectre of capital. "Class Struggle" is a narrative poem of a meeting Baraka had with Malcolm X and the Tanzanian Marxist Babu, who was later arrested and jailed.

> *Malcolm was murdered a month after the three of us met.*
> *And for a generation we slept, so many of us, what that really meant.*
> *We disappeared into islam and kawaida, into sections of truth that*
> *   each*
> *veered away toward fantasy. (HF 34)*

Baraka now interprets his relationship to Malcolm in a different way; holding on to Malcolm's legacy, he defines that legacy in the context of African and international socialism, and sees his own earlier version of Malcolm as a forerunner of Black cultural nationalism as a "fantasy." This is an important shift, which Baraka expressed more comprehensively in his essay "Not Just Survival: Revolution. A Brief Historical Investigation of Afro-American Drama" (UN 132). In the unpublished poem "Malcolm Remembered" (dated February 1977, 12 years after the assassination), Baraka addresses Malcolm as

> *Comrade Worker, Comrade*
> *Leader, Friend and visionary.*

An especially congenial atmosphere for Baraka's new poems is provided by the Newark band, "The Advanced Workers," who play sets from Bebop to Soul, and from Rhythm and Blues to avant-garde jazz, against Baraka's texts. Performance remains an important quality of Baraka's art; yet, as literature, Baraka's poems have not regained the strength of his early work. Although Baraka has renounced the reactionary anti-Semitic and antifeminist excesses of the nationalist poems, his postnationalist, Maoist work admits only occasional flashes of poetry, which are often overshadowed by hammering political slogans. What Baraka perceives as a political strength in his new commitment may well be a crucial poetic weakness: he knows *exactly* what he wants to say at all times.

3. NEW PLAYS: "THE NEW ARK'S A MOVERIN," "S-1," AND "THE MOTION OF HISTORY"

Baraka's drama of the 1970s is beset by similar problems. His sense of the social has widened. Posters announcing his new plays may include the phrase "poor whites are welcome" and performances may be double-billed with an Eisenstein movie. These radical changes in theatrical policy reflect Baraka's new and for many, surprising tenet that

White working class culture is closer to and more influenced by Black and third world cultures, all of which are opposed to and separate from the bourgeois (or "white" culture). (UN 121, p. 12)

Baraka's transitional play, "The New Ark's a moverin," first performed in Newark in February 1974, is meant to be a "political statement about the city,"[9] still from a nationalist point of view. The play is a mixture of ritual, agitprop, and Baraka quotations: it caricatures white and Black political figures in Newark, and contrasts scenes in which their follies and treacheries are exposed, with Baraka and Touré texts which envision a better world—one of "progressive perfection," of "Nationalism, PanAfrikanism, Ujamaa Socialism." The characters introduce themselves in short street verses which sound like introverted signifying, and expose their own shortcomings:

> IMPERIALE: (*Enters in Roman Toga with olive branch around his
> head*) (*To tune of "God Bless America"*)
> *I'm jelly belly ANT-Knee*
> *jelly belly ANT-Knee*
> *AntKnee Ant Knee*
> *AntKnee Captain Spaghetti*
> *to you–Antknee Antknee*
> *AntKnee Imperiale*
> *Imperiale-ism*
> *Imperiale-is my*
> *name—Imperialism is [my]*
> *Game.* (*UD 10, p. 2*)

"The New Ark" ridicules Black middle-class representatives—like
Helen Fullilove, "Full of Love / Love for white people"—but in
Baraka's old way, even quoting the whole poem "Black bourgeoisie." More sketches, pantomimes, and invectives against white
"liberals" are reinforced by slides of "famous white folk—liberals
. . . that niggers dig . . . Roosevelt, Kennedy, . . . Beatles . . .
Lincoln, . . . LBJ, Jesus, Stalin, Marx" (UD 10, p. 5). A city council "meeting" (consisting of introductions by members in the style
of the Imperiale introduction) is juxtaposed to Touré's reflections
on the political leader as a representative: "true political leaders of
Africa . . . can only be *committed men, fundamentally committed
against all the forms and forces of depersonalization of African culture* (UD 10, pp. 8–9).

The play's crucial sequence follows, as Mayor Gibson appears to
the sound of "Hail the Conquering Hero" and is questioned first by
a "crowd" of people, and then by a community leader, called "advocate" in the play.

> GIBSON: I'm the Mayor and must represent all the people.
> CROWD: Change our reality! transform our brutal reality!
> GIBSON: I need white votes. I cant be Black—My advisors (*They
> ballet twirl on set w/ great frog leaps*) say its wrong to be a
> Black racist!
> CROWD: We put you in. We worked to raise you in order to raise us
> all, we wanted a leader. Not a pleader!
> GIBSON: I'm the mayor. I'm a public official. I represent *all* the peo-
> ple. All All ALLLLLLL the peoples. (UD 10, p. 9)

The Black nationalist sentiment is unmistakable, but the questions raised cannot be answered satisfactorily within its framework.

> ADVOCATE: Change, Ken or we'll dump you
> (*people crowd around*) Represent Black needs the will of our
> people to change our lives or we'll dump you—cast you
> out—We elected you . . . mayor, not for you but for all of us
> and now you freeze to the title and seat like a statue creation of
> our enemies—represent our needs or we'll dump you
> Be our arms and brains or we'll put you down
> GIBSON: I cant represent just black people. Thats too limiting. (UD
> 10, p. 10)

The play ends with the advocate's plea that "all power should flow
from the will of the people" (UD 10, p. 10), and the chorus's
demand for a change. In many ways, "The New Ark's a moverin" is
more a continuation of "Junkies . . ." than a qualitatively new endeavor; the caricatures expose political vices, but the solutions offered are vague and confusing. Written in the year of Gibson's
reelection, the play neither endorses nor completely rejects him as
a candidate.

Two of Baraka's more recent plays, "S-1" and "The Motion of History"[10] go much further into the direction of Baraka's new politics
than the Gibson agitprop play. "S-1 (A Play in 26 Scenes) w/Music"
(UD 12) is dated "Jan-March 1976" in the 46-page manuscript. It is
a drama of much larger proportions than any of Baraka's previous
plays (with the exception of the unpublished "A Recent Killing").
The social picture is drawn with about fifty characters, ranging
from "Justice Thurman Marsh—Black Supreme Court Justice—
Black petit bourgeois elite" to "17th Century White indentured
servants, poor English folk," from two "Capitalists" of "the handful
of superrich who actually control America" to the Black communist
protagonists Lawrence "Red" Hall, "Member of the Central Committee, Revolutionary People Union" and Lillian "Lil" Hall, his
wife. The play is set in the very near future, as legislators pass the
"S-1" bill to curtail civil liberties. The Supreme Court declares the
bill legal, and an immediate campaign of repression ensues, in the
course of which "Red" is arrested by "Red Squad" policemen who
use Eliotic rhetoric. "Red" has been agitating for a multinational

communist party in America and addressing Black nationalists especially:

. . . we fight opportunism, we fight chauvinism. And we fight narrow nationalism too. . . . Some people who was bourgeois integrationists last year, we had to struggle with you against the cultural aggression that had you thinking you was Gregory Peck in Moby Dick or Audrey Hepburn in Sabrina Fair, now we got to struggle against your sudden narrow nationalism. (UD 12, scene 7, p. 12)

The passage of the S-1 bill strengthens the spirit of resistance, Red's party organization is growing. A reporter, Walt Stevens, becomes a sympathizer and realizes that

even those of us, the middle class who run the biggies errands who got to dress up and live in the suburbs . . . we don't own the means of production . . . we're just . . . lackies (UD 12, sc. 18, p. 37)

The crisis sharpens as limited warfare breaks out in central Europe and Russian and NATO ground forces battle each other, as Red had predicted.

Last scene is people clandestinely moving into a church . . . we can see a split level version of it, as people begin to file in, and it looks like a big meeting, a congress, is getting ready to take place. . . . (UD 12, sc. 26, p. 46)

The play ends with hope for a revolutionary organization of the people which will, in an extreme crisis, overthrow capitalist rule. The repeated slogan "The only solution is Revolution" summarizes the theme of the play, which takes the agitation against the "S-1" bill only as a stepping stone for its larger concerns. "S-1," which was performed in New York and Newark in the summer of 1976 (under Baraka's own direction), is strong in its satirical portraits of judges, legislators, and media owners, but unconvincing in its sloganeering agitation. It seems that Baraka has staked out a whole new territory of possible dramatic endeavor and tries to do too much in his first attempts.

"The Motion of History" (UD 11) is dated December '75–January 1976 in the manuscript. The play reviews the stages of Baraka's literary career and it is thus appropriate that it is the last work to be discussed here. While it shares some of the problems of

"S-1," it is a more complex attempt at creating a large-scale picture of historic situations of oppression and rebellion in America. The play, which has an appendix of historical sources, is an inventory of sketches of revolutionary activities in America, from Nat Turner to Malcolm X, from Denmark Vesey to Robert Williams. At times, the scenes are based on sources (for example, Walker's Appeal); in other instances they represent imaginative reinterpretations of American history (as in the creation of Bacon's rebellion as an interracial revolt against slavery and servitude). The reader who remembers Baraka's invectives against the civil rights movement of the 1960s will be especially surprised to find a strong and positive sketch of Chaney, Schwerner, and Goodman (UD 11, act I, scene 4, p. 3) and an homage to Martin Luther King (UD 11, IV-4, p. 42, and IV-12, p. 53). This wide range of historical material culminates in a contemporary plot which centers on the development of two ex-Bohemians who decide to go back home and to become revolutionaries in their own communities. At first, they are shown as de-ethnicized and alienated men who communicate in a language evocative of Baraka's lyrical prose:

> BLACK DUDE: . . . You see I grew up in this country, was a child here, went through school, exposed to some of it the bitterest agony of it like a halfmoon, half lit, half smart, half slick, half integrated. Where I'm at. Because for everything I carry there is another half to me. My fullest memory from a fullest self. Why? I'm here with you . . . but no there's something more, I know—
>
> WHITE DUDE: A half moon. You asked me my name, its Moriarty. I'm Irish-Italian on my fathers side, a Polish-Hungarian Jew on my mothers side. You slept with my sister, my wife and my father's colored friend's daughter. I'm a half moon too, in a way, though I don't know what you're talking about. Except there's a side a me didn't come in the hard steamers, a side of me aint a dirty immigrant, spit on . . . no Irish or dogs, no wops, no Polaks, no hunkies—
>
> BLACK: You're a hunkie? (UD 11, IV-4, p. 40)

This interchange recalls Baraka's drama of the divided self; the "Black dude" is struggling for a Black identity under his bourgeois façade, like Clay once did; and the "white dude" (Moriarty, as in

On the Road) gropes for his own legacy of political-ethnic opposition to "America," perhaps echoing Lula, who claimed that her mother was a communist (DS 19).

> WHITE: My grandfather was a miner at Ludlow, Colorado, 1914. Rockefeller sent his boys and shot him down, they drowned in their blood fighting for a higher wage. I was with Rocky, myself, and killed my own grandfather, and laughed at his red gown.
> BLACK: Yeh, Yeh, Hunky. I was the nigger that turned in Gabriel, and Vesey, that found Nat Turner and ran and told the massa quick as I could. I helt the dogs searching for Harriet Tubman. When I see niggers come in a place I'm sitting in I duck my head and pray they'll go away before people in the place make the comparison and see we's the same. . . .
> WHITE: I changed my name from Mataraz to Mature; from Rosenberg to Russell; from Anarchist to PBA; from Molly McGuire to John Birch. I cut off my nose three times, dyed my hair, and changed my voice to a soft musical duck belch.
> BLACK: Bite my lips, white powder my face, . . . and straighten comb is my pillow. I invented jazz for Paul Whiteman
> WHITE: He's the King of Jazz
> BLACK: I invented blues for Sophie Tucker
> WHITE: She's the Queen of Blues
> BLACK: I invented Swing for Benny Goodman
> WHITE: He's the King of Swing
> TOGETHER: And the Osmond Klan's the royal family of the teeny boppers. For Sure! (UD 11, IV-4, pp. 40–41)

The Black and white "half moons" share an ambivalence toward ethnic roles; in Baraka's traditional sense, they are "bodies" burdened by "names," but try to resist the results of their Americanization. The principle of laying bare the Hannibal under the Roman armor, the verb force under the "noun" Swing, is being extended to include de-ethnicized whites who are, "perhaps" (p. 42) in the "same morass." While the white Bohemian hesitatingly suggests "hedonism" as a way to "feel" a new identity, the Black dude takes bebop as a point of departure:

Religion died when bebop was born. And when I put on those windowshade glasses, tho I aimed to put on a good suit and get me a briefcase and ride the elevator to the top floor of the new negro building, still they'll be some trouble out of me. (UD 11, IV-4, pp. 41–42)

As Black and white halfmoons search for their identities, the scene changes to the march on Washington on a movie screen, through which white and Black dude stick their heads in order to hear the end of Martin Luther King's speech, "his shadow across them."

> I have a dream that one day little black children and little white children will walk together and play together, I have a dream that one day my children will be judged by the content of their character rather than the color of their skins, I have a dream . . .
>
> BLACK & WHITE: (*lights up*) We're playing together now.
>
> BLACK: But what's it mean? (UD 11, IV-4, p. 42)

The bombing of the children in Birmingham and Malcolm X's speech in response to those murders add a tone of confusion to the Bohemian life, which now appears as a hedonistic dance on the volcano.

> BLACK: We've got to do. . . . . .
> WHITE: What are you talking about? I think Malcolm X is . . .
> BLACK: There's something to be . . .
> WHITE: Malcolm X is . . . . . .
> BLACK: We should be doing. . . . . .no I should be who should be we should be what we. . . .what we. . . .
> WHITE: Malcolm X I saw Malcolm X on television talking to Kenneth Clark. . . . Andy Warhol made a new film called Sleep last night, it went on for 8 hours and showed a person you know what sleeping. Did you read Creeley Olson's new dance? Merce Bouborn really swung at the adulterousox last night you you listen to Tobey Kline's new burp Malcolm?
> (*it is now a party scene*)
> (*Negroes there too, superflous role.*)
> COUPLE: Eat drink and be merry. (*Whole crowd is saying that*) *they begin to go into a nonstop, high speed, kissing, dopesmoking, shoot up, seducing, drinking, artifaction scene. With the pictures of the civil rights movement burning around them.*) (UD 11, IV-5, p. 44)

After Malcolm X's assassination, Elijah Muhammad replaces Malcolm's political message with the story of Yacub and the white devil, familiar from "Black Mass" (UD 11, IV-8, pp. 46–47). In the next scene, the message of the Black Panther Party is equally garbled and "comes out of the two radios different," because of the interference of white voices.

> BLACK MAN: (*going up to the panther figures and listening intently.*
> . . . [*T*]*he voice cannot be heard clearly. They're saying:*
> WHITE VOICES: Take your job. . . .threaten your chil-
> dren. . . .blacks are animals. . . .take your job. : . .at least
> you're white. . . . you can get ahead . . . no perpetural servi-
> tude . . . tarzan . . . kingkong. willie best (*over the radio of
> the blacks it also comes out distorted, but they are sick of the
> voice) and the voice comes out in argument with the black voice*
> WHITE VOICE: Welcome turds . . . citizens (*black panther
> voice. . . .Malcolm voice. . . .*"Freedom, self defense black-
> nationalism") integration—not real; progress—to where the col-
> ored toilet; America offers—agony and death; Prosperity . . .
> slavery; All men are equal Emmett Till, Mack Parker, Birming-
> ham; With liberty and justice for all—poll tax, Scottsboro,
> sharecropper, 3/5ths of a man; —the land of the free and the
> home of the ku klux klan, racist police, roaches big as
> hounddogs. . . . crackers. . . . . . honkies. . . . . . .
> (UD 11, IV-9, pp. 48–49)

Karenga and Carmichael, Suni Muslims and Hippies round off the panorama of a confused and rebellious decade, in which King's last speech appears to be a true voice in the wilderness. This is all the more significant since Baraka mocked King's "I have a dream" in *Slave Ship*. The new socialist perspective leads to drastic rein-terpretations.

> DOCTOR KING: (*speaking to Sanitation Workers, brothers have sign "I
> AM A Man"*) Brothers, we have to see that we fighting some-
> thing bigger than just these poor ignorant municipal govern-
> ment officials of Memphis. We fighting the same people op-
> pressing the Vietnamese people. We fighting the same people
> who're crushing our brothers and sisters in South Afrika. If we

talk about peace and non-violence, then as some of our critics
have said, we need to ask the government to be peaceful and
non-violent. And in marching for your demands tho we have
always favored non-violence, we know you still got to show
these people you mean to get equality, to get justice, to get
your full due under the law. . . . I been to the mountain top.
. . . I've seen . . .
(Shot Rings out, King clutches his throat, and dies)
A LONG SILENCE—then
*(All around him, flashes of light, like molotov cocktails, and the rattle
of guns going off. Black people running in the street. Shooting.
Shootouts with police.* (UD 11, IV-12, p. 53)

Newly elected and appointed Black officials prove to be part of
the old corruption, as a scene with a Black police director indicates. After an elaborate black handshake and a Swahili welcome,
this police director is unwilling to investigate the death of a Black
man at the hands of the police. As Richie Moriarty and Lennie (the
white and Black dudes) come back to their homes, they begin to
ask questions which illustrate the many concrete contradictions of
capitalism. Independently, they attack racist and chauvinist notions
which separate whites from Blacks, in conversations with their own
peer groups, at their jobs, and at parents' meetings. In the last
scene, Lennie and Richie meet again at a political congress and listen to a speech by the representative of the Puerto Rican Revolutionary Alliance, who demands the founding of a Leninist "revolutionary vanguard party" (UD 11, IV-30, p. 75). The play ends as
"the delegates begin cheering and surging forward . . . Richie and
Lennie among them." In Baraka's new vision of the world, the motion of history is about to be fulfilled.

"The Motion of History" is Baraka's most complex attempt at
drama since *Dutchman*. It returns to a divided self (Len-
nie/Moriarty) and to the political legacies of the 1960s. Yet the
play, which was first performed on May 27, 1977, at the New York
Theater Ensemble, under the direction of Baraka's sister Kimako,
is unsatisfactory in its attempt to resolve dramatic conflicts and the
process of history with the *deus ex machina* of a Maoist congress.
The ending of "The Motion of History" is another indication of how

the certainty of Baraka's political conviction keeps him from developing literature with a literary logic of progression and resolution. Baraka still intends to merge political and aesthetic avant-gardism, but in his present works, politics often wins out over aesthetics.

Conclusion

A study of a living author cannot, properly speaking, have an ending. The process remains ongoing, the "same" keeps "changing." An understanding of Baraka is also part of this process of continuous change. At the same time, the possibility exists of entering into a dialogue with the author. It is therefore fitting to include excerpts from my conversation with Amiri Baraka (taped on December 17, 1976, in the building of the former NewArk Afrikan Free School) in the formal framework of this study about him.

Question: How would you describe your literary outlook today? Are there any writers you like to read today? What is your vision of your own literary future?

Answer: A lot of my preferences in terms of who I would read, writers whose works I have concern for, have changed. At this point, I am willing to read almost anybody. All the time. But there are very few people at this point whose work I follow a great deal. I read a Chinese short story writer, Lu Hsün, who has been, perhaps, the most inspiring discovery that I made in the last year. His short stories I find brilliantly done; and, of course, as far as my own political development is concerned, I find it verified. I have been studying books, political books and actually, doing a lot of reading in Marxism-Leninism rather than in fiction and poetry.

Q.: Your nonfictional interests are well reflected in *Unity & Struggle;* but I wondered about your old literary concerns, for example, your projection of a "Black Baudelaire."

A.: Ha!

Q.: . . . in the figure of Clay in *Dutchman?* Is this concern as dead as Clay (who, after all, was resurrected and became, as you suggested, a figure like Andrew Young)?

A.: That's him! In *Hard Facts*, Clay is Congressman William Clay of St. Louis.

Q.: Is there still a pleasurable relationship to reading and writing fictions?

A.: Yes. There are a lot of young writers around. For example, there are some younger Puerto Rican writers who are very good: Pedro Pietri, José Angel Figueroa, or Victor Hernandez Cruz.

Q.: Could you describe some of your present literary endeavors?

A.: Many of my books are now out of print or hard to get. I've started advertising *Hard Facts* in places like the *Village Voice*. When I printed a poem in there, I got a very good response, letters and book orders. I would assume that if I can sustain some kind of advertising myself, on a *consistent* basis, I can reach some people, move some people, at least make them understand that there have been a lot of changes.

Q.: This is like going back to the mode of distribution of *Preface* and *Yugen* in your Beat period.

A.: That is, I guess, the best way in the first place. That way you're not dependent on people who are finally not interested in what you're doing.

Q.: But you are also publishing above the little magazine bookstore circuit.

A.: I have collected the Congress of Afrikan People Ideological Papers, but I haven't been able to publish them. There is an Italian publisher who is interested in them. Another piece is appearing in *Temps Modernes*. I also just signed a contract with Morrow for the plays *Slave Ship*, "The Motion of History," and "S-1."

Q.: Did you revise *Slave Ship* in any way?

A.: No. It's just like it was; but it's been out of print for years. There were a couple of other plays that I wanted to print, "The Sidnee Poet Heroical" and "A Recent Killing." But they said that "Sid Poet" is libelous and "A Recent Killing" is just too long, though I made extensive cuts and revisions in "Kill-ing" based on the production by Woodie King and based on changes in the way I saw it. Still, it is a very long play. but I would have liked to see it printed.

Q.: In *Dutchman,* you utilized André Breton's *Surrealist Mani-festo;* and in your poetry you talked about "Santa Surreal." Are you still a surrealist?

A.: Surrealism in America becomes realism. The basis of my whole development has been to get a materialist, a scientific point of view. My writing is now based on that, and certainly what I want to look at and read. Therefore, it is very difficult for me to find many fictions that I really want to read, because much of it, philosophically, turns me off.

Q.: There are certain affinities between your own most recent po-etry and the poems of Langston Hughes in *Good Morning, Revolution.*

A.: Yes, I should have added that early Langston and Lu Hsün have really been the main inspirations in the last year or so. Langston's work in *Good Morning, Revolution* is an event, it is fantastic, absolutely contemporary, as strong as any work I have seen by an American poet and very carefully hidden by American literary marshals. His poems, like the one to China, to Lenin, they are really startling, because when you see those poems and you know that Langston was so clear, at that point, then you trace his whole development and disillusionment with the Communist Party USA, just like Richard Wright's disillusionment, just like so many other writers' disillusion-ment, then his trip to the House Un-American Activities Committee and at the end the things that he was doing, you might not be prepared for the strength of the work he was doing earlier. Again, we are talking about the problem of his-tory; we have to study Langston's work, study Richard Wright's work, and we also have to study what their rela-tionship was with the CP and its failure, and the kind of disillusionment of the Black intellectual and the white intellec-tual. I would like to see someone do a study of the 1920s and 1930s, Harlem Renaissance and the whole communist and

Marxist-Leninist routes and the whole proletarian drama thing. Hughes, for instance, is a fantastic playwright, and a lot of his works were very very "radical"—but a lot of this is hidden. You always find out what the Right did, you know, the literary "avant" of the Right, but what about the literary "avant" of the Left? That is a gap in American history.

Q.: There has been some reinterpretation of, e.g., McKay's search for a viable philosophical position in that period.

A.: The Blacks who have done work on that, a lot of times have used more nationalist approaches to it and a lot of the whites have used more academic approaches to it. But we really need a Marxist approach to it in order to find out what happened.

Q.: Have you done any historical work yourself?

A.: I wrote an essay last spring, "Not Just Survival, Revolution," a history of Afro-American drama.

Q.: What do you think is the result of the Black Arts Movement in the American theater?

A.: A lot of the stuff has just become "skin drama." That's what they are left with, based on the actual lack of an ideological development. A lot of it began as "skin drama." The Negro Ensemble Company: that was never anything but an attempt to co-opt the nationalist development.

Q.: You called them "Negro Pimps" in one of your nationalist essays.

A.: Right. Exactly. That's what that was; an attempt to put in blackface a straight bourgeois line. Now the whole nationalist theater washed away with the nationalist movement. The bourgeois aspect of it has gone straight to Broadway and Hollywood.

Q.: In that sense, the movement has been successful.

A.: The commercial aspect, the straight bourgeois aspect of it has been amazingly successful. Now there are about eight plays on Broadway. They've got everything from *Porgy and Bess* to *The Wiz, Colored Girls,* and *Bubbling Brown Sugar.* Bessie Smith! They really used it. They milked it! But I think the whole theater movement now, when it comes back, will be more clearly revolutionary. The American art scene, by the 1980s, will have developed a very clear revolutionary edge to it. It moves beyond the Black, beyond the neoexpressionist, the happenings, and combines all these elements to make statements about this society.

Q.: This seems to be a rephrasing of your concept of populist modernism, the merger of Melville, Joyce, the best writing in the modernist tradition with social consciousness. So let me go back to those literary figures who are attempting to work along such a line. Are you, for example, interested in Pablo Neruda or European socialist playwrights?

A.: This is a stream of concern I have had for a while. As a matter of fact, I just read Neruda's Nobel speech a couple of days ago. It is a very interesting speech, but he says it more indirectly, I think, than I would. Still, there are a lot of people in the world who are basically struggling to try to change things; and that is what I see my task as: to do that, *clearly*, in the medium of literature. I was not always focused on that. But that has always been the backbone of what I wanted to do. To make *literary* statements; but those statements had to contribute to *actually changing* it rather than just commenting on it.

Q.: You have always tried to be as far removed from a middle-class usability, co-optability as possible, sometimes finding yourself on roads which did not take you as far away as you had hoped. Is there not something in artistic constructs, however, that prohibits too blatant a procedure? In your recent works, you say things more "directly" than Neruda, but is that not, in the end, detrimental to the processes you are trying to stimulate?

A.: I think that's a particular philosophy, a bourgeois philosophy. What a writer has to do is to expose contradictions, to increase understanding that you can change. How you expose the contradictions, of course, is the method, is the art itself; and the question whether you attack directly or indirectly is the question of the art itself. Can you do it successfully is the question—whatever it is that you are attempting to do. And ultimately, is the political line that you are conscious of expressed as well as it can be expressed. All writers have their political line, but when you propose that you are a spokesperson for a particular ideology, then I think that you have two things going for you. At one point, it's positive, because you know *exactly* what it is that you are going to say at all times. I am now at the point where I know exactly what it is that I want to say all the time. Now the question is, *how* do you say that. The danger is that you become just a propagandist without the art. And Lu Hsün and Mao Tse Tung say that all art is propaganda, but not all propaganda is art. We want to make sure that our propaganda is art, that you have a unity of form and content, of artistic form and political content.

Q.: When I look at some of the poems in *Hard Facts,* I can see that, for instance in the "Christ" poem with the Langston Hughes echoes.

A.: That's a good parallel. I was shocked. I found Hughes's Christ poem after I wrote that poem. Once I saw his poem, I was startled. The problem that I see is that that is thirty years of actual struggle, personal struggle. Given a good socialist education, I would have *had* that to build on.

Q.: Lynn Hope might have recited it at The Graham.

A.: Absolutely. But without this, it keeps you more primitive. By the time you discover some things that you, *then*, could have used to develop a much more sophisticated method—you have just come to this conclusion—you find people came to this conclusion thirty years ago, a hundred years ago! That is the question again of not being able to benefit from history. And Langston Hughes is almost contemporary! He was the first major poet to acknowledge me. He sent me a letter and said that he liked some poems that he saw of mine, invited me up for coffee. I knew him, but I had never met him before.

Q.: You wrote an early review of *Tambourines to Glory;* and he wrote about the "Jones year" in *Black Magic* and wrote a funny review of *The Toilet.*

A.: Well, some of the stuff he didn't like; but he was very gracious from the beginning, very friendly.

Q.: But he did not pull any of his poems of the 1930s out of the drawers.

A.: No. If he had done that too, how much greater that would have been! But he had developed into another thing, too. At the end of his writing career, he was some kind of liberal spokesman. But he was always very friendly with me and, really, in a lot of ways an inspiration. He was a *Black* writer who was a *writer*. He wrote; that's what he did. He existed because he was a writer. Everybody knew his name; and whatever he had to say about his work. He was Langston Hughes, and he was him. Then when you discover after he's gone that he was a *great* writer, that is really staggering.

Q.: Back to the politics in your own works. In your new poetry it comes, perhaps, more naturally, although this may merely be the successful end of a long artistic struggle. But it is not the same in the plays. Isn't there a problem in what you just said: you seem to know *exactly* what you want to say so that in "S-1," e.g., the notion of an impending war in central Europe does not come out of the flow of the play, but is the result of an analysis at which you arrived *outside* of the play. Do you think that might be a more general problem in your new art?

A.: That's possible. I don't know. I reckon it is the problem of meshing gears—Mao says "learning to play the piano."

Q.: Well-tempered agitprop?

A.: It's the question of trying to get all the things in that you want in and of doing it naturally. Mao Tse Tung's work on art and literature, especially the Yenan forum, has been another inspiration. Some of my own pieces have, again, a clear basis; now the question is practising, doing it. "S-1," as you say, may have suffered from showing the wheels turning rather than showing the motion.

Q.: Back to the general question of art and politics, which seems to have been your eternal concern.

A.: Right.

Q.: How can one combine the best of the literary and the political. How do you envision this process for you today?

A.: The problem is finding forms that are organically suited to the contents. I have "forms" before my eyes here everyday. I am trying to write a radio play series that I want to bring on radio. I have a little radio program, it's supposed to be editorial, but we want to put on ten-minute radio plays every week, to see how that will work. Because that will be very very funny. Also people are getting very interested in radio plays, radio drama. The stuff that unfolds before your eyes: literally, this town is like a journal of *The American Tragedy*. Every day. It's right here.

Q.: Newark looks worse than much of New York. Walking here from the railroad station . . .

A.: It's pretty grim. It hasn't changed at all.

Q.: Still, I see this relationship to Newark through your work, which "poeticizes," even in its radicalism, place names such as Belmont Avenue in "The Screamers."

A; That was a real Newark story.

Q.: It's based on a real event, isn't it?

A.: Oh, yes. That joint is still there. It is now the Masonic temple. The theater that was next to it has been torn down. You see, Belmont and Spruce used to be the center of Black Life and now it's just—whew, destroyed. That was real, I guess that's why it is so pretty, I could write about it, it was vivid, cause it happened, and I could write my own interpretation of what it meant. But New York is a city. Newark is a town. It's the end of the road. It's an enormous source of strength of inspiration, too. It's like the only thing here is people. There is really nothing else here. The kinds of confrontations that they have in this system, in this society! But other than that it is people who you like or dislike and who have a really hard struggle. New York to me is like a confluence of so many things that you actually can be in New York and not be in America; you can be in the intellectual capital of the bourgeois world. Be absolutely kept away from what is happening in the United States. New York is a highly sophisticated, legendary place. I really love New York; I have contemplated moving other places, but the question of moving too far from New York has always stopped me. On the other hand, New York is so jaded with that, people begin to think that's the only thing that's happening in the world. I remember when we were in New York they used to say when you talk about Black people you had to talk about Harlem. That people who didn't live in Harlem didn't know anything about Black people. Fantastic. That was where Black folks were. Fantastic! In the world! If you didn't have much to do with Harlem, you really didn't have much to do with Black people.

Q.: Your interest in radio plays continues a longstanding interest in American popular culture, the immense power of popular images, the divinity of Lamont Cranston.

A.: That's very strong for me because, of course, I used to listen to those radio plays; I guess a lot of people of my generation did. I suppose it was what's now the TV thing. After school we would go out and play and then we would come back before dinner-time, at about quarter of five, and we would start listening. Every fifteen minutes they came on. 5, 5:15, 5:30, 5:45, 6, we'd eat. The Lone Ranger. That was like the literature of earlier times: that whole relationship to radio programs, serial radio culture. Popular culture to me remains the lifeblood of any kind of art. That is, taking from the people and giving it back to them.

Q.: But when you give it back, you have to politicize?

A.: That is the kind of problem I have been meeting performing with a musical group, The Advanced Workers. We'd go, let's say, to some nightclub, and they'd say: Jesus, they talk about communism! Or another guy would say: You know you are not playing avant-garde! You are playing rock 'n' roll. But I think that's peculiar, because to me avant-garde jazz, avant-garde music, has no basis without rhythm and blues, old American music, the Afro-American, Hillbillie—without that it doesn't have any basis, it is not valid. You can hear it, too, because they go further and further away from that real direct, concrete relation to reality and become very ephemeral. Ornette Coleman and Archie Shepp, to me, were stronger when they were closer to a real blues thing. What I always liked about Archie Shepp is that he always had a real growly barrelhouse kind of style like Ben Webster, Coleman Hawkins. At the same time, he would play some things that were not just that linear, straight base on the same chords. He would go out, move into different rhythms and I thought that was good; just to abandon the whole thunder of people, to me, is like disappearing into meaninglessness. It becomes very boring.

Q.: At this point, the modern composer and the avant-gardist jazz musician can shake hands. Did you, incidentally, ever write a letter to *The Floating Bear* and sign it "Anton Webern?" It sounded very much like you.

A.: Yes. I was identifying with Webern very heavily at the time, and I still like him very much. I do like avant-garde music. I also like modern American music, Elliot Carter or Charles Ives. Also Ravel. They have a sensuous kind of feeling. On the other hand, there are certain things that do not relate to anything, that become so abstract, so cerebral that I can't relate to them, and it becomes very boring. I don't like to be bored and then find a rationalization why it's important even though I am bored.

Q.: This is, then, the borderline where avant-garde becomes a commodity?

A.: It becomes a bourgeois decoration, an artifact; something that somebody can *have* or *not have*. It's not an organic need for the masses of people. But art should be that; no matter how difficult its themes or methods are, in the end it should be able to become an organic need. The question is not only raising people's level (which is correct) and, on the other hand, popularization (which is correct), the question is how to combine those two. Raising people's level and popularizing. So that what you have is a synthesis of the most advanced and the most popular. When you bring that together you have something that is really profound. I am writing this book on Trane now, trying to finish it (for years and years); and that's one of the things I'm coming to with Coltrane's music. How it changed. It reaches a point where it's very close, where it comes from the people, then goes into a form that is *advanced* but still drawn so much on the people that it comes together. In a fantastic form that is very advanced and very close to the people. But then it goes off into something else, becomes metaphysical, he begins Eastern religions, goes into OM, then it actually gets further and further away from the people and gets more and more boring, too. To see that kind of curve is what I am trying to see, the whole dialectic of that. Why did it happen. Then you can get an American version of a theory of art based on dialectical materialism but that uses something else as popular as Trane to show its popular origins and why it went away from those origins. That's what I'm trying to do now. I think it needs to be done, because when you listen to Trane, and I listen to his music constantly, I have most of his records, you can hear the changes and you can see why. He becomes much more self-conscious, much more me-centered, much more metaphysical, abstract, away from what's actually happening *here*. Working people, for instance, cannot sit for two hours listening to this—you've got to go to work. You've got something to do. That whole question of just being able to lay out there, with a little Marijuana and lay for hours, that's the petty bourgeois kind of thing.

Q.: You quoted Brooks Adams' distinction between the economic sensibility and the imaginary sensibility, and Van Wyck Brooks similarly separates visionaries from practical men. Once you follow that interpretation you may see the artist's opposition not merely directed against the bourgeoisie, but against *people* as they tend to substitute society within themselves.

A.: This self-absorption makes art completely abstract. I think that no matter how deep or profound I try to be, would like to be, there would always be something that someone seeing it would say: "Oh, that's what's happening," that it would make them laugh, make them cry, make them mad or happy, educate them, but not that abstract: "What is that about?" There are advanced forces, there are middle forces and there are backward forces among the people, too. I think that there is no doubt that what we are saying is going to get there, but the advanced are going to get it more quickly. They are searching for answers anyway. The average person: they may not dig everything, but they can dig most things.

Q.: Is this a reason why you stopped publishing prose fiction after *Tales?*

A.: I wrote a long and unsuccessful novel; unsuccessful also because I have not been able to publish it. Some of the things I talk about in the novel I need to talk about very badly, but I haven't been able to get far enough away from it to get close enough to it. You're still reacting to it as a person, it doesn't want to make you write, it wants to make you feel. It's a question of getting far enough away from something so that you can get close to it in literature and write about it in a very personal and intimate way, because I am no longer shattered by it.

Q.: Once you said "I see a bus full of people; I don't have to say I am a Negro seeing a bus full of people." Later you emphasized that you were, indeed, a Black man seeing a bus full of people. How important is the racial perspective to you now?

A.: How important is nationality to perception. Obviously, it adds something to it. It fixes it in a particular matrix. Ultimately, it is just a contributing factor, certainly not the principal factor, by no means. The question of national oppression of Black people is an important aspect, certainly of everything I have ever done. But now, I see the national question as part of the stranglehold that this particular system has on all life, all nationalities, the majority of working people. Now I can take a view that is not so subjective or chauvinistic. Finally it is a question of how people live, survive, develop. And I see that through a revolutionary process. But the question of Black liberation, what is that related to? You talked about Andy Young as Clay. We've come so far, in that sense. What's good about naming Young, and I hope Carter names a lot—I hope he names Gibson, Labor leaders, Barbara Jordan—because what that means is that it cuts away the illusion. In a little while, we are going to see that it's not going to change a thing. The masses of people are still going to suffer from it. But it cuts away the illusion from race. People will see that it's the whole *method* of doing things, whether it's got Black faces in it or white faces in it, that has to be altered, destroyed. Something else has to come in its place.

Q.: But as long as there are no "Black faces" in office, this is hard to recognize?

A.: Right. That's why Andy Young makes the system measurably stronger. But dialectically, he weakens it. Stronger, because they can then say, look, here is a man who was a civil rights leader, who fought in the streets, and he is now "in charge of the United Nations," of all our policies dealing with South Africa. On the other hand, he weakens it because the illusion is destroyed that the system would change if Blacks were only in it.

Q.: How do you envision real change in America?

A.: I only see it coming through revolutionary struggle, through armed struggle, a communist party, organizing the masses. I don't think real socialism will come any other way.

Q.: Do you see any chances for social democratic reforms and the electoral process?

A.: No. I think we will get more of it, but that will not be the transformation of society the masses need. That change will come only through armed struggle. The example of Chile is so important, because it shows you that you cannot be elected to really control a society. The army, the police remain in the service of the bourgeoisie. The economic crisis in America and in capitalist countries in general objectively pushes contradictions into the direction of a revolution.

Q.: Isn't there a basic lack of social consciousness in America, of perceiving oneself as part of a society?

A.: That's basically a petty bourgeois, middle-class thing. What has helped this particular ruling class is opportunism, the fact that this is the wealthiest society ever. It has been able to use the superprofits that it's made, predominantly by exploiting the Third World, but also by exploiting other peoples besides Third World Peoples, taking portions of those superprofits and actually bribing sections of the working class and actually making it settle for short change, social democracy. That's why these traitors are so deadly and dangerous. Because they are the preachers of negativity in the working class. Whether it is reform or racial chauvinism, or sexual chauvinism, they are the carriers of it, right into the working class. In Europe, they are up against a little sharper thing. Europe still has to put up more of a front than the United States. The U.S. has more money to spread out bribes. Europeans have to get more pro forma, reformatory "socialist"-type systems, because they don't have the money to spread out the bribes. Europe has to lurch to even more elaborate social democratic reforms to keep away communism. They have to more and more simulate socialism to keep it away. Pretend they are doing it so it won't come. The United States will do that, too, to a certain extent. The Jimmy Carter thing, what he had to say: mild, social democratic rhetoric.

Q.: In the 1960s, you were one of the writers who idolized the lumpenproletariat, advocated a "surrealist" abstract violence. How do you feel about that issue now?

A.: Sympathy with the lumpen is basically a petty bourgeois kind of thing. Lumpen have actually already been crushed by the system, they've been defeated. That infatuation with the debris of society . . .

Q.: "Young ruffians from the 3rd estate"

A.: . . . that's really just romanticism. It's the working class that is the backbone of the society's development and will be the spearhead of any kind of revolution. The working class, in its determination to "make it" in society, not to be crushed by it, to raise its children, to live, to fight for what they have and to live as well as they can, I think that's much more inspirational to me. That's the positive aspect of society. This is always a tendency in the petty bourgeoisie, the drunk, drugs thing; that happens to a lot of petty bourgeois intellectuals, which approximates a lumpen. They go right into that. Drunks, Junkies, staggering around.

Q.: The legacy of the Beat Generation and the Counterculture?

A.: Yes, exactly.

Q.: But if you see the crisis sharpening, do you not think that the lumpenproletarian base will actually widen?

A.: But the majority of the working class resists that. There are obviously marginal parts of the working class that do get lumpenproletarianized; but the masses of the workers, they resist that, resist it vigorously. The process of decay, of fabulous,

startling amounts of wealth hoarded away and, at the same
time, this abject, horrible poverty. So you live and you say:
I've got everything, but I am surrounded by mad people who
want to kill me!

. . .

Baraka has been called a "kind of civil rights Rorschach test" the
results of which must be varied since "what LeRoi Jones is depends on what and where you are."[1] To continue the metaphor,
however, Baraka represents a Rorschach test in which the ink spots
continually change their shape. This does not mean that our understanding of Baraka has to stop with the relativistic observation that
change is the only constant in his literary career.[2] The very dynamic which pushed Baraka from Beat poetry to political and ethnic protest, from Black Cultural Nationalism to Maoism, has an element of constancy in Baraka's antibourgeois cultural strategy of
populist modernism; but opposing American bourgeois culture had
to take different artistic shapes in order to reflect the drastic
changes in post-World War II America. By continually forcing himself to abandon roles in which he had become accepted by smaller
or larger audiences, Baraka fought the reification process that
would make him "the Beat poet," "the angry young man," or "the
Black nationalist." Baraka preferred the risk of losing artistic complexity (which he had achieved in the early 1960s) to the prospect
of becoming a man who would fight his targets only within the con-
fines of formal literature. He has been striving for unity of literature and life within and outside his poetry, drama, and prose.

As a result of this continuous yearning, his works may be "uneven"; but Baraka has become an important figure in political and
aesthetic avant-gardism; as a subtle and extremely individualistic
modernist poet and as political activist and orator; as a writer who
helped to modernize Black literature, liberating it from the
shackles of epigonic naturalism, by becoming a Bohemian
avant-gardist *and* an ethnocentric agitator; as a playwright who articulates the anxieties and identity crises of an artist with a petit
bourgeois background and proletarian-revolutionary leanings,
given to conflicting loyalties in approaching the dramatic collisions
of individual outsiders (ethnic, sexual, political, intellectual) and

social groups; as a writer who reflects the Eliot-Williams tensions and whose works exist in the "high modernist" tradition, yet who claims the spiritual legacy of American popular culture, from radio plays to comics, from horror movies to pulp magazines; as a writer whose commitment to himself made him a social figure with a mass audience; and, perhaps most importantly, as a visionary who also tries to be a practical man.

Baraka's life and art remain very much in process—the Rorschach "ink spots" are still fluid. This makes it difficult to predict where Baraka's development will lead. Any such statement would be, in Baraka's terms, simply another "noun" forced upon a "verb" reality. Yet if the "noun" Bohemian has any significance in describing Baraka's shifting positions, certain things remain to be seen: whether his present commitment is merely a left-wing swing on the antibourgeois pendulum, a countermovement to the right-wing swing of the 1960s; whether Baraka will find a more personal way of opposing the middle class than his rigidly impersonal slogans in the current issues of *Unity & Struggle;* and whether his persistent interest in Black music and in popular culture, his Beat style and advocacy of art-ing, will synthesize in new poems, plays, and fictions, in which his aesthetic capacities are able to balance his political convictions. But to attempt to answer such questions is to venture into the realms of speculation and prophesy, and where Baraka is going is less the concern of this book than where he has been.

Notes

INTRODUCTION

1. Cf. Edward Albee and Arthur Miller quoted by Pierre Dommergues, *Les U.S.A. à la recherche de leur identité: Rencontres avec 40 écrivain américains* (Paris: Grasset, 1967), pp. 439–40.

> *Arthur Miller:* Pur produit de la colère; artistiquement limité. . .
> *Edward Albee:* Jones n'a pas encore réussi à dépasser la colère. En soi, la colère est destructrice. Il faut l'organiser, la discipliner, la transformer en art.

2. From 1968 to 1974 Baraka also used the title "Imamu." In September 1974, Baraka gave me the following explanation of his name: "Imamu is the Bantuized version of the Muslim 'Imam,' literally someone who has read the Qran, a spiritual leader; Amiri is the Bantuized version of 'Ameer' ('prince'); and 'Baraka' is 'the blessed one.'" Baraka also related that "the name 'Ameer Baraka' was given to me by an orthodox Muslim, the same Muslim who buried Malcolm X, a man named Heshaam Jaàber; and Imamu the title was given to me by Maulana Ron Karenga." (From tape of UI 20.) In 1974, Baraka dropped the title "Imamu" and sometimes signed his articles in *Unity & Struggle* "Chairman Amiri Baraka." For clarity's sake I shall use the name Baraka throughout the book, although much of the literature discussed was first published, of course, under the name LeRoi Jones, and a few early works under pen names such as "Johannes Koenig," "John King," "Duke Mantee," or "Caliph John, the Mississippi Shiek."

3. Addison Gayle, Jr., quoted by Hollie West, "The Poetry of Black Experience," *Washington Post*, April 4, 1971, section H, p. 6. Cf. also H 248–49, R 29, UD 3 and HF 34.

4. According to Eberhard Brüning, Baraka is "ein engagierter Künstler par excellence," "Nachwort," *Amerikanische Protestdramen* (Berlin: Henschelverlag, 1972), p. 453. Addison Gayle, Jr., evaluates Baraka in *The Way of the New World: The Black Novel in America* (Garden City, N.Y.: Doubleday, 1975), p. 306, with the following comment: "Though his contributions in the area of literature are remarkable, his contribution in the area of commitment is even greater."

5. Quoted by Stephen Schneck, "LeRoi Jones . . . ," *Ramparts* 6, no. 12 (June 29–July 13, 1968), p. 18. This is also the source of our Mailer motto. In a conversation in 1977, Mailer called Baraka one of the greatest writers today and affirmed his appreciation of *Dutchman.*

6. In a poll published by *Negro Digest* in January 1968, the majority of 38 prominent Afro-American writers chose Baraka as the "most promising black writer," the "most important living black poet," and the "most important black playwright" (pp. 17–18).

7. As I am trying to show, this is not only the result of a white-black dichotomy, but also part of a troubled relationship between, in Van Wyck Brooks's terms, "visionaries" and "practical men." Cf. Quentin Anderson, "Practical and Visionary Americans," *The American Scholar* 45, no. 3 (Summer 1976), pp. 405–18.

8. For the use of this term cf. M. H. Abrams, *The Mirror and the Lamp: Romantic Theory and the Critical Tradition* (New York: Norton, 1958). Abrams draws a useful model of coordinates of art criticism, which I apply loosely to my discussion of Baraka.

UNIVERSE	universe-work: mimetic
WORK	work-work: objective
ARTIST AUDIENCE	artist-work: expressive
	work-audience: pragmatic

9. Further biographical sources are listed under "bibliographies" and "general criticism" in my bibliography; the works by Dippold, Fouch, and Hudson are most important. Baraka's own anthologized biographical notes are often revealing and humorous, but not always reliable. The article in *Current Biography,* the essays by Cecil Brown, Diane DiPrima, Isabel Eberstadt, David Llorens, Larry Neal, Jack Richardson, Stephen Schneck, and Jerry Tallmer, and the published interviews with Baraka provide many details of Baraka's career.

10. Jerry Tallmer, "Across the Footlights: The Making of LeRoi Jones," *New York Post,* May 10, 1964, p. 22. Cf. UN 36.

11. Ibid.

12. As a characteristic gesture of literary politics, Baraka tried to transform the "dumb industrial complex" (UN 38) of Newark into a Black nationalist "New Ark" which was to secure the new chosen people's survival through the apocalyptic "fire next time" that had been prophesied as the catastrophe after the deluge. This casts Baraka as what Cotton Mather might have called a "Noah Afro-Americanus."

13. Walter H. Waggoner, "Shift in Position is Hinted by King," *New York Times,* March 28, 1968, p. 40. See UD 11 for a recent, and rather positive King portrait by Baraka.

14. UN 103, the series of articles in *Unity & Struggle* (August 1974 to December–January 1975) against Don Lee, "Haki Madhubuti and Jitu Weusi . . . Two Reac-

tionary Nationalists," resembles much Panther agitation against Karenga's and Baraka's own "Pork Chop Nationalism." Cf. *The Black Panther* 3, no. 18 (August 23, 1969), p. 4; no. 19 (August 30, 1969), pp. 9–10; and no. 27 (October 25, 1969), p. 9. The June 1976 edition of *Unity & Struggle* contains a detailed self-critical reevaluation of Baraka's own commitments to Black nationalism, "A Summation and a Beginning: From Congress of Afrikan People to Revolutionary Communist League, M-L-M" (UN 134).

15. Baraka has, of course, elicited a wide range of critical responses: perhaps two thousand articles and reviews, two books, and several dissertations and M.A. theses. Theodore Hudson's *From LeRoi Jones to Amiri Baraka* is a solid and informative first book-length study with a detailed biographical essay. William C. Fischer's "The Pre-Revolutionary Writings of Imamu Amiri Baraka," *Massachusetts Review* 14, no. 2 (Spring 1973), contains some good interpretations of Baraka's works, but is not always convincing in its notion that Black cultural nationalism constitutes the ultimate *telos* of Baraka's development. Kimberly W. Benston's *Baraka: The Renegade and the Mask* is a more recent, often elucidating close reading of Baraka's works which continues Fischer's approach.

1. FROM BLACK BOURGEOISIE
TO BEAT BOHEMIA

1. Frazier, *Black Bourgeoisie*, pp. 226–27. What the Chicago school of sociology meant to Richard Wright, Frazier meant to Baraka.

2. This may, perhaps, explain why Baraka frequently focused his attacks on a Black bourgeoisie of the 1940s and 1950s. Since Frazier's critique a new Black bourgeoisie has emerged which can further its middle-class ends without resorting to the white-oriented world of make-believe. The change is readily apparent in the transformation of *Ebony*. It was discussed in *Black Scholar* 4, no. 4 (January 1973). Baraka's works since 1974 frequently agitate against this new middle class.

3. Donald Allen and Robert Creeley, eds., *The New Writing in the USA* (Harmondsworth: Penguin, 1967), p. 324. UN 38, p. 324.

4. *Current Biography* (May 1970), p. 18.

5. Isabel Eberstadt, "King of the East Village," *New York Herald Tribune*, December 13, 1964, p. 13.

6. Cf. Allen & Creeley, *New Writing*, p. 274.

7. Frazier, p. 230.

8. Cf. Joseph Satin, ed., *The 1950's: America's "Placid" Decade* (Boston:

Houghton Mifflin, 1960). Cf. also Massimo Teodori, *The New Left: A Documentary History* (Indianapolis, New York: Bobbs-Merrill, 1969), pp. 6–11.

9. Nan Robertson, "Dramatist Against Odds," *New York Times*, March 8, 1959, section ii, p. 3; and "Lorraine Hansberry, 34, Dies—Author of 'A Raisin in the Sun,'" *New York Times*, January 13, 1965, p. 25. Cf. Langston Hughes's famous polemic against such self-consciousness in "The Negro Writer and the Racial Mountain," *Nation* 122 (1926), pp. 692–94.

10. Edmund Wilson, *Axel's Castle* . . . (New York: Scribner, 1931; repr. 1959), pp. 297–98. Section 2 of "Consider This" is entitled "SYMBOLISM" (UP 17).

11. Quoted in *Axel's Castle*, p. 263.

12. Renato Poggioli, *The Theory of the Avant-Garde* (New York: Harper & Row, 1971), p. 113. Poggioli's phenomenology of the avant-garde is very helpful for an understanding of Baraka and the Black Arts Movement.

13. Cf. Poggioli, pp. 110–11. Baraka shares the American obsession with Christ-like protagonists in post-typological fiction.

14. "LeRoi Jones to Give Course on Playwriting at Columbia," *New York Times*, June 22, 1964, p. 22. According to Hudson, p. 78, this was the book which ultimately became *Home*.

15. Parry, *Garrets and Pretenders*, p. 8. Cf. *Axel's Castle*, p. 12.

16. Kreuzer, *Die Bohème*, pp. v and 281. My discussion of Bohemianism follows Kreuzer's phenomenology. I think that Kreuzer and Poggioli provide us with a much better framework for an understanding of Baraka than much Baraka criticism. And though only partly concerned with the Beat Generation, Kreuzer and Poggioli are far superior to the frequently polemic, flippant, and impressionistic accounts of the Beat Generation proper given by Bruce Cook in his chatty *The Beat Generation* (New York: Scribner, 1971) or by John Gruen's guidebook through *The New Bohemia* (New York: Grosset, 1967).

17. Kreuzer, p. 283.

18. Kreuzer, p. 289. See also Poggioli, pp. 30–40, 97–99, and *passim*.

19. Karl Marx, *Selected Works*, prepared by the Marx-Engels-Lenin Institute, Moscow, ed. by V. Adoratsky (New York: International Publishers, n.d.), vol. 2, p. 370. Marx's list contains the characteristic Bohemian catalogue: "Alongside decayed *roués* with doubtful means of subsistence and of doubtful origin, alongside ruined and adventurous offshoots of the bourgeoisie, were vagabonds, discharged soldiers, discharged jail-birds, escaped galley-slaves, swindlers, mountebanks, *lazzaroni*, pickpockets, tricksters, gamblers, *maqueraux*, brothel-keepers, porters, *literati*, organ-grinders, rag-pickers, knife-grinders, tinkers, beggars, in short the whole indefinite, disintegrated mass thrown hither and thither, which the French term *la Bohème;* from this kindred element Bonaparte formed the basis of the Society of December 10."

20. Kreuzer offers an interesting if somewhat perplexing graph in order to illustrate the politics of Bohemia, or, what is here called "aesthetic protest":

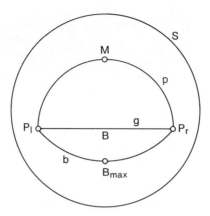

Within the varying historical situation ("S") the political spectrum ("p") reaches from the mainstream center ("M") both to the extreme left ("Pl") and the extreme right ("Pr"). The "world of Bohemia" ("B") is the area contained between the direct line from "Pr" to "Pl" ("g") and the arch ("b") leading through the point "Bmax."

> In that area of B, subjectively radical ultra-right and ultra-left tendencies interpenetrate and condition individualistic and unstable positions. . . . The arch-Bohemian viewpoint (Bmax) has the furthest possible distance from the middle M (maximally conforming with the system) on the arch p, and is also, as its direct antipode, related to it in an extreme, negativistic manner. And yet, the degree of unambiguous political deviation from the vertical central axis (M—Bmax)—the degree of unambivalent political deviation to the left or the right—equals zero in the case of Bmax. . . .

> Our total evidence supports, and our model concretizes, the notion that positions on arch b appear less "extreme" and yet more "radical" than Pl and Pr, because, firstly, they are structured paradoxically, constituted from divergent (opposite) tendencies of the Left and the Right, which makes a peaceful adaptation to the orthodox wing impossible, and secondly, because they show, to a differing degree, an anarchist influence which may radicalize itself to an absolutely antisocial attitude (Bmax), whereas the positions located on p have in common a striving toward power-protected social orders in the service of interest groups. (355–59)

Applied to our present purpose, Bmax on the model would indicate the ideal position of aesthetic protest. The model also suggests the inherent instability of Baraka's Bohemianism between extreme left and extreme right antibourgeois agitation.

21. In *Liberations: New Essays on the Humanities in Revolution,* ed. Ihab Hassan (Middletown: Wesleyan University Press, 1971), p. 102. Next quotation on the same page. For a reference to Georges Sorel in Baraka's works, see SD 53.

22. Reprinted on the inside front cover of the paperback reprint of Parry, *Garrets*.

23. It is here that the "myth of America" as promised land and as city on the hill converges with the fable of Bohemia as a sacred space. This confluence of New World rhetoric and Bohemian cult of art may have contributed to the dominance of that mode in American literature which has been described as symbolist, sacral, visionary, imaginary, individualist, and self-centered, and which attempted to "create through language an essentially imaginative environment," *A World Elsewhere*. (Cf. Poirier, pp. 3–49.) "Palestine" may be the etymological root of "Philistine."

24. "Disengagement: The Art of the Beat Generation," *The Beat Generation and The Angry Young Men*, ed. Gene Feldman and Max Gartenberg (New York: Citadel, 1958), p. 324.

25. Cf. Hans Magnus Enzensberger, "Die Aporien der Avantgarde," *Einzelheiten* (Frankfurt: Suhrkamp, 1962), p. 305.

26. (San Francisco, 1960), p. 4.

27. *Playboy* (June 1959), p. 31. Repr. in *A Casebook on the Beat*, ed., Parkinson (New York: Crowell, 1961), pp. 68–69.

28. "Advertisement for 'Notes Toward a Psychology of the Orgy,'" *Advertisements for Myself* (New York: Putnam–Berkley Medallion, 1966), pp. 389–90. The emphasis on the opposition of "sound" and "meaning" is important for Baraka's own aesthetic of "How You Sound??"

29. Myrdal analyzed the "white man's rank order of discrimination" which lists the "bar against intermarriage" in the first, and "discriminations in securing land, credit, jobs" in the last rank. Myrdal then observed that the "Negro resists least the discrimination of the ranks placed highest in the white man's evaluation and resents most any discrimination of the lowest level." *An American Dilemma: The Negro Problem and Modern Democracy* (New York: Harper, 1944), pp. 60–67. Cf. Calvin Hernton, *Sex and Racism in America* (New York: Grove Press, 1966).

30. *The Real Bohemia: A Sociological and Psychological Study of the Beats* (New York: Basic Books, 1961), p. 51. Reasons given by interviewees: Black men are "better lovers . . . more stud," or "Wow, are we a shocker."

31. *Advertisements for Myself* (New York: Putnam–Berkley Medallion, 1966), p. 321. Further references: p. 314, 321, 314. Cf. Nathan Huggins, *Harlem Renaissance* (New York: Oxford University Press, 1971), pp. 84–93.

32. Cf. Sterling A. Brown's influential essay, "Negro Character as Seen by White Authors," *Journal of Negro Education* 2 (January 1933), pp. 179–203, and his more recent "A Century of Negro Portraiture in American Literature," *Black and White in American Culture*, ed. Jules Chametzky and Sidney Kaplan (Amherst: University of Massachusetts Press, 1969), pp. 333–59.

33. "Color, Conscience and Crucifixion: A Study of Racial Attitudes in American Literature and Criticism," *Jahrbuch für Amerikastudien* 6 (1961), p. 42. Dixon is

the author of racist novels such as *The Clansman* (1905), which was popularized through D. W. Griffith's film *Birth of a Nation* (1915).

34. *Partisan Review* 25, no. 2 (Spring 1958), p. 311. The next quotation, from same page, is a reference to Ned Polsky's earlier reply to Mailer in *Dissent*.

35. "The Jig is Up!," *Waiting for the End: A Portrait of Twentieth-Century American Literature and Its Writers* (New York: Stein and Day, 1970), p. 133.

36. Aaron H. Esman, "Jazz—A Study in Cultural Conflict," *American Imago* 8 (1951), pp. 219–226, esp. 221–224. Norman H. Margolis, "A Theory on the Psychology of Jazz," *American Imago* 11 (1954), pp. 263–291, esp. 288. I am indebted to Lawrence Levine for the reference to these articles as a background to Baraka's first attachment to "avant-gardism." Cf. *Black Culture and Black Consciousness: Afro-American Folk Thought from Slavery to Freedom* (New York: Oxford University Press, 1977), p. 293.

37. Thus, Ted Joans, a Black beatnik, ironically describes his initiation as a Beat poet as the acceptance of an imposed creative identity in return for material rewards:

> Well, I'm not really a poet except for Allen Ginsberg who grabbed me one November day in nineteen fifty eight and said he was bored stiff with reading in the coffee shop and why didn't I do it because I was great. . . . I tell you I was scared silly at first but it was worked out and now I'm making more money than I ever made from my painting.

(*The Beat Scene*, ed. Elias Wilentz [New York: Corinth, 1960], p. 101.)

38. Thus, Baraka invoked Whitman against American academic poetry in UN 24, p. 89, and donned Dr. Fu Man Chu's robe in polemicizing against "The Colonial School of Melican Poetry" as enforced by Robert Bly and William Duffy in UN 25. It seems interesting to note that Baraka's first literary commitment to nationalism was more in the tradition of Emerson's "American Scholar" than of Marcus Garvey's Black Star Line.

39. Isabel Eberstadt's article with that title for a description of the imperial side of Baraka's Bohemian existence.

40. *The New American Poetry*, ed. Donald M. Allen (New York: Grove Press, 1960), pp. 387–88. Further references are given parenthetically. For an Olson paraphrase by Baraka, see H 182.

41. It would be interesting to pursue an American tradition from Poe's concept of short forms and from Emerson's notion of self to the Beat Generation. Poggioli discusses romanticism as a "precedent" of the avant-garde (46–52). And M. H. Abrams describes John Stuart Mill as the proponent of an extremely "expressive" aesthetic (21–25); and there are certain resemblances between Mill's relationship to Wordsworth and Baraka's to Kerouac. Thus, Mill criticized Wordworth's theory of poetry as "erroneous," since it did not emphasize spontaneity enough. And although he had different categories for prose writing, spontaneity was for Mill the touchstone for evaluating poetry.

What *is* poetry, but the thoughts and words in which emotion spontaneously embodies itself? (p. 119)

This process, which is more natural to lyrical than to epic poetry, can, according to Mill, only come about if the poet concentrates on his emotions rather than on the reality that caused them:

> If a poet is to describe a lion, . . . [h]e will describe him by *imagery*, that is, by suggesting the most striking likenesses and contrasts which might occur to a mind contemplating the lion, in the state of awe, wonder or terror. . . . Now this is describing the lion professedly, but the state of excitement of the spectator really. The lion may be described falsely. . . . and the poetry be all the better but if the human emotion be not painted with the most scrupulous truth, the poetry is bad poetry, i.e., is not poetry at all, but a failure. (pp. 107–8)

The truthful rendition of the poet's emotion also presupposes "the poet's utter unconsciousness of a listener":

> Poetry is feeling confessing itself to itself, in moments of solitude, and bodying itself forth in symbols which are the nearest possible representations of the feeling in the exact shape in which it exists in the poet's mind. (p. 109)

Baraka extended Mill's extremely expressive theory of poetry to all *short* forms of literature—the only ones that could be created spontaneously. Mill's ultimate rejection of Wordsworth's poetic practice was based on a serious use of Wordsworth's own theoretical demands—Mill discovered that Wordsworth's poetry "has little even of the appearance of spontaneousness: the well is never so full that it overflows" (p. 122). The quotations are taken from "What is Poetry?" and "Two Kinds of Poetry," *Mill's Essays on Literature and Society*, ed. J. B. Schneewind (New York: Collier, 1965).

42. *Mill's Essays*, pp. 109, 110.

43. *Theory*, p. 38.

2. PREFACE TO A TWENTY VOLUME SUICIDE NOTE: EARLY POETRY AND PROSE

1. Baraka also utilized this strategy in prose fiction, e.g. in "The Chase (Alighieri's Dream)" (T 1–4), in the "association complexes" of *The System of Dante's Hell*, and, less successfully, in the uncollected story, "The Man Who Sold Pictures of God" (UF 3).

2. "Love Poem" (UP 3) illustrates how this method can fail to achieve an effect beyond ludicrousness:

*I tryed to force myself on you like dogshit on a pair
Of new sneakers. . . .
    Sometimes I see you as clearly as the cars you
Get in Crackerjacks. . . .
Your mouth is open, and I can hear you as plainly as if
My dreams were suddenly equipped with high fidelity.*

3. Cf. Poirier, "Is There an I for an Eye," *A World Elsewhere*, pp. 50–92, and Baraka's frequent use of the pun, e.g., in IN 21 or F 32. A related pun is the frequent "sun/son" in Baraka's works, e.g. T 1 or B 200. Cf. Sacvan Bercovitch, *The Puritan Origins of the American Self* (New Haven: Yale University Press, 1975), pp. 64–65.

4. A roll call of some of the personages who appear, in quick succession, on the 40 pages of *Preface* helps us to identify some of the realms of Baraka's poetry. (1) Self: I, wife, daughter, sister, James Karolis, Ora Matthews, Sylvia. (2) Artists: Beat writers, Bosch, Cezanne, "F. Scott Charon," Couperin, Debussy, Hogarth, Sra. de Jimenez, Kafka, Leonardo, Prokofieff, Ravel, Rimbaud, Seurat, Strindberg, and Tschaikovsky. (3) Black musicians: Nat Cole, John Coltrane, Bessie Smith, Charlie Parker, Sonny Rollins. (4) Heroes and antiheroes: Christ, Dubarry, Gandhi, Hitler, Hulan Jack, Goody Knight, "Lincun," Oral Roberts, F. J. Sheen, the Sphinx, Tiresias. (5) Popular culture: Captain Midnight, Raymond Chandler, Charlie Brown, Dickie Dare, Dr. Fu Man Chu, Duke Mantee, The Lone Ranger, Mandrake, Nick Charles, Red Lantern, The Shadow (Lamont Cranston), Kate Smith, Superman, Tom Mix, Tonto, and Uncle Don.

5. UI 1, p. 21 Baraka also discusses the influences of Lorca, Olson, Pound, and Negro speech in this interview. The Eliot-Williams controversy is discussed in Reed Whittemore, *William Carlos Williams: Poet from Jersey* (Boston: Houghton Mifflin, 1975), pp. 170–71, 258–59, and 277–78. David Perkins' excellent work, *A History of Modern Poetry: From the 1890's to the High Modernist Mode* (Cambridge: Harvard University Press, 1976), summarizes Williams' opposition to Eliot in the very terms Baraka used: Eliot, propagated by the New Critics, represented an approach to literature that seemed " 'academic,' to separate literature from life" (p. 550).

6. Cf. Dippold, p. 79 and Lee A. Jacobus, "Imamu Amiri Baraka: The Quest for Moral Order," *Modern Black Poets*, ed. Donald Gibson, pp. 112–26. Eliot examples taken from *The Complete Poems and Plays: 1909–1950* (New York: Harcourt, Brace, 1952), pp. 3, 42–43, 38–39. For further Eliot echoes in Baraka, cf.

*I am a soul in the world: in
the world of my soul the whirled
light . . . ("The invention of comics" DL 37)*

as well as many bangs and whimpers from "Exaugural address" (UP 46) to the recent agitprop play "S-1" (UD 12), where Eliotic rhetoric is assigned to a police agent who arrests the protagonist Red (scene 9, p. 24). Even some of Baraka's anti-Semitism in the period of Black cultural nationalism may be termed Eliotic, e.g. in the "owner-jews" of "Black Art" (B 116).

7. The references to autoeroticism are numerous in the early works from "Vice" (P 28) to *The Baptism.* Cf. Hudson, p. 72.

8. At the root of the alienated outsider metaphor is, of course, not only the discriminated-against Black, but also the homosexual or bisexual whose secret identity transcends the categories of "MEN" and "WOMEN." This early poetic self-definition as an ethnic and sexual outsider was still maintained in *The Toilet* (the setting of which is foreshadowed in "Slice of Life"), but abandoned later, when it gave way to very strong pro-Black and antihomosexual sentiments. John Rechy, one of Baraka's *Moderns,* makes a similar connection in *City of Night* (New York: Grove Press, 1963), "The Professor: The Flight of the Angels," pp. 64–88.

9. Dudley Randall used the image of a "white unicorn" to criticize the position of universalism in Black literature: "A critic advises / not to write on controversial subjects / like freedom or murder, / but to treat universal themes / and timeless symbols / like the white unicorn. / A white unicorn?" ("Black Poet, White Critic" in Henderson, *Understanding the New Black Poetry,* p. 234.)

10. References to Baraka's sister Sandra Elaine, who has worked as a teacher and a performer, recur throughout Baraka's works, often suggestive of Black middle-class attitudes, but later also with different meanings; e.g., "Experimental Death Unit # 1" is dedicated to a "used to be dead sister," and *Tales* carries the inscription, "For Lanie whose heard boo coos."

11. Images of "hunting" often suggest Baraka's notion of creating as a process; cf. "Hunting Is Not Those Heads On The Wall," H 173–78.

12. It is perhaps significant that the boroughs chosen are the "whitest" of New York City; cf. "Belly rub is not Queens," DS 34.

13. Hulan Jack, also mentioned in H 37, was a Black New York Borough President who was convicted of conflict of interest and conspiracy to obstruct justice in December 1960; cf. *New York Times,* December 7, 1960, p. 1. The reference to Lord Greystoke is explicit: "A white hunter, very unkempt, / with long hair, / whizzed in on the end of a vine. / (spoke perfect english too.)" (P 7)

14. This exotic, big-hipped goddess is reminiscent of an archetypical mother figure (as, e.g., Mtalba in Saul Bellow's *Henderson the Rain King*). Dianne Weisgram traced the inversion of this mammal breast imagery in *Dutchman;* cf. "I'll rip your lousy breasts off" (Clay to Lula, DS 34) and *American Imago* 29, no. 3 (Fall 1972), pp. 225–28.

15. Cf. Fischer, p. 267; a fuller treatment of this theme, which is also reminiscent of James Baldwin's *Go Tell It On The Mountain,* is given in Baraka's play, *The Baptism.*

16. For an interesting parallel cf. Roi Ottley's discussion of the Harlem "Café-Au-Lait Society in '*New World A-Coming': Inside Black America* (1943; repr. New York: Arno Press, 1968), pp. 167–85.

17. *Axel's Castle,* p. 276. The original passage in *Oeuvres,* ed. Suzanne Bernard (Paris: Garnier, 1960), p. 217, is annotated by the editor with the remark: "*De*

faux nègres, c'est-a-dire des nègres déguisées en blancs, plus nègres, plus méchants que les véritables" (p. 460). Another translation is given in Oliver Bernard's bilingual edition, *Rimbaud* (Baltimore: Penguin, 1962), p. 309.

18. Suzanne Bernard points out the relationship with Montaigne's "Des Cannibales," (p. 460), considered by Hoxie Neale Fairchild to be one of the earliest sources of this concept. *The Noble Savage: A Study in Romantic Naturalism* (New York: Columbia University Press, 1928), pp. 15–21.

19. Letter of February 25, 1890; quoted by Suzanne Bernard, p. 460.

20. The word "north" on line 1 of P 22 is perhaps a misprint; it was emendated to read "south" in Allen's *New American Poetry* (p. 360) as well as in later anthologies.

21. Cf. Fischer, pp. 270–71. The title of the poem is taken from Sonny Rollins' first album; cf. also BM 52–55 and B 11. The title, "Look For You Yesterday," comes from Jimmy Rushing.

22. Lloyd W. Brown, "Comic-Strip Heroes, LeRoi Jones and the Myth of American Innocence," *Journal of Popular Culture* 3, no. 2 (Fall 1969), pp. 191–204; Fischer, pp. 271ff. Cf. also Lee A. Jacobus. The mass culture Baraka was exposed to is described with great care in Raymond William Stedman's *The Serials: Suspense and Drama by Installment* (Norman: University of Oklahoma Press, 1971); e.g., "box tops," p. 197, "Captain Midnight decoder," p. 202.

23. Alan Watts, *Beat Zen Square Zen and ZEN* (San Francisco: City Lights, 1959), foreword: "the experience of awakening (*satori*) is not to be found by seeking, and is not in any case something that can be acquired or cultivated."

24. Lorca's later poetry made the connection of Gypsy and Negro utilizing a Bohemian strategy that would have interested Baraka; e.g., "Ay, Harlem, Harlem, Harlem! / There is no sorrow like your oppressed eyes, / like your blood shuddering in the dark eclipse, / your garnet violence, deaf in shadow and dumb, / like your great king, prisoner in a janitor's uniform." Edwin Honig, *Garcia Lorca* (Norfolk, Conn.: New Directions, 1944), p. 89. Cf. T 19 and UI 1 (Ossman).

25. Baraka referred often to Radio City Music Hall (e.g., B 10, T 6); most recently, he returned to the Andrews Sisters "Working for the Yankee Dollar" in HF 32.

26. Fischer, p. 270. The title of the collection belongs, of course, to what Poggioli terms "the cult of bizarre titles" (p. 142) and makes the agonism of the writer the object of humorism.

27. Paul Blackburn, "The Grinding Down," *Kulchur* 3, no. 10 (Summer 1963), p. 9. Blackburn describes the journals of the Beat Scene in great detail and criticizes *Yugen* as a "coterie affair" with "uneven contents," since Baraka's "range of acceptance" was "too wide and loose to give other than marshy ground." For a complete listing of books and pamphlets edited by Baraka, see Dace's bibliography. For a Whitmanesque self-appreciation cf. Baraka's list of pertinent reviews "by" and "of" the poet, UN 33.

28. James Weldon Johnson Collection, Beinecke Rare Book and Manuscript Library, Yale University.

29. Letter to Ron Loewinsohn, October 26, 1959, James Weldon Johnson Collection.

30. "The Press of Freedom: The End of the Affair, or Beyond the Beat Generation," *Village Voice*, December 15, 1960, pp. 4, 12. John Fles also edited *The Trembling Lamb*, which contained Baraka's "System of Dante's Inferno" and an archetypical text in avant-gardism, Artaud's Van Gogh essay "The Man Suicided by Society." (Cf. Poggioli, p. 106.)

3. TO "CUBA LIBRE" AND *HOME:* FROM THE 1950s TO THE 1960s

1. "Toward a History of the New Left," *The New Left: A Collection of Essays,* ed. Priscilla Long (Boston: Extending Horizons, 1969), p. 6. Cf. Morris Dickstein's recent account of "New Shoots from Old Roots" in *Gates of Eden: American Culture in the Sixties* (New York: Basic Books, 1977.)

2. Baraka became regional New York chairman in 1961. "Committee on Cuba Elects," *New York Times,* November 11, 1961, p. 9.

3. For definitions of this term and for a valid representation of five theses characterizing the New Left, cf. *The New Left: A Documentary History,* ed. Massimo Teodori (Indianapolis and New York: Bobbs-Merrill, 1969), "Historical and Critical Notes," pp. 3–90. See also *The New Radicals: A Report with Documents,* ed. Paul Jacobs and Saul Landau (Harmondsworth: Pelican, 1967), with a chronology on pp. 319–31.

4. Dale L. Johnson, "On the Ideology of the Campus Revolution," *The New Left,* ed. Teodori, p. 123.

5. E.g., *Raise,* Baraka's collection of essays from 1966 to 1971, despises leftists and the "counter-culture" and barely mentions Vietnam. *Black Music* agitates against "Anti-Viet" protest (206–7).

6. For other accounts of this journey cf. Harold Cruse, *The Crisis of the Negro Intellectual* (New York: Morrow, 1967), pp. 354–58, Harold Cruse, *Negro Digest* 18, no. 1 (November 1968), pp. 24–25; Julian Mayfield, *Negro Digest* 17, no. 8 (June 1968), p. 10ff; and Robert Carl Cohen, *Black Crusader: A Biography of Robert Franklin Williams* (Secaucus, N.J.: Lyle Stuart, 1972), pp. 142–47. "Cuba Libre" was first published in *Evergreen Review* 4, no. 15 (November–December 1960), pp. 139–59; reprinted in *Kulchur* 1, no. 2 (Winter 1960), pp. 54–89; published in January 1961 as a pamphlet by the Fair Play For Cuba Committee; and included in *Home,* pp. 9–62.

7. H 52. According to Cruse's account Baraka "made a very favorable impression on the revolutionary intelligentsia of the Castro regime," *Crisis*, p. 356.

8. Whereas Stokely Carmichael emphatically advocated a "Solidarity with Latin America" against "Anglo society" (*Stokely Speaks* [New York: Vintage, 1971], pp. 101–10), both Robert F. Williams and Eldridge Cleaver turned from initial enthusiasm for Cuba toward criticism of Cuba's racial politics. Cf. David Nagy, "Castro Said to Snub Cleaver and Friends," *Washington Post*, December 10, 1969, and Cohen, *Black Crusader*, p. 210ff., as well as Williams' periodical, *The Crusader* 8, no. 3 (March 1967), pp. 6–8.

9. Cruse, *Crisis*, p. 356. Isabel Eberstadt, "King of the East Village," *New York Herald Tribune*, December 13, 1964, p. 15 (Sunday Magazine).

10. "Letter to the New Left," *The New Radicals*, ed. Jacobs and Landau, pp. 109–10.

11. Thus, the slogan of Baraka's Committee for a Unified NewArk was "Identity Purpose Direction," *The Black Collegian* 3, no. 4 (March–April 1973), pp. 22–24, 43. "Purpose" was also one of the seven tenets of Kawaida ("Nia"); cf. R 134.

12. The classification of Asia and Africa as "new" may refer to revolutionary independence movements of the Third World, but, perhaps more likely, to the Bohemian sense of novelty of "discovering" the rest of the world.

13. Baraka emphasizes the young age of Cuban government officials; H 33–35.

14. E.g., in 1965:

> "When I look at the President I see a big fat ugly faggot. Do you want to know how to judge a country's vitality? Well, stand Adlai Stevenson and Che [Guevara] naked against a wall, and ask any chick in the world who she would rather screw. Or stand Lyndon and Fidel against the wall." Quoted in: Leonard Bloom, "You Don't Have to Be Jewish to Love Leroi Jones," *Realist*, no. 59 (May 1965), p. 24.

15. Cruse, p. 358.

16. *The Selected Poems of William Carlos Williams* (New York: New Directions, 1963), p. 3.

17. Cf. UI 1, H 61–62, and T 19.

18. *Evergreen Review* 5, no. 20 (September–October 1961), p. 127.

19. Harry Ring, *How Cuba Uprooted Race Discrimination* (New York: Pioneer Publishers, 1961), p. 15. The declaration was also reprinted in the *New York Post*, April 25, 1961.

20. Cruse, p. 363. Cruse also argues that for Baraka, "anti-interracialism was equated not only with anti-whiteness, but with *hatred* of whiteness." (p. 364)

21. For a parallel to Robert F. Williams' story, cf. Keita Fodeba, "African Dawn," discussed by Frantz Fanon in *The Wretched of the Earth*, trans. Constance Farrington (New York: Grove Press, 1968), pp. 231–32. Baraka dedicated the poem

"Rhythm & Blues" (DL 44–47) to Robert F. Williams. In the 1976 play, "The Motion of History," Baraka dramatized Williams' message of self-defense and his expulsion from the NAACP in the context of political rebellions in America.

22. In a discussion of "The Roots of Violence," Baraka answered the question whether his audience was predominantly white with the short remark: "It would have to be." *Negro Digest* 13, no. 11 (September 1964), p. 20.

23. Cf. Ralph Ellison's similar comments in *Shadow and Act* (New York: Signet, 1966), p. 132, "The World and the Jug."

24. *Beyond the Blues: New Poems by American Negroes*, ed. Rosey E. Pool (Lympne Hythe Kent: Hand and Flower Press, 1962), p. 135.

25. Eberstadt, p. 20.

26. The word "Milne-burg" alludes to A. A. Milne, the author of *Winnie the Pooh* (1926), which is also the source of the name *The Floating Bear* (p. 136).

27. That is, "square" America; cf. the Gauguin motto of the section "Thieves" in SD 69: "Was I to have made this far journey, only to find the very thing which I had fled?"

28. Cf. Walter Allen's review of M, "What's New?," *New York Review of Books* 1, no. 10 (January 9, 1964), p. 11: ". . . if the words are used in their normal sense, [populist modernism] is a contradiction in terms."

29. Cf. Stephen Henderson's categories in *Understanding the New Black Poetry: Black Speech and Black Music as Poetic References* (New York: Morrow, 1973).

30. Cf. J. P. Dillard, *Black English: Its History and Usage in the United States* (New York: Random House, 1972).

31. It is interesting to note that Julius Lester arrived at opposite results in his attempt to define himself as an Afro-American writer against Western grammatical structures. Lester identifies the *verb* with Western culture and sides, instead, with the noun. "Cultural Nationalism," *Look Out Whitey! Black Power's Gonna Get Your Mama!* (New York: Grove Press, 1969), p. 88.

4. "WHO SUBSTITUTES FOR THE DEAD LECTURER?": POETRY OF THE EARLY 1960s

1. Cf. Eliot's "Ash-Wednesday," *Complete Poems and Plays, 1909–1962*, p. 65.

2. Fischer, p. 281.

3. *Partisan Review* 38, no. 3 (1971), p. 298. Cf. UI 1. Seen this way, the antagonism of *"An Agony. As Now"* is not only between inside and outside, Black and white, but also still between Williams and Eliot. For an interesting parallel to "A contract . . ." cf. SD 35–36.

4. William Carlos Williams, *Paterson* (New York: New Directions, 1948), "Author's Note," p. [i].

5. It is significant that Baraka read the poem for a recording: *LeRoi Jones and the New York Art Quartet* (New York: ESP-Disk, 1965). For paraphrases of themes of the poem, cf. H 218–19.

6. The argument for an ethnic identity is, of course, in the tradition of Baraka's opposition to the Black bourgeoisie.

7. In Baraka's works, "rain" often has the connotation of a Joycean epiphany (DL 20, 28, 42, 56). Umbrellas suggest an artificial shield from revelations. The image is also associated with Gandhi and the principle of nonviolence, which Baraka opposed.

8. In George du Maurier's novel *Trilby* (1894), the English-Irish heroine is hypnotized by the demonic Austrian Jew Svengali. Trilby becomes a singer, but she really remains Svengali's instrument all the time. The "Trilby intrigue" (DL 62) is an appropriate popular pattern for the Black artist who tries to extricate himself from white "hip"-notization (UP 55). Cf. Edgar Rosenberg, *From Shylock to Svengali: Jewish Stereotypes in English Fiction* (Stanford: Stanford University Press, 1960), pp. 234–261.

9. Cf. the discussion of the Egyptian theme by Glen Burns, who also analyzes "The Death of Malcolm X" (UD 3), in Alfred Weber and Siegfried Neuweiler, ed., *Amerikanisches Drama und Theater im 20. Jahrhundert*. Göttingen: Vandenhoek und Ruprecht, 1975, pp. 261–88. Baraka's prose piece, "The Campaign" (UN 54), which also develops the "button down" theme in the description of a "Nigger Doctor sitting on the board of education with a 12 button suit buttoning out reality" (p. 35), is accompanied by Paul Davis' interesting illustrations of the Egyptian theme. Baraka's nationalist polemic against C. Vann Woodward, lists Thoth among the "Occult Teachers of Black People" (UN 50).

10. *Soul on Ice* (New York: Ramparts Books, 1968), p. 15.

11. Donald Bogle's *Toms, Coons, Mulattoes, Mammies, and Bucks* is an informative background source for this aspect of Baraka. Willie Best was a film actor of the "amiable" Black stereotype, and in the tradition of Stepin Fetchit. Best starred in many 1930s movies under the "coon" name "Sleep'n'Eat" (cf. also DL 18–27). Mantan Moreland's screen stereotype was that of a "fantastic cowardly lion with an uncanny command of stagecraft" (Bogle 103). Buckwheat, from the 1927 movie, *Our Gang*, was a Black pickaninny, a "quiet, odd-ball type, the perfect little dumdum tag-along" (Bogle 27). *The Bronze Buckaroos* (cf. B 44) were Herbert Jeffrey and Artie Young as singing Black cowboys in a 1938 Western which imitated "the expected Tex Ritter–Gene Autry heroics and exploits" (Bogle 152). In *Home*, Baraka articulates this strategy of inversion, by which the underdog of popular cul-

ture becomes the hero: "when Charles . . . will . . . ask the black lackeys to help him out, it is high time the black man began to make use of the Tonto-syndrome, *i.e.*, leave The Lone Ranger to his own devices, and his own kind of death" (H 205).

12. According to the late Africanist Janheinz Jahn, the name Damballah "is compounded from 'Dan' (snake) or 'Dangbe,' the cult of the snake in heaven, that is, the rainbow, and 'Allada,' the name of that kingdom in South Dahomey from which came the dynasty of Abomey, founders of the kingdom of Dahomey. . . . Damballah is identified with St. Peter or St. Patrick. His symbols are the snake and the egg." *Muntu: The New African Culture* (New York: Grove Press, 1961), p. 40.

13. Newbell Niles Puckett, *The Magic and Folk Beliefs of the Southern Negro* (University of North Carolina Press, 1926; repr. New York: Dover, 1969), p. 178. Puckett was a source of BP.

14. Perhaps the only truly "political" poem of this period is the uncollected, quite un-Barakian "Exaugural Address" (UP 46), dated four days after the assassination of John F. Kennedy. The poem was printed on a separate sheet that was attached, apparently at the last minute, between two pages of Baraka's review of Allen Ginsberg's *Reality Sandwiches* in *Kulchur* (UN 27). This little-known poem speaks for itself.

EXAUGURAL ADDRESS

(for Jacqueline Bouvier Kennedy, who has had to eat too much shit)

All hopes of the sweet millennium
vanished into the insanity of television. The deaths
and lies, sweatings through the tube. The clutch
of mad things growing in the silence and anguish of crowds.
Three or four ratgnawed freaks speaking into their hands
about the justice of Godliness, which is nothing if it is not
completely unjust. The bang has become the weight of our culture.
Floating in the head or the arm. Getting through to the same places.
Altering the million consciousness flowers, who will be dead
when this is issued in world talk, from the submarine
of state. Now that it has submerged again, to survive
and sustain itself in the holy blue moisture of darkness.

What we had
we have not.
Dissolved
into the spooky signals
of Catholics.

Where we are
is a place, we did not ever
want to be.
Strangled

in the withered coffin
of public orgasm.

Trail.
Trail on out.

A ringing, and banging.
To stop all twisting.

From now on we will sit in nightclubs with jewish millionaires
listening to the maudlin political verse of a money narcissist.

And this will be the payback for our desires.
For history, like the ringing coin

that will not bend
when we bite it.

—*LeRoi Jones*
November 26, 1963

The review of *Reality Sandwiches* praises Ginsberg as "one of us" for unconventionality, provocativeness, and romanticism, and contrasts the in-group of Beats to "them," and specifically to Jacqueline Kennedy. Taking Ginsberg's lines "You're angry at me. For all my lovers? / It's hard to eat shit, without having visions" as a touchstone, Baraka asks ironically: "Who has not eaten shit? I'm afraid there are too many people who have not. Has Jacqueline Kennedy eaten shit? I hope not, because if she has, then eating shit can no longer be the measure. Dig?" (UN 27, p. 87). "Eating shit" is thus a consciously provocative metaphor for the Beat exclusivism of visionaries. The fact that *Kulchur* # 12 appeared shortly after the assassination of President Kennedy prompted Baraka to insert the poem "Exaugural Address" with the strange subtitle that is really an apology to Mrs. Kennedy. (Cf. also: Allen Ginsberg, *Journals: Early Fifties–Early Sixties*, ed. Gordon Ball [New York: Grove Press, 1977], pp. xx, 167, 275.)

5. FROM OFF-BOWERY TO OFF-BROADWAY: "THE EIGHTH DITCH (IS DRAMA," *THE BAPTISM*, AND *THE TOILET*

1. Baraka's first attempts at drama are lost in manuscript. An advertisement for a Montclair, N.J., performance of the early playlet "A Good Girl Is Hard to Find" (1958) was published on the inside cover of *Yugen* # 2; and the loss of "Revolt of the Moonflowers" (1959) is reported in *Dark Symphony: Negro Literature in America*, ed. James A. Emanuel and Theodore L. Gross (New York: Free Press, 1968), p. 513. "The Eighth Ditch (Is Drama" was first published in June 1961, in *The Floating Bear* # 9 (coedited by Diane DiPrima and Baraka), and first performed by The New York Poets' Theatre (cofounded by Baraka) at the Off-Bowery

Theatre in October 1961, under the title "Dante," on the same bill with DiPrima's *Discontent of the Russian Princess* and Michael McClure's *Pillow.* It was again presented at the New Bowery Theater in March 1964.

2. An echo in T 105 underlines this connection with Melville.

3. According to Jerry Tallmer ("The Kafka Blues," *New York Post,* March 16, 1964), the play is "about an interracial homosexual rape somewhere in an army tent." Michael Smith defended the play in the *Village Voice* against obscenity charges by describing it as "less sexually provocative than most advertising" ("Theatre: The Eighth Ditch," March 19, 1964, p. 11). According to Joseph LeSueur, the play was "so graphic, so specific, that the imagination had no place to go" (*The Floating Bear* # 15, p. [12]). Richard Gilman called "The Eighth Ditch" "a crude, distressingly vulgar segment of sodomistic vainglory which was presented as a one-act play" in his review of *SD,* "The Devil May Care," *New York Herald Tribune Book Week* (December 26, 1965), p. 9. Gerald Weales takes the play humorously as a funny treatment of the fraudulent counselors theme: "The middle-class boy wants a glimpse into the deep, mysterious underworld, and the streetboy simply wants to screw him; the first boy never knows the difference" (*The Jumping-Off Place: American Drama in the 1960's* [New York: Macmillan, 1969], p. 138). Most recently, Benston identified 46 with Baraka, opposing him to 64 and all the other characters in the play as the "totally *acted upon* 'object' " (p. 16).

4. Since 64 is "inside" 46, we may also view the relationship of 64 and 46 in terms of the "thing inside" and the shell. In conversation, Baraka concurred with an interpretation of 46 and 64 as being really "the same person," a "kind of schizophrenic thing." He added a possible social explanation for the dichotomy: "The different elements, that is, I guess, the petit bourgeois background caught between the working class and aspiring bourgeois." (From tape of UI 20, September 1, 1974.) Cf. Robert Rogers, *A Psychoanalytic Study of the Double in Literature* (Detroit: Wayne State U. Press, 1970), esp. pp. 18–31.

5. For parallel passages cf. "The Alternative" (T 13) and *The Toilet.*

6. J. R. Goddard, "Poet Jailed for Obscenity; Literary Magazine Hit. LeRoi Jones & Floating Bear," *Village Voice,* October 26, 1961, p. 3.

7. Ibid., p. 16. The *Voice* also points out that Baraka's father "ironically is a postal superintendent in New Jersey."

8. "Poet's Theatre Fights $25 Fine," *Village Voice,* January 11, 1962, p. 2.

9. "Floating Bear Floats Free," *Village Voice,* May 3, 1962, p. 3. Baraka was on the witness stand for 3½ hours; the prosecutor was Assistant to the US Attorney Gerald E. Paley.

10. *The Baptism* was written in the early 1960s and first produced by Present Stages at the Writer's Stage Theater in New York on March 23, 1964, in the middle of what Tallmer called "LeRoi Jones week in the theater"—a few days after the opening of "The Eighth Ditch" at the New Bowery, and the night before the

opening of *Dutchman* at the Cherry Lane. Jerry Tallmer, "LeRoi Jones Strikes Again," *New York Post*, March 24, 1964, p. 20. The Headline of the *Variety* notice on March 25, 1964, reads: "LeRoi Jones One-Acters an Off-B'way Epidemic." Langston Hughes called 1964 "The Jones Year" in his *Black Magic: A Pictorial History of the Negro in American Entertainment* (Englewood Cliffs, N.J.: Prentice Hall, 1971), p. 251.

11. On its opening night, *The Baptism* was on a double bill with Frank O'Hara's satirical attack on General Douglas MacArthur, "The General Returns From One Place to Another." *The Baptism* was first published, together with *The Toilet*, as Evergreen Playscript #10, on June 30, 1967. A slightly different, probably earlier version is at the library of SUNY at Stony Brook. The most striking variation in this version is on p. 9 of the 13-page script, where the homosexual speaks the lines that are given to the minister in the printed version: "Lemme see you turn this joint into the White House . . ." (BT 25).

12. Gerald Weales described *The Baptism* as Baraka's "most casually obscene play, . . . a hipster religious allegory, a play about the Second Coming, a religious-sexual exercise that is an extended, if implicit, pun on *coming*." *The Jumping-Off Place*, p. 140.

13. Jeanne-Marie A. Miller attempts to interpret *The Baptism* as an application of Baraka's theory of "The Revolutionary Theatre" (H 210–15) in "The Plays of LeRoi Jones," *College Language Association Journal* 14 (1971), p. 331ff. Maria K. Mootry, on the other hand, emphasizes that if "anyone in the play has 'soul,' it is the homosexual," yet she interprets the boy as "Black Power" and his message as "*There will be no second enslavement.*" *Negro Digest* 18, no. 6 (April 1969), p. 45.

14. *The Jumping-Off Place*, p. 140.

15. "Black Man as Victim," *Commonweal* 88, no. 15 (June 28, 1968), p. 436.

16. Michael Smith, "Theatre: Present Stages," *Village Voice*, March 26, 1964, p. 9.

17. Jerry Tallmer, *New York Post*, March 24, 1964, p. 20. The review ends, however, with the suggestion that the playwright "has yet to go from the potential to the kinetic in drama."

18. "Drama Mailbag: Again the Readers Argue LeRoi Jones," *New York Times*, December 14, 1969, section 2, p. 15.

19. *New York Times*, November 16, 1969, section 2, pp. 1, 7. Later reprinted under Baraka's own title "Nationalism Vs PimpArt" in R 125–32.

20. Mead, *New York Times*, December 14, 1969, section 2, p. 15.

21. For example, T 5–29. "Ray" as a spiritual part in a Black dualism is, of course, a creation of Claude McKay's *Home to Harlem*, which opposed Ray and the physical Jake. When Baraka discussed McKay in *Tales*, he could unequivocally side with Jake against Ray (T 96, cf. also T 131), but at the point of *The Toilet* and the early *Tales*, Baraka was still struggling for a balance between "Ray" and "Foots,"

or, perhaps, between "LeRoi" and "Jones." After all, spirituality and group identity were the two opposing ends from which the populist modernist and Bohemian tried to fight the bourgeoisie. For a more recent "Ray," cf. the plays of Ed Bullins.

22. Quoted by Judy Stone, "If It's Anger . . . Maybe That's Good," *San Francisco Chronicle*, August 23, 1964, p. 42. Cf. interview with Cecil Smith, *Los Angeles Times Calendar*, March 21, 1965, quoted by Weales, p. 141.

23. Stone, p. 42. Hudson takes this quote as a motto of his discussion of *The Toilet*.

24. Stone, p. 42. There is a (perhaps earlier) typescript version of *The Toilet* in the library at SUNY Stony Brook, which contains several suggestions for changes, apparently in Baraka's handwriting. Thus, the location of the play is moved from the second floor of the school building to the basement, underscoring the "nether world" (Mootry, p. 44) and the "underbelly" setting, and the character of Perry is changed to "(clowns)—strong." *The Toilet* was first published in *Kulchur* 3, no. 9 (Spring 1963), pp. 25–39; and this version, too, is not identical with that of the Evergreen Playscript; e.g., it reads "urinating" for "peeing."

25. *The Best Plays of 1964–65*, ed. Otis L. Guernsey, Jr. (New York, Toronto: Dodd, Mead, 1965), p. 244. This "Introduction" also appeared on the playbill of the famous 1964 production of *The Toilet*, directed by Leo Garen and with a naturalistic set designed by Larry Rivers. This production, a double bill with Baraka's *The Slave*, had originally been scheduled to open on Baraka's 30th birthday. Guernsey's version reflects Garen's production, which is often referred to as "first," although *The Toilet* was first performed by the Playwright's Unit of the Actor's Studio in 1962.

26. Guernsey, p. 24. This is only true for the *dramatis personae*, but not for the dialogue which points out color explicitly and implicitly.

27. "The Slave and The Toilet," *Village Voice*, December 31, 1964, p. 10.

28. Matthew Andrews, "Theatre," *Kulchur* 4, no. 17 (Spring 1965), p. 81.

29. "That Boy LeRoi," *New York Post*, January 15, 1965, p. 38.

30. This is Gerald Weales's speculative answer to his own observation that Baraka "is obviously using homosexuality to represent something else in this play" (*The Jumping-Off Place*, p. 141). Race may also be seen as a metaphor for class in *The Toilet*: Ray Foots is the petit bourgeois torn between bourgeoisie (white) and proletariat (Black).

31. Maria K. Mootry, p. 47.

32. *Soul on Ice*, p. 100.

33. Ulf Hannerz discusses theories about these male attitudes in his chapter on "Growing Up Male" in *Soulside: Inquiries into Ghetto Culture and Community* (New York & London: Columbia University Press, 1969). His analysis also contains interesting examples of street language and dozens as "rituals of obscenity." Cf. also Lawrence Levine, *Black Culture and Black Consciousness*, pp. 344–358.

34. In Garen's presentation of *The Toilet*, Karolis was played by Jaime Sanchez. As a result, many reviewers focused on the special relationship of Blacks and Puerto Ricans, which, of course, strengthened the "love story" reading. In the text of the play, there is no indication that James Karolis should be Puerto Rican. Martin Gottfried stretches the importance of Karolis' Puerto Rican background to ludicrousness: " 'The Toilet' is meant to wipe away any antagonisms between Negroes and Puerto Ricans . . . the two groups are basically loving each other. And they must join forces in reducing the American white to a bloody pulp." "Theatre," *Women's Wear Daily*, March 12, 1965.

35. The ending, according to Guernsey, reads: "Foots . . . runs to the sink and wets a paper towel. Foots kneels by Karolis' form, weeping, cradling the head in his arms, wiping the blood from Karolis' face." This alteration may have provoked Baraka's later disavowal.

36. Quoted in Michael T. Kaufman, "Jones Asks Votes, Not Rioting, to 'Take' Newark," *New York Times*, April 14, 1968, p. 60.

37. Mel Watkins, "Talk With LeRoi Jones," *New York Times Book Review*, June 27, 1971, p. 26. (UI 17)

38. The critical reception ranged from harsh denunciation to high praise. Ivan Morris called the playwright a Black Dr. Verwoerd in his review in *Vogue* (February 1, 1965), p. 98. C.W.E. Bigsby referred to *The Toilet* as a "barely stageable homosexual fantasy," in *Confrontation and Commitment: A Study of Contemporary American Drama, 1959–1966* (University of Missouri Press, 1968), p. 138. Robert Brustein similarly termed the play "a psychodrama, designed for the acting out of sado-masochistic racial fantasies" in *The New Republic* 152, no. 4 (January 23, 1965), p. 33. And Myrna Bain took the title and setting literally and saw "straight bathroom drama, with little if any plot and absolutely no uplift," in "Everybody's Protest Play," *National Review* 17, no. 12 (March 23, 1965), p. 249. On the other hand, Harold Clurman praised the play as a "study in hypocrisy," *The Nation* 200, no. 1 (January 4, 1965), p. 16; and the London *Times* saw the expression of rage "almost in choreographic terms" (January 25, 1965), p. 7.

39. Paul Hoffman, "D.A. Refuses to Act Against Off B'Way Play," *New York Post*, January 20, 1965, p. 27.

40. "Jones Plays 'Obscene' to Los Angeles Police," *Village Voice*, April 1, 1965, p. 10.

41. "You Don't Have to be Jewish to Love LeRoi Jones," *The Realist*, no. 59 (May 1965), p. 24.

42. In this aspect, the only comparable work is Shirley Clarke's film *The Cool World* (1964), based on a novel by Warren Miller; and Hughes (p. 38) and Lawrence P. Neal, *Liberator* 5, no. 2 (February 1965), p. 23, make that comparison. Five of the nine Black actors had been studying with Robert Hooks, the Clay of the 1964 *Dutchman* production, and "none of them had any previous stage experience" (Stuart W. Little, "LeRoi Jones Double Bill," *New York Herald Tribune*, November 12, 1964). Three of the actors in Garen's production of *The*

Toilet, however, had appeared in *The Cool World:* Hampton Clanton (Ray Foots), Gary Bolling (Willie Love), and Bostic Felton (Johnny Boy Holmes). For the importance of the city milieu, cf. Darwin Turner, "Negro Playwrights and the Urban Negro," *College Language Association Journal* 12, no. 1 (1968), pp. 19–25. Cf. also Robert Tener's suggestive remarks in *Modern Drama* 17 (1974), pp. 210–14.

6. *DUTCHMAN* AND *THE SLAVE*

1. The play was directed by Edward Parone and produced by "Theater 1964," an enterprise dedicated to the promotion of American plays in the European absurdist tradition. Started by Richard Barr, Clinton Wilder, and Edward Albee, Theater 1964 was originally called "Theater 1960" and changed its name every year. For the first month of the Cherry Lane production, *Dutchman* was performed in conjunction with Arrabal's *The Two Executioners* and Beckett's *Play;* these two plays were subsequently replaced by Albee's *The American Dream. Dutchman* was successful, ran well into 1965 and toured several cities in the United States and in Europe. Translated into several foreign languages (among them French, German, and Hungarian) and performed on various European stages, *Dutchman* (as *Métro fantôme*) proved particularly controversial and influential in France. *Dutchman* was also performed, sometimes by all-Black casts in theatres throughout Black America, starting with the Black Arts Repertory Theatre in Harlem. The play received the *Village Voice* Obie award as Best New American Play. *Dutchman* was first printed, together with *The Slave,* on August 19, 1964, by Morrow and reprinted in more than a dozen anthologies. Contemporary reviews are listed in Dace's bibliography. Except for the difficulties which the show had when performed on a double bill with *The Toilet* in Los Angeles, there are few reported interferences by authorities with *Dutchman.* In 1965, one of the American backers of the Italian theater festival at Spoleto "emerged from the first performance of *Dutchman* outraged by the violence of the language and indignant at what he described as the irresponsibility of the dramatist's point of view" ("Poets Applauded at Spoleto Fete," *New York Times,* June 28, 1965, p. 34). A French production of *Dutchman* at the Dramatic Center in Montpellier in 1968 was banned by the city's mayor as "audacious, erotic, politically violent" ("Drama is Banned; Theater Head Quits," *Minneapolis Star,* January 8, 1968, p. 11B). In New York, the attempts to film *Dutchman* were boycotted by subway authorities, and it became easier to shoot the film in England (Gene Persson, "Arguing 'Dutchman,'" *New York Times,* March 3, 1967, section 2, p. 14). In 1969 *Dutchman* was barred from a reading list of a Black authors high school course in San Francisco by Max Rafferty, superintendent of public instruction in California (Wallace Turner, "Books by Two Negroes Barred From San Francisco Schools," *New York Times,* August 26, 1969, p. 24). In 1970, a Washington theater filed a complaint with the Federal

Communications Commission against a television station which had stopped video-taping a performance of *Dutchman* because "the language was bad" and "there is too much kissing and we have young children watching this show" (*Studies in Black Literature* 1, no. 2 [Summer, 1970], pp. 87–88).

2. For descriptions of the formal characteristics of the theater of the absurd and the one-act play, cf. Martin Esslin, *The Theatre of the Absurd* (rev. ed., Garden City, New York: Doubleday & Anchor, 1969) and Diemut Schnetz, *Der moderne Einakter: Eine poetologische Untersuchung* (Bern & München: Francke, 1967).

3. Formally, these phrases indicate the reification process; but "the woman's face" also makes Lula a disembodied mask reminiscent of Baraka's Willie Best poems: "The face sings, alone / at the top / of the body" (DL 18); and by calling Clay "the man" Baraka may both be ironicizing Clay's white orientation and his struggle for manhood. Cf. Baraka's statement in *Home*: "*Dutchman* is about the difficulty of becoming a man in America" (H 188). Cf. also Doris Abramson's discussion of the play in *Negro Playwrights in the American Theatre, 1925–1959* (New York: Columbia University Press, 1969).

4. "Channel X: Two Plays on the Race Conflict," *New York Review of Books* 2, no. 8 (May 28, 1964), p. 12. Baraka rejected several elements of Roth's interpretation in a letter to the editor, *New York Review of Books* 2, no. 11 (July 9, 1964), p. 23, and, less directly, in H 186–88.

5. Willene P. Taylor, "The Fall of Man Theme in Imamu Amiri Baraka's (LeRoi Jones') *Dutchman,*" *Negro American Literature Forum* 7 (1973), pp. 127–30.

6. Edward Parone, who directed the Cherry Lane Production, included *Dutchman* in his anthology, *New Theatre in America* (New York: Dell-Delta, 1965), pp. 191–214. Hugh Nelson argued in "LeRoi Jones' *Dutchman*: A Brief Ride on a Doomed Ship," *Educational Theatre Journal* 20, no. 1 (February 1968), pp. 53–59, that there are "a few significant differences between the two texts" (53). He therefore bases his discussion on the "later version" of the Parone text. However, all his quotations are identical in both versions, and instead of Nelson's reference to "beauties dashing along through the city's entrails" (56, bottom), *both* versions read "beauties smashing. . . ." Some representative variants between the first edition ("Morrow edition," in the absence of an identifiable editor) and the Parone edition are:

(Morrow)	(Parone)
"the man has noticed the face" (4)	*"the man has noticed it"* (194)
"Yeah" (9, 12, etc.)	"Yeh" (196, 198, etc.)
LULA: "like your ol' rag-head mammy" (31)	LULA: "like our ol' rag-head mammy" (208)
"Oh sit the fuck down" (32)	"Oh sit down" (209)
"Open the door and throw his body out. (*They throw him off*) And all of you get off at the next stop" (37)	"Throw his body off between the cars —and the rest of you get off at the next stop." (212)

On the bottom of DS 27, there is a typographical error which can be emendated with the help of Parone:

CLAY: "Morbid. Morbid. You sure you're not an actress? All scribed?" (27)	CLAY: "I will. And is this all of our life together you've described?" (206)

The most significant departure of the Parone text from the Morrow version of *Dutchman* is the absence of the conductor from the last scene, though not from the list of characters (DS 37–38 vs. Parone 213–14).

7. Cf. Gerald Weales, *The Jumping-Off Place*, p. 139.

8. Earlier attempts to interpret *Dutchman* as drama of self include that of Diane Weisgram, who sees Baraka as "both Clay and Lula," *American Imago* 29, no. 3, (Fall 1972), 231, and that of Albert Bermel, who interprets Clay's death as a poetic suicide and Lula as "the fears and doubts that torment Clay." "The Poet as Solipsist: *Dutchman* by LeRoi Jones (1964)," *Contradictory Characters: An Interpretation of the Modern Theatre* (New York: Dutton, 1973), p. 254.

9. "Movie Mailbag: Fur Still Flies on 'Dutchman.' From LeRoi Jones," *New York Times*, March 12, 1967, section 2, p. 17: "Lula would make a better 'critic,' and is already, if you dig it, for say East Village Other and SDS (viz Grokville Estab.), she at least, is, at the time of. Crowther never knew what hit him." Cf. also Gene Palatsky, "Seeing the Lie," *Newark Evening News*, March 30, 1964; quoted in Louis Phillips, "LeRoi Jones and Contemporary Black Drama," *The Black American Writer*, ed. C.W.E. Bigsby, vol. 2 (Baltimore: Penguin, 1969), p. 212.

10. Parone edition, p. 209; cf. DS 31.

11. In the letter to the *New York Times* quoted in note 9, Baraka defended Clay's speech and identified with it to such an extent as to make it appear even more Black nationalist than it is: ". . . the 17 minutes of the play he [i.e., Crowther] missed are the 17 minutes it takes for the black man to say his long speech. (We are a different species, with different 'zones' of response, &c."

12. *Manifestoes of Surrealism* (Ann Arbor: University of Michigan Press, 1969), trans. by Richard Seaver and Helen R. Lane, p. 125. The Breton motto of this chapter appears on pp. 136–37.

13. Cf. *Masculine Feminine: A Film by Jean-Luc Godard*, ed. Pierre Billard (New York: Grove Press, 1969), pp. 52–57.

14. Cf. this section of Baraka's earlier poem "The A, B, C's (For Charles)":

> *Safe now, within the poem, I make my*
> *Indiscreet avowals, my indelicate assumptions*
> *As if this gentle fire that bathed my flesh*
> *was rancor, or fear, or any other of life's idiot progeny. (UP 31)*

15. George Knox, "The 'Mythology' of LeRoi Jones's *Dutchman*," *Interculture: A Collection of Essays and Creative Writing Commemorating the 20th Anniversary of the Fulbright Program at the Institute of Translation and Interpretation, Univer-*

sity of Vienna, ed. Sy M. Kahn & Martha Raetz (Wien, Stuttgart: n.d.), pp. 246–50.

16. Cf. Knox, also Tom S. Reck, "Archetypes in LeRoi Jones' Dutchman," *Studies in Black Literature* 1, no. 1 (1970), pp. 66–68; John Gassner and Bernard F. Dukore, eds., *A Treasury of the Theatre*, 4th ed., vol. 2 (New York: Simon & Schuster, 1970), p. 1274. George R. Adams, who published a psychoanalytic interpretation of *Dutchman* as "a literary expression of id-activity" ("Black Militant Drama," *American Imago* 28, no. 2 [Summer 1971], pp. 116–21), also attempted a typological interpretation, " 'My Christ' in *Dutchman*," *College Language Association Journal* 15, no. 1 (September 1971), pp. 54–58; cf. the article by Nelson mentioned in note 6. The archetypes in *Dutchman* are also indebted to popular culture; thus, one might argue that the sudden character shift of Clay and Lula is not only part of the absurdist tradition, but related to a *Superman* aesthetic, from mild-mannered Clark Kent to Superman (cf. R 20–21). *Dutchman* is rich in allusions to other figures of popular culture.

17. Cf. Julian C. Rice, "LeRoi Jones' *Dutchman*: A Reading," *Contemporary Literature* 12, no. 1(Winter 1971), p. 43; and Herbert Grabes, "LeRoi Jones (Imamu Amiri Baraka): *Dutchman*," *Das amerikanische Drama der Gegenwart* (Kronberg: Athenäum, 1976), p. 193.

18. Cf. Janheinz Jahn, *Muntu: The New African Culture*, trans. Marjorie Grene (New York: Grove Press, 1961), p. 45.

19. James Weldon Johnson, ed., *The Book of American Negro Poetry* (New York: Harcourt, 1922; repr. 1931), pp. 120–22. I am indebted to Robert Bone for suggesting this parallel. "The White Witch" is also the name of a ghost ship; cf. note 23, below.

20. Nelson's approach has been criticized by Robert L. Tener, "Role Playing as A Dutchman," *Studies in Black Literature* 3, no. 3 (Autumn 1972), pp. 17–21.

21. Sherley Anne Williams, *Give Birth to Brightness: A Thematic Study in Neo-Black Literature* (New York: Dial Press, 1972) pp. 106–7. Cf. also Hudson, p. 152.

22. Further interpretations of the title are of minor relevance. Since the days of Dutch-English rivalries, the word "Dutch" has retained a derogatory connotation in the English language. If Clay has "Dutch courage," Lula gives him "Dutch consolation." With the geographic ambiance of Harlem and Amsterdam Avenue, *Dutchman* may also obliquely refer to a Harlemite. Knox (pp. 250–51) called attention to the use of a Dutch Master Cigars poster in the movie version, and to Larry Rivers' painting, *Dutchmaster and Cigars* (1964). Also: "dada man" and, perhaps, "Ditchman" ("The Eighth Ditch").

23. Second edition (Edinburgh: Ballantyne, 1811). The word "Flying Dutchman" in the notes, p. 176. The poem is quoted by *The Poetical Works of Sir Walter Scott: With the Author's Introductions and Notes*, ed. J. Logie Robertson (London, Edinburgh, etc.: Henry Frowde, 1906). p. 389. Another connection between the Flying Dutchman and the slave trade is made in Celia Thaxter's "The Mystery," quoted in Fletcher S. Bassett, *Legends and Superstitions of the Sea and of*

Sailors in All Lands and at All Times (London: Sampson Low, 1885), p. 360; "The White Witch" as a spectral ship, p. 354. Cf. also John Livingston Lowes, *The Road to Xanadu: A Study in the Ways of the Imagination* (1927; repr. Boston: Houghton Mifflin, 1964), pp. 512–16; and Elisabeth Frenzel, "Der Fliegende Holländer," *Stoffe der Weltliteratur: Ein Lexikon dichtungsgeschichtlicher Längsschnitte* (Stuttgart: Kröner, 1963), pp. 282–84.

24. Baraka explained how he related the myth of the Flying Dutchman to his play in my interview of September 1, 1974: "The title is from the Flying Dutchman . . . not from Wagner, but from the myth, wherever I picked up the myth from, that myth of a ship that sailed around forever." He also said that the *situation* really is the Dutchman, not Lula or Clay. (UI 20)

25. Walter Höllerer recognized this relation and reprinted "Note from the Underground" next to his interpretation of *Dutchman*. *Modernes Theater auf kleinen Bühnen* (Berlin: Literarisches Colloquium, 1965), p. 126.

26. Gerald Weales, *The Jumping-Off Place*, p. 142. Michael Smith, "Theatre: The Slave and The Toilet," *Village Voice*, December 31, 1964, p. 10. Hoyt W. Fuller, "About *The Toilet* and *The Slave*," *Negro Digest* 14, no. 9 (July 1965), p. 50. Donald P. Costello, "Black Man as Victim," *Commonweal* 88, no. 15 (June 28, 1968), p. 439. For a thoroughly enthusiastic, though rather superficial reading see Richard Lederer, "The Language of Leroi Jones' 'The Slave,' " *Studies in Black Literature* 4, no. 1 (Spring 1973), pp. 14–16. *The Slave*, subtitled "A Fable in a Prologue and Two Acts," was first presented—together with *The Toilet*—on December 16, 1964, at St. Marks Playhouse in New York and first published—together with *Dutchman*—by Morrow in 1964. Of Baraka's plays of this period, it fared best with the authorities; there was no report of any interference by police, censors, or judges until the play was presented at a high school in Wellesley, Mass., on May 31, 1968, and charges of obscenity were filed against five teachers. Although no complaints were issued against the teachers, District Judge Daniel A. Rider ruled on September 10, 1968, that, indeed, "a crime" had been committed: "I find this to be an obscene play. It should never have been presented to anyone under the age of 18." This complicated decision made the presentation of *The Slave* to Massachusetts minors a crime, but refrained from trying to find any "criminals." J. Anthony Lukas, "Obscenity Fight Splits City of Wellesley After LeRoi Jones Play Is Given at High School," *New York Times*, September 10, 1968, p. 25; " 'Obscene' Play Counts Dropped," *The Minneapolis Star*, September 11, 1968, p. 9B; Thomas J. Cottle, "The Wellesley Incident: A Case of Obscenity," *Saturday Review* 52, no. 11 (March 15, 1969), pp. 67–68, 75–77 (esp. p. 76). *The Slave* was performed in Paris and Dakar (where it received the drama prize of the World Festival of Negro Arts in 1966); it was translated into French and German.

27. Using alcohol as a supportive element of character motivation is a "conservative" technique which many contemporary dramatists discard; cf. Schnetz, *Der moderne Einakter*, pp. 101–2.

28. According to Dippold's conversation with Baraka, October 10, 1970. Cf. Dippold, p. 175. For other discussions of the date of composition of *The Slave*, cf. Harold Clurman, "LeRoi Jones; Naughton's Alfie," *Nation* 200, no. 1 (January 4,

1965), p. 16; and Henry Hewes, "Crossing Lines," *Saturday Review* 48, no. 2 (January 9, 1965), p. 46.

29. In my interview with Hettie Cohen Jones, she told me that Leo Garen had asked her, to her dismay, for pictures of her daughters to be used for the stage set; she also reacted with great shock to the performance of the play.

30. Baraka's own interpretation of *The Slave* as rendered by Jack Newfield, "LeRoi Jones at Arms: Blues for Mr. Whitey," *Village Voice* (December 17, 1964), p. 12. Baraka continued: "That it shapes up as black against white is the way it is; it's not my doing. Guerrilla warfare by blacks is inevitable . . . in the North and in the South."

31. Sherley Anne Williams, *Give Birth to Brightness*, p. 125.

32. The essay was written in the month *The Slave* opened at St. Marks Playhouse. Rejected by the *New York Times* (which had originally commissioned it) and the *Village Voice*, it was finally published in three Black periodicals before its inclusion in *Home*. *Black Dialogue*, no. 1 (1965), pp. 5–6; *Liberator* 5, no. 7 (July 1965), pp. 4–6; *Negro Digest* 15, no. 6 (April 1966), pp. 20–24.

33. The argument for a "corporate godhead" is much more convincing in the case of Clay and Lula than in the "trinity" of Walker, Grace, and Bradford. Cf., however, Lloyd Brown's interesting argument for such an interpretation of *The Slave* as a drama of self in "Dreamers and Slaves: The Ethos of Revolution in Walcott and LeRoi Jones," *Caribbean Quarterly* 12, nos. 3 and 4 (September 1971), pp. 36–44.

7. *THE SYSTEM OF DANTE'S HELL* AND *TALES:*
FROM "MEMORY EPIC" TO
"THEORIES OF GOVERNMENT AND PROSE"

1. (New York: H. Gantt / Phoenix Book Shop, 1959), pp. 29–48. The title of the collection denotes the artist as a sacrificial lamb in the vein of Poggioli's agonism; interestingly, *The Trembling Lamb* also contains Artaud's essay, "The Man Suicided by Society" (discussed by Poggioli).

2. *Soon, One Morning: New Writing by American Negroes, 1940–1962*, ed. Herbert Hill (New York: Knopf, 1963), p. 323.

3. *A World Elsewhere: The Place of Style in American Literature* (New York: Oxford University Press, 1966), pp. 39–40.

4. Cf. Poirier, pp. 50–92; and Quentin Anderson, *The Imperial Self: An Essay in American Literary and Cultural History* (New York: Knopf, 1971), pp. 3–58.

5. *New American Story,* ed. Donald M. Allen and Robert Creeley (Harmondsworth: Penguin, 1971), p. 251.

6. First published in *Pa'Lante,* no. 1 (May 19, 1962), pp. 91–93. For a more detailed analysis of this story, see John O'Brien, "Racial Nightmares and the Search for Self: An Explication of Leroi Jones' 'A Chase (Alighieri's Dream),' " *Negro American Literature Forum* 7 (1973), pp. 89–90.

7. See John O'Brien, "Innovative Black Fiction," ms. p. 8. This identification with Christ is, of course, a Barakian literary strategy common to much American literature. "Ray" is, like a similar projection in Baraka's poetry, the "son of sun," and thus, by name, associated with the son of God. In addition to the typological Christic dimensions, Ray also shows affinities to Claude McKay's protagonist in *Home to Harlem,* which is discussed in T 131.

8. An inversion devised in analogy to Brooklyn singer Amy Camus, who became famous as a performer under the supposed "Incan" name Yma Sumac.

9. Like "Bubbles," "Eddie McGhee" or "McGee" was a childhood nickname of the author: "my father called me 'mcgee' " (SD 138).

10. Cf. *New American Story,* p. 274: "Born . . . in the dumb industrial complex of Newark, New Jersey."

11. First published in *Evergreen Review* 9, no. 36 (June 1965), pp. 28–29, 92–93. Baraka made several ironic references to the "rags to riches" myth Horatio Alger stands for; most recently in the anti-Kissinger poem "Horatio Alger Uses Scag" (HF 20).

12. This formula comes from "Me and My Captain," *The Negro Caravan: Writings by American Negroes,* ed. Sterling A. Brown et al. (1941; repr. New York: Arno Press, 1970), p. 471.

13. In *Stephen Hero,* Joyce "defines an epiphany as 'a sudden spiritual manifestation' when the 'soul' or 'whatness' of an object 'leaps up to us from the vestment of its appearance,' i.e., when the metaphoric potential of an object (or a moment, gesture, phrase, etc.) is realized." Daniel Gifford with Robert J. Seidman, *Notes for Joyce: An Annotation of James Joyce's Ulysses* (New York: Dutton, 1974), p. 36.

14. Jaap Kool, *Das Saxophon* (Leipzig: Weber, 1921), p. 264 (my translation). In "The Practice of the New Nationalism," Baraka takes the uses of the saxophone as an indication of the essential difference between Black and white: "So Adolph Saxe's invention of a dour lamentation sounding 'a-phone,' and that projection of it did not in the end say anything about what John Coltrane could produce." (R 159)

15. "De Profundis," *New York Times Book Review,* February 4, 1968, p. 36.

16. According to Baraka, the "hucklebuck" is a dance only Blacks can do: BP 199–200; cf. also UP 10 and SD 85.

17. Cf. Kerouac's "Essentials of Spontaneous Prose," discussed in chapter one. Lynn Hope, who is this center in "The Screamers," significantly wears a jewel.

18. *Kulchur* 4, no. 4 (Summer 1964), p. 85.

19. *Cane* (1923; repr. New York: Harper, 1969), p. 145.

20. The poem in "Answers in Progress" was later incorporated into the class opening exercises at the New Ark Afrikan Free School; cf. *Education Text* (Newark: Jihad, 1974), p. 14.

21. For more recent developments, cf. the conclusion and UI 21. Baraka's own retreat from publishing fiction in the sense of *Dante* or *Tales* can only be partially responsible for the comparative paucity of criticism in this area. It would be interesting to study Baraka's syntactic realization of "art-ing" as a verb force. A linguistic analysis of his prose might yield many examples of an exaggerated verb force, which compresses sentences by extending the functions of a verb in analogy to its gerund powers. E.g., "And their voices, all these other selves screaming for blood. For blood, or whatever it is fills their noble lives" (T 29). Or: "and they are left with only the old Southern tongue, which cruel farts like me used to deride their lack of interest in America" (T 47). Or: "With no music till Lynn finishes 'macking' with any biglipped Esther screws across the stage" (T 71).

8. BLACK CULTURAL NATIONALISM AND THE BLACK AESTHETIC

1. Cruse, *Crisis*, p. 466.

2. Stephen Schneck, "LeRoi Jones or, Poetics and Policemen or, Trying Heart, Bleeding Heart," *Ramparts* 6, no. 12 (June 29–July 13, 1968), p. 14.

3. Elenore Lester, "Jones boy . . . and girl click on stage," *Newark Star-Ledger*, January 3, 1965, pp. 5, 7, presents a Horatio Alger version of Baraka and his sister, who are both "making their mark in the theater" (5). As far as Baraka's career is concerned, "LeRoi has no objection to being produced on Broadway, but hasn't the slightest intention of changing his style or the content of his plays to meet the requirements of the commercial theater" (7). For other contemporary accounts, see "Jones Coming to Broadway," *New York Times*, May 11, 1965; and "LeRoi Jones's Work to Play on Broadway," Minneapolis *Tribune*, July 18, 1965.

4. "They Think You're an Airplane and You're Really a Bird! An Interview," *Evergreen Review* 12, no. 50 (December 1967), p. 53. (UI 7)

5. "LeRoi Jones and the Tradition of the Fake," *Dissent* 12 no. 2 (Spring 1965), p. 207.

6. Ibid., p. 209.

7. Richard A. Koenigsberg's letter of January 7, 1965, "The Jones Case," was writ-

ten in response to *Village Voice* articles on Baraka and notes Baraka's "hysterical fear, his defensiveness, and his inability to construct a good English sentence." Koenigsberg's tirade continues: "Lacking the ability to confront educated 'highbrows' on their own terms, he quickly becomes the maligned and justifiably offended Negro, shirking the responsibility of rationally and intelligently answering his critics" (4). One week later, Dick Higgins criticized Koenigsberg in another letter to the *Voice* (January 14, 1965, p. 4). Higgins saw in Baraka "less an individual artist than a spokesman for the new lumpenproletariat."

8. "The Adventures of Superiorman," (by "Bloom/Leonard"). *Realist*, no. 59 (May 1965), pp. 16–17.

9. Harry Gilroy, "Racial Debate Displaces Jazz Program," *New York Times*, February 10, 1965, p. 47.

10. For definitions and discussions of Black nationalism, cf., e.g., Robert L. Allen *Black Awakening in Capitalist America: An Analytic History* (Garden City: Doubleday, 1970); Theodore Draper, *The Rediscovery of Black Nationalism* (New York: Viking, 1970); and *Black Nationalism in America*, ed. Bracey, Meier, and Rudwick (Indianapolis and New York: Bobbs-Merrill, 1970).

11. Cf. Volkhard Brandes, *Black Brother: Die Bedeutung Afrikas für den Freiheitskampf des schwarzen Amerika* (Frankfurt: Melzer, 1971), esp. pp. 43–47. Cf. also William Lloyd Garrison's critique of the Colonization Societies and Imanuel Geiss, *Pan-Afrikanismus: Zur Geschichte der Dekolonisation* (Frankfurt: EVA, 1968).

12. For background information on the Nation of Islam, see E. U. Essien-Udom, *Black Nationalism: The Rise of the Black Muslims in the U.S.A.* (Chicago & London: Chicago University Press, 1963), reviewed by Baraka for *Kulchur* (UN 26); C. Eric Lincoln, *The Black Muslims in America* (Boston: Beacon Press, 1961); Elijah Muhammad, *Message to the Blackman in America* (Chicago: Muhammad Mosque No. 2, 1965).

13. Cf. *The Quotable Karenga* (Los Angeles: US Organization, 1967). "Black Cultural Nationalism," pp. 1–8. Karenga's metaphoric concept of nationhood ascribes an essential role to culture, which becomes a sublimation for land—not unlike the German nation of "poets and thinkers" of the 19th century; cf. Bernard Bell, *The Folk Roots of Contemporary Black Poetry* (Detroit: Broadside Press, 1974).

14. Quoted by Vivian Gornick, "An Ofay's Indirect Address to LeRoi Jones," *Village Voice* 10, no. 20 (March 4, 1965), p. 6.

15. Baraka considered this essay crucial enough to refer to it as a primary source on Malcolm X (R 29). If Balzac dreamed that his own mission was to terminate with the pen what Napoleon had begun with the sword (Poggioli, p. 115), then Baraka saw himself as the cultural executor of Malcolm's political will. In the passage quoted above, there is also a certain echo to Emerson's "landscape" in "Nature." Cf. Richard Poirier, *A World Elsewhere*, pp. 57–62.

16. "Jones Says Blacks Really Form A Nation," *Amsterdam News*, May 24, 1969, p. 69.

17. The five formulations of Black Power are taken from Robert L. Allen, *Dialectics of Black Power* (New York: Guardian Pamphlets, 1968), pp. 7–18; the examples from the resolutions passed are quoted by L. H. Stanton, "The Black Power Conference," *Liberator* 7, no. 8 (August 1967), pp. 8–9. See also, "Black Power Meeting Opens," *New York Times*, July 21, 1967, p. 34, and "The Many Meanings of 'Black Power,' " *New York Times*, July 23, 1967, section 4, p. 1.

18. *Quotable Karenga*, ed. Clyde Halisi and James Mtume (Los Angeles: US, 1967), p. 1.

19. Michael T. Kaufman, "Jones Asks Votes, Not Rioting, to 'Take' Newark," *New York Times*, April 14, 1968, p. 60. While Baraka used Malcolm's "ballot-bullet" formula, he also charged white leftists with inciting riots in the Black ghetto. *Los Angeles Free Press*, May 3–9, 1968, pp. 3, 5, 42. (UI 11)

20. "Conciliator at Black Parley," *New York Times*, March 13, 1972, p. 30. Cf. *Quotable Karenga*, p. 19.

21. The title is related to the concept of "razing" and "raising" discussed in connection with the "destruction" and "rebuilding" of Patterson (DL 11; chapter 4). Baraka's works in the cultural nationalist phase abound with hymnic references to the words *Raise Race Rays Raze*. Baraka's regular column in his monthly paper *Black NewArk*, and later, *Unity & Struggle*, was entitled "RAISE!!" and sound patterns around the words "race" and "Ray(s)" recur. The poem "Part of the Doctrine" (B 200) and the play "Bloodrites" (UD 7) represent the most comprehensive uses of the sound cluster from the title of the essay collection. The tendencies implied by the words may be roughly paraphrased in the following manner: "raise"—the avant-gardist; "raze"—the nihilist tendency; "rays"—the Emersonian, cosmic, autobiographic expression; "race"—the Black spirit of populist collectivity.

22. Cf. "Black Mass" (F 17–39), discussed in chapter nine, pp. 210–14.

23. Cf. R 132 and Baraka's comment about "terrible Marx on the dirty Lenin" (R 130).

24. Cf. Frazier, *Black Bourgeoisie*, p. 226.

25. "Maulana Ron Karenga Discusses US/Panther Conflict and the Tackwood Distortions," *Unity & Struggle* 3, no. 6 (June 1974), p. 7. "Unite the many to defeat the few" was a motto of *Unity & Struggle*.

26. *Quotable Karenga*, p. 22.

27. "Black Cultural Nationalism," *The Black Aesthetic*, ed. Addison Gayle, Jr. (Garden City: Doubleday Anchor, 1972), p. 32.

28. *The American Mercury* 15 (December 1928), pp. 477–81.

29. Richard Gilman, "Black Writing and White Criticism," *The Confusion of Realms* (New York: Random House, 1969), p. 18. Cf., however, Gilman's earlier, derogatory review of *Dante*, "The Devil May Care," *New York Herald Tribune Book Week*, December 26, 1965, p. 9.

30. *Jazz* 5, no. 1 (November 1966), p. 38 (UI 4).

31. Cf. the documentation of FBI-inspired clashes between Karenga's US and the Black Panther Party in the *Supplementary Detailed Staff Reports on Intelligence Activities and the Rights of Americans,* book III (Senate Report No. 94-755, Washington, April 23, 1976), pp. 186–223, and Baraka's self-critical assessment of the stages of Black cultural nationalism, "From Congress of Afrikan People to Revolutionary Communist League," *Unity & Struggle* 5, no. 6 (June 1976), p. 3 (UN 134).

32. Cf. Van Wyck Brooks's reflections on "Transnationalism," *The Writer in America* (New York: Dutton, 1953), pp. 86–108.

9. THE BLACKER ARTS: POETRY AND DRAMA OF BLACK CULTURAL NATIONALISM

1. Poggioli, *Theory* . . . , p. 193.

2. This frequently reprinted and discussed poem was first published in the Black monthly, *Liberator* 6, no. 1 (January 1966), p. 18. Baraka recited the poem for a 1967 recording on the Album *Sonny's Time Now,* brought out by Jihad Productions. It is noteworthy that while many of Baraka's reviewers of the 1960s and most Black critics today have pointed out the indulgence in anti-Semitic themes (more in B 54, 131, 161, etc.), white Baraka critics of the 1970s tend to shy away from such discussions and do everything to avoid facing quotations such as the one given before. While Esther Jackson and Theodore Hudson mention Baraka's anti-Semitism openly and directly, William Fischer discusses *Black Magic* without any reference to this rather important obstacle to "revolutionary" art. Kimberly Benston quotes from Baraka's "Black Art" four times; but, unwilling to confront the lines about "dagger poems in the slimy bellies / of the owner-jews" (B 116), or "Another bad poem cracking / steel knuckles in a jewlady's mouth" (B 117), Benston chooses to quote less ambiguously "revolutionary" lines repeatedly. If a critic explicitly praises Baraka's poetic establishment of "the racial myth which the earlier works have been building toward in fits and starts" (Benston, p. 133) and refrains from discussing such traditional racial myths as anti-Semitism, doesn't this mean that the Jew becomes a *pharmakos,* a sacrifice brought by white American critics on the altar of Black cultural nationalism?

3. This is perhaps an ironic allusion to Joyce Kilmer's popular poem, "A Tree," which Baraka also parodied in "Western Front": "Poems are made / by fools like Allen Ginsberg. . . . But only God . . . is clearly responsible" (B 81). Cf. also P 6–12.

4. The poem was first published in *Evergreen Review* 11, no. 50 (December 1967), p. 49. In the version reprinted in B 225, the word "shotguns" was omitted at the end of the second line.

5. "LeRoi Jones, Talk-in Attraction, Inveighs in Poetry and Prose," *New York Times,* October 4, 1966, p. 51. Cf. *New York Times,* July 15, 1967, p. 11, and October 29, 1967, section 2, p. 2.

6. Court transcript, "State of New Jersey v. Everett Le Roi Jones, Charles Mc-Cray and Barry Wynn," Essex County Court, Law Division: Criminal Indictment No. 2220-66, January 4, 1968, pp. 17–18. I am indebted to Theodore Hudson for sending me a copy of the complete transcript, which reads like a ritual drama.

7. Court transcript, p. 20. In the course of the interchanges, Baraka addressed the public and voiced strong anti-Semitic feelings, which was hardly reported in the newspaper accounts:

> DEFENDANT JONES: All these Jews are going to get you killed. I'll tell you that. All you police, remember who is getting you killed. It's these Jews. To you Italians and you Irish, these Jews are setting you up. That's the way it is. (p. 21)

8. *Time* 91, no. 2 (January 12, 1968), p. 14; *New York Times,* January 7, 1968, section 4, p. 6; *Newsweek* 71, no. 3 (January 15, 1968), p. 24.

9. "LeRoi Jones framed, charge 16 poets," *Los Angeles Free Press,* January 20–26, 1968, p. 2; signed by Ashbery, Corso, Creeley, DiPrima, Duncan, Ferlinghetti, Ginsberg, Koch, Levertov, McClure, Olson, Oppenheimer, Orlovsky, Sorrentino, Whalen, and Wieners. Robert Terrell, "Rights Leaders Rap LeRoi Jones' Judge," *New York Post,* January 6, 1968. "In Defense of LeRoi Jones," *Freedomways* 8, no. 1 (Winter 1968), p. 2. "Declaration of United Black Artists," *National Guardian,* January 20, 1968, p. 20. Baraka's own account, UN 44. "Jones is Acquitted of Weapons Charge in Newark Retrial," *New York Times,* July 3, 1969, p. 18.

10. For further information and an excellent framework concerning the uses of speech and music in Black poetry, cf. Stephen Henderson, *Understanding the New Black Poetry.*

11. A variant version of "It's Nation Time" is included in AC 101–3. The poem is also a parody of "It's Howdy-Doody time."

12. "T. T. Jackson sings" (B 105) is an example of an imitative dozens poem. T. T. Jackson, a Black street character in Baraka's play "A Recent Killing," reflects a tradition which has been recorded in many alternate versions; one that is strikingly similar to Baraka's Jackson is reprinted by Henderson, p. 36. Although Leslie Fiedler is right in his statement that Baraka tries to "close the gap between high art and Pop," he misses the dozens context and therefore erroneously assumes that "T. T. Jackson sings" provides, for Baraka, "an ironical shield against the surrender to triteness and sentiment which characterizes Smokey Robinson. . . ." Fiedler, "The Children's Hour: or, The Return of the Vanishing Longfellow: Some Reflections on the Future of Poetry," *Liberations: New Essays on the Humanistic Revolution* (Middletown: Wesleyan University Press, 1971), ed. Ihab Hassan, pp. 163–64.

13. After recording "Black Dada Nihilismus" on the album *LeRoi Jones and the New York Art Quartet* (ESP-Disk 1004), Baraka read several of his own poems

with musical accompaniment on the records *Sonny's Time Now* (Jihad Productions) and *Black and Beautiful: Soul and Madness* (Jihad).

14. Recorded on the album *Black and Beautiful* with additional text.

15. Recorded on the album *Black and Beautiful*. The background sound has a striking resemblance to Smokey Robinson's hit "Baby Baby."

16. "Death Unit" was first performed on March 1, 1965, under the direction of Baraka, at St. Mark's, but was subsequently performed at the Black Arts Repertory Theater/School. In connection with the publication of the play in the *East Side Review*, there was a small scandal: Baraka was reported to have assaulted Shepard Sherbell, the editor of the review, for failing to pay Baraka $100 in royalties for "Death Unit." Cf. Albert Ellenberg, "LeRoi Jones Accused of Beating Publisher," *New York Post*, July 30, 1966.

17. "Patting your foot" suggests a Black commonality in a ritual, and a "personal life rhythm." Cf. the essay "Poetry and Karma," which is closely related to the theme of "Death Unit," R 20; cf. also "Leadbelly Gives an Autograph" B 25–26.

18. Cf. the discussion at the end of chapter two.

19. For an account of the performance, cf. Paul Velde, "Pursued by the Furies," *Commonweal* 88, no. 15 (June 28, 1968), p. 441.

20. As a satire, *Jello* requires some familiarity with Jack Benny. Cf. Daniel Blum, *A Pictorial History of Television* (Philadelphia and New York: Chilton, 1959), pp. 30–33. A photoscript of a Jello commercial is included in Wallace A. Rose, *Best TV Commercials of the Year* (New York: Hastings House, 1967), pp. 52–53.

21. "The Day LeRoi Jones Spoke on Penn Campus What Were the Blacks Doing in the Balcony." *New York Times Magazine*, May 4, 1969, p. 58.

22. The play was first published, in an abridged version, in *Liberator* 6, no. 6 (June 1966), pp. 14–17, where Baraka was also trying to reach a Black audience.

23. *Message to the Blackman in America* (Chicago: Muhammad Mosque No. 2, 1965), pp. 110–11. Further references are given parenthetically. There are popularized accounts of this story, e.g. in Malcolm X's *Autobiography* and in Cleaver's *Soul on Ice*.

24. Cf. the discussion of "Black Dada Nihilismus," chapter four.

25. Mary Wollstonecraft Shelley, *Frankenstein* (repr. New York: Signet, 1965), p. 56.

26. Larry Neal first suggested a reading of the play as a critique of l'art pour l'art in "The Black Arts Movement," *The Drama Review* 12, no. 4 (Summer, 1968), pp. 36–37. Related to Baraka's criticism of Jack Benny as an "artist" in *Jello*, "A Black Mass" is very likely an example of Baraka's retrospective self-criticism as an individualist creator and "new critic" (R 119). The interpretation of "A Black Mass" as agitation not so much against white devils as against their Black "creators," was borne out by the Black audience response to the performances in Ernie McClintock's New York Afro-American Studio for Acting and Speech and in Robert

Hooks's Washington Black Repertory Theater: the reactions were comparable to those toward the horror films Baraka parodied; and verbal criticism was launched only against Jacoub.

27. F 41–63. Clayton Riley rates "Great Goodness" as highly as *Dutchman* in his introduction to *A Black Quartet: Four New Black Plays* (New York: Signet, 1970), p. xxii. "Great Goodness" was first performed at Spirit House in November 1967 and had a successful off-Broadway run as one play of "A Black Quartet" in 1969.

28. The description is based, in part, on the powerful production of *Slave Ship* under the direction of Gilbert Moses at the Brooklyn Academy of Music. Despite its "antiwhite" tendencies (the theater critic of the *New Yorker*, e.g., was included into the show as an imaginary bidder at a slave auction off stage), this performance impressed most critics who could conclude, with Eric Bentley, that from a socialist perspective, one can read *Slave Ship* "as a series of extremely vivid images of capitalist exploitation . . . I got my consciousness raised by a writer who (I must assume) wants me liquidated as a carrier of the white plague, and whom I disapprove of as a racist." "Must I Side With Blacks or Whites," *New York Times*, January 23, 1972, section 2, p. 1. Cf. also the observations of Bertolt Brecht's son Stefan *The Drama Review* 14, no. 46 (Winter 1970), pp. 212–19. *Slave Ship* was recently reprinted, with program notes and a Yoruba glossary, in *The Motion of History and Other Plays* (New York: Morrow, 1978), pp. 129–50.

29. The most famous pictorial representations were the numerous pig cartoons in *The Black Panther* paper, drawn by Emory Douglas, the party's minister of culture.

30. Cf. *New York Times*, April 14, 1968, p. 60; "New Script in Newark," *Time* 91 (April 26, 1968), pp. 18–19; and the discussion in chapter eight.

31. In addition to the unperformed and unfilmed video script, "The Death of Malcolm X" (UD 3), there are several movies and many video recordings of Spirit House activities. Even within his formal works, Baraka transcended genres; thus, *In Our Terribleness* is a melange of photographs, essays, poetry, and other "texts."

32. "Political Assassination," *The Black Panther* 3, no. 19 (August 30, 1969), p. 10.

33. "Papa Doc and the Truth About Haiti Today" and "Karenga and the Truth About 'US,' " *The Black Panther* 3, no. 27 (October 25, 1969), p. 9.

34. George L. Jackson, *Blood in My Eye* (New York: Random House, 1972), p. 36.

35. Costas Axios and Nikos Syvriotis, *Papa Doc Baraka: Fascism in Newark* (National Caucus of Labor Committees, 1973), p. 9.

36. "Message from the Chairman," *Fundisha* 1, no. 5 (part of *Black News* 2, no. 10, October 22, 1973), pp. 7–8.

37. Donald M. Allen and Robert Creeley, eds. *New American Story* (Harmondsworth: Penguin, 1971), p. 275; James W. Sullivan, "The Negro 'National Consciousness' of LeRoi Jones," *New York Herald Tribune*, October 31, 1965, p. 34.

38. Michael Mok, "LeRoi Jones (Baraka)," *Publishers Weekly*, September 11, 1972, p. 20.

10. MARXISM–LENINISM–
MAO TSE TUNG THOUGHT

1. The papers are marked "CAP IP" in the bibliography. They were scheduled for publication with Howard University Press in 1975, but have not yet appeared.

2. This notion is more in accord with Baraka's older anti-integrationist sentiment than with Mao Tse Tung thought. Inspired by Robert F. Williams, Mao issued a statement after the assassination of Dr. Martin Luther King supporting the struggle of Afro-Americans and the civil rights movement.

3. Baraka published Cabral and Touré in pamphlet form. He included excerpts from Cabral's "The Weapon of Theory" in the May 1974 issue of *Unity & Struggle*. Touré's widely discussed essay on "A Dialectical Approach to Culture" first appeared in *Black Scholar* 1, no. 1 (October 1969), the same issue that carried Baraka's "Black Value System."

4. Joseph F. Sullivan, "Gibson Called A 'Puppet' By Baraka in Open Split," *New York Times*, August 18, 1973.

5. UN 108. Baraka also called *Black World* "the tombstone of petty bourgeois reactionary nationalist thought" (UN 108), while he continued publishing in it. The reference to Muhammad Ali is in UN 111.

6. "Blueprint for Black Criticism," *First World* 1, no. 1 (January–February 1977), p. 43.

7. Ibid.

8. Ibid.

9. Crispin Y. Campbell, "Window on black officials," *Jersey Record*, February 18, 1974. Baraka also mentioned being involved in writing a collective play entitled "Black Power, or The Incredible Rocky," in 1974 (UI 20).

10. These plays, which I quote from their manuscript versions, UD 11 and UD 12, have recently been published, in a slightly altered form, in *The Motion of History and Other Plays* (New York: Morrow, 1978). My "S-1" quotations can be found on pp. 167–68, 197, and 206, and the references to "The Motion of History" are on pp. 80–81, 81–82, 83, 84–85, 89, and 94 of the Morrow version.

CONCLUSION

1. Cecil Brown, "About LeRoi Jones," *Evergreen Review* 75 (February 1970), p. 65, and "Apotheosis of a Prodigal Son," *Kenyon Review* 30, no. 122 (Issue 5, 1968), p. 661.

2. Don N. Menchise, "LeRoi Jones and a Case of Shifting Identities," *College Language Association Journal* 20, no. 2 (December 1976), pp. 232–34. Cf. also: Hollie E. West, "Amiri Baraka: Why a Distinguished Writer Can't Get Published," *Boston Evening Globe*, April 13, 1978, p. 2 (repr. from *Washington Post*).

Selected Bibliography

Note: Baraka rarely revised or rewrote his works. His collections contain, for the most part, identical reprints of poems, plays, short stories, and essays which had previously appeared in periodicals and anthologies. For this reason, works which are included in Baraka's collections (II A) are not also listed in their originally published form or in subsequently reprinted versions. This means that sections II B-F contain no references to works which were included in the collections listed under II A.

Despite its brevity, section II (arranged chronologically) aims at completeness; no published work by Baraka which has entered previous bibliographies (I) or general reference guides has been omitted, and the present bibliography contains several works by Baraka which have never appeared in any listing. Readers who are interested in bibliography, however, should turn to Ms. Dace's work for more complete references, which allow the reconstruction of printing histories of individual works through 1970.

Section III is selective and lists mostly those secondary sources and materials which are used in the text.

I. BIBLIOGRAPHIES AND BIBLIOGRAPHICAL INFORMATION

Baker, John, "LeRoi Jones, Secessionist, and Ambitious Collecting." *Yale University Library Gazette* 46, no. 3 (January 1972), pp. 159–66.

Benston, Kimberly W. *Baraka: The Renegade and the Mask.* New Haven and London: Yale University Press, 1976.

Cohn, Alan M. "Additions to Dace's LeRoi Jones (Imamu Amiri Baraka)." *Papers of the Bibliographical Society of America* 70 (1976), pp. 537–38.

Curley, Dorothy Nyren; Maurice Kramer; and Elain Fialka Kramer. "Jones,

LeRoi (1934–)." *A Library of Literary Criticism*, 4th edition. New York: Ungar, 1969. Vol. 2, pp. 160–64.

Current Biography 31, no. 5 (May 1970), pp. 16–18. "Jones, (Everett) LeRoi."

Dace, Letitia. *LeRoi Jones (Imamu Amiri Baraka): A Checklist of Works By and About Him.* London: Nether Press, 1971.

Dippold, Diane. LeRoi Jones: Tramp With Connections. Ph.D. diss., University of Maryland, 1971. University Microfilms 72-1663.

Fouch, Deborah Smith. *Everett LeRoi Jones (Imamu Ameer Baraka).* Atlanta: Center of African and African-American Studies bibliography 2, n.d. (Mimeogr.)

Gibson, Donald B., ed. *Five Black Writers: Essays on Wright, Ellison, Baldwin, Hughes, and LeRoi Jones.* New York: New York University Press, 1970, pp. 309–10.

Harte, Barbara, and Carolyn Riley, eds. *Contemporary Authors: A Bio-Bibliographical Guide to Current Authors and Their Works.* Vols. 21–22. Detroit: Gale Research Co., The Book Tower, 1969, pp. 277–80.

Hudson, Theodore R. *A LeRoi Jones (Amiri Baraka) Bibliography: A Keyed Research Guide to Works by LeRoi Jones and to Writings About Him and His Works.* Washington, D.C.: priv. publ., 1971.

Rush, Theressa Gunnels; Carol Fairbanks Myers; and Esther Spring Arata. *Black American Writers Past and Present: A Biographical and Bibliographical Dictionary.* Metuchen, N.J.: The Scarecrow Press, 1975. Vol. 1, pp. 50–56.

Schatt, Stanley. "LeRoi Jones: A Checklist to Primary and Secondary Sources." *Bulletin of Bibliography and Magazine Notes* 28, no. 2 (April–June 1971), pp. 55–57.

Turner, Darwin T. *Afro-American Writers: Goldentree Bibliographies in Language and Literature.* New York: Appleton Crofts, 1970, pp. 63–64.

II. PRIMARY SOURCES

A. Collected Works

P *Preface To A Twenty Volume Suicide Note.* New York: Totem Press/Corinth, 1961. 48pp. 27 poems.

BP *Blues People: Negro Music in White America.* New York: Morrow, 1963. 244pp. Music criticism—Afro-American history—Sociology.

M Ed. *The Moderns: An Anthology of New Writing in America.* New York: Corinth, 1963. 351pp.

DS *Dutchman and The Slave.* New York: Morrow, 1964. 88pp. 2 plays.

DL *The Dead Lecturer.* New York: Grove Press, 1964. 79pp. 37 poems.

SD   *The System of Dante's Hell.* New York: Grove Press, 1965. 154pp. Novel (20 sections of short fiction and one play, "The Eighth Ditch").

H   *Home: Social Essays.* New York: Morrow, 1966. 252pp. 24 essays.

SS   *Slave Ship.* Newark: Jihad, 1967. 13pp. Play.

BT   *The Baptism and The Toilet.* New York: Grove Press, 1967. 62pp. 2 plays.

A   *Arm Yourself Or Harm Yourself.* Newark: Jihad, 1967. 11pp. Play.

T   *Tales.* New York: Grove Press, 1967. 132pp. 16 stories.

BM   *Black Music.* New York: Morrow, 1967. 221pp. Collected music criticism, 1959–1966.

BF   Ed. with Larry Neal. *Black Fire: An Anthology of Afro-American Writing.* New York: Morrow, 1968. 670pp.

B   *Black Magic: Sabotage—Target Study—Black Art: Collected Poetry, 1961–1967.* Indianapolis and New York: Bobbs-Merrill, 1969. 225pp. 167 poems (incl. a few short prose pieces).

F   *Four Black Revolutionary Plays.* Indianapolis and New York: Bobbs-Merrill, 1969. 89pp. 4 plays.

J   *Jello.* Chicago: Third World Press, 1970. 38pp. Play and introductory essay.

IN   *It's Nation Time.* Chicago: Third World Press, 1970. 24pp. 3 poems.

     In Our Terribleness (Some elements and meaning in black style). Indianapolis and New York: Bobbs-Merrill, 1970. 171pp. (no pag.). Poems and prose pieces with photographs by Fundi (Billy Abernathy).

R   *Raise Race Rays Raze: Essays Since 1965.* New York: Random House, 1971. 169pp. 21 essays.

     Strategy and Tactics of a PanAfrican Nationalist Party. Newark: Jihad, 1971. 22pp. Essay.

AC   Ed. *African Congress: A Documentary of the First Modern Pan-African Congress.* New York: Morrow, 1972. 493pp.

SR   *Spirit Reach.* Newark: Jihad, 1972. 26pp. 13 poems.

     Crisis in Boston. Newark: Vita Wa Watu—People's War Publishing, 1974. 32pp. 2 essays.

HF   *Hard Facts.* Newark: Peoples War, 1975. 40pp. 28 poems and introductory essay.

     The Motion of History and Other Plays. New York: Morrow, 1978. 225pp. Three plays and an introduction.

Note: SD, T, and DL were bound in one volume and distributed under the title *Three Books by Imamu Amiri Baraka (LeRoi Jones)* (New York: Grove Press, 1975). The pagination is the same as in the original editions.

II. B. Uncollected Poetry

UP 1   "Slice of Life." *Yugen*, no. 1 (March 1958), p. 16.
UP 2   "Lines to Garcia Lorca." *Yugen*, no. 1 (March 1958), pp. 17–18. (Accessible in Langston Hughes, ed., *New Negro Poets U.S.A.* Bloomington: Indiana University Press, 1964, p. 55.)
UP 3   "Love Poem." *Birth*, no. 1 (Autumn 1958), p. 52. (Not identical with UP 37.)
UP 4   "Scenario." *Naked Ear*, no. 11 (1958), pp. [7–8].
UP 5   "The Gift of the Unicorn." *Epos* 10, no. 2 (Winter 1958), p. 7.
UP 6   "Central Park in Winter." *Quicksilver* 11, no. 4 (Winter 1958), p. 14.
UP 7   "The Last Roundup."*Hearse*, no. 5 (1959), p. [16]. Recorded April 17, 1959, Library of Congress Work Order 2831 (LoC 2831).
UP 8   "Oedipus Poem." *Odyssey* 1, no. 4 (1959), p. 56.
UP 9   "April 13 (for Tom)." *Penny Poems* 30 (1959).
UP 10 "Parthenos." *Yugen*, no. 4 (1959), pp. 23–26. LoC 2831.
UP 11 "Sonar Rhapsody II." LoC 2831 (1959).
UP 12 "Spring & Soforth." LoC 2831 (1959). Printed: *Penny Poems* 111 (1960).
UP 13 "Where is Mu?" LoC 2831 (1959).
UP 14 "The Shadow Waltz." LoC 2831 (1959).
UP 15 "I Sign For My Check On Thursdays." LoC 2831 (1959).
UP 16 "The Plumed Serpent." LoC 2831 (1959).
UP 17 "Consider This." LoC 2831 (1959). Printed excerpt: Daisy Aldan, ed. *A New Folder*. New York: Folder Editions, 1959, pp. 31–32.
UP 18 "For You." LoC 2831 (1959). Printed: *Jan 1st 1959: Fidel Castro*. New York: Totem Press, 1959, p. [4].
UP 19 "Metaphysical Ode to Birth." LoC 2831 (1959).
UP 20 "The Making of a Poem from a Paint Can." LoC 2831 (1959).
UP 21 "Columbia the Gem of the Ocean." LoC 2831 (1959).
UP 22 "Vision Provoked by a Strand of Hair." LoC 2831 (1959).
UP 23 "One last thing beat out with my tubular drum." LoC 2831 (1959).
UP 24 "Anything is Painting." LoC 2831 (1959).
UP 25 "Poem Writ in the Dark." LoC 2831 (1959).
UP 26 "March." *Combustion*, no. 10 (May 1959), pp. [7–8].
UP 27 "Epistrophe (for Yodo)." Elias Wilentz, ed. *The Beat Scene*. New York: Corinth, 1960, p. 56.
UP 28 "In JW's Rug." *Provincetown Review*, no. 3 (1960), p. [69].
UP 29 "A Paramount Picture (for Nick Charles)." *Neon Obit*, no. 5 (1960), p. [2].
UP 30 "Node." *Yugen*, no. 6 (1960), p. 38.
UP 31 "The A, B, C's (For Charles)." *Yugen*, no. 6 (1960), pp. 39–40.
UP 32 "Confucius Say." *Combustion*, no. 13 (May 1960), p. 3.
UP 33 "The Disguise." *Penny Poems* 155 (1961).
UP 34 "Sundance." *Trobar*, no. 2 (1961), pp. 27–28.
UP 35 "Axel's Castle." *Whetstone* 4, no. 2 (1961), p. 81.

UP 36   "The Parade . . . five themes for Robert Thompson: the southpaw; bo peep; 'x'; boswell; dr. jive." *Outsider* 1, no. 1 (1961), pp. 67–68.

UP 37   "Love Poem." Gregory Corso and Walter Höllerer, eds. *Junge amerikanische Lyrik*. München: Hanser, 1961, p. 156.

UP 38   "Note From the Underground." Gregory Corso and Walter Höllerer, ed. *Junge amerikanische Lyrik*. München: Hanser, 1961, pp. 158–60.

UP 39   "A Long Poem for Myself." *Locus-Solus* 3–4 (Winter 1962), pp. 13–14.

UP 40   "A Poem for Myself, The Fool." *Locus-Solus* 3–4 (Winter 1962), p. 19.

UP 41   "To a 25 Year Old King." *Nomad/New York*, no. 10–11 (Autumn 1962), pp. 23–24.

UP 42   "Riding and Shooting." *Nomad/New York*, no. 10–11 (Autumn 1962), pp. 25–26.

UP 43   "The Pimp." *Outburst*, no. 2 (1963), p. [17].

UP 44   "Charlie Parker: The Human Condition." Herbert Hill, ed. *Soon One Morning: New Writing by American Negroes, 1940–1962*. New York: Knopf, 1963, pp. 609–10.

UP 45   "In Wyoming Territory: In Wyoming Territory (a title); In Wyoming Territory (a veil); In Wyoming Territory (a story); In Wyoming Territory (Music of); In Wyoming Territory (Dance/Like/)." *The Floating Bear* 28 (1963), pp. [5–9].

UP 46   "Exaugural Address (for Jacqueline Bouvier Kennedy, who has had to eat too much shit)." *Kulchur* 3, no. 12 (Winter 1963), inserted between pp. 86 and 87.

UP 47   "Engines." *Imago*, no. 1 (February 1964), pp. 6–8.

UP 48   "DoubleFeel." *Fuck You: A Magazine of the Arts* 6, no. 5 (10) (April 1964), p. [35].

UP 49   "Archie and Them Other Cats." *Liberator* 4, no. 9 (September 1964), p. 16.

UP 50   "Nana: 1888–1963." *Red Clay Reader*, no. 1 (1964), p. 51.

UP 51   "Sunspots." *Red Clay Reader*, no. 1 (1964), p. 51.

UP 52   "Like Rousseau." *Poetry* 105, no. 3 (December 1964), p. 161.

UP 53   "Target Study." *Niagara Frontier Review*, no. 2 (Spring–Summer 1965), pp. 54–56.

UP 54   "Chapter." *Niagara Frontier Review*, no. 2 (Spring–Summer 1965), pp. 57–58.

UP 55   "The Heavy." *Niagara Frontier Review*, no. 2 (Spring–Summer 1965), p. 59.

UP 56   "Relurk." *Niagara Frontier Review*, no. 2 (Spring–Summer 1965), pp. 60–61.

UP 57   "Lefty." *Niagara Frontier Review*, no. 2 (Spring–Summer 1965), pp. 62–63.

UP 58   "Brides of the Captured." *Niagara Frontier Review*, no. 2 (Spring–Summer 1965), pp. 65–66.

UP 59   "The Scholar." *Black Orpheus*, no. 17 (June 1965), p. 49.

UP 60   "Theory." *Spero* 1, no. 1 (1965), p. 24.

UP 61   "The Occident." *Black Dialogue* 2, no. 5 (Autumn 1966), p. 27.

UP 62   "Indians." *Black Dialogue* 2, no. 5 (Autumn 1966), p. 28. Also in: *Floating Bear*, no. 35 (1968), p. [15]. (Not identical with B 211.)

UP 63   "A Traffic of Love." *Floating Bear*, no. 35 (1968). p. [16].

UP 64   "Old Men's Feet (For Dr. Koch)." *Floating Bear*, no. 35 (1968), p. [17].

UP 65   "Nick Charles Meets the Wolf Man." *Floating Bear*, no. 35 (1968), pp. [18–19].

UP 66   "West of Dodge." *Floating Bear*, no. 35 (1968), p. [20].

UP 67   "No Matter. No Matter, The World is the World." *Journal of Black Poetry* 1, no. 8 (Spring 1968), pp. 24–25.

UP 68   "Who Will Survive America? Few Americans, Very Few Negroes, No Crackers at All." *Negro Digest* 17, no. 9 (July 1968), pp. 20–21. Also in: *Black News* 1, no. 4 (1969).

UP 69   "The Evolver." *Negro Digest* 17, no. 11–12 (September–October 1968), pp. 58–59.

UP 70   "Spacepoem for Four Tones." *Black News* 1, no. 4 (1969).

UP 71   "For Maulana Karenga and Pharaoh Saunders." *Black Theatre*, no. 4 (April 1970), p. 7.

UP 72   "Black Power Chant." *Black Theatre*, no. 4 (April 1970), p. 35. (Also performed as ritual on stage.)

UP 73   "Tanguhpay." *Black Theatre*, no. 5 (1970), p. 57.

UP 74   "Move." Woodie King, ed. *Black Spirits: A Festival of New Black Poets in America*. New York: Vintage, 1972, pp. 24–26.

UP 75   "African Love History." Woodie King, ed. *Black Spirits: A Festival of New Black Poets in America*. New York: Vintage, 1972, pp. 30–33.

UP 76   "We Know Directions." *Black World* 22, no. 7 (May 1973), p. 40.

UP 77   "O K Shoot!" *Black World* 22, no. 7 (May 1973), p. 40.

UP 78   "US." *Black World* 22, no. 7 (May 1973), pp. 41–42.

UP 79   "In The Midst of Chaos." *Black World* 22, no. 7 (May 1973), p. 42.

UP 80   "Look Inside." *Black World* 22, no. 7 (May 1973), p. 43.

UP 81   "Habari Gani." *Black World* 22, no. 7 (May 1973), pp. 43–44.

UP 82   "African Revolution (Conakry, Guinea, February 4, 1973, after Amilcar Cabral's funeral)." *Black World*, 22, no. 7 (May 1973), pp. 44–48.

II. C. Uncollected Drama

UD 1   "Home on the Range." *The Drama Review* 12, no. 4 (Summer 1968), pp. 106–11.

UD 2   "Police." *The Drama Review* 12, no. 4 (Summer 1968), pp. 112–15.

UD 3   "The Death of Malcolm X." Ed Bullins, ed. *New Plays From the Black Theatre*. New York: Bantam, 1969, pp. 1–20.

UD 4   "Resurrection in Life." Unpublished. Performed in Harlem, August 24, 1969. (Alternate title: "Insurrection and Misplaced Love.")

UD 5   "Rockgroup." *Cricket*, no. 4 (December 1969), pp. 41–43.

UD   6   "Junkies Are Full of (SHHH . . .)." Woodie King and Ron Milner, ed. *Black Drama Anthology*. New York: Columbia University Press, 1971, pp. 11–23.

UD   7   "Bloodrites." Woodie King and Ron Milner, eds. *Black Drama Anthology*. New York: Columbia University Press, 1971, pp. 25–31.

UD   8   "A Recent Killing." Unpublished. First performed in New York, February 1973.

UD   9   "Sidnee Poet Heroical or If in Danger of Suit, The Kid Poet Heroical." Unpublished. Performed in New York, 1974.

UD 10   "The New Ark's a moverin." Unpublished. Performed in Newark, July 1974. Ms. 13 pp.

UD 11   "The Motion of History." Unpublished. Ms. 80pp., dated December '75–January 1976. (Published, together with SS and UD 12, in *The Motion of History and Other Plays*. New York: Morrow, 1978.)

UD 12   "S-1 (A Play in 26 Scenes) w/Music." Unpublished. Performed in New York, July 1976, and in Newark, August 1976. Ms. 46pp., dated Jan.-March 1976. (Published in *The Motion of History and Other Plays*. New York: Morrow, 1978.)

II. D. Uncollected Fiction

UF   1   "Suppose Sorrow Was a Time Machine." *Yugen*, no. 2 (1958), pp. 9–11.

UF   2   "Round Trip." *Mutiny* 2, no. 2 (Autumn 1959), pp. 79–81.

UF   3   "The Man Who Sold Pictures of God." Stanley Fisher, ed. *Beat Coast East: An Anthology of Rebellion*. New York: Excelsior Press, 1960, pp. 91–96.

UF   4   "God and Machine." Sonia Sanchez, ed. *We Be Word Sorcerers: 25 Stories by Black Americans*. New York: Bantam, 1973, pp. 9–12.

UF   5   "Neo-American." *Les Temps Modernes* 32, no. 361–62 (1976), pp. 368–89. Trans. by Odilon Cavat and Charlotte Brody.

II. E. Uncollected Nonfiction (except music criticism)

UN   1   "Correspondence" (re: Beat Generation). *Partisan Review* 25, no. 3 (Summer 1958), pp. 472–73.

UN   2   "Correspondence" (re: Kerouac's Essentials of Spontaneous Prose). *Evergreen Review*, no. 8 (Spring 1959), pp. 253–56.

UN   3   "Reviews: Books: Langston Hughes' *Tambourines to Glory*." *Jazz Review* 2, no. 5 (June 1959), pp. 33–34.

UN   4   "Hafaz Fellowships." *Yugen*, no. 5 (August 1959), p. 13.

UN 5   "Movie Review." *Jazz Review* 2, no. 10 (November 1959), pp. 50–51.

UN 6   "How You Sound??" *The New American Poetry: 1945–1960*, ed. Donald M. Allen. New York: Grove Press, 1960, pp. 424–25.

UN 7   Autobiographical note: "LeRoi Jones." *The New American Poetry: 1945–1960*, ed. Donald M. Allen. New York: Grove Press, 1960, p. 438.

UN 8   "Part of a letter from LeRoi Jones." *Beatitude*, no. 17 (October, November 1960), p. [21].

UN 9   Review of John Wieners' *The Hotel Wentley Poems. Kulchur* 1, no. 2 (Winter 1960), pp. 94–95.

UN 10   "Paterson Society Statement." (Single sheet, mimeogr.), Cambridge, Mass.: Paterson Society, February 27, 1961.

UN 11   "Revue." *The Floating Bear*, no. 2 (February 1961), pp. [7–8].

UN 12   "Diane . . ." (letter to Diane DiPrima). *The Floating Bear*, no. 5 (April 1961), p. [5].

UN 13   "A Note on the Twelve Poems" (by George Stanley). *The Floating Bear*, no. 6 (April 1961), pp. [7–8].

UN 14   "Note" (on Larry Rivers). *The Floating Bear*, no. 6 (April 1961), p. [10]. Pen name "Johannes Koenig" used.

UN 15   "Putdown of the Whore of Babylon (a Lamantia title)." *Yugen*, no. 7 (April 1961), pp. 4–5.

UN 16   "Public Notice" (on Marcus Garvey). *Yugen*, no. 7 (April 1961), p. 63; by Baraka and/or Hettie Cohen.

UN 17   "Milneburg Joys (or, Against 'Hipness' As Such)." *Kulchur* 1, no. 3 (Summer 1961), pp. 41–43.

UN 18   "Robert Creeley's *A Form of Women* and Michael McClure's *Hymns to St. Geryon*." [Book reviews.] *Kulchur* 1, no. 3 (Summer 1961), pp. 81–85.

UN 19   "La Dolce Vita." Movie review. *Kulchur* 1, no. 4 (Autumn 1961), pp. 85–90.

UN 20   "Hello, Ma I Glad I Win!" *The Floating Bear*, no. 20 (May 1962), pp. [1–2]; with Diane DiPrima.

UN 21   "Lieber Bär." *The Floating Bear*, no. 23 (1962). Satiric letter to the editor, signed "Anton Webern." [Not ascribed to Baraka by DiPrima]

UN 22   "Names & Bodies." *The Floating Bear*, no. 24 (1962), pp. [7–9]. Pen name Johannes Koenig used.

UN 23   "Voices from the Art World (Or, Bright Sayings)." *The Floating Bear*, no. 26 (1962), pp. [8–9]. By "Duke Mantee."

UN 24   "Two Yale Men." Reviews of Alan Dugan's *Poems* and Jack Gilbert's *Views of Jeopardy. Kulchur* 2, no. 7 (Autumn 1962), pp. 88–91.

UN 24a "Apple Cores." Newsletters from Greenwich Village published in *Wild Dog* (Pocatello, Idaho): 1 (April 1963), pp. 28–29; 2 (April 1963), pp. 26–27; 6 (29 February 1964), pp. 29–30; 7 (5 April 1964), pp. 1–2; 9 (July 1964), pp. 31–32; 13 (12 January 1965), pp. 1–2. Letters signed "Caliph John, the Mississippi Shiek" (sic). (Ascribed to Baraka by Alan M. Cohn and verified by Baraka.)

UN 25   "The Colonial School of Melican Poetry (or, 'Aw, man, I read those
         poems before . . .')" *Kulchur* 3, no. 10 (Summer 1963), pp. 83–84.

UN 26   "Uncle-Udom's Cabin." Review of E.U. Essien-Udom's *Black Na-
         tionalism: A Search for an Identity in America. Kulchur* 3, no. 11
         (Autumn 1963), pp. 88–90.

UN 27   Review of *Reality Sandwiches* by Allen Ginsberg. *Kulchur* 3, no. 12
         (Winter 1963), pp. 86–88.

UN 28   Review of *An Anthology of Chance Operations* by LaMonte Young
         and Jackson MacLow. *Kulchur* 4, no. 13 (Spring 1964), pp. 92–94.

UN 29   "Channel X." Letter to the editor. *New York Review of Books* 2, no.
         11 (July 9, 1964), p. 23.

UN 30   "The Black Man Has No Other Choice." *Progressive Labor* 3, no.
         12–13 (November-December 1964), p. [26].

UN 31   "Black Revolutionary Newspaper; Black America's Choice: Unite or
         Perish; What Information; Che; Surplus and Peoplization; Babu in
         Harlem, a Message . . .; The Year Behind and the Year Ahead;
         Coons for Fun and Profit." *In-Formation*, prepublication (January
         1965), pp. [1–8]. Ascribed to Baraka by Dace.

UN 32   "Black Arts." *Black Dialogue* 1, no. 2 (July-August 1965), p. 27.

UN 33   Autobiographical note. "LeRoi Jones." Paris Leary and Robert Kelly,
         ed. *A Controversy of Poets: An Anthology of Contemporary Poetry.*
         Garden City, N.Y.: Doubleday, 1965, p. 533.

UN 34   "LeRoi Jones Replies to Gertrude Wilson." *Amsterdam News*, No-
         vember 13, 1965, p. 3.

UN 35   Letter to the editor. *Time* 86, no. 26 (December 24, 1965), p. 4.

UN 36   "Philistinism and the Negro Writer." Herbert Hill, ed. *Anger, and
         Beyond: The Negro Writer in the United States.* New York: Harper,
         1966, pp. 51–61.

UN 37   "Poetry: Actual Sweet Black Fury." *Diplomat* 18, no. 198 (November
         1966), pp. 70–73.

UN 38   Autobiographical note. "LeRoi Jones." Donald Allen and Robert
         Creeley, eds. *The New Writing in the USA.* Harmondsworth:
         Penguin, 1967, pp. 324–25.

UN 39   "From LeRoi Jones." (Letter to the editor re: *Dutchman* film.) *New
         York Times*, March 12, 1967, section 2, p. 17.

UN 40   "Statement." *Journal of Black Poetry* 1, no. 4 (Spring 1967), p. 14.

UN 41   "The Structure of the Academy Is: Against, The Street, or Versus."
         The Floating Bear 34 (1967), pp. [15–17]. Pen name Johannes
         Koenig.

UN 42   "Newark Black Survival Committee Press Conference." *The Floating
         Bear*, no. 34 (1967), pp. [22–24]. Ascribed to Baraka by Dace.

UN 43   "Tauhid: Impulse A-9138." *Cricket*, no. 1 (1968), pp. 19–20.

UN 44   "LeRoi Jones' Graphic Account of Brutal Arrest and Assault." *Worker*
         (January 9, 1968), p. 3. Reprinted several times.

UN 45   "Communications Project." *The Drama Review* 12, no. 4 (Summer
         1968), pp. 53–57.

UN 46   "On Creativity." *Playboy* 15, no. 12 (December 1968), p. 137.

UN 47   "The Shift from Moderates to Militants: A Separate Path to Equality." (Contains statement by Baraka.) *Life* 65, no. 24 (December 13, 1968), p. 87.

UN 48 "Spirit House, Unity Creed." *Black News* 1, no. 4 (1969). With Yusef Iman.

UN 49 "Rise! Black Man." *Black News* 1, no. 4 (1969), p. 4.

UN 50 Letter to the editor. *New York Times Magazine*, May 11, 1969, p. 132. (Re: C. Vann Woodward.)

UN 51 Letter to the editor. *New York Times*, November 30, 1969, section 4, p. 38. (Re: "To Survive the Reign of the Beasts.")

UN 52 "The Coronation of the Black Queen." *The Black Scholar* 1, no. 8 (June 1970), pp. 46–48.

UN 53 "Black Woman." *Black World* 19, no. 9 (July 1970), pp. 7–11.

UN 54 "The Campaign." *Evergreen Review* 15 (February 1971), pp. 33–35.

UN 55 "Black (Art) Drama Is The Same As Black Life." *Ebony* 26, no. 4 (February 1971), pp. 74–82.

UN 56 "The Pan-African Party and the Black Nation." *The Black Scholar* 2, no. 7 (March 1971), pp. 24–32.

UN 57 "Crisis in Newark." *New York Times*, April 16, 1971, p. 37.

UN 58 "Toward Pan-Africanism in Tanzania: Independence Anniversary." *Black World* 21, no. 5 (March 1972), pp. 65–67.

UN 59 "Raise! Pamoja Tutashinda!," *Black New Ark* (April 1972), p. 4.

UN 60 "Black Revolutionary Poets Should Also Be Playwrights." *Black World* 21, no. 6 (April 1972), pp. 4–6.

UN 61 "Raise!! Pan-Africanism and Electoral Politics." *Black New Ark* (May 1972), p. 4.

UN 62 "The National Black Political Agenda." Ratified by the National Black Political Convention in Gary, May 6, 1972. (Baraka coauthor.)

UN 63 "Black and Angry." *Newsweek* 80, no. 2 (July 10, 1972), pp. 35–36.

UN 64 "Raise!!" *Black New Ark* (July 1972), p. 4.

UN 65 "Raise!!" *Black New Ark* (September 1972), p. 8.

UN 66 "Black Nationalism: 1972." *The Black Scholar* 4, no. 1 (September 1972), pp. 23–29.

UN 67 "Toward the Creation of Political Institutions for All African Peoples." *Black World* 21, no. 12 (October 1972), pp. 54–78.

UN 68 "Raise!! Education for Liberation!" *Black New Ark* (November 1972), p. 8.

UN 69 "Raise!! What They Don't Want You To Know!!!...... Facts & Figures On Kawaida Towers." *Black New Ark* (December 1972), p. 8.

UN 70 "Raise!! S. D. S. Intervenes at Kawaida Towers!" *Black New Ark* (January 1972), p. 8.

UN 71 "Raise!! Viewing The Body." *Black New Ark* (February 1973), p. 8.

UN 72 "Imamu Baraka's Trip to Guinea." *Black New Ark* (February 1973), p. 8.

UN 73 "Raise!! Struggle Continues." *Black New Ark* (March 1973), p. 8.

UN 74 "Raise!!" *Black New Ark* (April 1973), p. 8.

UN 75 "Black Art: Vincent Smith–African Painter in America." *Black New Ark* (May 1973), p. 7.

Selected Bibliography

UN 76   "Raise!! Nixxxing Nixxxon." *Black New Ark* (May 1973), p. 8.
UN 77   "Raise!!" *Black New Ark* (June 1973), p. 8.
UN 78   "Raise!!" *Black New Ark* (July 1973), p. 8.
UN 79   "Raise!! African Revolutionary Class-Value Analysis Pt. 1." *Black New Ark* (August 1973), p. 8.
UN 80   "Raise!!" *Black New Ark* (September 1973, "1st edition"), p. 8.
UN 81   "Raise!!", *Black New Ark* (September 1973, "2nd edition"), p. 8.
UN 82   "Message from the Chairman." *Fundisha: Congress of African People, National and International Edition*, vol. 1, no. 5 (included in: *Black News* 2, no. 10 [October 22, 1973], pp. 7–8).
UN 83   "Raise!!" *Black New Ark* (October 1973, "1st edition"), p. 8.
UN 84   "Raise!!! Ujamaa, Small Business, Socialism, & Capitalism." *Black New Ark* (Novemba [sic] 1973, "1st edition"), p. 8. Also published as a Congress of Afrikan People Ideological Paper (CAP IP).
UN 85   "Toward Ideological Clarity." *Black New Ark* (November 1973, "2nd edition"), p. [1]. (Also CAP IP.)
UN 86   "Raise!! Mickey Mouse Joins the Storm Troopers." *Black New Ark* (November 1973, "2nd edition"), p. 8.
UN 87   "Raise!! Pig, Neo-Pig / Insect-Opportunism / & Shakey Negro Liberals." *Unity & Struggle* (December 1973), pp. 7–8.
UN 88   "Delegates' Reception 1973." Newark, N.J. (1973), 6 pp. CAP IP.
UN 89   "Nationalism, PanAfrikanism, Ujamaa: Their Future in America." (c. 1973/74) CAP IP.
UN 90   "CAP Going Through Changes." (c. 1974) CAP IP.
UN 91   "Black Nationalism and Socialist Revolution." (c. 1974) CAP IP.
UN 92   "Kawaida, National Liberation and Socialism." (c. 1974) CAP IP.
UN 93   "Revolutonary Party: Revolutionary Ideology." (March 31, 1974) CAP IP.
UN 94   "Creating a Unified Consciousness." (c. 1974) CAP IP.
UN 95   "The Concept of a Black United Front." 2pp. CAP IP.
UN 96   "Raise!!" *Unity & Struggle* (January–February 1974), p. 8.
UN 97   "Raise!! Nationalist Aspects of National Liberation." *Unity & Struggle* (February–March 1974), pp. 12, 11.
UN 98   "Support the Kawaida Political Prisoners Bail Fund!!" *Unity & Struggle* (March 1974), p. 6. Reprinted in several subsequent issues of *Unity & Struggle*.
UN 99   "Raise!! The Meaning & Development of Revolutionary Kawaida." *Unity & Struggle*. Part 1: March 1974, p. 12; Part 2: April 1974 (1st edition), p. 12; Part 3: May 1974 (1st edition), p. 12. Also a CAP IP, 8 pp. (1974).
UN 100   "Black People and Imperialism." Newark, N.J., April 6, 1974. CAP IP.
UN 101   "Toward Ideological Clarity." May 24, 1974. CAP IP. (Abridged in: *Black World* 24, no. 1 (November 1974), pp. 24–33).
UN 102   "Raise!! National Liberation and Politics." *Unity & Struggle*. Part 1: June 1974, p. 12; Part 2: July 1974, pp. 12, 11.
UN 103   "Haki Madhubuti and Jitu Weusi . . . Individualism Brings Two

CAP Resignations." *Unity & Struggle*. Part 1: June 1974, p. 10; Part 2: July 1974, pp. 4, 11; Part 3: August 1974, p. 4; Part 4: September 1974, p. 4; Part 5: October 1974 (1st edition), p. 4; Part 6: October 1974 (edition 2), p. 8; Part 7: November 1974 (edition 1), p. 10; Part 8: December 1974 (edition 1); Part 9: December-January, 1974 / 75, pp. 7, 8; Part 10: January 1975 (edition 2), p. 10; Part 11: February 1975, p. 10.

UN   104   "Revolutionary Culture & the Future of PanAfrikan Culture." Newark, N.J., June 19–27, 1974. CAP IP.

UN   105   "Raise!! Black People and Imperialism." *Unity & Struggle*. Part 1: August 1974 (1st edition), pp. 12, 5; Part 2: September 1974, pp. 12, 11.

UN   106   "NEW ERA IN OUR POLITICS: The Revolutionary Answer to Neo-Colonialism in New Ark Politics." Newark, N.J. (c. 1974), 18 pp. CAP IP.

UN   107   "Raise!! Partially Evaluating The Legacy Of The '60's." *Unity & Struggle* (October 1974, 1st edition), p. 12.

UN   108   "Raise!! Needed: Black Socialist Intellectuals." *Unity & Struggle* (October 1974, edition 2), p. 12.

UN   109   "Some Questions About the Sixth Pan-African Congress." *Black Scholar* 6, no. 2 (October 1974), pp. 42–46.

UN   110   "Raise!! On Being Incorrect!" *Unity & Struggle* (November 1974, edition 1), p. 12.

UN   111   "Raise!! Sectarianism, Undermining, Secret Agents & Struggle." *Unity & Struggle* (December 1974, edition 1), p. 16.

UN   112   "The Position of the Congress of Afrikan People." (December 1974) CAP IP. Also in: *Black Scholar* 6, no. 5 (January 1975), pp. 2–15.

UN   113   "National Liberation + Politics." Newark, N.J.: 1974. CAP IP.

UN   114   "Raise! Boston March!" *Unity & Struggle* (December-January 1974/75, edition 1), pp. 16, 15, 13, 12.

UN   115   "Raise!! Black Liberation is a Struggle for Socialism!!!" *Unity & Struggle* (January 1975, edition 2), p. 12.

UN   116   "Raise!! Black Women's United Front and National Black Assembly Meetings Analyzed." *Unity & Struggle* (February 1975), pp. 12, 9.

UN   117   "The National Black Assembly and the Black Liberation Movement." *Black World* 26, no. 5 (March 1975), pp. 22–27. Also a CAP IP, 6 pp. (November 29, 1974).

UN   118   "Raise!!" *Unity & Struggle* (March 1975), p. 12.

UN   119   "Raise!! 2 Line Struggle Heads Up NBA." *Unity & Struggle* (April 1975), pp. 12, 7.

UN   120   "Raise!! Crime and the Minority Community." *Unity & Struggle* (April 1975, 2nd edition), pp. 12, 9, 10.

UN   121   "Raise!! Revolutionary Nationalism = Scientific Socialism." *Unity & Struggle* (May 1975, edition 1), pp. 12, 9, 7.

UN   122   "Raise!! Capitalism On Its Deathbed!" *Unity & Struggle* (June 1975, edition 1), pp. 12, 11, 9.

UN   123   "Raise!! The Liberation of Afrika Will Bring Imperialism to Its Knees, But It Will Lose Its Head On the Funky Streets of the

U.S.A.!" *Unity & Struggle*. Part 1: June 1975 (2nd edition), pp. 12, 11; Part 2: July 1975, pp. 12, 10.

UN 124 " 'Why I Changed My Ideology': Black Nationalism and Socialist Revolution." *Black World* 24, no. 9 (July 1975), pp. 30–42.

UN 125 "Needed: A Second Civil War." *Unity & Struggle* (August 1975), pp. 12, 11, 10.

UN 126 "Raise!! Against Some Bogus Types Posing as Revolutionaries." *Unity & Struggle*. Part 1: August/September 1975, pp. 12, 11; Part 2: October 1975, pp. 12, 11.

UN 127 "Statement on the National Black Assembly." *Black World* 24, no. 12 (October 1975), pp. 42–46.

UN 128 "Raise!! People's Opposition to Capitalist Lieutenant Ford Intensifies! Danger of War Between Superpowers Increases." *Unity & Struggle* (October 1975, 2nd edition), pp. 12, 11.

UN 129 "Raise!! U.S. 'Diplomacy' Doomed: Sinai Pact & China Visit Miss!" *Unity & Struggle* (November 1975, edition 1), p. 12.

UN 130 "Raise!! Amiri Baraka Resigns As Secretary General of the National Black Assembly. CAP Calls For Intensification Of Struggle Inside The National Black Assembly." *Unity & Struggle* (November 1975, 2nd edition), pp. 12, 6, 7.

UN 131 "Raise!! Imperialism and Revolution." *Unity & Struggle*. Part 1: January 1976, p. 12; Part 2: February 1976, pp. 12, 11; Part 3: March 1976, pp. 12, 11.

UN 132 "Not Just Survival: Revolution. (A Brief Historical Investigation of Afro-American Drama.)" Ms. 28pp. April 1976.

UN 133 "Raise!! Black Liberation Today." *Unity & Struggle*. Part 1: April 1976, p. 12; Part 2: May 1976, p. 12.

UN 134 "From Congress of Afrikan People to Revolutionary Communist League (M-L-M)." *Unity & Struggle* (June 1976). (Special issue on the history of Baraka's commitments since 1965.)

II. F. Uncollected Music Criticism

UM 1 "Showtime at the Old Corral: Buddy Tate at the Celebrity Club." *Jazz Review* 2, no. 3 (April 1959), pp. 11–13.

UM 2 "Record Reviews: Brownie McGhee, *McGhee Sings the Blues*, Folkways 3557." *Jazz Review* 2, no. 10 (November 1959), pp. 44–45.

UM 3 "Record Reviews: *Sonny Rollins and the Contemporary Leaders*, Contemporary M 3564." *Jazz Review* 3, no. 2 (February 1960), pp. 32–33.

UM 4 "Record Reviews: Snooks Eaglin, *New Orleans Street Singer*, Folkways FA 2476." *Jazz Review* 3, no. 3 (March–April 1960), pp. 23–24.

UM 5 "Record Reviews: *Cannonball Adderley Quintet in San Francisco*, Riverside RLP 12-311." *Jazz Review* 3, no. 5 (June 1960), p. 20.

UM 6 "Record Reviews: Jackie McLean, *Capuchin Swing*, Blue Note 4038." *Metronome* 78, no. 3 (March 1961), pp. 33–34.

314
Selected Bibliography

UM 7 "Note" (on John Coltrane). *Floating Bear*, no. 6 (April 1961), p. [12]. Pen name "Koenig" used.

UM 8 "Record Reviews: Lonnie Johnson, *Blues and Ballads*, Prestige Bluesville 1011; Oliver Nelson, *Screamin' the Blues*, Prestige New Jazz 8243." *Metronome* 78, no. 4 (April 1961), pp. 36, 38–39.

UM 9 "Records Reviews: Cecil Taylor, *The World of Cecil Taylor*, Candid 8006; Richard Williams, *New Horn in Town*, Candid 8003." *Metronome* 78, no. 5 (May 1961), pp. 36–38. First part of review included in *Black Music*.

UM 10 "Classics and All That Jazz." *Urbanite* 1, no. 3 (May 1961), pp. 8, 33–34.

UM 11 "Record Reviews: Muddy Waters, *At Newport 1960*, Chess LP 1449." *Metronome* 78, no. 6 (June 1961), p. 26.

UM 12 "The Truth About Nat Hentoff." *Urbanite* 1, no. 4 (June 1961), pp. 20–21, 33.

UM 13 "Jazz Records: Champion Jack Dupree, *Natural and Soulful Blues*, Atlantic 8045; Lightnin' Hopkins, *Lightnin' in New York*, Candid 8010; Lee Morgan, *Leeway*, Blue Note 4034." *Metronome* 78, no. 7 (July 1961), pp. 29–31.

UM 14 "Jazz Records: Roosevelt Sykes, *The Honeydipper*, Prestige Bluesville 1014." *Metronome* 78, no. 8 (August 1961), pp. 33–34.

UM 15 "How They Voted." (Votes in the International Jazz Critis Poll.) *Down Beat* 28, no. 16 (August 3, 1961), p. 44.

UM 16 "Jazz Records: Art Blakey, *A Night in Tunisia*, Blue Note 4049." *Metronome* 78, no. 9 (September 1961), p. 26.

UM 17 "Jazz Records: Dizzy Gillespie, *Gillespiana*, Verve 8394; Freddie Hubbard, *Goin' Up*, Blue Note 4056." *Metronome* 78, no. 10 (October 1961), pp. 35–37.

UM 18 "Blues Chronicle." *Metronome* 78, no. 11 (November 1961), pp. 30–32.

UM 19 "Jazz Records: Rocky Boyd, *Ease It*, Jazztime JT001; Hank Mobley, *Roll Call*, Blue Note 4058; Sonny Red and Clifford Jordan, *A Story Tale*, Jazzland JLP40." *Metronome* 78, no. 12 (December 1961), pp. 27–28, 31–32.

UM 20 "A Coltrane Trilogy." *Metronome* 78, no. 12 (December 1961), pp. 34–36.

UM 21 "James Waring & Dance Co." *Floating Bear*, no. 19 (April 1962), pp. [11–12].

UM 22 "How They Voted." (Votes in International Jazz Critics Poll.) *Down Beat* 29, no. 21 (August 2, 1962), p. 34.

UM 23 "Trumpet on the Way Up: Ted Curson." *Down Beat* 29, no. 23 (August 30, 1962), pp. 20, 37.

UM 24 "Jazz: Roy Palmer/Ike Rodgers, *Gut-Bucket Trombone*, Riverside RLP 150; Bobby Scott, *Joyful Noises*, Mercury MG20701 (Scott, piano w/orchestra); Memphis Slim and Willie Dixon, *At the Village Gate* (w/Pete Seeger), Folkways FA 2386; Howard McGhee, *Maggie's Back in Town*, Contemporary M 3596; *Sonny Terry's New*

Sound (The Jaw Harp in Blues and Folk Music), Folkways FS 3821; Joe Gordon, *Lookin' Good!*, Contemporary M 3597; Junior Mance, *At the Village Vanguard*, Jazzland JLP 41; Barney Kessel, *Let's Cook!*, Contemporary M 3603; Jazztet, *Here and Now*, Mercury MG20698; Phineas Newborn Jr., *A World of Piano!*, Contemporary M 3600; Duke Ellington, *All American*, Columbia CL 1790." *Kulchur* 2, no. 7 (Autumn 1962), pp. 95–97, 99–105.

UM   25   "Jazz: Present Perfect, The Gill Evans Orchestra, *Into the Hot*, Impulse A-9; Jimmy Woods, *Awakening!!*, Contemporary M 3605; Charlie Mingus, *Wonderland*, United Artists UAJ 14005; Miles Davis, *Miles Davis at Carnegie Hall*, Columbia CL 1812; Billie Holiday *The Golden Years* (in three LPs), Columbia C3L 21." *Kulchur* 2, no. 8 (Winter 1962), pp. 95–98, 100–1, 103–5.

UM   26   Letter to the editor. *Jazz* 2, no. 2 (February 1963), p. 23.

UM   27   "Jazz: *A History of Jazz: The New York Scene*, Folkways RBF RF-3; Gerry Wiggins, *Relax and Enjoy It*, Contemporary M3595; Peter Fountain, *Music From Dixie*, Coral CRL 757401; Bill Evans–Jim Hall, *Undercurrent*, United Artists UAJ 14003; Tadd Dameron, *The Magic Touch*, Riverside RLP 419; Count Basie, *The Legend*, Roulette R 52086; Roland Kirk, *Domino;* The Jazztet, *Another Git Together*, Mercury MG 20737; Sonny Rollins, *What's New*, (RCA Victor LSP-2572)." *Kulchur* 3, no. 9 (Spring 1963), pp. 90–96.

UM   28   "Record Reviews: John Coltrane, *Ballads*, Impulse A32; Sonny Rollins, *Our Man in Jazz*, RCA Victor LPM-2612." *Jazz* 2, no. 4 (April–May 1963), pp. 17–19. Second part of review included in *Black Music*.

UM   29   "Jazz Forum: Is 'The New Thing' Anything?" *Jazz* 2, no. 5 (June 1963), p. 15.

UM   30   "Record Reviews: Billy Mitchell, *This Is Billy Mitchell*, Smash MGS 27027." *Jazz* 2, no. 6 (July–August 1963), p. 20.

UM   31   "How They Voted." (Votes in International Jazz Critics Poll.) *Down Beat* 30, no. 16 (July 18, 1963), p. 32.

UM   32   "Record Reviews: Connonball Adderley, *Jazz Workshop Revisited*, Riverside RM 444." *Jazz* 2, no. 7 (September 1963), p. 18.

UM   33   "Jazz: Pee Wee Russell, *New Groove*, Columbia Cl 1985." *Kulchur* 3, no. 11 (Autumn 1963), pp. 91–92.

UM   34   "Jazz Forum: Which Musicians Do You Think the Most Influential in Jazz Today?" *Jazz* 2, no. 8 (October 1963), p. 12.

UM   35   "Jazz: John Coltrane, *Impressions*, Impulse A-42; Jackie McLean, *Let Freedom Ring*, Blue Note 4106; *Original Golden Hits of the Great Blues Singers*, Mercury MG 20826; The Swingle Singers, *Bach's Greatest Hits*, Philips PHM 200-097." *Kulchur* 3, no. 12 (Winter 1963), pp. 101–4.

UM   36   "The Jay Winners." (Votes in First Annual Jay Award Poll.) *Jazz* 3, no. 1 (January–February 1964), p. 10.

UM   37   "Record Reviews: Art Blakey, *Ugetsu–Art Blakey's Jazz Messengers at Birdland*, Riverside 464; Sonny Rollins and Coleman Hawkins,

Sonny Meets Hawk, RCA LPM-2712." *Jazz* 3, no. 1 (January–February 1964), pp. 15, 19.

UM 38 "Jazz Capsules: Wes Montgomery, *Boss Guitar*, Riverside RM 459." *Jazz* 3, no. 1 (January–February 1964), p. 20.

UM 39 "Caught in the Act: John Coltrane—Cecil Taylor—Art Blakey, Philharmonic Hall, Lincoln Center, New York City." *Down Beat* 31, no. 6 (February 27, 1964), p. 34.

UM 40 "Record Reviews: George Russell, *The Outer View*, Riverside RM 440." *Jazz* 3, no. 2 (March–April 1964), p. 17.

UM 41 "How They Voted." (Votes in International Jazz Critics Poll.) *Down Beat* 31, no. 23 (August 13, 1964), p. 34.

UM 42 [On "The Star-Spangled Banner."] *Fact* 2, no. 1 (January–February 1965), p. 15.

UM 43 "Archie Shepp Live." *Jazz* 4, no. 1 (January 1965), pp. 8–9.

UM 44 "Blues, Jazz and the Negro." *The American Negro Reference Book*, ed. John P. Davis (Englewood Cliffs, N.J.: Prentice-Hall, 1965), pp. 759–65.

UM 45 "How They Voted." (Votes in International Jazz Critics Poll.) *Down Beat* 33, no. 17 (August 25, 1966), p. 42.

UM 46 "Integration Music." *Cricket*, no. 4 (December 1966), p. 3.

UM 47 "Notes on Lou Donaldson and Andrew Hill." *Cricket*, no. 4 (December 1969), p. 46.

UM 48 "Phil Cohran-Affro Arts Theatre." *Cricket*, no. 4 (December 1969), pp. 55–56.

II. G. Selected Interviews and Panel Discussions

UI 1 "The Sullen Art: LeRoi Jones in conversation with David Ossman." *Nomad/New York*, no. 10–11 (Autumn 1962), pp. 20–22. Reprinted, in an altered version, in David Ossman, ed. *The Sullen Art: Interviews with Modern American Poets*. New York: Corinth, 1963, pp. 77–81.

UI 2 "Black Revolution and White Backlash." *National Guardian*, July 4, 1964, pp. 5–9.

UI 3 "The Roots of Violence: Harlem Reconsidered." *Negro Digest* 13, no. 10 (August 1964), pp. 16–26.

UI 4 "Jazz and Revolutionary Black Nationalism." (Panel discussion on December 29, 1965.) Serialized in *Jazz* from April 1966 through July 1967.

UI 5 "Détruire L'Amérique." Pierre Dommergues, *Les U.S.A. à la recherche de leur identité: Rencontres avec 40 écrivains américains*. Paris: Grasset, 1967, pp. 170–75.

UI 6 "An Interview with LeRoi Jones by Sidney Bernard." *Literary Times*, May–June 1967.

UI 7 "They Think You're an Airplane and You're Really a Bird!" Interview conducted by Saul Gottlieb. *Evergreen Review* 12, no. 50 (December 1967), pp. 51–53, 96–97.

UI 8 "Problems of Black Power: An Interview." Robert L. Allen and Astrid Sengstacke. *Guardian*, March 23, 1968, p. 3.

UI 9 "Art, Artist and Revolution: Part II of the Interview." *Guardian*, March 30, 1968, p. 6.

UI 10 "Everything's Cool . . . An Interview." Marvin X. *Black Theatre*, no. 1 (1968), pp. 16–23.

UI 11 "A Transcript of the April 12, 1968, CBS Broadcast." *Los Angeles Free Press* 5, no. 18 (May 3–May 9, 1968), pp. 1–42.

UI 12 "God Is Black! Islam and Black Art: An Interview with LeRoi Jones by Marvin X and Faruk, with a Foreword by Askia Muhammad Touré." *Black Theatre*, no. 2 (1969), pp. 11–19.

UI 13 "Die bezopften Liberalen müssen verrecken." *Der Spiegel*, August 18, 1969, pp. 114–20.

UI 14 "Is Democracy a White Man's Word? LeRoi Jones and John Akar." David Frost, *The Americans*. New York: Stein and Day, 1970.

UI 15 "Conversation. Ida Lewis and LeRoi Jones." *Essence* (September 1970), pp. 20–25.

UI 16 "What Is Black Theatre? Michael Coleman questions Imamu Amiri Baraka." *Black World* 20, no. 6 (April 1971), pp. 32–38.

UI 17 "Talk With LeRoi Jones. By Mel Watkins." *New York Times Book Review*, June 27, 1971, pp. 4, 24, 26–27.

UI 18 Baraka interviewed on "SOUL." Broadcast on November 8, 1972, Channel 13. Newark, N.J.

UI 19 "Interview: Imamu Amiri Baraka." *The Black Collegian* 3, no. 4 (March–April 1973), pp. 30–33.

UI 20 Tape-recorded conversation with Baraka, September 1, 1974 (Werner Sollors).

UI 21 Tape-recorded conversation, December 17, 1976 (Werner Sollors).

III. SELECTED SECONDARY SOURCES AND MATERIALS

Abrams, M. H. *The Mirror and the Lamp: Romantic Theory and the Critical Tradition*. New York: Norton, 1958.

Abramson, Doris E. *Negro Playwrights in the American Theatre, 1925–1959*. New York, London: Columbia University Press, 1969.

Adams, George R. "Black Militant Drama." *American Imago* 28, no. 2 (Summer 1971), pp. 107–28.

—— " 'My Christ' in *Dutchman*." *College Language Association Journal* 15, no. 1 (September 1971), pp. 54–58.

"Adventures of Superiorman, The." *Realist*, no. 59 (May 1965), pp. 16–17.
Allen, Donald M., ed. *The New American Poetry: 1945–1960*. New York: Grove Press, 1960.
Allen, Donald, and Robert Creeley, eds., *The New Writing in the USA*. Harmondsworth: Penguin, 1967.
Allen, Robert L. *Black Awakening in Capitalist America: An Analytic History*. Garden City: Doubleday, 1970.
—— *Dialectics of Black Power*. New York: Guardian Pamphlets, 1968.
Allen, Walter. "What's New?" *New York Review of Books* 1, no. 10 (January 9, 1964), p. 11.
Alsop, Steward. "American Sickness." *Saturday Evening Post* 241 (July 13, 1968), p. 6.
Anderson, Quentin. *The Imperial Self: An Essay in American Literary and Cultural History*. New York: Knopf, 1971.
—— "Practical and Visionary Americans." *The American Scholar* 45, no. 3 (Summer 1976), pp. 405–18.
Andrews, Matthew. "Theatre." *Kulchur* 4, no. 17 (Spring 1965), p. 18.
Arnold, Martin. "Black Power Meeting Opens." *New York Times*, July 21, 1967, p. 34.
Axios, Costas, and Nikos Syvriotis. *Papa Doc Baraka: Fascism in Newark, including a special appendix Why the CIA Often Succeeds, by Hermyle Golthier, Jr.* National Caucus of Labor Committees, 1973.
Bain, Myrna. "Everybody's Protest Play." *National Review* 17, no. 12 (March 23, 1965), pp. 249–50.
Baldwin, James. *Go Tell It On The Mountain*. New York: Knopf, 1953.
Bassett, Fletcher S. *Legends and Superstitions of the Sea and of Sailors in All Lands and at All Times*. London: Sampson Low, 1885.
Beatitude Anthology. San Francisco: City Lights, 1960.
Bell, Bernard. *The Folk Roots of Contemporary Black Poetry*. Detroit: Broadside Press, 1974.
Bellow, Saul. *Henderson the Rain King*. Greenwich, Conn.: Fawcett, repr. 1965.
Benjamin, Walter. *Versuche über Brecht*. Frankfurt: Suhrkamp, 1966.
Bentley, Eric. "Must I Side With Blacks or Whites." *New York Times*, January 23, 1972, section 2, p. 1.
Bercovitch, Sacvan. *The Puritan Origins of the American Self*. New Haven and London: Yale University Press, 1975.
Bermel, Albert. *Contradictory Characters: An Interpretation of the Modern Theatre*. New York: Dutton, 1973.
Bernard, Oliver, ed. *Rimbaud*. Baltimore: Penguin, 1962.
Bigsby, C. W. E. *Confrontation and Commitment: A Study of Contemporary American Drama, 1959–1966*. University of Missouri Press, 1968.
Bigsby, C. W. E., ed. *The Black American Writer*. 2 vols. Baltimore: Penguin, 1969.
Billard, Pierre, ed. *Masculine Feminine: A Film by Jean-Luc Godard*. New York: Grove Press, 1969.
Blackburn, Paul. "The Grinding Down." *Kulchur* 3, no. 10 (Summer 1963), pp. 9–18.

Bloom, Leonard. "You Don't Have to Be Jewish to Love Leroi Jones." *Realist*, no. 59 (May 1965), p. 24.

Blum, Daniel. *A Pictorial History of Television*. Philadelphia and New York: Chilton, 1959.

Bogle, Donald. *Toms, Coons, Mulattoes, Mammies, and Bucks: An Interpretive History of Blacks in American Films*. New York: Bantam, 1974.

Bone, Robert A. "De Profundis." *New York Times Book Review*, February 4, 1968, p. 36.

—— *The Negro Novel in America*. New Haven and London: Yale University Press, 1958.

Bracey, John H., Jr.; August Meier; and Elliot Rudwick, eds. *Black Nationalism in America*. Indianapolis and New York: Bobbs-Merrill, 1970.

Brandes, Volkhard. *Black Brother: Die Bedeutung Afrikas für den Freiheitskampf des schwarzen Amerika*. Frankfurt: Melzer, 1971.

Brecht, Stefan. "LeRoi Jones' *Slave Ship*." *The Drama Review* 14, no. 46 (Winter 1970), pp. 212–19.

Breton, André. *Manifestoes of Surrealism*. Ann Arbor: University of Michigan Press, 1969. Trans. Richard Seaver and Helen R. Lane.

Brooks, Van Wyck. *The Writer in America*. New York: Dutton, 1953.

Brown, Cecil. "About LeRoi Jones." *Evergreen Review* 75 (February 1970), pp. 65–70.

—— "Apotheosis of a prodigal son." *Kenyon Review* 30, no. 122, issue 5, 1968, pp. 654–61.

—— "Black Literature and LeRoi Jones." *Black World* 19, no. 8 (June 1970), pp. 24–31.

Brown, Lloyd W. "Comic-Strip Heroes, LeRoi Jones and the Myth of American Innocence." *Journal of Popular Culture* 3, no. 2 (Fall 1969), pp. 191–204.

—— "Dreamers and Slaves: The Ethos of Revolution in Walcott and LeRoi Jones." *Caribbean Quarterly* 12, no. 3–4 (September–December 1971), pp. 36–44.

—— "LeRoi Jones (Imamu Amiri Baraka) as Novelist: Theme and Structure in *The System of Dante's Hell*." *Negro American Literature Forum* 7 (1973), pp. 132–42.

Brown, H. Rap. *Die Nigger Die*. New York: Dial Press, 1969.

Brown, Sterling A. "Negro Character as Seen by White Authors." *Journal of Negro Education* 2 (January 1933), pp. 179–203.

Brüning, Eberhard, ed. *Amerikanische Protestdramen*. Berlin: Henschelverlag, 1972.

Brustein, Robert. "Three Plays and a Protest." *New Republic*, 152 (January 1965), pp. 32–33.

Campbell, Crispin Y. "Window on Black Officials." *Jersey Record*, February 18, 1974.

Carmichael, Stokely. *Stokely Speaks*. New York: Vintage, 1971.

Capouya, Emile. "States of Mind, of Soul." *New York Times Book Review*, November 28, 1965, pp. 4, 42.

Chametzky, Jules, and Sidney Kaplan, eds. *Black and White in American Culture*. Amherst: University of Massachusetts Press, 1969.

Cleaver, Eldridge. *Soul on Ice.* New York: Ramparts Books, 1968.

Clurman, Harold. "LeRoi Jones." *Nation* 200 (January 4, 1965), pp. 16–17.

Cohen, Robert Carl. *Black Crusader: A Biography of Robert Franklin Williams.* Secaucus, N.J.: Lyle, Stuart, 1972.

Colbert, Alison. "A Talk With Allen Ginsberg." *Partisan Review* 38, no. 3 (1971), pp. 289–309.

"Committee on Cuba Elects." *New York Times,* November 11, 1961, p. 9.

"Conciliator at Black Parley." *New York Times,* March 13, 1972, p. 30.

Cook, Bruce. *The Beat Generation.* New York: Scribner, 1971.

Cook, Mercer, and Stephen E. Henderson. *The Militant Black Writer in Africa and the United States.* Madison, London: University of Milwaukee Press, 1969.

Costello, Donald P. "Black Man as victim." *Commonweal* 88, no. 15 (June 28, 1968), pp. 436–39.

Cottle, Thomas J. "The Wellesley Incident: A Case of Obscenity." *Saturday Review* 52, no. 11 (March 15, 1969), pp. 67–68, 75–77.

Cruse, Harold. *The Crisis of the Negro Intellectual.* New York: Morrow, 1967.

"Declaration of the United Black Artists." *National Guardian,* January 20, 1968, p. 20.

Dickstein, Morris. *Gates of Eden: American Culture in the Sixties.* New York: Basic Books, 1977.

Dillard, J. P. *Black English: Its History and Usage in the United States.* New York: Random House, 1972.

DiPrima, Diane. *Memoirs of a Beatnik.* New York: Travellers Companion, 1969.

Dommergues, Pierre. *Les U.S.A. à la recherche de leur identité: Rencontres avec 40 écrivains américains.* Paris: Grasset, 1967.

"Drama is Banned; Theatre Head Quits." *Minneapolis Star,* January 8, 1968, p. 11B.

"Drama Mailbag: Again the Readers Argue LeRoi Jones." *New York Times,* December 14, 1969, section 2, p. 15.

Draper, Theodore. *The Rediscovery of Black Nationalism.* New York: Viking, 1970.

DuBois, W. E. B. "Criteria of Negro Art." *The Crisis* 32, no. 6 (October 1926).

—— *The Souls of Black Folk.* Repr. New York: Fawcett, 1968.

du Maurier, George. *Trilby.* 1894.

Eberstadt, Isabel. "King of the East Village." *New York Herald Tribune,* December 13, 1964, pp. 14–15, 18, 20.

Eliot, T. S. *The Complete Poems and Plays: 1909–1950.* New York: Harcourt, Brace, 1952.

Ellenberg, Albert. "LeRoi Jones Accused of Beating Publisher." *New York Post,* July 30, 1966.

Ellison, Ralph. "The Blues." *New York Review of Books* 1, no. 12 (February 6, 1964), pp. 5–7.

—— *Shadow and Act.* New York: Signet, 1966.

Emanuel, James A., and Theodore L. Gross, eds. *Dark Symphony: Negro Literature in America.* New York: Free Press, 1968.

Empson, William. *Seven Types of Ambiguity.* New York: New Directions, 1947.

Enzensberger, Hans Magnus. *Einzelheiten.* Frankfurt: Suhrkamp, 1962.

Essien-Udom, E. U. *Black Nationalism: The Rise of the Black Muslims in the U.S.A.* Chicago and London: Chicago University Press, 1963.

Esslin, Martin, *The Theatre of the Absurd.* Rev. ed., Garden City: Doubleday, 1969.

"Excerpts from Affidavit Sworn by Naomi Eftis, Producing Director of Back Alley Theater, Inc." *Studies in Black Literature* 1, no. 2 (Summer 1970), pp. 87–88.

Fairchild, Hoxie Neale. *The Noble Savage: A Study in Romantic Naturalism.* New York: Columbia University Press, 1928.

Fanon, Frantz. *The Wretched of the Earth.* New York: Grove Press, 1968. Trans. Constance Farrington.

Feldman, Gene, and Max Gartenberg, ed. *The Beat Generation and The Angry Young Men.* New York: Citadel, 1958.

Fiedler, Leslie. *Waiting for the End: A Portrait of Twentieth-Cetury American Literature and Its Writers.* New York: Stein and Day, 1970.

Fischer, William C. "The Pre-Revolutionary Writings of Imamu Amiri Baraka." *Massachusetts Review* 14, no. 2 (Spring 1973), pp. 259–305.

Fisher, Stanley, ed. *Beat Coast East: An Anthology of Rebellion.* New York: Excelsior Press, 1960.

Fles, John. "The Press of Freedom: The End of the Affair, or Beyond the Beat Generation." *Village Voice,* December 15, 1960, pp. 4, 12.

Fles, John, ed. *The Trembling Lamb.* New York: Phoenix Book Shop, 1959.

"Floating Bear Floats Free." *Village Voice,* May 3, 1962, p. 3.

Frazier, E. Franklin. *Black Bourgeoisie: The Rise of a New Middle Class.* New York: Free Press, 1957.

Frenzel, Elisabeth. *Stoffe der Weltliteratur.* Stuttgart: Kröner, 1963.

Fuller, Hoyt W. "About *The Toilet* and *The Slave.*" *Negro Digest* 14, no. 9 (July 1965), p. 50.

Gassner, John, and Bernard F. Dukore, ed. *A Treasury of the Theatre.* 4th ed. Vol. 2. New York: Simon & Schuster, 1970.

Gayle, Addison, ed. *The Black Aesthetic.* Garden City: Doubleday, 1972.

—— *Black Expression Essays By and About Black Americans in the Creative Arts.* New York: Weybright and Talley, 1969.

—— *The Way of the New World: The Black Novel in America.* Garden City: Doubleday, 1975.

Geiss, Imanuel. *Panafrikanismus: Zur Geschichte der Dekolonisation.* Frankfurt: Europäische Verlagsanstalt, 1968.

Gibson, Donald B., ed. *Five Black Writers: Essays on Wright, Ellison, Baldwin, Hughes, LeRoi Jones.* New York: New York University Press, 1970.

—— *Modern Black Poets: A Collection of Critical Essays.* Englewood Cliffs: Prentice-Hall, 1973.

Gifford, Dan, with Robert J. Seidman. *Notes for Joyce: An Annotation of James Joyce's Ulysses.* New York: Dutton, 1974.

Gilman, Richard. *The Confusion of Realms.* New York: Random House, 1969.

—— "The Devil may care." *New York Herald Tribune Book Week,* December 26, 1965, p. 9.

Gilroy, Harry. "Racial Debate Displaces Jazz Program." *New York Times,* February 10, 1965, p. 41.

Ginsberg, Allen. *Howl and Other Poems.* San Francisco: City Lights, repr. 1970.

Goddard, J. R. "Poet Jailed for Obscenity; Literary Magazine Hit. LeRoi Jones and Floating Bear." *Village Voice,* October 26, 1961, p. 3.

Gornick, Vivian. "An Ofay's Indirect Address to LeRoi Jones." *Village Voice,* March 4, 1965, pp. 5–6, 16–17.

Gottfried, Martin. "Theatre." *Women's Wear Daily.* March 12, 1965.

Grabes, Herbert, ed. *Das amerikanische Drama der Gegenwart.* Kronberg: Athenäum, 1976.

Gruen, John. *The New Bohemia: The Combine Generation.* New York: Grosset and Dunlap, 1967.

Guernsey, Otis L., Jr., ed. *The Best Plays of 1964–65.* New York, Toronto: Dodd, Mead, 1965.

Hannerz, Ulf. *Soulside: Inquiries into Ghetto Culture and Community.* New York and London: Columbia University Press, 1969.

Hare, Nathan. *The Black Anglo-Saxons.* New York and London: Collier, 1965.

Harrison, John R. *The Reactionaries: Yeats, Lewis, Pound, Eliot, Lawrence: A Study of the Anti-Democratic Intelligentsia.* New York: Schocken, 1967.

Hassan, Ihab, ed. *Liberations: New Essays on the Humanities in Revolution.* Middletown: Wesleyan University Press, 1971.

"Helluva Way To Go." *Times Literary Supplement,* November 1, 1966, p. 777.

Henderson, Stephen E. *Understanding the New Black Poetry: Black Speech and Black Music as Poetic References.* New York: Morrow, 1973.

Hernton, Calvin C. *Sex and Racism in America.* New York: Grove Press, 1966.

Hewes, Henry. "Crossing Lines." *Saturday Review* 48, no. 2 (January 9, 1965), p. 46.

Higgins, Dick. "Letter to the editor." *Village Voice,* January 14, 1965, p. 4.

Hill, Herbert, ed. *Anger, and Beyond: The Negro Writer in the United States.* New York: Harper, 1966.

—— *Soon, One Morning: New Writings by American Negroes.* New York: Knopf, 1963.

Höllerer, Walter, and Gregory Corso, eds. *Junge amerikanische Lyrik.* München: Hanser, 1961.

Höllerer, Walter. *Modernes Theater auf kleinen Bühnen.* Berlin: Literarisches Colloquium, 1965.

Hoffman, Paul. "D.A. Refuses to Act Against Off B'way Play." *New York Post,* January 20, 1965, p. 27.

Honig, Edwin. *García Lorca.* Norfolk, Conn.: New Directions, 1944.

Howe, Irving. "New Styles in 'Leftism.'" *Dissent* 12, no. 3 (Summer 1965), pp. 295–323.

Hudson, Theodore. *From LeRoi Jones to Amiri Baraka: The Literary Works.* Durham: Duke University Press, 1973.

Huggins, Nathan. *Harlem Renaissance.* New York: Oxford University Press, 1971.

Hughes, Langston. *Black Magic: A Pictorial History of the Negro in American Entertainment.* Englewood Cliffs: Prentice-Hall, 1971.

—— *Good Morning, Revolution: Uncollected Social Protest Writings.* Ed. and introd. Faith Berry. New York, Westport: Hill, 1973.

—— "The Negro Writer and the Racial Mountain." *Nation* 122 (1926), pp. 692–94.

—— *New Negro Poets, U.S.A.* Bloomington, Indiana University Press, 1964.
—— "That Boy, LeRoi." *New York Post*, January 15, 1965.
"In Defense of LeRoi Jones." *Freedomways* 8, no. 1 (Winter 1968), p. 2.
Jackson, Esther M. "LeRoi Jones (Imamu Amiri Baraka): Form and Progression of Consciousness." *College Language Association Journal* 17, no. 1 (September 1973), pp. 33–56.
Jackson, George L. *Blood in My Eye.* New York: Random House, 1972.
Jackson, Kathryn. "LeRoi Jones and the New Black Writers of the Sixties." *Freedomways* 9 (1969), pp. 232–48.
Jacobs, Paul, and Saul Landau, eds. *The New Radicals: A Report with Documents.* Harmondsworth: Penguin, 1967.
Jahn, Janheinz. *Muntu: The New African Culture.* New York: Grove Press, 1961. Trans. Marjorie Grene.
—— *Neo-African Literature: A History of Black Writing.* New York: Grove Press, 1968. Trans. Oliver Colburn and Ursula Lehrburger.
Johnson, James Weldon, ed. *The Book of American Negro Poetry.* New York: Harcourt, 1922. Repr. 1961.
Johnson, James Weldon. "The Dilemma of the Negro Author." *The American Mercury* 15 (December 1928), pp. 477–81.
"Jones Coming to Broadway." *New York Times*, May 11, 1965.
"Jones is Acquitted of Weapons Charge in Newark Retrial." *New York Times*, July 3, 1969, p. 18.
"Jones Play 'Obscene' to Los Angeles Police." *Village Voice*, April 1, 1965, p. 10.
"Jones Says Blacks Really Form A Nation." *Amsterdam News*, May 24, 1969, p. 69.
Karenga, Ron. *The Quotable Karenga.* Los Angeles: US, 1967.
"Karenga and the Truth About 'US.' " *Black Panther* 3, no. 27 (October 25, 1969), p. 9.
Katz, Shlomo. "LeRoi Jones' Teutonic Accent." *Midstream* 12, no. 4 (April 1966), pp. 78–80.
Kauffmann, Stanley. "LeRoi Jones and the Tradition of the Fake." *Dissent* 12, no. 2 (Spring 1965), pp. 207–12.
Kaufman, Michael T. "Jones Asks Votes, Not Rioting, to 'Take' Newark." *New York Times*, April 14, 1968, p. 60.
Keil, Charles. *Urban Blues.* Chicago: University of Chicago Press, 1966.
King, Woodie, and Ron Milner, eds. *Black Drama Anthology.* New York and London: Columbia University Press, 1971.
Klinkowitz, Jerome. "LeRoi Jones (Imamu Amiri Baraka): *Dutchman* as Drama." *Negro American Literature Forum* 7 (1973), pp. 123–26.
Knox, George. "The 'Mythology' of LeRoi Jones's *Dutchman.*" *Interculture: A Collection of Essays and Creative Writing Commemorating the 20th Anniversary of the Fulbright Program at the Institute of Translation and Interpretation, University of Vienna.* Ed. Sy M. Kahn and Martha Raetz. Wien, Stuttgart: n.d.
Koenigsberg, Richard A. "The Jones Case." *Village Voice*, January 7, 1965.
Kool, Jaap. *Das Saxophon.* Leipzig: Weber, 1921.
Kreuzer, Helmut. *Die Bohème.* Stuttgart: Metzler, 1968.

Leary, Paris, and Robert Kelley, eds. *A Controversy of Poets: An Anthology of Contemporary American Poetry.* Garden City: Doubleday, 1965.

Lederer, Richard. "The Language of Leroi Jones' 'The Slave.'" *Studies in Black Literature* 4, no. 1 (Spring 1973), pp. 14–16.

"LeRoi Jones Accused of Beating Publisher." *New York Post,* July 30, 1966, p 3.

"LeRoi Jones—A Fierce and Blazing Talent." *New York Herald Tribune,* April 12, 1964, p. 26.

"LeRoi Jones framed, charge 16 poets." *Los Angeles Free Press,* January 20–26, 1968, p. 2.

"LeRoi Jones's Work to Play on Broadway." *Minneapolis Tribune,* July 18, 1965.

"LeRoi Jones, Talk-in Attraction, Inveighs in Poetry and Prose." *New York Times,* October 4, 1966, p. 51.

"LeRoi Jones to Give Course on Playwriting at Columbia." *New York Times,* June 22, 1964, p. 22.

Lester, Elenore. "Jones boy . . . and girl click on stage." *Newark Star-Ledger,* January 3, 1965, pp. 5, 7.

Lester, Julius. *Look Out Whitey! Black Power's Gon' Get Your Mama!* New York: Grove Press, 1969.

LeSueur, Joseph. Review of "The Eighth Ditch." *The Floating Bear,* no. 15 (1961), p. [12].

Levine, Lawrence. *Black Culture and Black Consciousness.* New York: Oxford University Press, 1977.

Lincoln, C. Eric. *The Black Muslims in America.* Boston: Beacon Press, 1961.

Little, Stuart W. "LeRoi Jones Double Bill." *New York Herald Tribune,* November 12, 1964.

Llorens, David. "Ameer (LeRoi Jones) Baraka." *Ebony* 24 (August 1969), pp. 75–33.

Long, Priscilla, ed. *The New Left: A Collection of Essays.* Boston: Extending Horizons, 1969.

Lowes, John Livingston. *The Road to Xanadu. A Study in the Ways of the Imagination.* 1927; repr. Boston: Houghton Mifflin, 1964.

Lubbers, Klaus, ed. *Die amerikanische Lyrik: Von der Kolonialzeit zur Gegenwart.* Düsseldorf: Bagel, 1974.

Lukas, Anthony. "Obscenity Fight Splits City of Wellesley After LeRoi Jones Play Is Given at High School." *New York Times,* September 10, 1968, p. 25.

McKay, Claude. *Home to Harlem.* New York and London: Harper, 1928.

McPherson, James M., *et al.,* eds. *Blacks in America: Bibliographical Essays.* Garden City: Doubleday, 1971.

Mailer, Norman. *Advertisements for Myself.* New York: Putnam-Berkley Medallion, 1966.

Malcolm X. *The Autobiography of Malcolm X.* With the assistance of Alex Haley. New York: Grove Press, 1965.

"Many Meanings of 'Black Power,' The." *New York Times,* July 23, 1967, section 4, p. 1.

Margolies, Edward. *Native Sons: A Critical Study of Twentieth-Century Negro American Authors.* Philadelphia and New York: Lippincott, 1968.

Marx, Karl. *Selected Works.* Prepared by the Marx-Engels-Lenin-Institute, Moscow, ed. V. Adoratsky. New York: International Publishers, n.d.

Mays, Mardess. "LeRoi Jones: A study of his writings." Master's thesis, Department of English, Howard University, 1966 (typed ms.).

Mead, Taylor. "Drama Mailbag: Again the Readers Argue LeRoi Jones." *New York Times*, December 14, 1969, section 2, p. 15.

Menchise, Don N. "LeRoi Jones and a Case of Shifting Identities." *College Language Association Journal*, 20, no. 2 (December 1976), pp. 232–34.

Mill, John Stuart. *Mill's Essay on Literature and Society*. Ed. J. B. Schneewind. New York: Collier, 1965.

Miller, Jeanne-Marie. "The Plays of LeRoi Jones." *College Language Association Journal* 14, no. 3 (March 1971), pp. 331–39.

Milne, A. A. *Winnie the Pooh*, 1926.

Mitchell, Loften. *Black Drama: The Story of the American Negro in the Theatre*. New York: Hawthorn, 1967.

Mok, Michael. "LeRoi Jones (Baraka)." *Publishers Weekly*, September 11, 1972, p. 20.

Mootry, Maria K. "Themes and Symbols in Two Plays by LeRoi Jones." *Negro Digest* 18, no. 6 (April 1969), pp. 42–47.

Morris, Ivan. "Notebook: Theatre—The Slave and The Toilet." *Vogue*, February 1965, p. 98.

Muhammad, Elijah. *Message to the Blackman in America*. Chicago: Muhammad Mosque of Islam no. 2, 1965.

Myrdal, Gunnar. *An American Dilemma: The Negro Problem and Modern Democracy*. New York: Harper, 1944.

Nagy, David. "Castro Said to Snub Cleaver and Friends." *Washington Post*, December 10, 1969.

Neal, Lawrence P. "The Black Arts Movement." *The Drama Review* 12, no. 4 (Summer 1968), pp. 31–37.

—— "Development of LeRoi Jones." *Liberator* 6, no. 1 (January 1966), pp. 4–5; and no. 2 (February 1966), pp. 18–19.

—— "LeRoi Jones' The Slave and The Toilet." *Liberator* 5, no. 2 (February 1965), pp. 22–23.

"Negro militant with a talent for plays." *Times* (London), January 25, 1965, p. 7.

Nelson, Hugh. "LeRoi Jones' *Dutchman*: A Brief Ride on a Doomed Ship." *Educational Theatre Journal* 20, no. 1 (March 1968), pp. 53–59.

Newfield, Jack. "LeRoi Jones at Arms: Blues for Mr. Whitey." Village Voice, December 17, 1964, pp. 1, 12.

Nichols, Charles H. "Color, Conscience and Crucifixion: A Study of Racial Attitudes in American Literature and Criticism." *Jahrbuch für Amerikastudien* 6 (1961).

" 'Obscene' Play Counts Dropped." *Minneapolis Star*, September 11, 1968, p. 9B.

O'Brien, John. "Innovative Black Fiction: The Problem of LeRoi Jones." Ms., 10pp.

—— "Racial Nightmares and the Search for Self: An Explication of LeRoi Jones' 'A Chase (Alighieri's Dream).' " *Negro American Literature Forum* 7 (1973), pp. 89–90.

O'Hara, Frank. *Lunch Poems*. San Francisco: City Lights, 1964.

Oliver, Edith. "Off-Broadway: Over the Edge." *New Yorker*, April 4, 1964, pp. 78–79.

Osborn, Jim. "The White Man Can Not Dance." *Los Angeles Free Press,* June 14–20, 1968, p. 20.

Ottley, Roi. *'New World A-Coming.' Inside Black America.* 1943; repr. New York: Arno Press, 1968.

"Papa Doc and the Truth About Haiti Today." *Black Panther* 3, no. 27 (October 25, 1969), p. 9.

Parkinson, Thomas, ed. *A Casebook on the Beat.* New York: Crowell, 1961.

Parry, Albert. *Garrets and Pretenders: A History of Bohemianism in America.* New York: Covici, 1933.

Paul, Eugene. Review of *Tales. Liberator* 7, no. 12 (December 1967), p. 7.

Perkins, David. *A History of Modern Poetry: From the 1890's to the High Modernist Mode.* Cambridge: Harvard University Press, 1976.

Persson, Gene. "Letter to the editor: Arguing 'Dutchman.' " *New York Times,* March 3, 1967, section 2, p. 14.

Podhoretz, Norman. "The Know-Nothing Bohemians." *Partisan Review* 25, no. 2 (Spring 1958).

"Poets Applauded at Spoleto Fete." *New York Times,* June 28, 1965, p. 34.

"Poet's Theatre Fights $25 Fine." *Village Voice,* January 11, 1962, p. 2.

Poggioli, Renato. *The Theory of the Avant-Garde.* New York: Harper and Row, 1971.

Poirier, Richard. *A World Elsewhere: The Place of Style in American Literature.* New York: Oxford University Press, 1966.

"Political Assassination." *Black Panther* 3, no. 19 (August 30, 1969), p. 10.

Pool, Rosey E., ed. *Beyond the Blues: New Poems by American Negroes.* Lympne Hythe Kent: Hand and Flower Press, 1962.

Puckett, Newbell Niles. *The Magic and Folk Beliefs of the Southern Negro.* University of North Carolina Press, 1926; repr. New York: Dover Press, 1969.

Randall, Dudley. "System of Dante's Hell." *Negro Digest* 15, no. 5 (March 1966), pp. 52–53.

Rechy, John. *City of Night.* New York: Grove Press, 1963.

Reck, Tom S. "Archetypes in LeRoi Jones' *Dutchman." Studies in Black Literature* 1, no. 1 (1970), pp. 66–68.

Resnick, H. S. "Brave New Words." *Saturday Review* 50 (December 9, 1967), pp. 28–29.

Rice, Julian C. "LeRoi Jones' Dutchman: A Reading." *Contemporary Literature* 12, no. 1 (1971), pp. 42–59.

Rigney, Francis J. *The Real Bohemia: A Sociological and Psychological Study of the Beats.* New York: Basic Books, 1961.

Richardson, Jack. "Blues for Mr. Jones." *Esquire,* June 1966, pp. 106–8, 138.

Riley, Clayton, ed. *A Black Quartet: Four New Black Plays.* New York: Signet, 1970.

Rimbaud. *Oeuvres.* Ed. Suzanne Bernard. Paris: Garnier, 1960.

Ring, Harry. *How Cuba Uprooted Racism.* New York: Pioneer Publishers, 1961.

Robertson, Nan. "Dramatist Against Odds." *New York Times,* March 8, 1959, section 2, p. 3.

Rose, Wallace A. *Best TV Commercials of the Year.* New York: Hastings House, 1967.

Rosenthal, M. L. *The New Poets: American and British Poetry Since World War II.* New York: Oxford University Press, 1967.

Roth, Philip. "Channel X: Two Plays on the Race Conflict." *New York Review of Books* 2, no. 8 (May 28, 1964), pp. 10–13.

Sartre, Jean-Paul. *What is Literature.* New York: Harper, 1965. Trans. Bernard Frechtman.

Satin, Joseph, ed. *The 1950's: America's "Placid" Decade.* Boston: Houghton Mifflin, 1960.

Schneck, Stemphen. "LeRoi Jones or, Poetics and Policemen or Trying Heart, Bleeding Heart." *Ramparts* 6, no. 12 (June 29–July 13, 1968), pp. 14–19.

Schnetz, Diemut. *Der moderne Einakter: Eine poetologische Untersuchung.* Bern, München: Francke, 1967.

Scott, Sir Walter. *The Poetical Works. With the Author's Introductions and Notes.* Ed. J. Logie Robertson. London, Edinburgh: Frowde, 1906.

Shelley, Mary Wollstonecraft. *Frankenstein.* New York: Signet, 1965.

S[mith], M[ichael] (?). "Threatre: The Eighth Ditch." *Village Voice,* March 19, 1964, p. 11.

Smith, Michael. "Theatre: Present Stages." *Village Voice,* March 26, 1964, p. 15.

—— "Theatre: The Slave and the Toilet." *Village Voice,* December 31, 1964, pp. 10–11, 15.

Stanton, L. H. "The Black Power Conference." *Liberator* 7, no. 8 (August 1967), pp. 8–9.

Starke, Catherine Juanita. *Black Portraiture in American Fiction: Stock Characters, Archetypes, and Individuals.* New York, London: Basic Books, 1971.

State of New Jersey v. Everett Le Roi Jones, Charles McCray and Barry Wynn. Essex County Court, Law Division. Criminal Indictment No. 2220-66. January 4, 1968.

Stedman, Raymond William. *The Serials: Suspense by Installment.* Norman: University of Oklahoma Press, 1971.

Stone, Judy. "If It's Anger . . . Maybe That's Good." *San Francisco Chronicle,* August 23, 1964, p. 42.

Sullivan, James T. "The Negro 'National Consciousness' of LeRoi Jones." *New York Herald Tribune,* October 31, 1965, p. 34.

Sullivan, Joseph F. "Gibson Called A 'Puppet' By Baraka in Open Split." *New York Times,* August 18, 1973.

Supplementary Detailed Staff Reports on Intelligence Activities and the Rights of Americans. Book III. Senate Report no. 94-755. Washington, D.C., April 23, 1976, pp. 186–223.

"A Survey: Black Writers Views On Literary Lions and Values." *Negro Digest* 17, no. 3 (January 1968), pp. 10–89.

Tallmer, Jerry. "Across the Footlights: The Making of LeRoi Jones." *New York Post,* May 10, 1964, p. 22.

—— "LeRoi Jones Strikes Again." *New York Post,* March 24, 1964, p. 20.

—— "The Kafka Blues." *New York Post,* March 16, 1964, p. 16.

Taylor, Willene P. "The Fall of Man Theme in Imamu Amiri Baraka's (LeRoi Jones's) *Dutchman.*" *Negro American Literature Forum* 7 (1973), pp. 127–30.

Tener, Robert L. "Role Playing as A Dutchman." *Studies in Black Literature* 3, no. 3 (Autumn 1972), pp. 17–21.
—— "The Corrupted Warrior Heroes: Amiri Baraka's *The Toilet.*" *Modern Drama* 17 (1974), pp. 207–15.
Teodori, Massimo. *The New Left: A Documentary History.* Indianapolis and New York: Bobbs-Merrill, 1969.
Terrell, Robert. "Rights Leaders Rap LeRoi Jones' Judge." *New York Post*, January 6, 1968.
Toomer, Jean. *Cane.* 1923; repr. New York: Harper, 1969.
Tryford, John. "Who is LeRoi Jones? What is He?" *Trace*, no. 65 (Summer 1967), pp. 294–98.
Turner, Darwin. "Negro Playwrights and the Urban Negro." *College Language Association Journal* 12, no. 1 (1968), pp. 19–25.
Turner, Wallace. "Books by Two Negroes Barred From San Francisco Schools." *New York Times*, August 26, 1969, p. 24.
Velde, Paul. "Pursued by the Furies." *Commonweal* 88 (June 28, 1968), pp. 14–19.
"Village Voice 'Obies,' 1963–1964, The." *Village Voice*, May 28, 1964, p. 1.
Waggoner, Walter H. "Shift in Position is Hinted by King." *New York Times*, March 28, 1968, p. 40.
Wardle, Irving. "On the Negro in the American Theatre." *Times* (London), February 14, 1968.
Watts, Alan W. *Beat Zen Square Zen and ZEN.* San Francisco: City Lights, 1959.
Weales, Gerald. "The Day LeRoi Jones Spoke on Penn Campus, What Were the Blacks Doing in the Balcony?" *New York Times Magazine*, May 4, 1969, pp. 38–40.
—— *The Jumping-Off Place: American Drama in the 1960's.* New York: Macmillan, 1969.
Weber, Alfred, and Siegfried Neuweiler, eds. *Amerikanisches Drama und Theater im 20. Jahrhundert. American drama and theater in the 20th century.* Göttingen: Vandenhoek & Ruprecht, 1975.
Weisgram, Dianne H. "LeRoi Jones' *Dutchman:* Inter-racial Ritual of Sexual Violence." *American Imago* 29, no. 3 (Fall 1972), pp. 215–32.
West, Hollie. "The Poetry of Black Experience." *Washington Post*, April 4, 1971, section H, p. 6.
Whittemore, Reed. *William Carlos Williams: Poet from New Jersey.* Boston: Houghton Mifflin, 1975.
Wilentz, Elias. *The Beat Scene.* New York: Corinth, 1960.
Williams, Robert F. *Listen, Brother!* New York: World View Publishers, 1968.
Williams, Sherley Anne. *Give Birth to Brightness: A Thematic Study in Neo-Black Literature.* New York: Dial Press, 1972.
Williams, William Carlos. *Paterson.* New York: New Directions, 1948.
—— *The Selected Poems.* New York: New Directions, 1963.
Wilson, Edmund. *Axel's Castle: A Study in the Imaginative Literature of 1870–1930.* New York: Scribner, 1931; repr. 1959.

Index

Smith, Kate, 54
Smith, Michael, 111
Snodgrass, W. D., 30, 31
Snyder, Gary, 36, 61
Social worker mothers, 124-25, 164
Sorel, Georges, 20, 29, 267n21
Sorrentino, Gilbert, 3, 166
Spellman, A. B., 3
Spirit House, 5, 207
Stade, George, 4
Stalin, Joseph, 238
Stanley, George, 34
Stein, Gertrude, 21
Stevenson, Adlai, 275n14
Strindberg, August, 2, 122-23
Suicide, 42, 57, 58-61, 63, 84-87, 112,
  128, 195, 274n30
Sun Ra, 170, 204, 210, 212
Superman, 54
Surrealism, 78, 93-94, 117, 125-28, 130,
  162, 249
Svengali, 91
Swenson, May, 31
Swing, 27, 81, 161, 242

Tambo, 93
Tarzan, 45, 46, 108, 208, 244
Tate, Allen, 75
Taylor, Cecil, 142
Thomas, Dylan, 146
Thoreau, Henry David, 1, 49
Till, Emmett, 244
Tintoretto, 16
Tonto, 56; see also Lone Ranger, The
Toomer, Jean, 2, 78, 168-69, 187
Touré, Sekou, 185, 225, 237
Toussaint L'Ouverture, 93
Trees, 46-47, 51, 168, 198, 294n3
Trilling, Lionel, 31
Trotsky, Leon, 23
Tucker, Sophie, 242
Turner, Darwin, 284n42
Turner, Nat, 1, 217, 241, 242
Twain, Mark, 2, 78 (Pudd'nhead Wilson)
Typology, see Adam, Jesus, and New
  Ark
Tzara, Tristan, 139

Uncle Don, 61, 103
Uncle Tom, 122, 125, 129, 149, 150, 209,
  217
Updike, John, 31, 166
Urban League, 164, 184

Vesey, Denmark, 93, 135, 241, 242
Villiers de l'Isle-Adam, 16
Violence: Baraka's image, 1; Sorel and,
  20; Mailer's "Negro," 26, 27; against
  Liberal intellectuals, 30-32; against
  sensitivity, 77; poetic advocacy of,
  88-89, 126-27; vengeful racial, 90-92;
  surrealist, 93-94; as a perversion of
  love, 99-100, 102, 111, 120; and repression of homosexuality, 113-115; victim of violent racism, 121; venting
  pent-up, 126; art as a perversion of,
  127; and change in America, 137; and
  foodsmells, 145; against a homosexual,
  146-49; dozens transformed into, 153;
  in "The Screamers," 162-66; espousal
  of lumpenproletarian, 173; anti-
  Semitic, 198; and "Black People!,"
  199-202; orderly military, 208; and
  revolution in Slave Ship, 217

Wagner, Richard, 16, 130
Walker, David, 135, 241
Ward, Douglas Turner, 184
Warhol, Andy, 76, 107, 243
Washington, Booker T., 150
Washington, George, 183
Watergate, 229, 235
Weales, Gerald, 106, 210
Webern, Anton, 256
Webster, Ben, 255
Wedekind, Frank, 129
Welk, Lawrence, 179
Wells, H. G., 50
Weston, Jessie, 40
Whalen, Philip, 22, 36, 61, 100
Whiteman, Paul, 242
Whitman, Walt, 2, 31, 34, 39, 43, 61, 75,
  233, 234
Whittemore, Reed, 271n5
Wieners, John, 34, 36, 37